THE UNEASY PARTNERSHIP

The Dynamics of Federal, State, and Urban Relations

Edited,
with Introductions,
by Richard D. Feld
and
Carl Grafton
University of Houston

NATIONAL PRESS BOOKS

First edition 1973

Library of Congress Catalog Card Number: 72-97844

International Standard Book Numbers:
0-87484-250-6 (paper)
0-87484-251-4 (cloth)

Manufactured in the United States of America

National Press Books
850 Hansen Way, Palo Alto, California 94304

The Uneasy Partnership was set in Times Roman
and Helvetica by Applied Typographic Systems
and was printed and bound by the George Banta
Company. Nancy Sears designed the book and
Jim M'Guinness designed the cover. The editors
were Alden C. Paine and Gene Tanke; Michelle
Hogan supervised production.

Contents

Acknowledgements

Many persons have assisted us in completing various portions of this book. We are indebted to John C. Bollens of the University of California, Los Angeles and Alan Saltzstein of the University of Houston who provided guidance and encouragement in the early stages of this project. We wish to thank Alden C. Paine who proved that a publisher can be efficient, considerate, and helpful. Michelle Hogan has expertly translated our manuscript into the finished product. We are grateful to the authors and publishers who cooperated with us in arranging publication of their work in this collection. Virginia Wren, Sandra Smith, Jaye Patton, and Kai Sorensen were extremely helpful in typing and assembling the manuscript.

Finally, a special word of thanks to Naomi Feld, who assisted with proofreading and editing, but most important, demonstrated outstanding patience and understanding during the long days of work required for preparing the final manuscript for publication.

Of course, we alone are responsible for any errors contained herein.

Richard Feld

Carl Grafton

Editors' Introduction

The topic of federal-state-local relations has always received a great deal of attention in the United States. Of late, city mayors have laid the blame for pollution on adjoining cities; revenue sharing is an issue of widespread concern; presidents of large universities are frequently seen testifying before congressional committees about the effects of federal research programs on higher education; and Washington bureaucrats often complain that their programs are paralyzed by state and local officials.

Few books have been written on this topic, and most of them emphasize historical and theoretical aspects of federalism. Relatively little space is devoted to a major concern of working government officials: the nature of federal-state-local relations and the solution of specific problems of public policy.

The list of current public policy questions which involve federal-state-local relations is long and impressive: pollution; transportation (automobiles in cities, air traffic snarls, disintegration of railroads); energy shortages (sulfur-free coal, natural gas, fuel oil, electricity); a ponderous and uncoordinated welfare system; urban problems (provision of services, governmental fragmentation, fiscal disparities); and higher education (impact of federal research on state universities). Solutions to these and many other problems can only be found by coordinating the work of federal, state, and local agencies. Since relationships between these agencies are important, and are often characterized by intense conflict, we believe that they are worth examining. Our goal in this book has been to look at these relationships in the light of specific policy problems. Since these policy problems are all rather technical in nature, we decided that an anthology would be the best vehicle for the task.

THE MEANING OF AMERICAN FEDERALISM

Federalism has been defined in a variety of ways. One writer suggests that federalism implies "an association of states which have been founded for certain purposes, but in which the member states retain a large measure of their original independence."[1] More simply, it has been suggested that federalism is "a device for dividing decisions and functions of government."[2] All definitions of federalism include the idea of division of powers. It is this concept which separates a *federal* from a *unitary* (or centralized) form of government. To quote Richard Leach: "Each level of government in a federal system insists upon its right to act directly upon the people. Each is protected constitutionally from undue encroachment or destruction by the other."[3]

The division of powers among governmental units can be accomplished in one of two ways. In the United States, virtually all the powers of the federal government are listed, with the remaining powers being left to the regional (state) government. The opposite is found in Canada, where powers of the regional (provincial) governments are listed, and the remainder is left to the national government. Regardless of the system employed, federalism implies a lack of total control by the national government, and introduces a degree of uncertainty concerning how the powers of government are to be divided.

Federalism has been a cornerstone of American government since the founding of the Republic. Several reasons account for this:

1. It was a necessity, representing the only way by which a group of independent states could be induced to surrender part of their sovereignty in order to form a nation.

2. It was part of the heritage of strong local self-government that was retained from experience in Great Britain and government in the colonies.

3. It allowed a degree of experimentation with a variety of governmental formats, and took into consideration the diversity of socioeconomic characteristics found among the states.[4]

EVOLUTION OF FEDERALISM IN THE UNITED STATES

One of the basic rules guiding the operation of American federalism is set forth in Article Ten of the Constitution: "Those powers not delegated to the United States by the Constitution, nor prohibited by it to the States, are reserved to the States respectively, or to the people."

In the early years of our Republic, this formula was relatively easy to follow, because distinctions could usually be made between functions that were national in character (such as defense) and those which were regional or local (such as education). Recently, particularly in the past seventy years, this distinction has not been as sharp. Daniel Elazar has shown that the twentieth century contains six rather distinct periods of intergovernmental relations, which move toward more and more state-federal interaction:[5]

1. *Period of Transition (1895-1911).* Characterized by experimentation in collaboration among governmental units.

2. *Progressive Agrarianism (1911-1921).* Established the foundations for twentieth-century cooperative federalism through Woodrow Wilson's New Freedoms programs.

3. *Normalized Entrenchment (1921-1930).* Republican domination resulted in continuation of existing cooperative programs but no new ventures.

4. *Crisis-Oriented Centralism (1931-1945).* A major increase in federal activities brought about by the New Deal.

5. *Non-Centrist Restoration (1946-1961).* A period of expansion of cooperative programs, large increases in state expenditures, and increased concern with the role of the states in the federal system. The term Cooperative Federalism was coined by the Eisenhower administration during this period.

6. *Concentrated Cooperation (1961-1969).* An increased emphasis on federal encouragement of state programs, and a growing trend toward centralization of many government activities. The term Creative Federalism was used by President Lyndon Johnson to describe this period.

Recently, we have entered a phase which President Nixon calls the New Federalism; there has been a reemphasis on state participation in federal programs, the formulation of a program of revenue sharing with the states, and an attempt to decentralize the administration of federal activities.

PROBLEMS OF THE FEDERAL SYSTEM

In the third paragraph of this Introduction we listed some major substantive problems facing the federal system, such as pollution and the urban crisis. The success or failure of the federal system in dealing with them hinges on the ability of federal, state, and local governments to coordinate their activities. In reporting the results of a survey of federal and state officials involved in the application of various federal grant programs, Leach comments: "The most frequently occurring words in the views of both sets of officials are *function, program, activity, administration,* in considering all of which *collaboration* and intergovernmental *relations* are fundamental."[6]

Federalism has many virtues and many drawbacks. It is a flexible political system in a nation characterized by immense diversity. But this flexibility, exemplified by state and local autonomy, is also the source of many difficulties as government officials wrestle with the problems which beset the country today. This book is concerned with both the virtues and the drawbacks of the federal system as it confronts some of the most difficult public policy problems ever to face any political system. And coordination is the key concept in the analysis of federalism and public policy.

In an article reprinted in our first chapter, James L. Sundquist distinguishes between two types of coordination—horizontal and vertical. Horizontal coordination refers to the process of "consultation, sharing of information, and negotiation among equals."[7] Horizontal coordination (or the lack of it) is particularly critical in the realm of pollution politics. Here we often find that in any given city only a small fraction of pollution can be controlled by city regulation; in many instances pollution is generated by manufacturing plants in neighboring cities or automobiles licensed in another state. When horizontal coordination breaks down, vertical coordination must be established. For Sundquist vertical coordination refers to the settlement of a conflict at one level of a social system by the decision of a central figure at a higher level. Coordination can take place at any and all points in the process of formulating and administering a program. And "vertical coordination" is not necessarily synonymous with "central government take-over." Vertical coordination can operate at any degree of centralization. For example, we will see in the readings that federal coordination of state and local pollution regulation activities is heavily dependent on state and local cooperation.

THEORIES OF FEDERALISM

The reader may note that we have placed little emphasis on theories or models of the federal system. We share Richard Leach's atheoretical approach to the study of federalism. While various theories and models of federal systems are interesting and have considerable value from an academic and political standpoint, they shed little light on the day-to-day realities of federal-state-local relationships which are the concern of this book.

PLAN OF THE BOOK

The first chapter of this book provides an overview of the American federal system, and gives details about the nature of the many problems it faces. Chapter Two concentrates on federal-state-local fiscal relations, with special emphasis on revenue sharing. Chapter Three, entitled "The Role of the States," stresses the continuing importance of state government and suggests means by which the ability of states to respond to the needs of their constituencies can be enhanced. In Chapter Four we examine the "urban crisis." Here the numerous problems confronting local government are noted and ways by which the federal system can alleviate these difficulties are described. The nation's welfare program is discussed in Chapter Five. Chapter Six focuses on the impact of federal aid and research programs on state universities and state higher-education coordination systems. The topic of the seventh chapter is the interaction between federalism and technological development (for example, pollution, the energy crisis, and weather modification). Chapter Eight, the concluding segment of the book, attempts to assess the future of the federal system.

Obviously, there are many other topics which could have been included in this list. Public primary and secondary school finance, public health care and delivery systems, urban and regional planning, and mass transit, are just a few that readily come to mind. In selecting our topics, choices had to be made, since space limitations precluded detailed treatment of every aspect we might wish to cover. Hopefully, the readings we have selected will clearly illustrate the workings of the American federal system, and motivate the reader to seek out information concerning other areas of interest that have not been examined.

Each chapter opens with an introductory essay. These essays have several purposes, which include providing background information necessary to place the articles in their appropriate context, demonstrating their relevance to contemporary events and issues, and pointing out their implications for the formulation and execution of public policy. The introductions also briefly highlight the main points in each of the chapter's articles and note the relationships between them and their relationship to other sections of the book. This information should emphasize the diversity of issues involved in the functioning of the federal system, and reinforce the idea of the interaction between these issues that is constantly present.

[1]Kenneth C. Wheare, *Federal Government* (New York: Oxford University Press, 1947), p. 1.

[2]Morton Grodzins, "The Federal System," *Report of the President's Commission on National Goals: Goals for Americans* (New York: American Assembly, Columbia University, Prentice Hall, Inc., 1960), p. 265.

[3]Richard H. Leach, *American Federalism* (New York: W. W. Norton, 1970), p. 1.

[4]For a general discussion of these and other points relating to the origin of U.S. federalism, see Brooks Graves, *American Intergovernmental Relations* (New York: Charles Scribner's Sons, 1964), pp. 1–31.

[5]Daniel Elazar, "The Shaping of Intergovernmental Relations in the Twentieth Century," *Annals of the American Academy of Political and Social Sciences,* May 1965, pp. 11–22.

[6]Leach, *American Federalism,* p. 18.

[7]James L. Sundquist and David W. Davis, *Making Federalism Work* (Washington: The Brookings Institution, 1969), p. 17.

Chapter ONE

Federalism in Transition

INTRODUCTION TO CHAPTER ONE There is little need to point out that the federal system is large. Virtually any measure adopted can illustrate this point. One yardstick is the number of employees serving in all levels of government. In 1970, the federal government had a total of nearly 3 million civilian employees. The number of employees on the state and local level (including school districts) is even larger: as of 1970, over 8.5 million persons were so classified.

Another indicator is expenditures made by the various governmental entities. In fiscal year 1971, the federal government spent approximately $215 billion for a variety of services ranging from national defense to educational assistance. State and local expenditures are also impressive: in 1970, state governments spent over $68 billion, while municipalities spent an additional $23 billion.

Table 1 illustrates the increase in expenditures by the federal government on programs that are intergovernmental in nature.

These figures describe some, but not all, of the impact that governmental growth and spending has had upon the American system of government. Other measures, such as the number of new programs adopted by all levels of government, the number of recipients of various public assistance programs, and the increasing demands for revenues by the public sector could all testify to the increasing involvement of government in our day-to-day activities.

TABLE 1 Increase in Federal Aid Expenditures to State and Local Governments, 1959–73

Fiscal year	Federal aid			
		As a percent of		
	Amount (millions)	Total Federal outlays	Domestic Federal outlays[a]	State-local revenue[b]
1959	$6,669	7.2	15.9	12.3
1960	7,040	7.6	16.4	11.6
1961	7,112	7.3	15.4	11.0
1962	7,893	7.4	15.8	11.3
1963	8,634	7.8	16.5	11.6
1964	10,141	8.6	17.9	12.4
1965	10,904	9.2	18.4	12.4
1966	12,960	9.7	19.2	13.2
1967	15,240	9.6	19.5	14.2
1968	18,599	10.4	20.9	15.8
1969	20,255	11.0	21.3	15.3
1970	23,954	12.2	21.9	15.9
1971	29,844	14.1	23.5	17.9
1972 estimate	39,080	16.5	25.8	21.1
1973 estimate	43,479	17.6	27.0	21.1

[a]Excluding outlays for defense, space and international programs.
[b]*"Governmental Finances in 1969–70,"* Bureau of the Census.

Source: *Special Analysis, Budget of the United States, Fiscal Year 1973, Table P-5, p. 245.*

In recent years, technological advances, new political alignments, economic dislocations, and patterns of population growth have resulted in additional changes in the character of the federal system.

One change has been the increased emphasis placed on the needs of the cities by both the federal and state governments. On the federal level, this has been reflected by new programs such as Model Cities, Mass Transit Grants, and the War on Poverty. Reapportionment of state legislatures and the growth of urban population in many states has resulted in state governments also beginning to recognize the importance of programs for city residents.

Another change has been the deep involvement of the federal government in areas once thought to be totally the concern of state or local governments. These areas include education, police protection, pollution, and public health.

In the past decade, there has also been increased attention given to methods for decentralizing the large federal bureaucracy and providing more effective management of federal programs.

Finally, and perhaps most important, policy makers at all levels have demonstrated increased awareness of the many interrelationships that exist in the formulation and execution of governmental policy. At the same time, they have also recognized the interdependence of the constituent units in the federal system and the need for eliminating the friction and confusion that often result in dealings between them.

In keeping with the points noted above, the three selections in this introductory chapter center upon a common theme which runs throughout the entire book: that American federalism is still undergoing a period of rapid transition, a metamorphosis which will ultimately result in a new pattern of governmental relationships which borrow from the past but appear radically altered from those of the present.

READINGS IN THIS CHAPTER

Changing Patterns of Federalism: Merriam

The first article is written by a person who has combined academic, governmental, and business careers. Having served as Assistant to the President, and Deputy Director of the Budget Bureau in the Eisenhower administration, Robert Merriam has first-hand experience upon which to base his judgments of the strengths and weaknesses of the federal system. His article, which is drawn from a lecture presented under the auspices of the Graduate School of the U.S. Department of Agriculture, summarizes problems such as lack of coordination between the levels of government, uncertainty concerning the objectives of governmental officials administering various programs, and lack of sufficient financial resources to enable state and local governments to carry out necessary domestic programs. He then outlines some of the more recent approaches being used in attempting to solve these problems. These include the Intergovernmental Relations Act of 1968, the establishment of the Urban Affairs Council, and the decentralization of various federal programs.

He concludes by arguing that while such measures have been important, they do not go far enough. Thus, even more attention to the operation of the federal system must be given by the president and the Congress, and we must also start the painful process of rethinking our national priorities so that domestic needs are given increased weight.

Intergovernmental Relations—An Overview: Rosenthal

This selection, which is drawn from the lead article of a symposium on intergovernmental relations featured in the *Public Administration Review*, is a survey of scholarly literature in the field of intergovernmental relations, with particular emphasis on grant-in-aid programs. The article contains a discussion of the question of federal versus states rights and how this debate affects current activities. The role of the Advisory Commission on Intergovernmental Relations is mentioned, and Rosenthal advocates increased study of ways to facilitate cooperation between the constituent units of the federal system. The controversial topic of revenue sharing is also reviewed.

In the final sections of his article, Professor Rosenthal outlines several suggestions for removing impediments to increased intergovernmental cooperation. These are in the area of fiscal and accounting procedures, coordination of programs, and elimination of restrictive constitutional provisions on the state and local levels. He also suggests consideration of two other ideas: The reestablishment of a governmental commission to study federal-state-local procedures, and the creation of regional commissions which would coordinate programs on an area-wide basis.

Coordination in the Federal System: Sundquist and Davis

In the Introduction to this book, we noted that one of the most difficult problems facing the federal system is that of coordination. As Sundquist and Davis point out, the need for finding some mechanism to enable government to bring order out of confusion has become all the more pressing in the 1970s, as governmental agencies attempt to administer the large number of intergovernmental programs initiated during the past decade.

One area where this lack of coordination is immediately apparent is in aid to the cities. Using the Model Cities and War on Poverty Programs as examples, Sundquist and Davis illustrate the bureaucratic confusion and lack of effectiveness caused by the poor cooperation between agencies (such as the Department of Housing and Urban Development and the Office For Economic Opportunity) administering these programs. Similarly, they show that many rural-based development projects are also ineffective because of this same lack of coordination between agencies, such as the Departments of Agriculture, Labor, and Commerce.

In suggesting several ways by which greater coordination and effectiveness can be achieved, the authors argue that these or other equally effective measures must be adopted; the ability of the federal system to respond to the domestic needs of our nation is at stake.

1 Federalism in Transition: The Dynamics of Change and Continuity

Robert L. Merriam

From: *Federalism Today*, published by the Graduate School Press of the U.S. Department of Agriculture (1969), pp. 5–16. Reprinted by permission of the author and publisher.

Robert Merriam is currently chairman of the Advisory Commission on Intergovernmental Relations.

I speak to you today from the protected vantage-point of an "Olympian" observer, watching the kaleidoscope of events unfold but without any day-to-day responsibility at any one of the base points of our Federal system. However, having been involved rather intimately at all levels of government, from precinct worker to Presidential Assistant (with even a short stint at the UN), I hesitantly lay claim to some understanding of the problems confronting the widely diverse units of government and the political power structure supporting them.

The problem of dynamic federalism is nothing more than creating a rational structure to find and channel money, through the efforts of human beings, to perform functions uniquely assigned to the public sector for the betterment of all. With this objective, we become committed to the proposition–and will continue ever more rapidly, I hope–that even in our complex modern society we can evolve a "government of, by and for the people."

A "new" federalism can have meaning only in this context. It requires the meshing of the often-ponderous wheels of government, with all its lethargy and built-in resistance, so as to rationalize a governmental structure which provides a better life for all our people. Such a structure can only be erected through the imaginative use of governmental powers, an enormous amount of bone-crunching, and the destruction or diminution of some powerful vested interests. I would hope we are aware of and up to coping with the enormity of the problem, because no longer can we afford the luxury of an inefficiently operating Federal system. The problems of race and transportation and air pollution and poverty and jobs and schools and a decent place in which to live can only be attacked intelligently on a coordinated basis.

But let us step back a moment for a quick view in perspective. In a sense, the title of this lecture is a misnomer because federalism always has been in transit. As Hamilton reminded us in his concluding essay in the *Federalist Papers*, in quoting the 18th century philosopher David Hume:

"To balance a large state or society, whether monarchial or republican, on general laws, is a work of so great difficulty, that no human genius, however comprehensive, is able, by the mere dint of reason and reflection, to effect it. The judgments of many must unite in the work; experience must guide their labor; time must bring it to perfection; and the feeling of inconveniences must correct the mistakes, which they inevitably fall into, in their first trials and experiments."

The basic premise of the American Federal system is that a strong national government should unify and coordinate the national purposes and endeavors, supplemented by vigorous, autonomous State and local units exercising primary governmental functions in their respective spheres. The States, which out of necessity formed the Union, proposed in the Constitution a way to establish this system.

From the simple Constitutional division of powers between Nation and States ("The powers not delegated to the United States by the Constitution, nor prohibited by it to the States, are reserved to the States respectively, or to the people"), our path begins. We have been in transit ever since, but the forms of change themselves have changed.

1. Judicial change has played its forceful role in cycles, from the outset. The early decisions of the Marshall-dominated Supreme Court struck down State legislation considered contrary to the Constitution, broadly interpreted the "implied" powers of the National Government, and upheld the supremacy of the National Government in interstate commerce. The latest phase of the judicial cycle from school segregation to one-man, one-vote decisions, re-emphasizes judicial change once again.

2. National aid to the States commenced slowly with the land grants, to the present $25 billions spread across 160 major programs based on

more than 400 separate congressional authorizations, and administered by 21 Federal agencies with more than 150 Washington-based bureaus and 400 regional and field offices.

3. One problem was "solved" by war, with 617,000 Americans slain in the process of resolving supremacy of national constitutional power, and with widespread constitutional change resulting.

4. New techniques adapted into law have been a vital part of the transition. Most notable undoubtedly has been the income tax (which like many of you, I suspect, occupied your speaker late into last night).

5. Strong Presidents, beginning with a reluctant Jefferson (whose Louisiana Purchase stretched the Constitution) through the two Roosevelts battling first industrial monopoly and then collapse, dramatically shaping the "new" federalism.

6. Weak States and proliferating local governments and problems have been a significant negative force at work: 30,000 governments, including 3,049 counties; 35,000 plus municipalities, towns, and townships; 20,000 independent school districts; and another 20,000 special districts for water supply, sewerage, road building and the like; all now receiving $25 billions in Federal aid and an additional $100 billions in local tax monies.

But even the tempo of change is changing. As we peer ahead toward the fast-approaching 200th anniversary of our Federal system and the 2000th calendar year, we see the geometric progression of the knowledge, technology, industrial, and population explosions, all descending upon us. We see by the year 2000 a Gross National Product of $2 trillion (in 1969 dollars), a doubled population (but perhaps finally leveling off), a continued industrial centralization (Anti-Trust Division notwithstanding), and a corresponding urban agglomeration. This is the dynamics of change we must now cope with.

But all of us are aware of both the trends and the problems. Commissions galore have dramatically highlighted them. What we really must ask is how we organize for the tasks ahead. What are the practicalities and realities of political life? Should we junk the Federal system and place all power and responsibility in the hands of the National Government? Should we shift vast powers back to the States and localities? What can we do about a system which at the moment is neither adequately meeting current needs nor planning for future problems?

Going from generalities to specifics is never easy. This is the task to which most of you in this audience so capably devote yourselves daily. The key is to place into broad context, with defined purpose, these daily actions and decisions.

I'd like to start with some general observations about what I will call "the spirit of government" needed in the years ahead.

From the Federal government it means willingness at both the executive and legislative levels to undo the "papa knows best" concept. In the States it means somehow bursting the chains of parochialism and agrarianism so prevalent in many of our State legislatures. And at the local level it means a willingness to really face up to, and to batter head-on, the dual, but now interrelated, problems of suburb vs. central city and black vs. white.

The "new" federalism will require a re-examination of the purposes of governing.

For example, I have long thought that both legislative and executive groups at all levels of government tend to occupy far too much of their all-too-little time immersed in their own bits of trivia. A Congress which passes more private bills than public laws, a State legislature which occupies too much of its time with administrative minutiae, and a city council which worries more about driveway permits than the quality of educational standards in the city, all contribute to the breakdown of effective government. The same may be said for many executive actions.

Having noted the generalities, I suggest that we look at recent trends in federalism. A few bright spots illuminate an otherwise rather gloomy horizon. In 1953 President Eisenhower sponsored, and the Congress approved, the first formal governmental review of our Federal system since the Constitutional Convention. While in terms of results it could be said that a mighty effort created a mouse, a start was made. A later Federal-State Action Committee perhaps put to rest for all time the notion that some neat sorting out of governmental functions could be made. But this Committee did begin an important dialogue which in part contributed to the formation in 1959 of the Advisory Commission on Intergovernmental Relations. It was the first statutory "mixed" commission of the Federal, State, and local officials with public members. Its monumental studies offer us a continuing glimpse into the future. As its last annual report noted:

"At the beginning of 1969, the Nation continues its search for a New Federalism–dedicated to balance; designed to correct structural, functional, and fiscal weaknesses; and rooted in a vital partnership of strong localities, strong States, and a strong National Government. Federalism, after all, seeks to enhance national unity while sustaining social and political diversity. The partnership approach is the only viable formula for applying this constitutional doctrine to late Twentieth Century America. Yet, this approach can succeed only if all of the partners are powerful, resourceful, and responsive to the needs of the people. The alternative is a further pulverizing of State and local power, and the consequent strengthening of the forces of centralization."

The Intergovernmental Cooperation Act of 1968 potentially is another significant development at the Federal level. First of all, it requires the setting up of a better communications and information service between the National Government and the States regarding grants-in-aid requested or approved for agencies within the States. It also authorizes Federal agencies, at cost, to provide specialized or technical services to requesting State or local governments.

Title IV of this Act has far wider implications. It provides that:

"All viewpoints–national, regional, State, and local–shall, to the extent possible, be fully considered and taken into account in planning Federal or federally assisted development programs and projects. State and local government objectives, together with the objectives of regional organizations, shall be considered and evaluated within a framework of national public objectives, as expressed in Federal law, and available projects of future national conditions and needs of regions, States, and localities shall be considered in plan formulation, evaluation, and review.

"To the maximum extent possible, consistent with national objectives, all Federal aid for development purposes shall be consistent with and further the objectives of State, regional, and local comprehensive planning. Consideration shall be given to all developmental aspects of our total national community, including but not limited to housing, transportation, economic development, natural and human resources development, community facilities, and the general improvement of living environments."

It is probably fair to say that when and if fully implemented, this represents the biggest "carrot" dangled before State and local governments to date. Although the Act does not mention the term, it potentially could add up to nationwide planning. But the problems of implementation remain to be solved. And the realization that such legislation is required speaks for itself.

There are other promising developments. The President has formed an Urban Affairs Council, and has chosen as his assistant in these matters an unusually knowledgeable person, Mr. Moynihan. This is a culmination of increasing Cabinet-level concern with State and local affairs in recent years. The increased emphasis on regional councils of Federal Government officials, and even the designation of common regional boundaries for at least some Federal agencies are other actions long overdue. As President Nixon observed in taking these steps: "Greater decentralization should contribute to closer cooperation and coordination between Federal agencies and State and local governments since decision-making will be closer to the non-Federal agencies directly responsible for delivery of services." Decentralization, however, too often is discussed largely in negative terms, in the context of minorities or poverty groups, or as a substitute for "lack of confidence" in government.

At the State and local levels still-feeble stirrings are noted. I am privileged at the moment to be co-chairman of one such effort in Illinois —The Commission on Urban Area Government. Our task is to present to the Governor, legislature, and a pending Constitutional Convention recommendations relating to structure, functions, and financing of the State and its local governments in the nine metropolitan regions of Illinois. Similar studies in New York, Minnesota, Maryland and elsewhere have met with varied results, some disastrous. A common lesson from these studies is that better coordination of government services requires simultaneous, or at least parallel, action at all levels of the Federal system.

Intergovernmental compacts and less formal cooperation have also been utilized, sometimes successfully. Cooperative actions by local governments within an area, "metro" annexation, consolidation of city and county, all have been tried, again with scattered success. But progress has been minuscule compared with the mounting needs for a coordinated government response to the problems of polluted air, miserable transportation, segregated living, inadequate housekeeping services, and aging communities.

Where, then, are we heading? How do we get there? Who will take the lead in mounting the effort to get us there? I start my answer with a few basic premises:

1. Our Founding Fathers did not want, nor do we, a monolithic governmental structure with all policies and implementation directed from one place.

2. The Federal system as written and developed is both desirable and workable, but requires drastic restructuring.

3. The answer is not that of vertical rearrangement (i.e., returning this or that function to one level of government or the other), but rather of horizontal readjustment (i.e., combining responsibilities of various levels of government to focus on specific problem areas.)

To carry out these objectives, I suggest a "National Urban Plan" which by supplying central goals and objectives may be the only chance we have left to achieve effective local decision-making. The steps are these:

First, the President should develop and present to the Congress a "National Urban Plan" for dealing with our urban problems in their totality. This Plan should clearly delineate areas of appropriate national interest, make recommendations for an allocation of resources to meet these needs, and propose the legal, organizational, and fiscal means for achieving the objectives.

It is important that the national interest in our Federal system, its workings, and the urban problems now straining its workability, all be the object of national attention. The dialogue must be focused on the whole problem, not on isolated pieces which have been the subject of discussion and legislation in the past.

The fiscal dividend which we all hope will present itself shortly makes the timing of this endeavor most urgent. Lacking an overall plan and recommended priorities in allocating resources, the Congress again will be faced with piecemeal decisions in which special interests are likely to score more heavily than their claims should allow.

The Urban Affairs Council provides a vehicle for developing a total urban plan for the President's consideration, perhaps assisted by the Advisory Commission on Intergovernmental Relations and other interested organizations. When we realize that urgent domestic needs (heavily in urban areas) demand annual expenditures (at today's prices) of tens of billions of dollars (*Fortune* magazine recently totaled up $57 billion required annually for education, medical care, welfare reforms, crime control, inner cities, suburban sprawl, eyesores, mass transit, and pollution control), the enormity of the problem is magnified.

Second, to focus attention on the "National Urban Plan" and to assist in its implementation, the President should exercise vigorous leadership and the moral suasion which only he can bring to bear, to rally widespread public support for his Plan. He should convene special sessions with the Conference of Governors and other organizations of State and local officials to explain his Plan and elicit support for it. He particularly should urge the Governors to put their own machinery in the best working order (for without adequate State and local organization and planning, who will receive and implement the Plan?). The President also must seek the support of the business community, the labor movement, church and civic leadership, the academic community, and, of course, the general public.

The enormity of this "selling" job is only exceeded by the size and gravity of our urban problems. Only with a dramatic and comprehensive attack on the problem can sufficient enthusiasm ever be generated to bring it to reality. But we have attacked with vigor and success other great challenges to our way of life, from war to depression. Who is to say we should not try here?

Third, the Congress should enact overall guidelines for restructuring our legal, organizational, and fiscal arrangements to implement this national plan. The antiquated grant-in-aid program must be converted to a new fiscal aid or sharing plan with the minimum of niggling restrictions and a concentration on matters of overriding national interest, such as integration, minimum educational standards, and balanced services. The "carrot" of Federal funds must be more aggressively used to require not only area-wide planning but also area-wide coordination of local governmental functions. And along with this, the Congress must require even further consolidation and coordination of Federal executive agencies to match the impositions on the local communities.

A few examples are in order of what might be included in this "National Urban Plan." Interchangeability among government personnel at all levels could easily be expedited by a nationally organized or sponsored recruiting and retirement program. We could have an integrated national management of public finances through creation of a central banking mechanism for financing long-term capital investments at the various levels of government, developing uniform standards for local taxing practices, and a series of block grants (or a tax) *not* earmarked for special purposes. A "national support budget" could set overall levels of expenditures required to put certain defined minimum levels of public service into effect at various echelons of government. Criteria for local public transportation which measure the cost of new expressways against the cost of mass transportation could be developed. Standards for conservation or urbanized land areas and new town development could be formulated. Minimum educational standards could be evolved. Even a plan to break up the ghettos could be considered.

Bitter medicine you say? But the disease is virulent. Impractical? Not politically feasible? Too dangerous; likely to result in domination by the National Government?

Well, first of all, the National Government in thousands of ways, in hundreds of thousands of words written into regulations, and in the form of billions of dollars a year, is deeply involved in urban affairs today. In the second place, the present tangled, ponderous system is not meeting urgent urban needs. Finally, already some of the more gloomy academic observers are predicting the death of the Federal system, and a few are urging its demise in favor of central governmental control of everything. I, for one, am not yet ready to accept this alternative. But it will be the only alternative without drastic action such as proposed here.

In summary, in 1787 a Federal system was erected to avoid the chaos of our Confederation of States. Our embryonic Government was tottering on the brink of disaster. From that day forward we have practiced allocation of national resources, whether it be land or other natural resources, our economic or our human resources. In the last 25 years we have added to this priority-making process an allocation based on our changed role in the world in which we live. Currently, we are in the midst of another vigorous debate about the allocation of resources for defense (the ABM). Must we not learn rationally to apply the same criteria to the overall allocation of resources to make our communities liveable?

2 The Current Scene: Approaches and Reproaches

Albert H. Rosenthal

From: *The Public Administration Review*, Vol. 28 (1968), pp. 3–9. Reprinted by permission of the author and publisher.

Albert Rosenthal is Professor of Political Science at the University of New Mexico. He has written several articles dealing with American federalism.

An evaluation of intergovernmental relations today might be taken from the opening lines of Charles Dickens' *Tale of Two Cities*. It seems to be "the best of times" or "the worst of times," depending on one's point of view. Perhaps it is both.

On one hand, there is little doubt that the grant-in-aid device, originated in the early 1800s but coming into real significance with the depression programs of the 1930s and geometrically increasing to the present time, has provided a mechanism by which national programs could be instituted or strengthened while state governments continued as the major administrative level for these programs. The public assistance and employment security programs afford striking examples of massive federal financial participation with first-line administration by the state governments.

Professor Daniel J. Elazar puts this case strongly in the following statement:

> The federal principle has been adapted to a dynamic society which has developed in mankind's most dynamic period. It may some day be said that, indeed, it was the federal principle that provided the basis for

> the survival of the American government as a free government during these difficult times. American federalism has been able to combine strength at the center with local control and reasonably uniform national progress with opportunities for local diversity.[1]

Also, on the plus side, Professor Wayne Vasey points out that the federal grant system has greatly stimulated the strengthening of state governments: "One might argue, on the other hand, that in the exercise of this particular responsibility state and local governments have flourished only since they began to receive aid on a large scale from the national government."[2]

A third group of supporters of the present grant-in-aid approach reflects a pragmatic rather than philosophic view. This group, including a wide range of state and local program officials and their professional constituents and interest groups, points out that state and local financial resources are not adequate to bear the cost of the programs adopted during the past 30 years. This is demonstrated despite the fact that state and local indebtedness has increased many times over the comparable increase in federal indebtedness during the same period.

Also on the plus side, the present period is marked by a great deal of ferment and activity. Congressional subcommittees have held hearings in which significant points of view have been aired; the Advisory Commission on Intergovernmental Relations has continued its work, has developed over 30 useful publications on this subject, and early this year will be publishing a significant document entitled *Fiscal Balance in the American Federal System;* and new programs to work in this area have been recently established such as the states' Urban Action Center and the Institute on State Programming for the 70s. The significant question is, "What will come of all this?"

"STATES RIGHTS" ARGUMENT

On the negative side, extremist critics of present-day intergovernmental relations charge usurpation of "states rights" by the federal government, particularly when they oppose the particular program or value system being advanced by the grant programs. Here the opponents of federal-state "cooperative" programs could quote Lewis Carroll's *Alice's Adventures in Wonderland,* in which Alice describes the luncheon of the owl and the panther:

> I passed by the garden and watched with one eye,
> How the owl and the panther were sharing a pie.
> The panther took pie crust and gravy and meat,
> While the owl had the dish as its share of the treat.

Excellent studies of grants-in-aid as a tax equalization device by Professor Byron Johnson and others and the periodic studies by the Office of Government Reports of the Bureau of the Census show that the "have not" states, mainly those of the Rocky Mountains and the South, receive appreciably more in federal subsidies than they pay in federal taxes. These studies, however, seem not to have been widely distributed, read, or believed in those states. It is currently considered by some to be "good politics" in the Rocky Mountain states to air the old saw: "We send a dollar to Washington and get back fifty cents. Why don't they let us administer our own programs in our own way?"

The fact is, of course, that the citizens in these states receive about a dollar and a half for every dollar collected in federal taxes. The "have" states, such as New York, Illinois, Michigan, and California, pay more than their share to make up the difference. This oversimplified statement of the facts concerning federal grants vis-à-vis taxes simply points up the irony of the antifederal sentiment evidenced in the Rocky Mountain states and in the South. Firsthand observation of this view moved the then recently appointed Secretary of Interior to state: "However, it is more difficult to explain the anti-federal government movement in the West for our region has always had a special and uniquely profitable relationship with the government in Washington."[3]

Herbert Block, in an address at Columbia University, described his impression of the generally held view toward federal government:

> Not corruption, injustice or inequities in representation, but the federal government itself, and most particularly the Executive and Judicial branches, is made out to be some kind of enemy. The local government may do things for you—like paving roads, even though this is generally done mostly with federal funds—but those "bureaucrats" in Washington take from you."[4]

These examples are presented simply to illustrate the wide range of evaluative views concerning the effectiveness and desirability of intergovernmental relations in the United States today. As in most issues, the constructive position is found somewhere between the extremes.

No one seriously proposes the elimination of federal subventions to the states. But problems in the present system—composed of some 170 different programs for grants-in-aid, using varying standards and formulas, and expending over $16 billion in the current fiscal year—have stimulated many different proposals.

In 1952 the so-called "stringless grant" was suggested. In 1958 Wisconsin's Congressman Melvin Laird initiated a bill for a general federal subsidy to the states, but the House Ways and Means Committee did not report the bill out of Committee. In 1964 Professor Walter Heller, shortly before he resigned as chairman of the Council of Economic Advisors, developed a variation of the "stringless grant." His proposal was also essentially a revenue sharing plan.[5] In 1966 two Wisconsin congressmen, Melvin Laird and Henry S. Reuss, presented proposals along the same line.[6] In December 1967 Governor Nelson A. Rockefeller revived the campaign for federal-state revenue sharing and proposed that cities be included in the plan. He stated that existing federal grant programs offer states and cities "too much complexity and rigidity, but not enough cash." He estimated that state and local expenditures would continue to increase faster than federal expenditures and that state and local government costs would rise from the present $75 billion to $119 billion by 1975.[7]

Several task forces have been at work both inside and outside the government to find acceptable alternatives. The President's Advisory Commission on Intergovernmental Relations has issued several thoughtful proposals for rationalizing the present grant structure but has achieved only limited White House or Congressional support. It is hoped that the recommendations of the ensuing report of the Advisory Commission on Intergovernmental Relations will be given more attention and action than has been given to earlier proposals.

At the 1967 National American Society for Public Administration Conference in San Francisco, on the subject of "Intergovernmentalizing the Great Society," several papers stressed the need for: (1) an appreciation of the need and value of the grant programs in many areas; (2) the need to rationalize the extensive network of grants which has developed piecemeal and sporadically during the past 30 years; (3) possible uses of the Federal Executive Board approach which has demonstrated on a limited scale the promising values of coordination in the field; and, (4) the need to consider some innovative and dramatically new approaches to the administration of federal grants, such as that afforded by the concept of the Regional Economic Commissions.

One of the earliest and most consistent contributors to the body of knowledge in the intergovernmental relations field is Dr. William Anderson, distinguished professor of political science, now professor emeritus at the University of Minnesota. The following symposium opens with Dr. Anderson's reaction to bill S. 1236 entitled the Tax Sharing Act of 1967, submitted by Senator Howard H. Baker, Jr. In his considerations, Professor Anderson also evaluates the related, although somewhat different, proposal by Professor Walter W. Heller. Because this approach, as already indicated, is looked upon by many people as "the answer" to many of the problems which developed in the grant-in-aid programs, the response by as eminent an authority as Dr. William Anderson is of timely value and significance. To the questions raised by

Dr. Anderson may be added the fact that the revenue-sharing proposals are not addressed to some of the most troublesome characteristics that have developed in the administration of the grant-in-aid programs.

Proponents of revenue sharing stress the lack of financial resources of the states and suggest a federal subsidy as a means of meeting this problem. Many states have not utilized potential fiscal resources to the fullest.[8] However, there is no doubt of the current financial difficulty, not only of the state governments but at federal and local levels as well, in providing the public services demanded by citizens living in an increasingly complex and urbanized society.

Some state and local governments are having difficulty in raising even the matching amounts called for by many grant programs.[9] None of the tax-sharing or unrestricted grant proposals contemplates complete elimination of all grant programs. To substitute the block, unrestricted grant would not only require an astronomical amount of money if the present levels of services or activities are to be maintained, but would also cancel out many of the values of the grant system—the very reasons why it was adopted.

Both the problems and approaches to their solution growing out of the major issues, inconsistencies, and irritations in the present system have been described by the reports of the President's Advisory Commission on Intergovernmental Relations, the Hearings and Reports of the Committees and Subcommittees of the Senate and the House of Representatives, and numerous commissions and institutes.[10]

There are those who have stated that the revenue-sharing proposals beg the real question of how to improve the administration of federal grant programs, which have specific purposes reflecting carefully considered and adopted national policy, seeking to achieve, *inter alia:* (1) the establishment of new programs by providing financial incentives for states to participate in these programs; (2) the strengthening or enlargement of existing programs; (3) the supplementation of state financial resources in particular specified areas where state governments are desirous of installing or enlarging a program but are limited by the lack of adequate funds; (4) the achievement of tax benefit equalization among the states to counterbalance the lack of financial tax resources in particular areas; and (5) for purposes which may be unique in particular program areas. The first value is most obvious in the health field. Cancer, tuberculosis, heart, and similar programs were initiated in most states on the basis of available federal funds. The second and third values are clear when one views the development of the road and airport programs. The fourth value is pointed up by the truism that areas with the greatest needs frequently have the least resources. The fifth is illustrated by the civil defense program which remained dormant in most states until given the impetus of grants made available for this purpose.

PROBLEMS IN ADMINISTRATION

If the concept of the grant program is to be maintained, it is apparent that the attention must be given to the less spectacular, but nonetheless highly significant, problem areas in the *administration* of the present grant programs. A first step would be made in broadening the categories in such fields as health and welfare. The present specific grant programs, known in health as the "anatomical" grants and in welfare as the "categories," cause difficulties all the way through the administrative structure down to the social worker who must wrestle with standards of eligibility for Old Age Assistance, Aid to Familes with Dependent Children, and the like, rather than work toward the primary purpose of meeting the needs of the whole person or the total family. It is encouraging to note that the Department of Health, Education and Welfare and its constituent agencies are moving toward the consolidation of related grant programs. Table 1 affords, in an oversimplified way, some examples of relatively obvious defects in the present myriad of categorical, formula, project, and other federal grant programs and summary suggestions for their improvement.

The correction of the administrative faults which have developed because of the disparate way the separate grant programs have developed would do much to increase the programs' effectiveness and to maintain state and local support for the grant approach.

ALTERNATIVES

Perhaps a President's Commission on Administrative Management similar to the 1937 Brownlow Commission—with attention focused on both the policy and administrative impediments to effective intergovernmental relations and with qualified staffs and task forces working intensively for a period of a year or two—might develop the kind of information and momentum necessary to overcome inertia and special-group interests which retain the present program. To capitalize on the knowledge and expertise already developed, the chairmen, members, and able professional staffs of the Advisory Commission on Intergovernmental Relations, the Council of State Governments, and the Congressional Subcommittees on Intergovernmental Relations should be included in the Commission membership, task forces, and staffs.

Another possible alternative was pointed out by former Health, Education and Welfare Secretary John Gardner in testimony before the Senate Committee on Government Operations in 1966. He pointed out that unless state and local government administration improved, federal agencies would seek to set up their own network of local instrumental-

TABLE 1 Federal Requirements Impeding Administration of Grant-in-Aid Programs

Impediment	*Approach to Improvement*
Coordination:	
Related federal programs have duplicative, overlapping, and inconsistent provisions and requirements particularly obvious when several federal programs deal with one state agency.	Legislative inconsistencies call for joint congressional committee study and congressional action.
Public assistance and child welfare (state welfare departments); and public health and children, health (state health departments).	Administrative regulations can be modified at agency level.
Organization:	
"Single state agency"[a] requirement restricts flexibility of state organization pattern.	Eliminate the "single state agency" concept to permit greater flexibility of state organization of counterpart programs.
Personnel:	
State merit program is effective in some areas but does not provide national recruitment or other needed devices.	Shift emphasis of state merit system program from detailed regulations to the development of a positive personnel program such as providing nationwide recruitment and training services in scarcity fields.
Budget:	
Timing of grants frequently does not consider budgets at appropriate schedules of state governments. Many state governments utilize biennial appropriations.	State budget and appropriation schedules should be considered in scheduling recurrent grant approvals. Extend two-year grant approvals, presently in road program, to other programs.
Accounting:	
New programs require extensive guidance for adequate accounting to meet audit requirements.	Provide constructive accounting service particularly in the establishment of new programs.
Excessive time periods required for maintenance of accounting records.	Establish program to reduce time full accounting records must be maintained.
Audit:	
Delayed audits create many difficulties.	Maintain audits on as "current" a basis as possible (within two-year period). Develop program of federal acceptance of state audits where performed under approved standards and with federal spot checks.

Impediment	*Approach to Improvement*
Information: Governors and state legislative staffs frequently do not have adequate information concerning grants and requirements.	Provide system for provision of periodic information concerning grants to governors and state legislatures with: (a) advance copies sent to governors and heads of state agencies, and (b) summary information pointing up major changes and trends.
Reporting: Excessive periodic and special reporting requirements impede program operations.	Establish program of continuous review of periodic reporting requirements. Examine necessity for large number of special reports. Seek to consolidate in periodic reporting system.
State Legal Restrictions: Federal requirements frequently do not take account of state constitutional and legal provisions.	Establish state-by-state review of legal and constitutional restrictions preventing governor or state agency from full utilization of federal grants. Adjust grant requirements with realistic time period to permit constitutional or legal change.

[a]That one agency of state government must be charged with final authority both for administering the particular program within the state and in dealing with the federal agency.

ities. Secretary Gardner stated, "State and local governments might then become vestigial–an outcome I would regard as most regrettable."[11]

Almost exactly 30 years ago, V. O. Key, Jr., cautioned against the use of direct federal administration as an alternative to the grant-in-aid approach. Writing during the earliest years of the expanded grant-in-aid approach, he stated:

> The achievements of direct federal administration are not so striking as to make federal assumption an inviting alternative to the grant system. The governance of a nation of continental proportions is a matter for which no simple blueprint and specifications are available. The grant system builds on and utilizes existing institutions to cope with national problems. Under it the states are welded into national machinery of sorts and the establishment of costly, parallel, direct federal services is made unnecessary. A virtue of no mean importance is that the administrators in actual charge of operations remain amenable to local control. In that way the supposed formality, the regularity, and the cold-blooded efficiency of a national hierarchy are avoided. The grant system is admittedly an expedient. It must be judged, however, not by the ideal, but by

its concrete achievements. In all probability, the functions promoted by it would not have been performed on the same scale or with the same degree of effectiveness had the federal-aid scheme not been devised.[12]

Casting about for other alternatives for innovative methods of achieving the purposes of grants-in-aid but without many of the observed disadvantages of this system, [some writers] propose the establishment of regional commissions composed of both federal and state personnel which avoid identification of representing either of these levels. Federal grant-in-aid officials are sometimes chagrined when they visit a state counterpart office to hear one of the state officials say, "Quiet, here come the 'Feds'." In parallel, federal officials, particularly in professional fields such as education or public health, frequently speak with some disdain of the administrative and professional competence of their counterparts at state levels. Consequently, the concept of the regional commissions which are not identified as "federal" or "state" bears careful consideration and close observation of its use in the administration of the Public Works and Economic Development Act of 1965.[13]

Title V of the Act calls for the establishment of regional commissions composed of one federal member known as the "federal co-chairman" (appointed by the President, with the consent of the Senate) the one member from each participating state in the region. The state members of the commission elect a co-chairman of the commission from among their number. While the law provides for the use of the concept of the regional commissions for planning the extensive works projects program, the same approach and the use of the same type of administrative apparatus might be considered for the administration of the federal public assistance program, public health, vocational rehabilitation, water, air pollution, road, airport, construction, and other programs. . . .

As the realities of program operation reveal the interdependence of each level of government on the other for the achievement of national, state, and local goals, the area of intergovernmental relations affords an added dimension for intensive study, research, and innovation.

[1]Daniel J. Elazar, *The American Partnership* (Chicago: University of Chicago Press, 1962), p. 339.

[2]Wayne Vasey, *Government and Social Welfare* (New York: Henry Holt & Co., 1958), p. 39.

[3]Address by Secretary of the Interior Stewart L. Udall, University of New Mexico, February 6, 1964.

[4]Herbert L. Block, Elmer Davis Memorial Lecture, Columbia University, December 3, 1963. For a different view, see Kilpatrick, Cummings, and Jennings, *The Image of the Federal Service* (Washington, D.C.: The Brookings Institution, 1964), pp. 239–41.

[5]Cf. Walter W. Heller, *New Dimensions of Political Economy* (Cambridge: Harvard University Press, 1966), ch. 3.

[6]James L. Kilpatrick, " 'Stringless Grants' to States Suddenly Boil," *Minneapolis Star*, December 1, 1966.

[7]Ted Knapp, "Tax Sharing Drive Opened by Rockefeller," *Albuquerque Tribune,* December 2, 1967.

[8]The draft copy of the ACIR report on *Fiscal Balance in the American Federal System*, published early in 1968, states: "A policy calling for greater State tax effort in most States and a greater local tax effort in some States can be justified on the grounds that States–and many localities–have considerable untaxed revenue potential." Chapter 7, pp. 7–45.

[9]This is the premise of HUD's Model Cities program, which provides subventions for the matching amounts in certain selected areas.

[10]Cf. *Advisory Commission on Intergovernmental Relations*, Eighth Annual Report, Jan. 31, 1966, and the extensive research publications of the Advisory Commission; U.S. Senate Committee on Government Operations, Subcommittee on Intergovernmental Relations, *Catalogue of Federal Aid to State and Local Governments*, 89th Congress, 1st Session, 1965; House of Representatives, Committee on Government Operations, Intergovernmental Relations Subcommittee, *To Establish an Advisory Commission on Intergovernmental Relations,* 86th Congress, 1st Session, 1959; House of Representatives, Committee on Government Operations, *Advisory Commission on Intergovernmental Relations, The First Five Years,* House Report #1457, 89th Congress, 2nd Session, 1966; Council of State Governments, Chicago: *The Council, 1964,* and publications of the Council.

[11]Roscoe Drummond, "State-Federal Revenue Sharing," *St. Paul Dispatch*, December 6, 1966.

[12]V. O. Key, Jr., *The Administration of Federal Grants to States* (Chicago: Public Administration Service, 1937), p. 383.

[13]Public Law 89-136, 89th Congress, S. 1648, August 26, 1965.

3 The Problem of Coordination in a Changing Federalism

James L. Sundquist, with the collaboration of David W. Davis

In the nineteen-sixties the American federal system entered a new phase. Through a series of dramatic enactments, the Congress asserted the national interest and authority in a wide range of governmental functions that until then had been the province, exclusively or predominantly, of state and local governments. The new legislation not only established federal-state-local relations in entirely new fields of activity and on a vast scale but it established new patterns of relationships as well.

The massive federal intervention in community affairs came in some of the most sacrosanct of all the traditional preserves of state and local authority—notably education and, in 1968, local law enforcement. It included major national programs in new fields of activity like manpower training and area economic development, as well as new aid for established functions of local goverment like mass transportation, water systems, and sewage treatment plants. Moreover, in the Economic Opportunity Act of 1964 and again in the model cities program of 1966, the Congress for the first time authorized aid to local communities for a virtually

James L. Sundquist is a member of the staff of Brookings Institution and is author of the study *Politics and Policy: The Eisenhower, Kennedy and Johnson Years.* (1968) David W. Davis was also a member of the Brookings staff until leaving to become Director of the Office of Public Services of the City of Boston.

unrestricted range of functions, subject only to a general definition of purpose in the former case and a limitation by geographical area in the latter.

The transformation of the federal system in the 1960s can be seen in the dramatic rise in the number of federal grant-in-aid programs. The Advisory Commission on Intergovernmental Relations lists ninety-five areas of state and local activity for which federal grants-in-aid were available during the period 1966–68. In only ten of these areas had federal aid been initiated prior to 1930. Another seventeen areas were opened during the New Deal years. Twenty-nine more were added in the first fifteen years of the postwar period. But thirty-nine—or 41 percent of the total—were added in just six years, from 1961 to 1966.[1]

The transformation is reflected also in the expanded volume of federal grants to states and local communities under both new and old legislation. In a dozen years it has risen more than fivefold, from less than $5 billion to an estimated $25 billion in the 1970 fiscal year. It has risen also as a proportion of federal expenditures and of state-local revenue. . . .

Finally, the changing character of the federal system is evidenced in a shift of emphasis in the pattern of federal-state-local relationships in grant-in-aid programs. Characteristic of the legislation of the 1960s are forthright declarations of national purpose, experimental and flexible approaches to the achievement of those purposes, and close federal supervision and control to assure that the national purposes are served. Some earlier grant-in-aid programs are in this pattern too—urban renewal, for example—but typically the pre-1960 programs were cast in a different mold.

Before 1960 the typical federal assistance program did not involve an expressly stated *national* purpose. It was instituted, rather, as a means of helping state or local governments accomplish *their* objectives. It was the states that set the goal of "getting the farmers out of the mud" through improved state highway networks; federal highway aid was made available simply to help them reach that goal sooner. Communities needed hospitals and sewage treatment plants and airports; the leading lobbyists for expansion of federal assistance for community activities were the national organizations of municipal officials, and they sought it for specific and accepted functions of local government.

Policy making for the established functions, in the older model, remained where it resided before the functions were assisted—in the state and local governments. Federal review and control, accordingly, sought primarily the objectives of efficiency and economy to safeguard the federal treasury, and did not extend effectively to the substance of the programs. Even controls for purposes of assuring efficiency could be loose, because the programs called for a substantial state or local contribution—usually 50 percent—and it could be assumed that the sponsoring governments, in their vigilance against waste of their own money, would automatically protect the federal government too. Funds were distributed among the states on a formula basis, and the states—within broad statutory guidelines—determined the allocation among communities within the states. Where state plans had to have federal approval they were rarely rejected. The federal agencies saw their role as one of technical assistance rather than control. They would offer advice, and "work with" the states to improve their programs, but they would not substitute their policy judgment for that of the recipient agencies. Moreover, the state agencies organized potent national associations with the dual mission of lobbying for more federal money and resisting every suggested extension of federal control, through appeals to the Congress if necessary.

In the newer model the federal grant is conceived as a means of enabling the federal government to achieve *its* objectives—national policies defined, although often in very general terms, by the Congress. The program remains a *federal* program; as a matter of administrative convenience, the federal government executes the program through state or local governments rather than through its own field offices, but the motive force is federal, with the states and communities assisting—rather than the other way around. . . .

Achievement of a *national* objective requires close federal control over the content of the program. Projects are therefore individually approved; the state or community is not assured of money automatically through a formula apportionment.[2] On the other hand, in order to accomplish the national objective the federal government must make certain—through one means or another—that sufficient and appropriate proposals are initiated. Accordingly, federal agencies aggressively promote the program, solicit applications, and provide extensive technical assistance, either directly or by financing the employment of consultants. As further inducement, the federal contribution is raised well above the 50 percent that was characteristic earlier; it commonly begins at 100 percent and often remains there.[3] Since the states and communities have little or no financial stake in the undertaking, the expenditures must be closely supervised by the federal government from the standpoint of economy as well as substance.

Where the federal objectives are broadly defined and highly experimental—for example, the war on poverty—the federal agencies are given leeway as to what state or local agencies they will deal with and what specific activities they will finance. In these circumstances the federal government may find it expedient to deal with established organs of local government; or to foster the creation of wholly new bodies at the community level whose loyalty will be primarily to the federal agencies that finance them and who can be counted on to adhere to federal policies; or even to use private organizations as the local instrumentalities for the execution of federal programs. The money is thus put "more precisely on target" than it would be if distributed in the old fashion, through the state.[4]

The transition from the older to the newer model was not, of course, an abrupt one. Before the 1960s, as already noted, programs like urban renewal were devised on the second model; and some statutes of the 1960s embodied more features of the former model than the latter—notably Title I of the Elementary and Secondary Education Act of 1965, under which funds are distributed among the states by formula and projects are approved at the state rather than the federal level (although the federal grant is 100 percent). In both periods, individual programs might incorporate elements of both models. Nevertheless, in the 1960s the mix changed. Before that decade, new programs characteristically embodied more features of the early model; in the 1960s, more features of the latter. . . .

THE DEMAND FOR COORDINATION

When the federal structure was transformed in the 1960s, it was not recast according to anybody's master plan. Nobody had one. Indeed, in the enactment of the new programs of federal assistance, scant attention was paid to the pattern of federal-state-local relations that was emerging. At every level—in the executive department, in the White House, in the Congress—the concentration was upon the substance of the legislation; the administrative language was inserted almost incidentally. "We have no organizational philosophy, only a program philosophy," one high federal official put it. In the absence of a common doctrine, the structure of federalism embodied in a particular bill reflected the ideas of whatever particular group of legislative draftsmen worked on that particular measure and what laws they used as precedents. Each statute had its own administrative strategy. Some programs followed the older model of federalism; most were patterned on the new. Formula grants coexisted with project grants. Established agencies vied with new ones as the recipients of the federal funds, in a welter of relationships and patterns that varied from agency to agency and from program to program.

By the mid-1960s, governors, mayors, and federal officials alike began raising their voices against the "proliferation" of federal programs and agencies and the "confusion" and "lack of coordination" in the administration of the grant-in-aid programs. The rise in criticism coincided with the peak years of enactment of new grant authorizations and particularly with the gathering momentum of the war on poverty. Under that banner a host of new programs was being launched and a new institution—the community action agency (CAA)—was being created in each community, with uncertain relations to local governments and to other existing institutions. . . .

In March 1966, Senator Edmund S. Muskie of Maine, chairman of the Senate subcommittee on intergovernmental relations, presented a detailed analysis of the coordination problem at all levels of government and a series of proposed remedial measures, which he said had growr out of a three-year subcommittee study. He told the Senate:

> We found substantial competing and overlapping of Federal programs, sometimes as a direct result of legislation and sometimes as a result of empire building. Similar competition and duplication were found at the State and local levels. We learned that too many Federal aid officials are not interested in, and in fact are even hostile to coordinating programs within and between departments, and that they are reluctant to encourage coordination and planning at State and local levels. These conditions frequently and predictably result in confusion and conflicting requirements which discourage State and local participation, and adversely affect the administrative structure and fiscal organization in these jurisdictions. . . .
>
> In short, we found conflict between professional administrators at the Federal level and less professional administrators at the State and local levels, between line agency officials and elected policymakers at all levels, between administrators of one aid program and those of another, between specialized middle-management officials and generalists in the top-management category, and between standpat bureau heads and innovators seeking to strengthen the decision-making process at all levels.
>
> The picture, then, is one of too much tension and conflict rather than coordination and cooperation all along the line of administration—from top Federal policymakers and administrators to the State and local professional administrators and elected officials.[5]

The senator proposed new coordinating mechanisms at every level of the federal government. At the top, he proposed a national intergovernmental affairs council, patterned after the National Security Council, to serve as "an operating mechanism for developing the President's policies of program coordination, and overseeing their implementation." At the departmental level, he called for a deputy undersecretary or his equivalent in each department with "full-time responsibility for coordinating aid programs on a departmental, interdepartmental, and inter-governmental basis." At the regional level, he endorsed a suggestion for a federal regional coordinator who would be responsible directly to the executive director of the national council. At the local level, he noted, an administration bill then pending provided for an office of federal coordinator in each city.[6] In introducing a bill embodying some of these proposals, in June, Senator Muskie warned, "We are headed for trouble in the building of the Great Society if we do not pull the Federal Establishment together and develop a more positive attitude of helping State and local governments meet their increasing public needs."[7] In hearings in November he drew admissions from members of the Cabinet and the budget director that the problem of coordination was serious. "In almost every domestic program we are encountering crises of organization," Secretary of Health, Education, and Welfare John W. Gardner told the Muskie subcommittee. "Coordination among Federal agencies leaves much to be desired. Communication between the various levels of government–Federal, State and local–is casual and ineffective. State and local government is in most areas seriously inadequate."[8]

The criticism continued throughout the remainder of the Johnson administration. In March 1968, for example, Mayor Henry W. Maier of Milwaukee, appearing on a national television show, protested that "a whole maze of some thirty possible agencies involving the city, the county, the state, and the Federal Government, and yes, the private sector" might be dealing with the welfare problems of a single family, and went on: "The thing is duplicated from top to bottom. We have now a general in HUD, we have a general in OEO, we have a general in HEW, at the top, and each one of these generals goes down the line to deal with the generals at the county level, the city level, the private sector. And I think that what we ought to have is . . . something that parallels a Joint Chiefs of Staff, starting at the top, some models of coordination going down to the bottom. . . ."[9] And later in that year both party platforms took cognizance of the administrative problems. The Republicans promised "a complete overhaul and restructuring of the competing and overlapping jumble of Federal programs to enable state and local governments to focus on priority objectives." The Democrats pledged to "give priority to simplifying and streamlining the processes of government, particularly in the management of the great innovative programs enacted in the 1960s." Acknowledging the existence of "duplication, administrative confusion, and delay," the platform pledged to "seek to streamline this machinery by improving coordination and management of federal programs."

A DEFINITIONAL DIGRESSION

In all the discussion the constantly recurring objective has been "coordination." The word, however, is one of many definitions, and it has been used in many senses. Coordination is sometimes a process, sometimes a result. Federal agencies are coordinated, so are levels of government, so are programs and projects.

In terms of process, coordination may be lateral—consultation, sharing of information, and negotiation among equals, a type of coordination that has been labeled "mutual adjustment."[10] Or it may be the settlement of a conflict by the decision of a "coordinator." Or it may be a combination of these—a process in which lateral coordination is expedited, facilitated, and even coerced by leadership and pressure from an independent or higher level coordinator.

Coordination may take place during the planning stage of a project or program, particularly if the planning process is a comprehensive one. By definition the elements of a properly drafted comprehensive plan are mutually consistent, mutually reinforcing, and hence coordinated. Through the planning process, conflicts can be defined early and resolved before, rather than after, programs go into operation. In some discussions, therefore, the words "planning" and "coordination" may be used almost interchangeably. The planning process itself can be either lateral or hierarchical or both; the plan can be assembled by equals who mutually adjust its elements, or it can be centrally drawn by planners and then adopted and enforced by those with authority to decide, or it can grow out of a combination of these. But coordination takes place in operations, too, after the plans are finished. Thus, training, job development, and placement organizations coordinate their handling of the same trainees; and welfare, health, rehabilitation, and other agencies coordinate their work by arranging for the cross referral of clients. The coordination may be lateral and voluntary or, if the agencies report to a common superior, it may be achieved through central direction.

In terms of result, coordination means consistency, harmony, mutual reinforcement, the absence of conflict and duplication. It may mean the consolidation of separate projects or programs into single undertakings serving the purposes of more than one program, agency, or government. It may mean, conversely, the division of single programs into clearly demarked segments that do not overlap, as in the apportionment of a training program among training agencies. Coordination may be spatial—the optimum physical relation of activities with one another, as in the assembly of related service agencies in a common neighborhood center, or the coordination of shoreline recreation and access road development with reservoir construction, or the expansion of transportation systems to serve new employment areas. It may be sequential, as in the scheduling of training of employees to coincide with the opening of a new plant. It may pertain to both space and time, as in the concentration of services in an urban renewal area when residents are displaced.

Given all these usages of the word, the objective of coordination has come to embrace in public discussion a wide range of improvements in interagency, intergovernment, interprogram, and interproject relationships—indeed, almost any change in organization, relationships, policies, practices, projects, or programs that will resolve whatever conflict or hiatus in the federal-state-local chain of relationships the user of the term may happen to be concerned with. A term whose meanings are so broad, so loose, and so varied may seem virtually without meaning at all. But there *is* a problem—recognized by Presidents, Cabinet members, governors, mayors, and observers of every station. The use of a single term to describe the problem is a recognition that, in all its many and varied aspects, it is still a *single* problem. It should be described, then, by a single word; another might be used, but "coordination" serves the purpose. In this study the term is used—as in contemporary jargon—as a convenient shorthand for any or all of a range of related concepts. . . .

DEVICES FOR COORDINATION: IN WASHINGTON

As the need for coordination began to be felt by planners and administrators within the federal government—and as external criticism mounted—the government responded by moving to create an elaborate structure of coordination, both in Washington and at the community level (with some innovation, too, at the regional and state levels). In doing so, the government chose to rely almost wholly upon systems of mutual adjustment rather than of central direction, upon what could be attained through negotiation among equals rather than through the exercise of hierarchical authority.

At the Washington level the government designated coordinators—not one but several, each with responsibility for coordination in a particular field but without power to enforce coordination. Two of the coordinators were assigned on a geographical basis; the Secretary of Housing and Urban Development was made responsible for coordinating urban development programs and the Secretary of Agriculture for coordinating rural development programs. The Appalachian Region Commission and the five other regional commissions subsequently established had responsibility, however, for coordinating development programs in their designated regions, and the Secretary of Commerce was charged with coordinating their work and regional development in general. Beyond that were functional coordinators in a series of fields—the director of the Office of Economic Opportunity for antipoverty programs, the Secretary of Labor for manpower programs, the Secretary of Health, Education, and Welfare for programs in those fields insofar as other departments or agencies were involved. In 1965, coordinators were being designated with such frequency and regularity that one of them referred to the group irreverently as "the coordinator-of-the-month club."

The coordinating authority was assigned to the department and agency heads by statute or executive order, usually in restrained language —but language broad enough, and indefinite enough, to cover all of the aspects of coordination discussed above. Recognizing that Cabinet members cannot exert power over one another, the documents proceeded in two ways: they authorized the coordinator to "assist" or "advise" the President in the exercise of the presidential coordinating power; and they established mechanisms for lateral coordination and negotiation of agreements—Cabinet-level interdepartmental committees with fixed membership, initially, and later a "convener" procedure by which the coordinator was empowered to call meetings and representatives of the other agencies were directed to attend. The first of the coordinators—the director of OEO—was established by law in the Executive Office of the President in order that he might partake of the President's coordinating authority, and the President initially announced that the director would be the presidential "chief of staff" for the war on poverty. If he had so functioned, there might conceivably have been no need for other coordinators; in fact, however, he did not develop his chief of staff role, nor is there evidence that the President really tried to use him in that capacity. OEO became absorbed instead in organizing and operating the Job Corps and setting up community action agencies and became, in effect, one more operating agency of the government. On matters of coordination the director of OEO negotiated with Cabinet members as their equal, not as their superior. . . .

In addition to all these, President Johnson designated Vice President Humphrey as his liaison officer with the nation's mayors, and the director of the Office of Emergency Planning (later the Office of Emergency Preparedness) as a central point of contact for governors and other state officials.[11]. . .

DEVICES FOR COORDINATION: IN THE COMMUNITIES

Essentially, of course, the Washington negotiations were not centered upon the division of power and responsibility in Washington but their division among competing institutions in the country's thousands of communities. And this reflects the essence of the issue. As the headquarters of an army exists only to direct and support the army in the field, where the battle is, so the whole federal grant-in-aid structure exists only to influence and support what goes on in the communities. The ultimate purpose of coordination at every level of that structure is to harmonize programs and projects, and interrelate them constructively, at the point of impact–in the communities. But it is not federal programs only that must be interrelated. Federal programs must be coordinated not only with one another but also with state programs, the community's own public programs, and private endeavors of all kinds. If there were no federal grants-in-aid, coordination would need to be achieved locally in any case, and that would be the responsibility of community institutions. The addition of federal assistance programs only complicates the job of those community institutions; it in no way transfers the responsibility for the coordination process itself from the community to the federal government. Accordingly, much of the discussion that treats lack of coordination as a *Washington* problem, or a *federal field* problem, is misdirected. It is a community problem; conflict among federal agencies in Washington or in the field is important because, but only because, it affects the ability of community institutions to achieve coordination.

The proliferation and vast expansion of federal assistance programs in the 1960s soon overwhelmed the local coordinating institutions that were in existence–local governments, primarily, and area planning bodies, and such private organizations as councils of social agencies. Communities, aided in some instances by the states, had been proceeding slowly to strengthen their institutional structures for purposes of coordination. States had authorized multijurisdictional planning and development bodies, both in metropolitan and in rural areas, and these were struggling into being. A few cities were experimenting with new institutional devices (the predecessors of OEO's community action agencies) aimed at mobilizing into a concerned effort the many public and private agencies that were attacking the problems of poverty and slums. But in general, community institutions–urban and rural alike–were unequal to the demands of the new national programs for leadership, planning, and coordination at the community level. It soon became apparent to the planners of those programs that the weakness of the community institutions was itself *a national problem* that demanded a national solution, because in the absence of an adequate local institutional structure the national programs designed for the solution of substantive community problems would be bound to fail.

But, in the absence, once again, of an organizational philosophy, no one solution was devised for the problem of community-level coordination. Almost as many solutions were conceived as there were federal agencies grappling with the problems of community development. Each agency developed its own strategy of community organization, and the competing strategies were separately recommended to the Congress and enacted into law or separately established by agency authority. The "coordinator of the month" at the Washington level created his counterpart "coordinating structure of the month" at the community level—and jurisdictions overlapped in the communities as in the capital. By 1967 more than a dozen types of federally initiated, local coordinating structures could be counted. OEO had its community action agencies (CAAs); HUD, its city demonstration agencies (CDAs) under the model cities program; Agriculture, its resource conservation and development (RC&D) projects, rural renewal projects, rural areas development (RAD) committees; technical action panels (TAPs), and concerted services coordinators; Commerce, its economic development districts (EDDs) and overall economic development program (OEDP) committees; Labor, its cooperative area manpower planning system (CAMPS) and its concentrated employment program (CEP); the Appalachian Regional Commission, its local development districts (LDDs); and HEW, its comprehensive area health planning agencies. In addition, four agencies (HUD, Labor, HEW, and OEO) jointly were organizing pilot neighborhood centers. Finally, in 1968, HUD was given authority to sponsor nonmetropolitan districts (NMDs) in cooperation with Agriculture and Commerce. To complicate the situation further, several of the states had designed coordinating mechanisms of their own, which were related only imperfectly to the patterns being developed by the federal government, and local jurisdictions had formed councils of governments (COGs) and metropolitan and nonmetropolitan planning bodies.

The federally initiated community mechanisms differed not just in name, structure, and function but also in the elements of the communities' social, economic, and political structures upon which they were based. Each reflected the particular clientele of its parent agency, as well as that agency's administrative traditions and customary channels of communication. Thus, HUD relied on elected officials, particularly urban mayors, and built its mechanisms around local governments—but even so, in the case of model cities, required creation of the city demonstration agencies. The Office of Economic Opportunity, skeptical of the treatment that its clientele, the poor, would receive at the hands of local government, created in its community action agencies a new kind of institution whose control was to be shared by public officials, representatives of private organizations, and the poor themselves (although some of the agencies were, at least in name, departments of the city governments). The Department of Commerce established its relationships with business leaders and other elements of community "power structures," and the Appalachian Regional Commission—a federal-state agency—

followed the same pattern. The Department of Agriculture, with its tradition of direct field operations, tended to rely upon its own employees, supported by committees of rural leaders. The Department of Health, Education, and Welfare, accustomed to dealing with local communities only through the states, followed that course in setting up its community-level planning bodies in the field of health. The Department of Labor likewise looked primarily to its principal state counterpart, the state employment service, although in the concentrated employment program it chose to bypass the states and rely upon the community action agencies as sponsors.

By 1967 the cry for coordination that was rising from governors, mayors, and other participants in the federal system at all levels was directed less toward the need for coordinating federal programs as such than to the need for bringing order to the maze of coordinating structures that federal agencies were independently propagating. That became the substance of the treaty-negotiating sessions among Cabinet departments. They negotiated the jurisdictional claims of their community counterparts–without the presence of community representatives at the bargaining table. OEO and Labor worked out, for example, the relation in each community between the concentrated employment program, the community action agency, and the state employment service. OEO and HUD entered into bilateral negotiations on relationships between the community action and city demonstration agencies (although a presidential assistant finally umpired the dispute). HUD, Agriculture, and the Economic Development Administration (Commerce) jointly considered the guidelines for establishing nonmetropolitan districts under the 1968 act (although HUD finally issued the guidelines without awaiting agreement on all particulars).

The federal agencies pressed the claims of their community counterparts as their own, for in a very real sense they were. The position of the counterpart in the community determined the status of the parent agency in Washington. OEO depended upon the community action agencies as much as the agencies depended upon OEO; if they were lost, or subordinated, then OEO would be the loser too. If Agriculture's agencies were recognized as the coordinators in the rural communities, then Agriculture would be the coordinator of rural development in Washington. And so on. Consequently, the federal agencies, in their struggle for status and authority, pressed their conflicting strategies of community organization within the communities themselves, promoting the creation or the aggrandizement of their client counterparts. Communities were being pressed and torn by the conflicting demands of federal agencies. "Our city is a battleground among federal Cabinet agencies," a local model cities director told us. And the battle went on without benefit, except intermittently on an ad hoc basis, of an umpire with the power to reconcile conflicts and enforce order among the battling agencies.

THE FEDERAL SYSTEM AS A SINGLE SYSTEM

. . . The federal system is an intricate web of institutional relationships among levels of government, jurisdictions, agencies, and programs—relationships that comprise a single system, whether or not it is designed as one. The time has come for the Congress and the executive branch to take that system seriously—to stop making changes in any part of that system, by law or administrative order, without considering the impact of those changes upon the system as a whole. The federal system is too important—to the national objectives and community objectives alike—for the country to continue to accept as the structure for that system whatever happens to emerge from the power struggles and treaty negotiations among mutually jealous federal agencies and the random outcome of piecemeal legislative processes. The federal system is too important to be left to chance.

[1]Advisory Commission on Intergovernmental Relations, *Fiscal Balance in the American Federal System* (1967), Vol. 1, Table 22, pp. 140–44. The 95 areas included 379 separate categorical grant offerings, by the Advisory Commission's count of Jan. 1, 1967. Of these, 219 had been added in the four-year period 1963–66, 109 of them in 1965 alone. Additional programs have, of course, been enacted since then, including assistance for crime prevention and control in the Omnibus Crime Control and Safe Streets Act of 1968.

[2]Of the 379 grant-in-aid authorizations in effect on Jan. 1, 1967, some 280 were project grants, by the definitions of the Advisory Commission on Intergovernmental Relations; 99 were formula grants. Well over half of the project grant authorizations—160 of the 280—were enacted in the three-year period 1964–66. In contrast, more than half of the formula grants authorizations—53 of the 99—were enacted before 1963. Advisory Commission on Intergovernmental Relations, *Fiscal Balance in the American Federal System*, Vol. 1, Table 23, p. 151.

[3]See *ibid.*, Table 24, pp. 156–57, for tabulation of program matching ratios by years of origin of programs.

[4]Charles E. Gilbert and David G. Smith, "The Modernization of American Federalism," in Murray S. Stedman, Jr. (ed.), *Modernizing American Government: The Demands of Social Change* (Prentice-Hall, 1968), p. 140. In pp. 135–41 they review the changing character of federal grant programs.

[5]*Congressional Record*, Vol. 112, 89 Cong. 2 sess. (1966), p. 6834.

[6]The demonstration cities and metropolitan development bill. Protests from mayors led to elimination of the office by the Congress before the bill was passed.

[7]*Congressional Record*, Vol. 112, 89 Cong. 2 sess. (1966), p. 13228.

[8]*Creative Federalism*, Hearings before the Subcommittee on Intergovernmental Relations of the Senate Government Operations Committee, 89 Cong. 2 sess. (1966), p. 267.

[9]Comments on Meet the Press, National Broadcasting Co., March 3, 1968.

[10]Charles E. Lindblom, *The Intelligence of Democracy* (Free Press, 1965), p. 24, offers a tentative definition of coordination: "A set of interdependent decisions is coordinated if each decision is adapted to the others in such a way that for each adjusted decision, the adjustment is thought to be better than no adjustment in the eyes of at least one decision-maker." His book is an analysis of the methods, and comparative advantages in various circumstances, of two general types of coordination processes—"central coordination," or coordination by a decision maker (plus, of course, combinations of the two). His sympathies lie with mutual adjustment.

The San Francisco Federal Executive Board, Oakland Task Force, *An Analysis of Federal Decision-Making and Impact: The Federal Government in Oakland* (August 1968), pp. 181–88, offers three coordinative models, called "central direction," "mutual interaction," and "adaptation." The last two models appear to be subtypes of Lindblom's "mutual adjustment" model.

[11]President Nixon has given these related assignments to the same man, Vice President Agnew.

Chapter TWO

Fiscal Federalism

INTRODUCTION TO CHAPTER TWO This chapter deals with financial relations between federal, state, and local governments. There are many aspects to federal-state-local financial relations (most of which are covered in the chapters on higher education, welfare, and urban problems), but since 1960 this topic has tended to revolve around the issue of revenue sharing. At first glance, revenue sharing would not appear to be the kind of issue that could generate intense interest and widespread news coverage. The reason for it is that a debate about fiscal federalism in general and revenue sharing in particular quickly transforms itself into a debate about urban problems (such as welfare, mass transportation, racial strife, and pollution), the quality of education for the poor in America, the relative efficiency of state and federal bureaucracies, and a host of other problems. Indeed, this multi-problem quality of fiscal federalism may account for much of the difficulty that President Nixon has had in getting his revenue sharing proposals passed by Congress.

Under the many revenue sharing plans which have been proposed in the last fourteen years the federal government would give money to all the states on an annual basis with few restrictions concerning how the money would be spent. Former Representative Melvin R. Laird (R, Wis.) introduced the first revenue sharing bill in 1958. The idea was refined and popularized by economist Walter Heller in 1960. Thus the first two leading proponents of revenue sharing were a conservative Republican politician and a liberal Democrat academician; revenue sharing has, from the very beginning, cut across familiar partisan and ideological lines.

Heller's version (which came to be known as the Heller Plan) was very simple. Each year the federal government would place one or two percent of the federal individual income tax base (net taxable income) into a trust fund. The fund would be similar to trust funds which handle Social Security and highway construction monies. The money would be distributed among the states on the basis of population. Heller recognized that local governments deserved some of the funds, but writing in 1966 he could not decide "whether to leave the fiscal claims of localities to the mercies of the political process and the institutional realities of each state or to require a pass-through to them."[1]

The Heller Plan permitted the states and localities nearly complete freedom in the use of their money; they would be subject only to normal accounting procedures and Title VI of the Civil Rights Act. But, after arguing for minimal federal controls on shared funds, he added a critical point: "Those who fear that some states will simply use the revenue shares to rest on their fiscal oars would put in a further condition: that the shares of those states which lowered their fiscal effort would be reduced."[2] All widely discussed revenue sharing plans have featured a clause along these lines.

But why should the federal government collect money and then give a portion of it to the states? Would it not be simpler for the states to collect their own taxes? Proponents of revenue sharing argue that state and local responsibilities have grown beyond their abilities to collect adequate revenues. State and local governments have heavy and in some cases exclusive responsibilities in the fields of highway and street construction, education, health and welfare, sanitation, and police and fire protection. Major revenue sources for state and local governments are property, sales, and income taxes. Property and sales taxes are regressive and extremely unpopular. In many states it is impossible to raise them without great political danger to incumbent governors and legislators. Income taxes are more progressive but they are also unpopular, and the income tax field is largely dominated by the federal government. Furthermore, many state constitutions contain strict limitations on tax rates, and the constitutions can be changed only with great difficulty. Thus, say revenue sharing proponents, state and local governments lack sufficient funds to fulfill their responsibilities.

The weak financial condition of state and local governments has long been recognized and dealt with through federal grants-in-aid for specific programs, including health care, education, and highway construction. Federal grants totaled $24.4 billion in fiscal 1972. They have been very useful, but their operation has been accompanied by charges of excessive federal control and red tape. Revenue sharing promises a predictable, reliable, and automatically growing source of money with few controls and little red tape. Other arguments for (and against) revenue sharing are found in the first three articles in this chapter.

President Lyndon Johnson favored revenue sharing, but his support was not made public because of Vietnam budget pressures and a political fluke.[3]

In August 1969 President Richard Nixon's revenue sharing ideas were submitted to Congress (S 2948 and HR 13982) and referred to the Senate Finance Committee and the House Ways and Means Committee, but the bills did not even receive hearings. However, an alternative bill (S 2483) submitted by Senators Edmund Muskie (D, Maine) and Charles E. Goodell (R, N.Y.) was the subject of hearings before Muskie's Government Operations Subcommittee on Intergovernmental Relations.

The Muskie-Goodell bill had much in common with the Nixon proposal. First, there were almost no spending restrictions on shared revenues. Second, the shared revenues would not be funneled through the normal appropriations process (through the House Appropriations Committee and the Senate Appropriations Committee). Instead, the money would be appropriated by the act creating revenue sharing; it would be a permanent appropriation which the two appropriations committees could not affect. Third, the money would be distributed to the states, which would in turn be required to distribute the money to localities according to formulas set forth in the law. Fourth, the money would be distributed among the states according to population and tax effort. Generally speaking, "tax effort" refers to the intensity or severity of taxation in a governmental unit. Tax effort is normally measured by some ratio of the amount of taxes paid to per capita wealth. Thus a poor state with low taxes may exercise the same tax effort as a wealthy state with high taxes.[4]

The first two points of the Muskie-Goodell and Nixon plans were identical with the original Heller Plan. The second two points were somewhat different: Heller was undecided about distribution formulas for localities and he originally favored distribution among the states strictly according to population without reference to tax effort.

There were two major differences between the 1969 Nixon and Muskie-Goodell plans. First, the Muskie-Goodell plan would have provided more money to be shared ($3 billion compared with $500 million for the first year). Second, the Muskie-Goodell plan would have required that twice as much money be passed through to localities. The Muskie-Goodell plan also placed heavier emphasis on large cities. These differences reflected the liberal urban orientation of Muskie and Goodell, and, more particularly, the urban orientation of the Democratic Party. Nixon placed more emphasis on states because more states than cities had strong Republican Party influence (Republican governors or Republican-dominated legislatures).

But these differences were of little consequence because any revenue sharing legislation had to be processed by the House Ways and Means Committee chaired by long-time revenue sharing foe Wilbur Mills (D, Ark.) who refused to hold hearings in 1969 or 1970. According to his public statements, Mills' opposition stemmed from his conception of governmental responsibility; he felt that a unit of government which spends money should be required to raise most of it. Mills' opposition was shared by ranking minority member of the Ways and Means Committee John W. Byrnes (R, Wis.) who focused on Walter Heller's original conception that shared revenues would come from surpluses in the federal budget. Byrnes argued that federal deficits made revenue sharing fiscally unwise; in other words, he claimed that the federal government did not have revenues to share.

In 1971 President Nixon submitted a revised and expanded two-part revenue sharing plan. One part (entitled "general revenue sharing") was very similar to his 1969 version; the formulas were nearly the same, and the amount of money shared with states would be 1.3 percent of taxable personal income instead of the 1 percent in the original plan. In the 1971 version the 1969 formulas were applied to 90 percent of the total money shared with the states; a state which created its own formula for sharing money with the localities (where the plan was approved by localities representing a population majority of the state), would become eligible for the remaining 10 percent. The Treasury Department calculated the amounts of money to be shared by each state. For example, New York would receive 10.68 percent or $534 million. Of this, 51.43 percent would be distributed among New York localities. Maine would receive only 0.458 percent or $22.8 million. In Maine, localities would receive 45.46 percent.

The second part of the 1971 plan (entitled "special revenue sharing") consisted of $11 billion in loosely earmarked funds to be given to the states as follows:

Law enforcement	$0.5 billion
Manpower training	2.0 billion
Urban community development	2.0 billion
Rural community development	1.0 billion
Transportation	2.6 billion
Education	3.0 billion

Only $1 billion of these funds would be newly appropriated; the remaining $10 billion was already being spent for existing programs. Shifting them to revenue sharing would allow more state and local control of funds.

But Wilbur Mills and John Byrnes remained opposed to the Nixon plan although Mills mentioned that he would favor a revenue sharing plan that would focus its aid on the cities. In November 1971 Mills and nine other members of the Ways and Means Committee introduced their own revenue sharing bill. A slightly revised version of this bill (HR 14370) was approved by the Ways and Means Committee in April 1972 by a vote of 18-7. The distribution formulas in this bill were much too complex to be described here; they included such factors as total state tax effort, state income tax effort, state population, urban population, and inverse per capita income (with the poorest states favored). The formulas tended to favor states and localities with Democratic Party majorities.

In the Rules Committee and on the House floor the Mills bill ran into the opposition of George Mahon (D, Tex.) chairman of the Appropriations Committee. Mahon objected to both the Mills and Nixon bills because they sought to appropriate money, thus short circuiting his own committee. In addition, representatives from states without income taxes opposed the heavy emphasis on distribution of money to states with income taxes in the Mills bill. Despite this opposition, the bill was approved by the House by a vote of 274-122.

After the House vote the bill was sent to the Senate Finance Committee, the Senate counterpart to the Ways and Means Committee. The Senate Committee made drastic changes in the bill which reflected the fact that a majority of the committee members came from relatively poor rural states. This bill was passed by the Senate. The differences between the House and Senate bills were compromised by a conference committee, and President Nixon signed the bill in October, 1972.

READINGS IN THIS CHAPTER

Introduction: Deil S. Wright

Wright describes the broad outlines of fiscal federalism. In fiscal 1971 federal aid to the states totaled $30.7 billion. Most of this money was transmitted in the form of federal grants. A major difference between grants and revenue sharing is that grants are designed to support specific programs such as Model Cities or special health care programs, and revenue sharing means that the federal government would give sums of money to the states with no (or few) strings attached. Wright describes other differences, and presents some arguments for and against revenue sharing.

Revenue Sharing, Pro and Con: ACIR and Banfield

Deil Wright presents an objective analysis of the advantages and disadvantages of revenue sharing. Two articles, by the Advisory Commission on Intergovernmental Relations (ACIR) and Edward Banfield, provide sharply conflicting and clearly defined points of view.

The ACIR focuses on urban problems and comes down hard in favor of a massive revenue sharing program. It argues that we are in the midst of an urban fiscal crisis of ever-increasing severity. In the past two decades many relatively wealthy people and industries have abandoned cities for the suburbs. The result is black, poor, disintegrating core cities surrounded by white, wealthy, rapidly growing suburbs which contribute little to the core on which they feed. This situation is exacerbated by concentrations of "high cost citizens" in the core. Thus revenue sources are drying up and urban government costs continue to increase. According to the ACIR, existing federal and state aid programs are inadequate. It concludes that revenue sharing (in addition to other solutions) is essential.

The controversial political scientist Edward Banfield disagrees with this analysis. He argues that the urban fiscal crisis is largely mythical. The problem, he says, is not the *ability* of states and cities to finance themselves, but, rather, their ability to finance programs desired by various reformers.

In analyzing the proper level of federal aid to states and cities, Banfield makes the important distinction between "those state-local needs that are in some sense national [and] those that are not." For example, migration of poor rural people into the cities (what the ACIR calls "high cost citizens") is not strictly an urban phenomenon, and state and federal money should be contributed to their maintenance. Water pollution is another trans-governmental problem which must be shared. Nevertheless, argues Banfield, there are many state and local needs which should be paid for by state and local governments. Furthermore, he argues that many trans-governmental problems such as welfare should not be handled with revenue sharing; the welfare problem could more efficiently be solved by creating a federal welfare program. Banfield also examines pressure group alignments for and against revenue sharing.

School Funding and the Value-Added Tax: Grafton

In 1971 two federal courts and the California Supreme Court declared that each state must provide equal educational opportunities for its children regardless of where they live in the state. The local property tax was the target of these decisions. The property tax is the major source of funds for secondary and primary schools, and, since property values vary widely from one school district to another, school quality (and educational opportunity) varies as well.

These decisions will require that state governments assume extra financial burdens. Secretary of Health, Education, and Welfare Elliot Richardson has speculated that these burdens will require federal aid to education financed by a national value-added tax. In this article, the court decisions are analyzed and property and value-added tax characteristics are discussed.

[1]Walter W. Heller, "New Dimensions of Political Economy" in Thomas R. Dye (ed.), *American Public Policy* (Columbus: Charles E. Merrill, 1969), p. 581.

[2]*Ibid.*, p. 582.

[3]President Johnson had intended to announce his support of revenue sharing, but when someone in his Administration leaked this to the press, Johnson (who hated news leaks) remained silent.

[4]In the Nixon Plan a given state would receive money determined by the formula $S = (P \times R/I)/A$ where S = the state's fraction of the total revenue to be shared, P = population of the state, R = revenues obtained by state and local units of government, I = total personal income earned by the state's residents, and A = the sum of $P \times R/I$ for all 50 states and the District of Columbia. R/I is the tax effort index. A state which increased its taxes and therefore increased revenue (R) would clearly increase its fraction of the shared revenue (other things being equal). Also, poorer states with low total personal incomes (I) would receive a disproportionate amount of money. Total revenue to be shared would start at a fraction of 1 percent of personal taxable income and rise to 1 percent by fiscal 1976. This would produce approximately $5 billion in 1976. Distribution of money within a given state would be determined by two formulas:

$L = M/G$, where L = the fraction of revenue sharing funds received by a given state which must be passed through to localities, M = locally gathered tax revenues excluding school and other special districts, and $G = M +$ state-gathered tax revenues excluding liquor store sales, public utilities, and insurance trust funds.

$H = C/F$, where H = a fraction of revenue sharing money going to a particular locality, C = locally gathered tax revenues excluding "business" operations such as transit or water systems, and F = the total of all locally gathered tax revenues in the state. The localities would receive an average of approximately 30 percent of a given state's revenue sharing money. States could change the $H = C/F$ formula by obtaining the agreement of two-thirds of the localities both by number of localities and the fraction of locally gathered tax revenues.

4 Federal Revenue Sharing: Problems and Prospects

Deil S. Wright

A convenient and even necessary starting point for discussing any type of federal aid is a useful classification scheme of the various forms of federal aid to state and local governments. For purposes of clarity and policy significance the utility of several three-category breakdowns is suggested. At one level federal aids can be grouped as: A. Loans and guarantees, B. Grants-in-aid, and C. Revenues shared. The grant component in the above grouping can be further sub-divided into three elements: (1) categorical, (2) consolidated, and (3) block. Likewise, the revenue sharing component can be split three ways: (1) pre-existing, (2) special, and (3) general revenue sharing items.

Brief descriptive comments about these groupings are in order. It is helpful, however, to grasp the dollar magnitudes in each of these components as presented in the current and proposed budget. Table I presents the estimated dollar amounts for fiscal 1971 and 1972 as contained in the 1972 budget. Two prominent policy conclusions emerge from these tabulations for the fiscal year 1971. The first is the overwhelming reliance on the grant-in-aid as the major mechanism for intergovern-

From: *Public Affairs Comment* of the Institute of Public Affairs, The University of Texas, July 1971. Reprinted by permission of the author and publisher.

Deil S. Wright is Professor of Political Science at the University of North Carolina at Chapel Hill.

mental aid. A second, for the same fiscal year, is the equally heavy reliance within the grant sector on categorical grants rather than consolidated or block grants. The $29.1 billion being spent for categorical grants in 1971 include 175 major programs, over 500 specific sub-authorizations, and about 1,300 federal assistance activities providing money figures, application deadlines, precise contracts, and use restrictions.

GRANTS AND SHARED REVENUES: ANATOMICAL DIFFERENCES

There are three major differences between grants-in-aid and shared revenues. First, grants are annually-appropriated specified amounts whereas shared revenues are fluctuating amounts of a predetermined revenue source or tax base that normally does not require annual legislative action for transfer to and expenditure by the receiving unit. Second, grants are almost uniformly conditional. That is, they prescribe expenditure restrictions, e.g., allocation to a specific function or program, matching requirements, and conformity to a previously-approved plan. Shared revenues place minimal restrictions on the manner in which recipients use funds. Third, grants have a built-in programmatic aim; their conditional character orients them to specific program goals. Shared revenues, on the other hand, are intended as general or unrestricted interlevel aid.

The central feature of the grant device is its *conditional character;* it limits or restricts the way in which the funds may be used. The restrictions invariably apply to the substantive or program use of monies and normally entail other conditions as well, such as matching, advance planning, prior approval, accounting, reporting, personnel qualifications, etc.

The degree of program constraint provides a basis for identifying three types of federal grants in descending order of restrictiveness. Grants may be (1) categorical, (2) consolidated, or (3) block. The block grant is the widest in scope of the three types. Its funding is limited only to a broad functional purpose, such as education, health, law enforcement, or welfare. The consolidated grant is a hybrid form somewhere between the block and categorical types. As the term implies, it represents a grouping, combining, or consolidation of former categorical grants into a larger, broader program that subsumes the previous narrow categories.

Until recently, consolidated and block grants were an academic matter, of interest largely to scholars and state and local officials seeking reform. The only significant example of a consolidated grant is the comprehensive health planning and services program. This program came into being in 1966 with the passage of P.L. 89–749 abolishing more than a dozen categorical disease grants (such as heart, cancer, tuberculosis) and establishing a single consolidated grant to cover the broad range of health services. Two examples of block grants presently exist. One is the model cities legislation enacted in 1966 to develop a coordinated attack on urban ills in a target area within a city. The second involves the allocation of funds to states under the Omnibus Crime Control and Safe Streets Act of 1968.

Past examples of revenue sharing are few and far between in the panoply of federal assistance programs. Presently, there are nine revenue sharing programs in the natural resources field and these total less than $300 million. In 1970, President Nixon proposed a modest start on unrestricted or general revenue sharing amounting to $500 million on a fiscal year basis. The recommendation, of course, was not approved. For 1972, and beyond, the President has offered more striking and unprecedented departures. An appreciation of the magnitude of the shift is obtained by comparing the 1971 and 1972 figures in Table 1.

TABLE 1 Forms of Federal Aid: 1971 and 1972 Comparisons

	Estimated Outlays (billions of dollars)			
Type of aid	*Fiscal 1971*		*Fiscal 1972*	
A. Loans and Guarantees (Net)		$ .4		$ .3
B. Grants-in-Aid (Total)		30.0		24.4
1. Categorical	$29.1		$24.2	
2. Consolidated (Health)	.2		.2	
3. Block (LEAA, Model Cities)	.7		–	
C. Revenue Sharing (Total)		.3		13.9
1. Pre-existing (Mostly Natural Resources)	.3		.3	
2. Proposed: Special Revenue Sharing	–		9.6	
3. Proposed: General Revenue Sharing	–		4.0	
Grand Total of Federal Aid		$30.7		$38.6

Source: Adapted from *Special Analyses–Budget of the United States, Fiscal Year 1972*, Table P-9.

On a full fiscal year basis general revenue sharing will approximate $5.0 billion but will distribute about $4.0 billion in 1972 if enacted by this session of the Congress. Of equal or greater significance are the "special" revenue sharing amounts estimated at $9.6 billion in fiscal 1972 and at $11.4 billion annually after 1972.

General revenue sharing probably needs little explanation. The President's 1971 plan specifies that 1.3 percent of the federal personal income tax base ($5.0 billion) be placed in a trust fund to be distributed among the states on the basis of population weighted by state-local tax effort (i.e., high tax effort states would receive more). Mandatory pass-through provisions require local sharing in direct proportion to local governments' shares of combined state local taxes. Intra-state distributions, unless specified differently by state legislatures, are based on percentages of general revenues raised by local units in the respective states, e.g., a city collecting 5 percent of all local revenues in the state would receive 5 percent of the pass-through money in that state.

The President's *special* revenue sharing proposals deserve far more extensive and intensive comment than time and space allow. There are six broad functions for which funds will be "shared" in the following approximate full-year amounts:

Function	Amounts in Billions	Number of Programs Consolidated
Education	$ 3.0	33
Transportation	2.6	28
Law Enforcement	.5	2
Rural Community Development	1.0	39
Urban Community Development	2.0	11
Manpower Training	2.0	17
Total	$11.1	130

These groupings represent the consolidation of 130 categorical grants into six major functions or programs. The actual or potential semantic confusion may already be apparent to the casual observer. If this grouping or collapsing of categorical grants does occur, why not call the end result a "consolidated" grant, or perhaps even a block grant where such broad functions justify the term, e.g., education, law enforcement, urban community development?

There seems to be slender justification for the "revenue sharing" term since the funds for these functions are not tied to a tax source or base. Also, since the amount allocated to each function is dependent on the annual congressional appropriations process, the term "grant" appears more appropriate and accurate.

On the other hand, the term "revenue sharing" is defensible for at least three reasons: (1) the dollar magnitudes of the amounts; (2) the absence of matching requirements and other "strings" attached to the special revenue sharing moneys; and (3) the political salability of "revenue sharing" rather than "grants."

To illustrate only the political factor, it is a fact of current political life that revenue sharing is an "in" or "swinging" idea in many quarters of the national capital and in hinterland capitols, courthouses, and city halls. "Grants," on the other hand, is a bland, sluggish, unleavened term. It lacks political pizzaz. If it carries any emotional overtones, they are negative connotations stemming from critiques of grant proliferation, grantsmanship, and grant management jungles. In retrospect and given the status of "grant" affairs, the Administration's choice of novel but somewhat inconsistent terminology seems advisable and judicious.

A PROBLEM ANALYSIS OF REVENUE SHARING: ARGUMENTS FOR AND AGAINST

In place of a long list of pros and cons on revenue sharing, I would prefer to focus attention on five fundamental features or problem areas of our political system that revenue sharing is intended to influence. These system-level problems provide one basis for compiling a summary balance sheet on the assets and liabilities of revenue sharing. The problem areas are identified by the mnemonic code of five R's–Resources, Reliability, Relationships, Results, and Responsiveness.

Resources. On the credit side, the central aim of the revenue sharing, both special and general, is to secure a better match of funds and functions. The figure of $10 billion is mentioned as the current state-local revenue gap. The $6 billion in new money ($5 billion general and $1 billion special) is the Administration's response. It has proved successful in generating enthusiastic lobbying by many governors and mayors, although the latter have been less supportive of the special revenue sharing proposals. Perhaps the most significant plus for the general proposal is the revenue growth factor. The amount shared hinges on the personal income tax base, an economic indicator that rises more rapidly than total GNP.

On the debit side, a central criticism of revenue sharing is the separation of revenue-raising responsibility from the authority over resource allocation. This charge proceeds from what may be called the "pain-pleasure thesis." Simply put, it asserts that the pleasure of spending public funds should be linked with the pain of raising those same resources. This thesis is an amalgam of utilitarian-based political propositions and protestant, puritanical parsimony.

Revenue sharing clearly runs counter to the pain-pleasure thesis. The prime question on this issue, however, is not the degree of contradiction but the degree to which one subscribes to the psychology of government incorporated in the thesis. There are two viewpoints held by some members of the Congress that reinforce sentiments sympathetic to the pain-pleasure thesis. One is the ignorance, skepticism, or downright distrust of state and local governments. A second, and perhaps dominant, concern is over the loss of congressional control. As one senator commented, "I'm concerned about the aspect of revenue sharing that permits them to spend it any way they wish." The heart of revenue sharing is that "them," state and local governments, will have broad discretion to allocate the shared resources as they see fit. This raises a central and continuous political question: Who shall decide? In turn, it poses the issue of the responsibility or reliability of state and local government.

Reliability. Will state and local governments use shared revenues in a reliable and responsible manner? On the negative side, there are charges that state and local governments are leaky purses or low-gauge sieves into which choice federal funds should not be poured. Some non-results with Title I of the Elementary and Secondary Education Act and the loose handling of some Law Enforcement Assistance Administration funds give credence to the claims.

Overlapping, duplication, mismanagement, waste, and inefficiency are seen as chief features of local government. This is not an idle or ill-considered outlook. Wholesale reform and reorganization of local *and* state government have been specified as conditions for receiving general revenue sharing funds in a bill introduced by Congressman Henry Reuss (D, Wisc.). The full particulars of Reuss' views and his "State and Local Government Modernization Act" appear in his book *Revenue-Sharing: Crutch or Catalyst for State and Local Governments?*[1] Senator Hubert Humphrey has introduced a similar bill in the Senate.

What can be said on the plus side of the ledger for responsible, reliable state-local governments and revenue sharing? Will it, as the Administration contends, make the nation stronger because of the increased vitality of its state and local governments?

Two points deserve attention. First, both forms of revenue sharing are designed and aimed toward general purpose units of governments. Special districts and even school districts are bypassed. Second, within these general governments the chief executives are the focal officials. The President's messages, supporting materials, and the bills encourage and anticipate broad discretion exercised by governors, county executives (or commissioners), and mayors. Important involvement by legislative bodies is not precluded and in some ways it is fostered. But executives are clearly expected to occupy center stage in making major choices under revenue sharing proposals.

Relationships. The present and future linkages between units or levels of government are the focus of attention under this topic. What effects would revenue sharing have on the relationships among or between governmental jurisdictions? This question forces us to set the proposal within the larger context and issues encompassed by the term "intergovernmental relations." What is the fundamental nature and modal pattern of relationships among units of government in the American multi-jurisdictional political system? We should be quick to add a qualifying or clarifying comment. Strictly speaking, there are no such events we can call inter-*governmental* relations; there are only relationships among officials who govern. How will these relationships be altered by revenue sharing? Only the most gross and panoramic observations can be offered.

On the debit side, it is possible that revenue sharing could lead not only to increased dependence of state-local officials on Washington-based decisions but also to a greater degree of subservience. Such consequences might result from the following sequence of events. Revenue sharing might increase the tendency of state or local officials to "appeal upstairs," that is, to carry their case for funds to Washington more frequently than they now do. The initial broad-based, flexible-use character of the funds might be eroded through informal bargains struck in the chambers of the Congress. The Congress, as a result of more intense and intimate contact with state-local officials, may be drawn deeper into detailed deliberations and decisions of the entire state-local political sector.

On the positive side, it can be argued that revenue sharing is a key clause in a new "Declaration of Interdependence." (Since we are nearing the bicentennial of the first declaration, it seems only appropriate that we give thought to the elements of a new credo.) A central tenet of revenue sharing is its explicit if not implicit recognition of the convergent and interdependent character of contemporary federalism in the U.S. It not only posits a "bringing together" but a "binding together."

We can adopt the metaphor of the internal combustion engine to help make the point. The velocity (or scope) of all governments has increased, and there has been an accompanying increase in the compression ratio. Governments and their officials are closer and more compacted (a) than in the past and (b) than most people realize. The governmental engine is powered by money, and revenue sharing would help furnish the correct mix of fuel to operate this new-technology vehicle.

On balance, and to my own way of thinking, revenue sharing holds greater promise as a recognition of interdependence than a concession of overdependence.

Results. Will money allocated through revenue sharing secure greater effectiveness than funds spent or channeled in another manner? Will the money go where it is "needed?" Will it be spent for programs that are top priority concerns? Will it be used to reduce taxes? What kind of revisions in spending programs and service levels might revenue sharing precipitate?

It is much easier to state than to respond to these difficult (and perhaps unanswerable) questions. Furthermore, we should note that these may not cover the most pertinent policy questions.

A few economists have done some systematic and insightful writing on selected aspects of revenue sharing. To the extent that I can read what they are saying, and read it correctly, I interpret their results negatively. Do not count on revenue sharing to have a strong stimulative effect on state-local outlays. It would be almost totally additive, that is, state-local spending would be increased by nearly the exact amount of the funds shared.

Two other comments deserve mention. First, recent evidence on the effects of grants-in-aid reveals that they are much less stimulative than long suspected, especially in the highway and welfare fields. Second, it is worth observing that revenue sharing without any matching requirements would not, in the aggregate at least, produce significant substitutive effects, i.e., state-local tax reduction. The elasticity of service demands is evidently high and widespread.

It is clearly not easy to ascertain a plus or minus sign on the expected results or effects of revenue sharing. No doubt the chief difficulty stems from the elusiveness and inconclusiveness of our measurement capabilities when we ask about "needs," "priorities," and "service levels." The balance sheet result on "results" is, therefore, a draw, with small entries on both sides of the ledger.

Responsiveness. One approach to the matter of responsiveness is to consider the manner in which government reacts to public demands. Another is to consider the content of governmental actions from the citizen's standpoint. What are the direct impacts of a program or policy on the individual and the body politic? It is mainly from the latter standpoint that we discuss revenue sharing and responsiveness.

A persistent query in the President's speeches, messages, and supporting documents is: "How will revenue sharing bring government closer to the people?" The response to this question has been varied but one that comes to mind goes as follows: "The President's program for revenue sharing is designed to provide major benefits to the individual citizen through units of local government rather than unresponsive special districts and agencies. The individual will find his voice in government strengthened and the upward pressures on his State and local taxes reduced by a program of shared resources."

This statement implies three types of citizen impacts as a consequence of revenue sharing. The first is structural and recalls earlier comments about general versus special governments. The suggestion of greater citizen control can be clearly inferred. Control, however, is in large measure contingent on participation. Both the latter and the former are indicated by how "the individual will find his voice in government strengthened." Exactly how this will occur because of revenue sharing is not specified. The presumption appears to be that each citizen will somehow acquire a new niche or added leverage that was absent prior to its adoption. Here is an area that calls for more extensive elaboration and precision to support the responsiveness argument.

The third type of responsiveness indicated in the above quotation involves the impact of taxes. Here some evidence is available to show the impact on citizens of the tax shift and expenditure effects that would probably accrue from revenue sharing. Briefly, and omitting considerable complex economic evidence, the following points can be made:

1. Revenue sharing would be likely to moderate state-local tax increases.

2. State-local outlays financed by revenue sharing would come from the progressive federal tax sources rather than from the more regressive state and local taxes.

3. The estimated incidence of benefits from state-local expenditures is heavily pro-poor. That is, the bulk of state-local outlays, e.g., education, health-hospitals, and welfare, are made largely on behalf of lower income citizens.

On at least one aspect of responsiveness, tax-expenditure effects, revenue sharing may be claimed an asset. A small additional entry might be made for a structural feature, general government. But on the citizen control and participation elements, no credits can be tallied. The overall summary on the responsiveness factor is an asset balance. . . .

CONCLUDING COMMENTS

Candor, a combination of both involvement and detachment, plus the perspective produced by 15 years of intergovernmental "watching," compel the writer to offer a few final summary observations.

Revenue sharing is an issue with a comparatively short political life. It has been seriously discussed as a viable national alternative for only seven or eight years. Compare it with two or more decades of discussion before action on national health care plans and general aid to education. It is a relative newcomer to the top of the national political agenda.

The partisan political palatability of revenue sharing is not yet firmly established. It crosses and subordinates party lines at the state-local levels, but it lacks similar fluidity on the Potomac scene. An explicit revenue sharing plank appeared in the 1964 and 1968 Republican platforms. In 1968, the Democratic platform said, "We must seek new methods for states and local governments to share in federal revenues . . ." This qualified endorsement leads to a suggestion that revenue sharing proponents secure an unequivocal positive statement in the 1972 Democratic platform. A recent study of party platform pledges from 1944 through 1964 found that when both parties promised action on an issue that pledge was redeemed 85 percent of the time.

Despite the heavy descriptive emphasis of this discussion the author's biases and personal judgments have intruded, as they should. Let me make my position explicit and clear. I count myself among those favorable to revenue sharing. At the same time, I find myself among a smaller and amorphous group somewhat pessimistic about its passage, particularly in the short run. Although the hues of the picture should be bright, realism suggests shades of gray.

In a larger sense and in the longer run, however, one can be optimistic, ignoring for the present Keynes' trenchant comment: "In the long run we are all dead!" First, the President's bold and significant proposals have created a state of flux and a readiness to act (or react) in the Congress on pressing intergovernmental fiscal issues. The inputs to the Congress are regularly far different than the outputs. But there are excellent prospects for some positive action from the 92nd Congress. A second note of optimism concerns the long-range prospects for revenue sharing. It seems only a matter of time until some forms of special and general revenue sharing are on the statute books. This is said without callousness and with concern for what happens in the state-local finance sector in the meantime. We may come much closer to the "progress through chaos" route than we wish. But progress we will. Move forward we must.

Both currently and in the long run revenue sharing represents a relatively uncharted course. Like all policy choices there is an element of the unknown and a necessity for confidence in one's past and positive expectations about the future.

[1]Henry S. Reuss, *Revenue-Sharing: Crutch or Catalyst for State and Local Governments?* (New York: Praeger Publishers, 1970), 170 pp.

5 Restoring Fiscal Balance in the Federal System

The Advisory Commission on Intergovernmental Relations

From: *Urban America and the Federal System* (Washington: Superintendent of Documents, 1969), pp. 7–18.

The Advisory Commission on Intergovernmental Relations is a governmental agency composed of representatives of the national, state, and local governments, plus private citizens. It conducts research and issues studies on numerous topics relating to the federal system.

References to "the urban fiscal crisis" are commonplace. In practically any issue of big city newspapers there are reports about critical budgetary and tax problems that face the central city and other local governments in the metropolis. . . .

Yet it is nearly as commonplace that major urban areas account for most of the Nation's wealth and income. Metropolitan areas, having but two-thirds of the total population, account for: four-fifths (80 percent) of all bank deposits; more than three-fourths (77 percent) of the value added by manufacturing; three-fourths (75 percent) of all personal income in the Nation; . . . and seven-tenths (70 percent) of all values officially assessed for property taxation.[1] Personal income per person averages half again more in metropolitan areas than elsewhere in the United States—in 1966, $3,314 compared with $2,236 per person.[2]. . .

WHY A LOCAL FISCAL CRISIS?

But if it is clear—as so many measures attest—that metropolitan areas are so typically "better off," it is no less true that most of the problems besetting urban America show up most sharply in these areas. The answer to this seeming paradox is to be found in a growing fiscal imbalance within our federal system—a disorder that is most apparent among the jurisdictions in metropolitan areas in general and in the dire fiscal plight of many of the nation's central cities in particular. This intergovernmental fiscal imbalance is the product of many factors—conditions that either increase the "tilt" or prevent a restoration of balance:

1. A progressive political fragmentation of the tax base of most metropolitan areas—a fiscal splintering that places powerful constraints on the ability of local jurisdictions to raise revenue and creates a radical mismatch of resources between the "have" and "have not" jurisdictions within the same metropolitan area.

2. Misallocation of responsibility for financing education and public welfare programs—a factor that causes a severe tax overload for many jurisdictions. This year the local tax base will be forced to underwrite over half of the estimated $32 billion bill for public elementary and secondary education and approximately $1.5 billion for public welfare costs.

3. The constant local revenue crisis caused by the fact that urban expenditure demands and especially big city demands consistently outpace both the growth in the nation's income and the "automatic" increase in local taxes.

4. A lopsided Federal aid system, under which, despite its steadily growing fiscal superiority, the Federal Government has failed to develop a balanced system of support for State and local government. Heavy Federal emphasis on narrow categorical-type aid has unduly restricted State and local budgetary powers while intensive Federal use of the personal income tax has discouraged effective State use of this prime revenue source.

5. Faulty State aid systems that often aggravate rather than compensate for the growing fiscal disparities among local governments within the metropolitan areas.

6. A defective local property tax, the shortcomings of which (unequal assessments, regressive incidence and adverse land use effects) become increasingly apparent as local governments are forced to make more intensive use of this levy.

7. Limited revenue potential to be derived from local nonproperty taxes and user charges due to the limited jurisdictional reach of local governments coupled with their extreme vulnerability to interlocal competition. These limitations, particularly in metropolitan areas, severely constrict the possibilities of any particular local government from mounting an "operation bootstrap," of which rugged individualists still like to dream.

Countervailing Economic and Political Trends

While each of these factors has made its contribution to the general state of fiscal imbalance, two countervailing trends–one economic and the other political–merit special attention. These trends are reflected most dramatically in two fiscal facts; with each passing year the fiscal supremacy of the National Government becomes more apparent and the fiscal plight of many of America's central cities becomes more desperate. The economic trend–the growing interdependency of the nation–gives the Federal tax collector, equipped with the most productive tax and the broadest geographical reach, the best opportunity to tap the growing affluence of the national economy. The political trend–the progressive subdivision of the metropolitan area into more and still more governmental units–works in precisely the opposite direction. It both constricts the tax reach of the local jurisdictions and saddles the "have nots" (usually the central cities) with enormously disproportionate burdens. . . .

Fiscal Consequences

The worst features of the mismatch of needs and resources are now clearly apparent in the growing social, economic, and fiscal disparities among local jurisdictions in the great metropolitan areas of the Northeast and Midwest. At one extreme are the "big losers"–usually the central cities–"stuck" with an extremely anemic tax base and confronted with rapidly mounting expenditure demands incident to the governing, educating and "welfaring" an increasing proportion of relatively poor, black families. At the other extreme are the "big winners"–those white suburban jurisdictions wealthy enough to be able to underwrite a superior public educational system with a below average tax effort.

The Political-Fiscal Dilemma

The ultimate cause of this radical mismatch of needs and resources is political–State and Federal policy-makers are unable to muster sufficient support necessary either to prevent this head-on collision of economic and political forces or to provide sufficient compensation for damages to the local victims. The inability to engineer consent, in turn, can be traced to a political-fiscal dilemma. A strong tradition of local home rule ordinarily blocks any attempt to bring needs and resources into better alignment via the administrative centralization approach–i.e., creation of a metro-type government or the shifting of all responsibility for certain high cost functions such as education or welfare to the State or National Government. On the other hand, popular support for a "Puritan" ethic that discourages the divorce of tax and expenditure responsibility ordinarily stands in way of a "fiscal" decentralization solution–i.e., the transfer of Federal funds to State and local government on a "no strings" basis or for State assumption of virtually all the responsibility for financing education while leaving wide policy discretion in the hands of local school boards. . . .

Grim Fiscal Outlook for Central Cities

. . . The findings of a recent Advisory Commission study of metropolitan fiscal disparities clearly substantiate the widespread belief that most of our major cities are now in a desperate situation.

1. The central cities, particularly those located in the industrial Northeast and Midwest, are in the throes of a deepening fiscal crisis. On the one hand, they are confronted with the need to satisfy rapidly growing expenditure requirements triggered by the rising number of "high cost" citizens. On the other hand, their tax resources are increasing at a decreasing rate (and in some cases actually declining), a reflection of the exodus of middle and high income families and of business firms from the central city to suburbia.

2. The concentration of high cost citizens in the central city is dramatically underscored by public welfare statistics. For example, 27 percent of Maryland's population is located in Baltimore, yet 72 percent of Maryland's AFDC expenditures is to be found in that city. By the same token, Boston, with 14 percent of Massachusetts' population, accounts for 40 percent of that State's AFDC expenditure.

3. A clear disparity in tax burden is evident between central city and outside central city. Local taxes in the central cities are 7.5 percent of income; outside the central cities only 5.6 percent of income. Higher central city taxes are reinforcing the other factors that are pushing upper income families and business firms out of the central city into suburbia.

4. On the educational or "developmental" front, the central cities are falling farther behind their suburban neighbors with each passing year. In 1957 the per pupil expenditures in the 37 metropolitan areas favored the central city slightly–$312 to $303 for the suburban jurisdictions. By 1965, the suburban jurisdictions had forged far ahead–$574 to $449 for the central cities. This growing disparity between the central city and suburban school districts takes on a more ominous character in light of the fact that the central city school districts must carry a disproportionately heavy share of the educational burden–the task of educating an increasing number of "high cost" underprivileged children. Children who need education the most are receiving it the least!

5. On the municipal service or "custodial" front, the presence of "high cost" citizens, greater population density, and the need to service the needs of commuters force central cities to spend far more than most of their suburban neighbors for police and fire protection and sanitation services. The 37 largest central cities had a non-educational (municipal)

outlay of $232 per capita in 1965–$100 greater than their suburban counterparts.[3]

The situation for most central cities takes on an even more dismal cast because there is little prospect for a *voluntary* solution arising from within the metropolitan area. Suburban political leaders can generally be counted upon to oppose stoutly any proposal that would call for a significant redistribution of resources such as an area-wide tax with a strong equalization twist to aid the central city. By the same token, suburban leadership can be expected to view with a jaundiced eye any major redistribution of burdens, i.e., the rezoning of suburban land to permit low income central city families to obtain public or low cost housing in suburbia. . . .

TOO LITTLE AND TOO LOPSIDED: THE STATE AND FEDERAL AID RESPONSE

In theory at least the States and the National Government–armed with superior fiscal resources–could have intervened and radically reduced local fiscal tensions. They could have responded to the challenge created by the widespread collapse of the balanced municipality and the rise of the lopsided metropolitan jurisdiction by rifling high-powered aid on the basis of need and local fiscal capacity into the coffers of the most "disadvantaged" localities and school districts.

In practice, there is little evidence to suggest that State and Federal aid combined has materially slowed down (let alone reversed) the forces working to increase metropolitan fiscal disparities. On the contrary, there is considerable evidence to suggest that State school aid and tax sharing policies in particular have had the effect of throwing gasoline on the fires. Federal mortgage insurance, highway and other grant-in-aid policies have had an equally incendiary effect. In addition, so-called "impact aid" to school districts often has tended to widen fiscal and social disparities in urban education.

Because of little or no explicit recognition of educational and municipal overburdens, most State aid programs increase the central city–suburban educational resources gap. By the same token, the not uncommon State practice of sharing a part of its tax receipts with local government on the basis of taxpayer residence also both promotes the cause of metropolitan political splintering and increases the gap between the "have" and "have not" communities.

One of the dramatic illustrations of this anti-equalization effect is found in Wisconsin's present system for sharing personal income tax receipts with its municipalities. In 1966, the high income residential suburbs in the Milwaukee metropolitan area received a $100.94 per capita share of the State personal income tax compared to $18.62 for the central city of Milwaukee and $18.47 per capita share for the area's low income residential suburbs. In order to provide a slim fare for its poorest jurisdictions Wisconsin has to set out a banquet for its richest municipalities!

To the extent that State and Federal aid programs have equalizing effects they are usually indirect–the by-products of a specific program designed to help poor people rather than direct results of programs designed to find and to help poor local jurisdictions *per se*. Because the poor increasingly tend to cluster together in the same municipality within a metropolitan area, any State or Federal program with a direct poverty orientation is bound to have an inter-local equalization effect, albeit of an indirect nature.

It may also be argued that any Federal program designed to prevent indigency also has a beneficial and indirect equalizing effect on local and State finances. In this case the Federal social insurance program–OASDI–must be cited as an important force working in the right direction.

Nevertheless, even after all of the State and Federal programs with the most indirect equalization effects are thrown on the scales, the fact remains that outside financial help has not come in sufficient magnitude to turn the fiscal tide for the nation's hard pressed central cities. . . .

RESTORING FISCAL BALANCE

Two great goals–decentralized decision-making and the equitable distribution of the costs and benefits of domestic government–challenge any effort to secure fiscal balance in our federal system. Add to this perennial dilemma the remarkable political, social and economic diversity to be found across the land and it becomes readily apparent that there is no sure-fire formula for fiscal salvation in our federal system.

Nevertheless, it is becoming apparent that believers in the federal system will have to take certain corrective actions because two powerful and closely related forces–urbanization and growing economic interdependence–are making it increasingly difficult to reconcile the twin goals of governmental decentralization and fiscal equity.

With each passing day the growing economic interdependence of the nation enhances the fiscal and tax superiority of the National Government. This fact and the predisposition of the Congress to attach detailed expenditure strings to its grants threaten the goal of decentralized decision-making. On the other hand, the forces of urbanization have burst municipal boundaries in most areas leaving in their wake glaring fiscal disparities among jurisdictions within the same metropolitan area. The political splintering along income and racial lines is akin to giving each rich, middle class, and poor neighborhood the power to tax, spend, and zone. Such decentralization of power can and does play hob with the goal of social justice.

In those metropolitan areas where the forces of urbanization have ruptured the local governmental shell, it is becoming increasingly apparent that federalism's second line of defense–the States–will have to take on many of the classical political and fiscal functions once performed by the old balanced municipality.

ACIR Recommendations—A Summary

The Advisory Commission's proposals for restoring fiscal balance call for strong positive action by both Federal and State governments:

1. To insure an equitable distribution of the costs and benefits of public elementary and secondary education and public welfare by broadening the geographic base of support for these two programs. Specifically this involves:
   a. As a long-range objective, State assumption of virtually all of the cost of financing public elementary and secondary education.
   b. National Government assumption of complete financial responsibility for public assistance, including Medicaid.

2. To harness the growing fiscal power of the National Government in behalf of our system of shared power, the Commission, in its report on *Fiscal Balance in the American Federal System,* has called for the development of a balanced program of Federal support for State and local governments that includes:
   a. Federal revenue sharing with State and local governments.
   b. Streamlining of the Federal categorical aid system.

3. To expedite the development of an effective and equitable State and local revenue system:
   a. Federal income tax credit for State income tax payments.
   b. Balanced State use of income and sales taxes.
   c. Property tax rehabilitation.

4. To enable the States to play a key role in equalizing local resources, State aid programs should:
   a. Take account of variations in local fiscal capacity.
   b. Develop "a systems approach" to State grants to local governments. . . .

[1]U.S. Bureau of the Census, *Statistical Abstract of the United States: 1968* (Washington, D.C.: 1968), pp. 883–86, 910, and 911; and U.S. Department of Commerce, *Survey of Current Business* (Washington, D.C.: August 1968), p. 32.

[2]*Survey of Current Business* (August 1968), p. 33.

[3]This analysis was conducted by Professor Seymour Sacks of Syracuse University and appears as a part of the Advisory Commission's study *Fiscal Balance in the American Federal System* (A-31; October 1967), Vol. 2.

6 Revenue Sharing in Theory and Practice

Edward C. Banfield

From: *The Public Interest*, No. 23, Spring 1971, pp. 33–45.

Edward Banfield is Professor of Political Science at the University of Pennsylvania. He is an author of several books including *Political Influence* and *The Unheavenly City*.

How one evaluates revenue sharing will depend upon what one takes the central issues to be. Oddly enough, what must appear to many people to be *the issue*—namely, how to keep the cities and states from going bankrupt—is not properly speaking an issue at all.

Mayor Lindsay has long tried to give the impression that catastrophe lies just ahead unless the federal government provides "massive" additional financial support. Recently other political leaders have been saying the same thing. "Countless cities across the nation," Mayor Gibson of Newark told the press recently, are "rapidly approaching bankruptcy." Governor Rockefeller, after having been informed of the Administration's latest plans, remarked that the federal government must do even more to prevent the states and cities from "virtually falling to pieces." Meanwhile Governor Cahill of New Jersey was telling a joint session of his legislature that "the sovereign states of this nation can no longer supply the funds to meet urgent and necessary needs of our citizens, and institutions and our cities." A day or two later Senator Humphrey in a single sentence made two of the most outstanding rhetorical contributions. The cities, he said, are "mortally sick and getting sicker" and the states "are in a state of chronic fiscal crisis."

In fact, the revenue-sharing idea was, at its inception, the product of exactly such forebodings. Back in 1964, when Walter Heller and Joseph Pechman proposed it, many well-informed people expected that state and local governments would soon be in serious financial difficulties while at the same time the federal government would be enjoying a large and rapidly growing surplus. The war in Vietnam was expected to end soon and, if federal income tax levels remained unchanged, the normal growth of the economy and the increase of population would yield large increases in revenue year after year. Thus, while the federal government fattened, the state and local governments would grow leaner and leaner. Because of rising birthrates and population movements, the demands made upon states and localities for all sorts of services, but especially schools, would increase much more rapidly than would their ability to raise revenue. Whereas the federal government depends largely upon the personal income tax, the yield of which increases automatically with incomes, state and local governments depend mainly upon sales and property taxes, which are inelastic. This being the outlook, it seemed sensible to make up the expected deficit of the state and local governments from the expected surplus of the federal government. Heller and Pechman proposed to do this by giving the states a claim on a fixed percentage of federal taxable income, subject to the requirement that a fair amount "pass through" the states directly to the cities. The idea quickly won wide acceptance. Both political parties adopted revenue-sharing planks, and in 1968 some 90 revenue-sharing bills were introduced in Congress.

What happened, however, was not what was expected. Federal expenditures rose unexpectedly (defense spending was cut, but increases in the numbers of persons eligible for social security together with higher payment levels and unexpectedly high costs for Medicaid took up the slack) and, because of the recession, tax collections fell off. Instead of a surplus the federal government faced a deficit. State and local governments meanwhile fared better than expected. Legislatures and electorates were surprisingly ready to approve new taxes and higher rates. In 1967, for example, the states increased their tax collections by 15 percent, and in 1968 they increased them by another 15 percent. Cities also found it possible to raise more revenue than they had expected. Between 1948 and 1969 state-local expenditures increased in real terms from 6.7 percent of Gross National Product to about 10 percent. For some time they have been the fastest growing sector of the economy. The credit rating of the cities has improved, not worsened. With respect to the 50 largest cities, only three (New York, Boston, and Baltimore) received lower ratings from Moody's Investment Service in 1971 than in 1940 and many (including Chicago, Los Angeles, and Cleveland) received higher ones.

Dangerous as even short-run predictions in these matters have proved to be, it therefore seems safe to say that no "fiscal crisis" looms for most states and cities. In 1975, according to an estimate cited in a recent article by Richard Musgrave and A. Mitchell Polinsky, state and local expenditures will reach $119 billion. Assuming that federal aid increases at no more than the normal rate of recent years, this will leave a short-fall of $17 billion. Eleven billion of this will be made up from normal borrowing. The remaining deficit of $5 billion, Musgrave and Polinsky say, "could be met by a 5 percent increase in tax rates at the state-local level, an increase which seems well within the reach of state-local governments . . ." As more and more state governments adopt income tax laws, their revenues will be less dependent upon the vagaries of legislatures and electorates. Moreover, thanks to the recent decline in the birthrate, the principal item of state-local expense–schooling–will for at least a decade be considerably less than had been expected.

INABILITY OR UNWILLINGNESS?

The "fiscal crisis" issue is spurious if defined as the inability (economic, organizational, legal or even political) of the states–and therefore in a sense of the cities, which are their legal creatures–to support public services at high and rising levels. It is real, however, if defined as their unwillingness to support many of these services at what most reformers deem minimum-adequate levels. Presumably what Governor Cahill meant to tell the New Jersey legislature was something like this: "Any proposal to raise state and local taxes to what everyone would consider satisfactory levels would surely be voted down." The issue, then, has to do with using federal revenue to raise the level of services above the level that, given the realities of state and local politics, would otherwise exist. In other words, it concerns the amount and kind of income redistribution that the federal government should undertake.

That the federal government, and not state-local ones, should be primarily responsible for any income redistribution has long been generally accepted. In recent decades this principle has been used to justify giving federal aid to states and localities in spectacularly increasing amounts. As John M. De Grove has pointed out, the increase was ten-fold in the last 20 years, four-fold in the last 10, and two-fold in the last five. In 1970 federal aid to states and cities reached an all-time peak of over $24 billion. The question therefore is not *whether* they should be aided but (a) by how much and (b) on what principle of distribution.

In considering what is involved in this, it is necessary to distinguish those state-local needs that are in some sense national from those that are not. That millions of poor rural people have moved to the cities is not something that the taxpayers of the cities should bear the entire financial responsibility for; apart from fairness, there is another consideration—presumably the nation as a whole will be injured if these millions do not receive adequate school, health, police, and other services that only state and local governments can provide. This is one argument that may justify large additional federal support for the states even though they could—if they would—raise the necessary money themselves. Some state-local needs, however, are in no sense national. Most pollution control and much highway construction is in this category. Why, one may ask, should the people of New York be taxed to pay for cleaning up a river in Vermont? As Dick Netzer has remarked in his excellent *Economics and Urban Problems,* ideally such non-national needs should be met by the development of regional governmental agencies, interstate in some cases and metropolitan in others, that can collect taxes and distribute benefits with a view to whatever public is affected—and to that public only. Unfortunately, such jurisdictions do not exist and it is politically impossible to create them. There is, however, as Netzer points out, a substitute for them—namely, the state governments. So when mayors and governors demand *federal* aid for non-national purposes, they do not have a persuasive case. Not only is it unfair to shift the cost of essentially state-local benefits to the national public; it is also very wasteful, for when someone else is to pay the bill, the natural tendency is to be prodigal. (Since Uncle Sam is to pay, why not build the bridge or sewerage system twice as big and four times as costly as necessary?)

Still, there unquestionably do exist truly national needs which urgently require increases in federal aid. But aid to whom? Revenue sharing is not a self-evident proposition. In dealing with the redistribution problem, the Nixon Administration itself has consistently put the emphasis on aiding individuals rather than governments. Shortly after taking office it exempted persons below the poverty line from paying federal income taxes. In its first two years its main effort was to bring into being the Family Assistance Plan, the effect of which would be to reduce those income inequalities that in large part constitute the "crisis of the cities."

Looking at revenue sharing from this standpoint, there is much to be said against it. Compared to the existing federal grant-in-aid programs, it would be much less redistributive.[1] The existing programs are redistributive because grants are generally awarded on the basis of some criteria of need. The shared revenue, on the other hand, would be distributed to states and cities on the basis of population and tax effort. This means that the wealthier states (in terms of per capita income) would benefit; the poorer states would not. Moreover, it is not likely that all of the money that went to the richer states would end up in the pockets of its neediest citizens. Such features of revenue sharing make for complications.

Under the present grant programs, for example, New Yorkers pay in taxes much more to the federal government than they get back in grants from it. In 1967, the per capita personal income tax paid from New York state to the federal government was $433 whereas the grants received in 1968 amounted to only $120 per capita. In North Dakota it was the other way around; there the per capita personal income tax payment was $177 and per capita grants were $357. On the basis of these figures, a New York politician (say Senator Javits) might decide that revenue sharing is a big improvement over the grant system. After all, under the Administration's proposed plan, New York state, which accounts for 10.98 percent of the national income, would get 10.68 percent of the shared ('general') revenue, whereas under the present grant system it gets only (the figure is for 1968) 8.6 percent. On the other hand, an Arkansas politician (say Wilbur Mills, Chairman of the House Ways and Means Committee) might conclude that revenue sharing is a very bad idea. Arkansas, which accounts for .67 percent of the national income and gets (1968) 1.46 percent of the federal grants would, under revenue sharing, get only .86 percent of the $5 billion.

In the last decade or so, the movement of poor people from the country to the city has made income redistribution an intra-city, or rather intra-metropolitan area, problem, as well as an interstate one. Of the $17 billion granted in the fiscal year 1968, $10 billion went to metropolitan areas. Some of the largest grant programs—especially OEO, Model Cities, and Title I of the Elementary and Secondary Education Act of 1965—put money mainly or entirely in so-called poverty areas. From the standpoint of the people who live in these areas, revenue sharing is subject to exactly the same objection that it is subject to in Arkansas: i.e., that it will give these areas less than they would get if the same amount were distributed under the existing grant programs. As Governor Sargent of Massachusetts has pointed out, the wealthy suburb of Newton would get $1,527,668 of the $5 billion that the Administration proposes to share, whereas Fall River, a city that is really poor, would get only $827,760. One way to meet this objection, at least in part, would be to declare small cities, most of which are well-off suburbs, ineligible to share in the fund. Two years ago, the Intergovernmental Relations Advisory Commission suggested limiting eligibility to cities of 50,000 or more but it has since been realized that this would leave more than 40 percent of all cities without an incentive to support the plan. The small suburbs are disproportionately Republican, of course, and this must also be taken into account by the Nixon Administration.

That a state like Arkansas or a city like Fall River would rather have $5 billion distributed under the existing grant programs than under revenue sharing is quite irrelevant if, as some observers claim, Congress could not possibly be persuaded to increase the total of grants by any such sum. Those who think that the Administration must "come up with something new" if it is to have any chance of getting "massive" new money for the cities will presumably conclude that $5 billion in revenue sharing is preferable to, at best, a few hundred million more in grants.

Of course the choice need not be between revenue sharing and grants. There are indications that Congress might be willing to assume the costs of certain social programs, especially welfare. Insofar as the object is to redistribute income, it would certainly make more sense to allot the $5 billion to welfare than to revenue sharing. This has been the Administration's position all along. Family assistance, not revenue sharing, was, and presumably still is, its first love.

A "NEW FEDERALISM"?

From the standpoint of the Administration, the central issue is neither the alleged "fiscal crisis" nor the problem of income redistribution. Rather it is the direction in which the federal system is to develop. From his first statement on the subject (August 13, 1969), the President has emphasized the need to create what he calls a New Federalism. Revenue sharing, he said when he first proposed it, would "mark a turning point in federal-state relations, the beginning of the decentralization of governmental power, and the restoration of a rightful balance between state capitals and the national capital." By the end of the decade, he predicted, "the political landscape of America will be visibly altered, and state and cities will have a far greater share of power and responsibility for solving their own problems." In his recent State of the Union Message, he went even farther. He was proposing, he said, a New American Revolution, "a peaceful revolution in which power will be turned back to the people—in which government at all levels will be refreshed, renewed, and made truly responsive. This can be a revolution as profound, as far reaching, as exciting, as that first revolution almost 200 years ago."

One of the things that caused the President to think along these lines was the rapid and continuing growth that has been—and still is—taking place in the number of federal grant-in-aid programs. As he pointed out in his 1969 message, this growth has been 'near explosive'; between 1962 and 1966, he said, the number of categorical grant programs increased from 160 to 349. There was no reason to think that the rate of increase would slow down, much less stop, of its own accord; but unless it *did* slow down, categorical programs would soon number in the thousands. Revenue sharing was one of the means by which the Administration hoped to slow it down. Instead of creating more categorical programs, Congress would be asked to give the money to the states and cities "with no strings attached." Along with revenue sharing, the President asked for authority to order consolidations of categorical programs, provided that Congress did not within 60 days disapprove his orders. He also proposed a Manpower Training Act which (among other things) would have permitted the consolidation of about 20 more or less competing manpower programs and would have given the governors of the states a good deal of control over the consolidated program.

All of these measures had a common rationale–to simplify the structure of federal aid to the states and cities in order to bring it under control and reduce waste. With hundreds of grant programs, each with its own laws and regulations, no central direction is possible. Cabinet officers cannot keep track of–let alone exercise policy direction over–the many and varied programs for which they are responsible. Governors cannot find out what federal money is coming into their states or what is being done with it. The largest cities employ practitioners of the new art of "grantsmanship," in some instances with great success; many small cities, however, finding that they must apply to scores, or even hundreds, of programs, each with its own special requirements and each administered by a different bureaucracy, have more or less given up any hope of getting much help. The system, if it can be called that, is as wasteful as it is frustrating. A state or local government cannot trade a project that is low on its priority list for one that is high. Perhaps it can get $20 million for an expressway that it does not want but not $200,000 for a drug addiction project that it wants desperately. This involves a double waste: first in what is taken (local authorities can rarely refuse money that is "free") and second in the foregone benefits of desirable projects for which grants are unavailable.

The proposals in the State of the Union Message represent elaborations of those put forward in 1969. "General" revenue sharing differs from the revenue sharing then proposed only in amount and in the percentage (now 48) to be "passed through" to the cities. "Special" revenue sharing is (despite the confusing terminology) nothing but consolidation of categorical programs on an all-at-once, comprehensive basis rather than on a piecemeal one. As everybody presumably knows by now, a few categorical programs would be eliminated and most of the others grouped into six super-categories (urban community development, rural community development, education, manpower training, law enforcement, and transportation) each under a cabinet officer. Under "special" revenue sharing, grants-in-aid would be distributed among states and local governments on the basis of need as in the past, but the distribution would be according to an agreed-upon formula (or rather formulae because each super-category would have its own) rather than as the result of (among other things) grantsmanship, endurance, "clout," and chicanery–criteria that cannot be excluded at present. Under the plans so far announced (in the nature of the case these are incomplete and somewhat tentative) some interests are bound to gain and others to lose. Mayor Hatcher of Gary, Indiana, for example, has complained that his city would lose about one-fourth of the $150 million a year that it now receives. To such complaints the Administration has replied that it will hold in reserve a fund from which to make up any losses that local governments may suffer because of changes in distribution formulae.

ORGANIZED BENEFICIARIES

There is no doubt that state and local officials enthusiastically favor consolidating and simplifying the grant system and giving them (the officials) wide discretion in deciding the uses to which federal aid should be put. Congressmen, too, are well aware of the faults of the present system, and many have spoken out against it. Nevertheless, there is reason to think that proposals to change the system fundamentally will not prove acceptable now or later, no matter who proposes them or what their merits.

It must be remembered that every one of the categorical programs (the most recent estimate is 550) has its organized beneficiaries–not only those who receive grants but also those who are paid salaries for administering them. These beneficiaries have a much livelier interest in maintaining and enlarging their special benefits than the generality of taxpayers–unorganized, of course–has in curtailing them. If there happens to be a grant program for re-training teachers in secondary schools having high drop-out rates, it is safe to say that there exists an organization that will exert itself vigorously to prevent the consolidation of that program with others. It is safe to say, too, that no organization exists to put in a good word for the consolidation of the teacher-retraining program with other manpower programs.

From the standpoint of organized interests, dealing with Congress and the Washington bureaucracies (a few key Congressmen and administrators are usually all that matter to any particular interest) is vastly easier and more likely to succeed than is dealing with the legislatures and governors of 50 states, not to mention the officials of countless cities, counties, and special districts. This consideration alone might well be decisive from the standpoint of organized labor, which knows just where to go and whom to see in Washington, even if the political complexions of the state and local governments were exactly the same as that of the national government. In fact, of course, they are not; some interests that are well received and can make themselves heard in Washington–organized labor, minority groups, the poor–would be ignored in certain state capitols and city halls.

Interest groups will not be the only, or probably the most important, defenders of the grant system, however. Congressmen–especially those on important committees–are fond of categorical programs for at least two reasons. One is that they constitute answers to the perennial question: What have you done for me lately? A narrowly defined category is ideal from this standpoint. It is custom-made to suit the requirements of some key group of constituents and the Congressman can plainly label it "from me to you." Revenue sharing, whether "general" or "special," altogether lacks this advantage. It gives benefits not to constituents directly but in wholesale lots to state and local politicians who will package them for retail distribution under their own labels, taking all of the credit.

Congressmen also like categorical programs because of the opportunities they afford to interfere in administration and thus to secure special treatment, or at least the appearance of it, for constituents among whom, as Jerome T. Murphy shows in his case study of the politics of educational reform (*Harvard Educational Review,* February 1971) state and local as well as federal agencies sometimes figure prominently. These opportunities are plentiful because the Congressmen see to it that "ifs," "ands," and "buts" are written into the legislation in the right places, and because administrators are well aware that every year they must respond in public to whatever questions may be asked in appropriations and other hearings. Wanting to stay on the right side of those members of Congress with whom they must deal, administrators frequently ask them for "advice." Perhaps it is not too much to say that the categorical system constitutes a last line of defense against what many Congressmen regard as the usurpation of their function by the executive branch.

As this implies, the present coldness of Congress to President Nixon's revenue-sharing proposals is not to be explained solely or perhaps even mainly on the ground that he is Republican and Congress is Democratic. The crucial fact is that his proposals would involve a large-scale shift of power from Congress to the White House. *No* Congress would like that, although sooner or later one may feel compelled to accept it.

Revenue sharing would also shift power to governors and mayors. To hear some of them talk, one might think that they would like to have the federal government dismantled and the pieces turned over to them. In fact, most of them are likely to find excuses for not accepting powers that may be politically awkward–and what ones may not?

In his valuable book, *The American System*, the late Morton Grodzins provides some evidence on this point. He tells at some length the story of the Joint Federal-State Action Committee, which President Eisenhower created in 1957 after a flight of oratory (". . . those who would be free must stand eternal watch against excessive concentration of power in government . . .") to designate federal functions that might be devolved to the states along with revenue to support them. The Committee was a very high level one; it included three members of the Cabinet, the Director of the Bureau of the Budget, and a dozen governors. After laboring for two years, it found only two programs that the federal government would give up and that the states would accept–vocational education and municipal waste treatment plants. As Grodzins explains, the difficulty was not so much that the federal agencies could not be persuaded to give up functions as that the governors would not accept them. They would not take the school lunch program, for example, because doing so would involve a fuss about parochial schools, and they would not take Old Age Assistance because they knew that the old people's lobby would not like having it transferred to the states. Modest as the Committee's two proposals were and strongly as President Eisenhower backed them, Congress turned them down.

Whether state and local governments would make good use of the federal funds if given them "with no strings attached" is much doubted by career civil servants in Washington and by what may be called the good government movement. State and city governments, it is frequently said, are in general grossly inefficient and in many instances corrupt as well. The charge is certainly plausible–one wonders whether New York City, for example, has the capacity to use wisely the large amounts that it would receive. The fact is, however, that no one really knows what the state and local governments are capable of. And even if their capacity should prove to be as little as the pessimists say it is, may it not even so be superior to that of the present system *as it will be in another decade or two?*

Administrators in Washington generally assume that the management capacity of state and local governments can be much improved by provision of special grants to strengthen the staffs of the chief executives and by teaching the techniques and advantages of comprehensive planning. The lessons of the last 10 years give little support to this assumption, but the Administration is nevertheless proposing a fund of $100 million for more such efforts. In my judgment the results are bound to be disappointing. It is the necessity of working out compromises among the numerous holders of bits and pieces of power on the state-local scene that is the main cause, not only of "inefficiency," but of corruption as well. Giving governors and mayors authority over the spending of federal funds would, by strengthening their political positions, reduce the amount of compromising that they must do and the amount of corruption that they must pretend not to see if they are to get anything done. In this way it would contribute more than anything else to increasing the coherence (to use the word that is favored among planners) of state-local programs. The $100 million in management assistance that the federal government proposes would probably work in the very opposite direction. In practice if not in theory, giving "technical assistance" usually means maintaining and extending the influence of the federal agencies.

THE PROSPECT BEFORE US

Insofar as there would be a real devolution of power to governors and mayors–and therefore, as the President said, to the people who elect them–the Administration's proposals could bring the federal system closer to what the Founding Fathers intended it to be. In my opinion, this is a consummation devoutly to be desired. There is no denying, however, that the short-run effect of decentralization of power would be to take a great deal of pressure off those state and local regimes, of which there may be many, that have no disposition to provide essential public services on an equitable basis or at what reasonable people would regard as adequate levels. This is a powerful objection. It may, however, only be a temporary one. Within a very few years, the political arithmetic of every sizable city and every industrial state will be such as to give politicians strong incentives to take very full account of the needs and wishes of those elements of the electorate that have been, and in some places still are, neglected.

Still, given the political realities that I have mentioned–a public opinion that favors income redistribution but is divided as to how far it should go and how costs and benefits should be apportioned; tax boundary lines inappropriately drawn but not susceptible to being redrawn; hundreds of federal agencies having programs to protect; interest groups even more numerous and with more at stake in the status quo; interstate and intra-metropolitan area differences of interest; Congressmen loath to see their powers diminished; governors and mayors equally loath to accept responsibilities that can be avoided–it is not to be expected that any quick or clear-cut settlement will be found for the issues that revenue sharing raises.

I expect that the federal government will continue to play a larger role in raising revenue for all sorts of purposes. As Julius Margolis has pointed out, the larger and more diverse the "package" of expenditure (or other) items that a government presents to its voters, the harder it is for the people to make their decisions on the basis of self-interest as opposed to ideology. This being the case, those who want to win acceptance for proposals that would not be accepted if self-interest were the criterion always try to include them in packages that are sufficiently large. That is, they prefer to have decisions made on a city-wide rather than a neighborhood basis, on a state-wide rather than a city-wide one, and on a national rather than a state one. It seems to me that the changing class character of the population reinforces this tendency. As we become more heavily upper-middle class, we are increasingly disposed to regard general principles (or ideology, as Margolis calls it), not self-interest, as the proper criterion.

If the federal government will have an ever-larger part in raising revenue, it is not likely to have an ever-smaller one in spending it. He who pays the piper calls the tune. To be sure, he may choose to permit, or even to require, others to do some calling when the number of tunes to be called is inconveniently large, and by so doing he may make everyone better off. The essential fact is, however, that the state governments can be what Governor Cahill called them–sovereign–only if they do what he says they cannot do–supply the funds to meet the urgent and necessary needs of their people. I myself am strongly in favor of the reforms that the President has proposed because I think they represent the largest improvement over the present situation that it is reasonable to hope for. I do not, however, share his expectation that these reforms will bring about "a historic and massive reversal of the flow of power in America." Indeed, in the event–unlikely, I am afraid–that his proposals are accepted and carried into effect, I would be very surprised if first Mississippi and then New York did not discover that they are ruled as much as ever by national public opinion, acting through national institutions–the Presidency, Congress, the Supreme Court–and that this opinion and these institutions, the White House most of all perhaps, will in the years ahead assert conceptions of the national interest more vigorously than ever.

[1]What is under discussion at this point is the so-called "general" revenue-sharing proposal: that is, the $5 billion, to start with, that would go to states and cities with "no strings attached." This is to be distinguished from "special" revenue sharing, which is the grant system much reorganized and with $1 billion in "new" money added to it.

7 A Federal Value-Added Tax?

Carl Grafton

Interest in federal revenue sharing has been stimulated by recent court decisions striking down the local property tax as the major basis for supporting primary and secondary schools. As a result of these decisions, the Nixon Administration is studying the possibility of sharing with states revenue from a national value-added tax (VAT) for partial support of schools. This paper deals with questions generated by the court decisions and the possibility that VAT will be adopted: Why do the federal courts object to the local property tax? Who pays property taxes? Can the states satisfy court requirements without federal assistance? What are the characteristics of VAT and how does VAT compare with the property tax? How does VAT compare with other taxes?

Source: Original article prepared for this volume.

Carl Grafton is Assistant Professor of Political Science at the University of Houston. He is the author of *The Politics of Higher Education.*

THE COURTS AND THE LOCAL PROPERTY TAX

Throughout United States history, schools have been primarily subject to local control and local financial support. Local control of schools has taken on the aspect of an honored tradition. States have assumed responsibility for maintaining minimum standards; teacher qualifications, textbook options, the number of school days, and a variety of other things are often decided at the state level. States also provide money to ensure that school districts will be able to meet state standards. The state share of support (excluding federal money) ranges from 8.9 percent in New Hampshire to 95.7 percent in Hawaii, with a national average of 43.7 percent.[1] But beyond state minimum standards and financial support, schools are nearly always locally controlled and funded.

The local property tax is the major source of support for schools. The major difficulty with the property tax is that some school districts are wealthy and others are poor. For example, Deer Park, Texas (in Harris County) includes a massive industrial complex on the Houston Ship Channel. In 1971 the Deer Park tax roll contained $453 million in property and only 7,000 students. In contrast, the North Forest school district (also in Harris County) had a $150 million tax roll and about 18,000 students. Disparities between Texas counties, are even greater than between districts. The result of this is that wealthy school districts tax themselves at relatively low rates and still spend a great deal on schools on a per pupil basis. On the other hand, poor districts must tax themselves at very high rates and even then they raise less money than their wealthy neighbors. Thus in Deer Park in the 1969–70 school year, property taxes levied per pupil were $1,013 while North Forest raised only $175. The state of Texas, like most other states, provides assistance to the poorer school districts. In the case of North Forest, approximately $270 per pupil was provided by the state. Deer Park receives little state assistance. Despite state (and federal) aid, North Forest spends half as much as Deer Park on a per pupil basis. *And these are two school districts within one county.*

On December 24, 1971, a federal court using a three judge panel ruled in *Rodriguez v. San Antonio Independent School District* that the Texas system of public school financing is unconstitutional because the highly unequal per pupil expenditures provide unequal educational opportunities. According to the panel, "The state may adopt any financial scheme desired, so long as the variations in wealth among the governmentally chosen districts do not affect the spending for the education of any child."[2] Educational opportunities afforded children must not be "a function of wealth other than the wealth of the State as a whole."[3] The defendants in the case were the Texas Board of Education and Education Commissioner J. W. Edgar. Assistant Attorney General Pat Bailey served as counsel for the defense. Bailey maintained that the present system allows parents to decide the level of school support in each particular district. The judges responded by saying that this argument "lost sight of the fact that the state had actually limited local choice in school financing by guaranteeing that some districts will spend low while others will spend high."[4] Bailey also argued that federal assistance provides some leveling between rich and poor districts. The judges rejected this argument on two grounds. First, federal assistance does not in fact equalize the districts. Second,

> defendants have not adequately explained why the acts of other governmental units should excuse them from the discriminatory consequences of state law. [The case of *Hobson v. Hansen* countered Bailey's argument by noting that federal aid to education statutes] are manifestly intended to provide extraordinary services at the slum schools, not merely to compensate for inequalities produced by local school boards in favor of their middle income schools. Thus they cannot be regarded as curing any inequalities for which the Board is otherwise responsible.[5]

Finally, Bailey argued that the plaintiffs wanted "socialized education."[6] The judges replied that "Education, like the postal service, has been socialized, or publicly financed and operated, almost from its origin. The type of socialized education, not the question of its existence, is the only matter currently in dispute."[7] This was a unanimous decision.

The judges also decided that if the legislature fails to change education financing to fit the equality standard, the court "will take such further steps as may be necessary to implement both the purpose and the spirit of this order."[8]

The Texas decision was identical to earlier findings made by the California State Supreme Court in August 1971, and by the U.S. District Court in Minnesota in October 1971, except that the California and Minnesota decisions lacked the threat described in the preceding paragraph.

In December 1971, Secretary of Health, Education, and Welfare Elliot Richardson speculated that the federal government might accept a major share of public school costs if it is found that the property tax can no longer be used.

IS THE PROPERTY TAX UNCONSTITUTIONAL FOR SCHOOL SUPPORT? IS FEDERAL ASSISTANCE ABSOLUTELY NECESSARY?

Some journalistic descriptions of the California, Minnesota, and Texas court decisions convey the impression that the property tax has been ruled unconstitutional and that massive federal assistance to primary and secondary schools is inevitable. Both impressions are incorrect. The system presently used in Texas and nearly all other states could be made to fit court requirements. It might work in the following manner. A decision would be made at the state level concerning desired standards of education. This could be expressed in terms of cost per pupil. This would not be a simple decision for at least two reasons. First, costs are different in various parts of a state. School operating costs may be much higher in urban areas. On the other hand, good teachers may be unwilling to isolate themselves in a place like Smithville, Texas without very high salaries. A single statewide per student cost figure would not be sufficient. Second, costs for unusual programs vary widely. For example, special programs for disadvantaged or especially talented children are likely to be twice as expensive as routine programs. Despite these difficulties, basic per-student expense figures could be established using sophisticated cost analysis techniques.

Once per student costs are calculated, how could they be funded consistent with court decisions? One author suggests an equal tax effort in each school district of the state and state financial assistance.[9] The local tax effort could be in the form of a property tax at one rate over the entire state. In those districts in which the local property tax does not produce sufficient funds to meet the state standard, state aid would be provided. This system would fit court requirements and it is little different from present arrangements. A major difference is the provision for an equal local property tax burden. Under the present system, the burden varies widely among districts. A second difference is that under this system, average per-student expenditures might be much higher because people in areas like Deer Park would insist that their schools be maintained at the high quality level to which they are accustomed. This would not be possible without raising the quality of all other districts in the state. Under the present system, citizens of Deer Park are indifferent about education in less fortunate districts; under the court-ordered system (whatever form it takes), Deer Park will be forced to lend its political support to other districts to achieve overall high levels of support.

In the 1969–70 school year, Texas state and local expenditures totaled $1.60 billion. Since total enrollment was 2,597,204 students, average state and local per pupil expenditures were about $615. What would be the additional cost if the average were raised near to Deer Park standards of about $900? The total cost would be $2.34 billion, or an additional $0.74 billion.[10]

An important drawback of the equalization system described above is that it relies on the property tax, which many people find objectionable. (For the major arguments against the property tax see the section below entitled "The Property Tax".) Another possibility is a complete takeover of school funding by the state without property tax support. In its discussion of full state funding the Advisory Commission on Intergovernmental Relations recommends "That local property taxpayers must be relieved of substantially all of the burden of underwriting the non-federal share of education; that state assumption of such costs is the most likely route to the provision of equal educational opportunity; and that local policy-making authority over elementary and secondary education must be retained."[11]

Various scholars have raised two major objections to full state funding: first, it would produce intense legislative agony, and, second, it would bring about state control of schools.

There is no doubt that a shift to full state funding without use of a property tax would be an unpleasant experience to most legislatures. In Texas, based on 1969–70 levels of support, this would mean additional state expenditures of $0.77 billion. If Deer Park levels are assumed, it would mean an additional $1.51 billion. For perspective, the reader should know that total state expenditures in Texas in 1969 were $2.51 billion and the largest single source of revenue, the sales tax, brought in $0.44 billion. A quantum jump of this sort would require creation of a corporate income tax or personal income tax, and, of course, creation of new taxes is anathema to politicians. A shift from property taxes to sales, personal income, or corporate profits taxes would mean that many powerful people (in any state) would lose a great deal of money. The resulting pressures and counter-pressures would produce a multi-dimensional battle of great ferocity, and many political careers would suffer as a result. Proponents of full state funding argue that legislative pain should not deter us from lessening our reliance on the highly obnoxious property tax. In practice, we would probably find that a move to full state funding would be accompanied by a state property tax; this would be the least painful approach consistent with a policy of full state funding.

The second major objection to full state funding is that it would eventually be accompanied by state control over curricula (the man who pays the piper calls the tune). We will see later that this argument also arises when federal aid to education is discussed. According to Paul D. Cooper, school superintendents in Delaware (which has 90 percent state school funding) have as much freedom as officials of other states having lower levels of state aid.[12] The ACIR argues that full state funding will free local administrators from "the necessity of 'selling' local bond issues and tax rate increases" and will allow them to devote more time to the important business of providing quality education for children.[13] ACIR also argues that public sentiment in favor of local control of education is so strong that any threat of state control will be resisted and defeated.

There is no way to settle this question here. We cannot determine with certainty how far state (or federal) control would go if full state (or federal) funding were instituted. The ACIR-Cooper position sounds convincing, and *at present* it is probably valid; the author is unaware of significant numbers of educators who advocate state or federal control over schools except in the realm of racial integration. But no one can say what the *future* would bring with full state or federal funding. Read any magazine article or book concerning a major social issue (for example, racial tension, crime, or pollution) and you will probably find a recommendation that the issue can be partially resolved through changes ("improvements") in school curricula. Local school boards and administrators stand at the focal point of enormous pressures and counterpressures, and the intensity of this situation is likely to increase in the future. With full state or federal funding, interests which are not satisfied by local decisions will probably press their cases at state or federal levels. It is impossible to predict the result.

Returning to the questions with which this section began, the property tax can be used as a basis for a constitutionally sound funding system. And federal assistance is not necessary; states can handle funding for revised systems which would be approved by the courts. Indeed in 1968–69 several states provided rather high percentages of non-federal money to their schools: Hawaii, 95 percent; Delaware, 82 percent; Alabama, 75 percent; New Mexico, 86 percent; North Carolina, 76 percent; and Washington, 75 percent.[14] And the state of Texas has no corporate or personal income tax, either one of which would be sufficient to cover any increased state burden even at Deer Park standards. Nevertheless, a great deal of attention is being given to the idea of increased federal aid to the schools via the value-added tax. We turn now to an examination of property taxes and value-added taxes.

THE PROPERTY TAX

Economist John F. Due evaluates the property tax in terms of several categories: revenue requirements of local governments, administrative feasibility of alternative taxes, equity, administration of the property tax, and economic effects. Due argues that the property tax is a mainstay of local governments, and that other major taxes (excise, sales, or income) are too expensive to administer at the local level. He concludes: "A property tax, centering on real property, is almost imperative for the local governments if they are to retain some financial autonomy."[15]

Due is less generous with the property tax in terms of equity. There are a variety of ways to judge the equity of a tax, but two of the major ones are "ability to pay" and the "benefit principle." "Ability to pay" refers to the general principle that some individuals and institutions can afford to pay higher taxes than others, and that those who can afford to pay more should pay more. The "benefit principle" refers to the fact that specific government services often benefit some people more than others and that people who benefit more should pay more. Neither of these standards is perfectly clear nor are they completely consistent, but they are useful guides for judgment.

Wealth in the form of property is certainly one legitimate measure of ability to pay. However, the property tax as it actually operates falls far short of being a fair measure of ability to pay. It has many drawbacks. First, it concentrates on real estate and virtually ignores other types of property. Second, it ignores debts outstanding against property, so that a person just beginning to pay the mortgage on a $30,000 house pays the same property tax as another person who owns his house outright. Third, most studies indicate that the property tax is regressive relative to income. This means that lower income property owners tend to pay higher property taxes as a percentage of income than higher income property owners. This is because higher income property owners have less of their income and wealth devoted to property than lower income property owners. Also, insofar as the tax on business property acts as a sales tax, it is also regressive; low income people spend most of their income and thus pay a sales tax on nearly their entire income whereas high income people spend only part of their income (saving or investing the remainder) and thus pay a sales tax on only part of their income. In this connection, perhaps the toughest burden of the property tax rests on elderly persons living on fixed incomes (e.g., pensions) who own the home they lived in during the peak income earning period of their lives. In many cases, the property tax is sufficient to drive such people from their homes.

The first two drawbacks listed above–that the property tax ignores personal property and that it ignores debts outstanding against property–could be eliminated, but they probably will remain; personal property taxation is extremely unpopular because of invasion of privacy, and taking debts into consideration would add greatly to the complexity and expense of tax administration. Property tax regressivity could be eliminated through the use of a progressive tax, and the extra burden on retired, fixed income homeowners could be eased with little difficulty.

The benefit principle adds another dimension to property tax evaluation. Since many government services are designed to preserve and protect real property, it seems reasonable that real property owners should pay some special tax. However, the benefit principle applies only to those government activities (such as police and fire protection) which directly benefit real property owners. Thus the benefit principle does not apply to support of schools.

Due's next criterion for evaluation of the property tax is the way in which it is administered. It is the most poorly administered major tax in the United States. The major difficulty is that assessments of property values are wildly inaccurate in most cities and counties. This is caused by a combination of poorly trained assessors and various political pressures, but there is no reason why the situation could not be improved.

Economic effects represent the final point of property tax evaluation. The property tax tends to discourage economic activities which make especially heavy use of large amounts of taxable items. Of particular interest to political scientists, the property tax tends to encourage people to build homes outside high tax areas (the "city limits") thus contributing to the "flight from the cities" which is seriously harming many urban centers. It is difficult to evaluate the seriousness of this criticism of the property tax, but two considerations lead the author to suspect that it is of relatively little importance. First, living in the suburbs of large cities imposes costs in terms of lost time in commuting and travel expenses, and, second, the flight from the cities has many other causes, including fear of city crime and a search for better schools. It is quite possible that factors such as this heavily outweigh the property tax.

A FEDERAL VALUE-ADDED TAX

The value-added tax operates in various countries in a number of forms, but according to Carl Shoup it is basically a tax "on the value that a business firm adds to the goods and services that it purchases from other firms."[16] Value-added is "the difference between the sales proceeds [gross receipts] and the cost of the materials, etc., that it has purchased from other firms."[17]

According to Edwin S. Cohen, VAT was first applied to all types of businesses, including retail stores, in Denmark in 1967. It had been applied earlier in France to all types of businesses except retail stores. In addition to Denmark, the complete VAT is now used in Sweden, Norway, and all Common Market countries. Cohen's explanation of the operation of the European VAT is identical to Shoup's theoretical definition.

A specific example may clarify the nature of VAT. To completely understand the example, the reader should perform the calculations with pencil and paper while referring to Figure 1. Company A is in the business of mining and refining clay. Company A sells a glob of refined clay to Company B for $100. Thus value added by Company A is $100 (disregarding for simplicity the cost of equipment used to refine the clay). In this case the value-added tax rate is assumed to be 10 percent. Company B pays the 10 percent ($10) to Company A which pays it to the government.

Company B produces ash trays out of the glob of clay and sells them to Company C for $200. Company C pays a tax of 10 percent on its $200 purchase ($20) to Company B. Company B deducts the $10 it paid to Company A from the $20 it received from Company C and pays the difference ($10) to the government. Notice that the money received by the government at this stage ($10) is 10 percent of the value added by Company B ($100). The government now has $10 from the tax on value added by Company A and another $10 from the tax on value added by Company B which totals $20 up to this point in the process.

Company C is in the business of decorating the ash trays, and it sells them to a retail store for $500. The store pays $50 extra to Company C. Company C subtracts $20 from the $50 and pays $30 to the government. Again, the money received by the government at this stage is 10 percent of value added by Company C. The government now has $50.

Finally, the retail store sells all the ash trays to consumers for a total of $700. Purchasers pay a total of $70 to the retail store. The retail store then deducts the $50 it paid to Company C from the $70 it received from the consumers and pays the difference ($20) to the government. The government ends up with a total of $70. Notice that the end result of this process ($70 to the government) is the same as if there was simply a 10 percent retail sales tax.

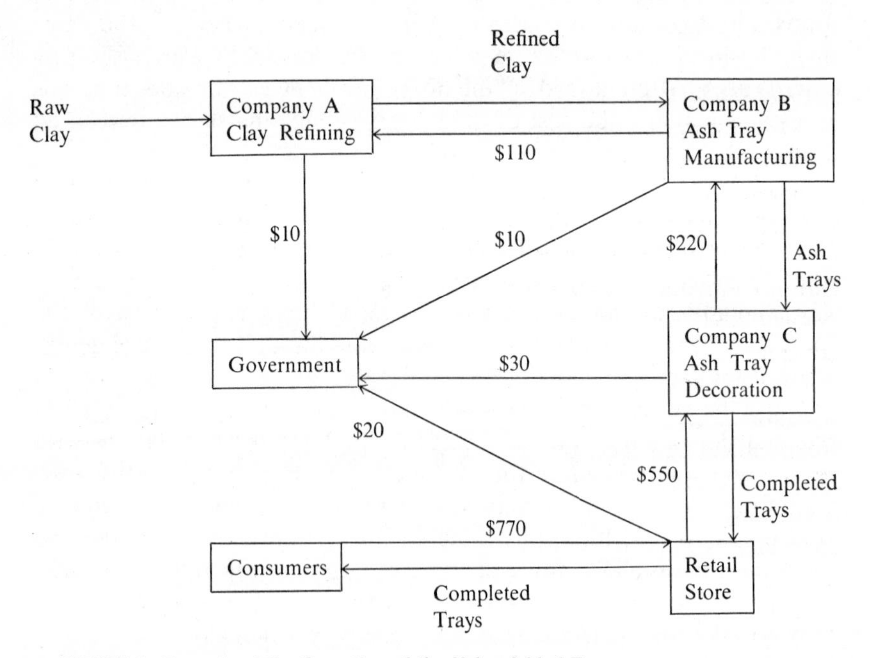

FIGURE 1 Example of the Operation of the Value-Added Tax

Nor does the simplified nature of this example change the basic conclusion. A more complex and realistic example involving purchases by the various companies of capital equipment would produce the same result.

What would happen if there was no tax at the retail level? In our example, the retail store would pay $50 to the government. Thus the government would still end up with $10+$10+$50=$70. Would the retail store absorb the $50? This would depend on the degree of competition and the elasticity of demand for the product, but we could expect the $50 to be at least partially passed on to consumers in the form of higher prices for ash trays. According to the President's Task Force on Business Taxation: "The value-added tax is a universal, identifiable item of cost, and hence may be expected to be reflected in prices charged. But depending on elasticities of demand and supply for a particular product and for alternatives to it, a change in even the most universal cost items may, under competitive pressures, be partially absorbed by a producer by lowering his pre-tax price. Nonetheless, the value-added tax is widely regarded as, by and large, shifted forward to final customers."[18] James A. Papke's analysis is the same: "the federal TVA [value-added tax] is nothing more than a disguised retail sales tax."[19]

Like the sales tax, VAT is regressive in the simple form described in the example. However, both the sales tax and VAT can be made proportional (or nearly so) by not taxing food or by providing a tax credit.[20] France uses a four-rate VAT which varies from 4 percent on food to 33 ⅓ percent on luxuries. Germany uses 5.5 percent on food and other items and 12 percent on other goods and services. On the other hand, Denmark has a single VAT rate of 15 percent and Sweden uses 17.65 percent.[21]

In the United States, labor unions and liberal groups tend to oppose sales tax increases and favor income taxes because income taxes are nearly always at least proportional and can easily be made progressive. But in Denmark and Sweden where VAT was recently raised from 12.5 percent to 15 percent and 11.1 percent to 17.65 percent, respectively, labor unions supported the increases. They justified this apparently paradoxical behavior by arguing that the benefits of the government spending were focused disproportionately to lower economic classes in the form of free medical care and free education (the benefit principle). American labor unions and most liberals have never been much impressed by this argument, and the scattered responses to Secretary Richardson's VAT speculations indicate that union-liberal opposition to a serious national VAT proposal would be strong.

Scandinavian countries have found that a single rate VAT is simpler to administer than a multi-rate VAT. In Denmark the VAT return is printed on a post card. Tax returns in multi-rate countries are longer and more complex although not unmanageable. None of the European countries have adopted a tax credit system like that described in footnote 20.

What effect does adoption of VAT have on price levels? The European experience is difficult to evaluate. Prices rose after value-added taxes were imposed, but they rose at a wide variety of rates for different products. A major difficulty in analyzing the price impact of VAT in Europe is that the value-added taxes were often imposed at the same time that other taxes were being removed. And various wage increases were also going into effect when VAT was imposed. Variations in monetary policy added further to the complexity. Despite the ambiguity of the European experience, there is every reason to believe that a U.S. VAT would be shifted to consumers in the manner of a sales tax.

CONCLUSIONS

Change is coming in most state systems of school finance in the United States. In terms of educational opportunities for children residing in poor school districts, the change will be a revolution. But a national value-added tax probably will not be adopted because federal aid to education is not absolutely necessary, and because the combined opposition of the left and right, described earlier, will be strong. However, greater federal aid to education financed by the income tax will probably accompany increased state education expenditures. On the state and local levels we will probably see less, but nevertheless continued, reliance on the property tax for major education financing. There will be less reliance on the property tax because an equal property tax burden throughout most states cannot support schools at what will probably be higher average levels. But the property tax will continue to be a major source of funds for several reasons. First, long term local school autonomy may depend on local financial autonomy. Second, politicians generally favor minimal decisions; they will try to satisfy court requirements with the least possible change. Third, the property tax is a rich source of funds in an area of state and local spending that gobbles up money.

As alternative methods of school financing are discussed, we will probably see increased criticism of property tax administration and regressivity; this attention may bring gradual improvements.

Many states faced with increased educational burdens will turn to new taxes. States which lack personal or corporate income taxes will create them, and states in which all major types of taxes already exist will be obliged to increase rates.

[1]Paul D. Cooper, "State Takeover of Education Financing," *National Tax Journal,* XXIV (1971), p. 339.

[2]*Demetrio P. Rodriguez et al. v. San Antonio Independent School District et al.,* Civ. A. No. 68-175-SA, U.S. District Court, December 23, 1971, *Federal Supplement,* April 10, 1972.

[3]*Ibid.* [5]*Ibid.* [7]*Ibid.*

[4]*Ibid.* [6]*Ibid.* [8]*Ibid.*

[9]Cooper, *op. cit.,* pp. 346–51.

[10]Texas Education Agency, *Annual Statistical Report 1969–70* (Austin: Texas Education Agency, 1971).

[11]Advisory Commission on Intergovernmental Relations, *State Aid to Local Government* (Washington: Advisory Commission on Intergovernmental Relations, 1969), p. 15.

[12]Cooper, *op. cit.,* pp. 350–51.

[13]Advisory Commission on Intergovernmental Relations, *loc. cit.*

[14]Cooper, *op. cit.,* p. 349, taken from *Public School Finances,* U.S. Department of Health, Education and Welfare, Office of Education, 1969.

[15]John F. Due, *Government Finance* (Homewood: Richard D. Irwin, 1963), p. 368.

[16]Carl S. Shoup, *Public Finance* (Chicago: Aldine, 1969), p. 251.

[17]*Ibid.*

[18]The President's Task Force on Business Taxation, "Business Taxation" (Washington: U.S. Government Printing Office, 1970), p. 63.

[19]James A. Papke, "Discussion," *National Tax Journal* XXIV (1971), p. 415.

[20]A tax credit can be provided which essentially omits from taxation the first (say) $500 in purchases. With this example, a sales tax on $500 in purchases would be $25, assuming a 5 percent rate. The $25 can be paid to individuals through the income tax system (for administrative simplicity). A credit like this can easily eliminate sales tax or VAT regressivity.

[21]Edwin S. Cohen, "Foreign Experience with a Value Added Tax," *National Tax Journal* XXIV (1971), pp. 400–401.

Chapter THREE

The Role of the States

INTRODUCTION TO CHAPTER THREE The states form the cornerstone of American federalism. Our entire political system is based upon the concept that they, as well as the national government, exercise power and make the policy decisions of government. As we noted in Chapter One, the power of the states has varied throughout our nation's history. At one point they were ascendant, with the federal government a weak partner; at another, they were at their nadir, with the national government assuming virtually all the powers once in their exclusive domain.

At present, the states are facing many challenges which will severely test their ability to survive as viable units of government. These challenges are being hurled from many directions:

1. *Growth in Population.* More people mean demands for additional services, creating the need for higher expenditures. States are also faced with problems caused by the particular way in which the population is growing. There are increases in the proportion of residents in urban areas, the number of young in society, and in the number of aged citizens. Each of these groups require greater outlays for services than their size alone would indicate. Another aspect of population growth involves the shifting racial balance in many of the cities and suburbs within the states. Tension caused by recent population movements further adds to the difficulties of government.

2. *Changes in the Economy.* Industrialization has brought many benefits to society. However, many states have discovered that economic growth by itself is not necessarily desirable, since it is often accompanied by environmental problems, as well as social and economic dislocations. Rapid technological growth has also meant that the states are most dependent upon the national economy and policy decisions of the national government. The unemployment crisis that struck Seattle and the state of Washington after Boeing's loss of the SST contract is an example of this point.

3. *The Revenue Crisis.* The increasing demands of the citizenry has led one state after another to the brink of bankruptcy. Most have now adopted broad-based taxes on sales and income, and there is a continuing search for new sources of revenue. High federal taxes and the reluctance of people to pay additional levies has intensified this dilemma.

4. *The Political Challenge.* As a result of reapportionment of state legislatures and the interest by many segments of society that had not previously participated in politics (such as the young and minority group voters), there has been a constant demand for change in the operation of state government, and frequently, a large turnover of elected officials.

DIVERSITY AMONG THE STATES

One often tends to forget the degree of diversity in social, political, and economic systems that exists among the states. Table 1 indicates how selected states differ with regard to several characteristics.

From the standpoint of federalism, the many differences in cultural backgrounds or environment of the states are equally important. Daniel Elazer has commented extensively on this last point, and has devised a classification system which describes three types of political cultures:

1. The *individualistic culture*, which emphasizes a utiiitarian approach to government. In its view, government is instituted primarily to handle those functions demanded by the people it is created to serve, and does not become unnecessarily involved in the affairs of society as a whole.

2. The *moralist culture,* which stresses the notion of the public welfare as a basis for democracy. Government is evaluated by the degree to which it advances the "public good" and in terms of honesty and dedication to the public welfare of those who govern.

3. The *traditionalistic culture,* which reflects an attitude that approves of a hierarchical society and assumes that those at the top of the social structure will take a special interest in government and play a dominant leadership role.[1]

In terms of the federal system, this diversity in political culture and socio-economic characteristics has a special significance. Because of

TABLE 1 Comparative State Indexes

Index	N.Y.	Vt.	Wis.	Neb.	Fla.	Miss.	Cal.	Ore.	U.S.
per. cap. income (1970)[a]	$4797	3491	3772	3700	3584	2561	4469	3700	3910
per. cap. rev. (1969)[a]	$ 788	619	611	558	497	417	795	624	567
per. cap. exp. (1969)[a]	$ 817	637	651	530	485	436	777	625	578
per pupil exp. (1969–70)[b]	$1420	1031	988	649	923	534	1067	1022	926
sel. service reject rate (% reject) 1970[a]	57.9%	49.2	39.7	41.3	49.3	52.5	45.2	37.2	45.7
av. wkly. earnings-manuf. (1970)[a]	$ 135	120	146	135	119	98	150	148	134
% urban (1970)[a]	85.6%	32.2	65.9	61.5	80.5	44.5	90.9	67.1	73.5
murder rate per 1000 (1970)[c]	5.4	3.1	1.9	2.7	10.5	8.7	5.4	3.1	6.1

[a]U.S. Government, Statistical Abstract, 1971.
[b]U.S. Dept. of Health, Education and Welfare, *Digest of Education Statistics,* 1970.
[c]Federal Bureau of Investigation, 1971.

these features, considerable heterogeneity is introduced into the system and the possibility for intergovernmental friction and dispute is greatly increased.

A NEW ROLE FOR THE STATES

Many observers have commented upon the role of the states in the federal system. However, despite nearly 200 years of debate, complete agreement on the specifics of this role still have not been reached. This is partly because contradictory forces are at work. States are jealous of the powers they still retain and refuse to entirely relinquish their responsibilities in fields such as education and welfare. Yet, political and fiscal pressures are forcing them to rely more heavily than ever before on the national government to provide the funds needed to carry out these responsibilities.

One of the areas in which the states have the greatest opportunity to exercise a new leadership role is in offering solutions to the problems of their cities. As the following chapter will indicate, this can be accomplished in several ways: by increased technical assistance, financial aid, constitutional changes that allow greater local governmental autonomy and flexibility, and by providing the political leadership necessary to overcome the broad range of social and economic difficulties found in urban areas.

Many changes will have to be made in order to enable the states to cope with the demands of the twentieth century. The weakness of state government and ways of eliminating these deficiences have been pointed out by many authors, including those included in this chapter. Each of the points they raise is important, but perhaps most crucial is the attitude of elected officials and the citizens of each state. In order for reform to succeed, there must be a willingness to make the necessary changes, and the desire to assume a more equal share of the federal partnership.

READINGS IN THIS CHAPTER

Modernizing State Government: The Committee for Economic Development (CED)

The CED report represents a broad look at the role of the states in the federal system. It suggests that while they have important functions to perform, there has been an inability or unwillingness to accomplish many objectives. Some of the reasons for this include: (a) lack of adequate geographic boundaries; (b) outmoded governmental structures; (c) inadequate use of resources; and (d) political weakness. In later sections of the report, recommendations for strengthening state governments are included, covering such areas as constitutional revision, strengthening of the executive, streamlining state legislatures, and improving the performance of political parties.

Reform of State Legislatures: Citizens Conference on State Legislatures

The Citizens Conference is a non-partisan research organization concerned with the problem of strengthening state legislatures. The present selection emphasizes the importance of state government, and the handicaps it faces when trying to function within the federal framework. The considerable variation in quality of legislatures is noted, and a method for evaluating legislative performance is proposed. Because of the powerful role played by legislatures in the budgetary process, in the passage of legislation, and in the formulation of state goals, the Conference argues that it is vital to strengthen this institution so that state government as a whole will be improved.

The Cost of Political Confusion: Herbert Alexander

An examination of the party system in America reveals an illogical, often inefficient, pattern with virtually no semblance of uniformity. Because of the fragmented nature of American politics that results in parties operating on three levels (national, state, and local) it is imperative that the machinery of elections, candidate selection, party finance, and platform formulation function smoothly if chaos is to be avoided. In recent years, there has been a continual effort to restructure the system of party finance so as to eliminate major abuses in the system and encourage greater participation. Herbert Alexander points out that several areas still need further attention: campaign costs, ethics legislation, nominating procedures, and party rules. He notes, however, that in each instance although many people are aware that problems exist, few positive steps are being taken to insure that changes will be effected.

[1]Daniel Elazar: *American Federalism; A View From the States* (New York: Crowell, 1972), Chapter 4.

8 Modernizing State Government

The Committee for Economic Development

From: *Modernizing State Government* (New York: Committee for Economic Development. 1967). pp. 10-19. Reprinted by permission of the publishers.

The Committee for Economic Development is a research organization concerned with a wide range of issues facing American government and society.

THE STATES AND THE FEDERAL SYSTEM

The concept of federalism is deeply embedded in the theory and practice of American government. Federalism encourages diversity in choice of priorities and institutional forms. It counters any tendency toward monolithic centralization of power in the national government, since the states are political as well as legal entities and may be used to rally public opinion against ill-considered national measures. And it provides a training ground for recruitment and development of public leadership.

The weaknesses of the federal system, as it actually operates, are equally obvious. States with small populations, or low densities, or chronic economic distress, or poor educational patterns find it increasingly difficult to provide modern public services. Moreover, as economic and social institutions expand in scale, ever-widening fields of human activity lend themselves poorly to management or control by the several states. State boundaries, fixed by history, are not based on current social and economic realities. The potential for interstate cooperation exists, but has not been vigorously exploited.

Any fundamental change in the tripartite division of powers and functions between national, state, and local levels may seem unimaginable. Yet, major changes in the basic character of the federal system have already taken place. Alterations have been gradual, with consequences often unforeseen. The federal system has proven remarkably flexible, permitting us to overcome its deficiencies by adroit use of ingenious devices. Nevertheless its complexities have created serious frustrations. Federalism cannot operate successfully without competent and effective governmental institutions *at all levels*. This elusive goal has not been attained and at times, particularly with respect to the states, it has seemed to move farther beyond reach.

The states form the keystone in the arch of the federal system—the bridge between local governments concerned with community problems and a central government dealing with nationwide issues. There is some validity in the facetious comment that our three-level federalism leaves "the national government with the money, local governments with the problems, and the states with the legal powers." However, most states have access to resources sufficient to satisfy the basic service needs of their citizens. The wealthier states can deal independently with many serious economic and social problems. But few state governments have sought to collaborate with their major cities—or with other local units—in meeting critical local necessities. Many states have been more active in seeking new types and larger amounts of federal aid than in modernizing either their own revenue systems or those of their local units.

The values inherent in American federalism can and should be preserved. Effective and responsive state governments would support local efforts to solve pressing community issues, and could command a larger share of the Gross National Product (GNP). This outcome cannot be anticipated if the American people continue to disregard the imperative need to reform the legislative, executive, and judicial institutions of their states.

POWERS AND FUNCTIONS OF THE STATES

Scholars have made much of the national government's expansion through exercise of its delegated powers over interstate commerce, national defense, international affairs, taxation, and appropriations for "the general welfare." But the national government has redelegated some of its powers and functions back to the states—permitting or encouraging them to act where federal authority is legally paramount, as in the maintenance of national guard units or the regulation of insurance companies with interests crossing state lines. The pressures of world politics are likely to command an increasing proportion of the energies within the national government, making assumption of a larger state role in domestic management a logical possibility.

Many vital matters are within state jurisdiction. States have broad regulatory powers over persons and property. They charter corporations, control the terms of business contracts, license trades and professions, grant land titles, protect private and civil rights, regulate utilities, and set the legal framework of family organization through marriage, divorce, support, and adoption legislation. Authority to limit the uses of land and other property in order to abate water and air pollution or other dangers to the public health resides in the states. Building codes and zoning plans rest on state powers. The manner of use or failure to exercise these powers should not obscure their existence.

In the daily exercise of their sweeping authority, state and local governments manage the bulk of civil government operations in the United States. Universal public education is mandated, regulated, and largely financed by them. Higher education is also heavily state supported. Highways are constructed mostly by the states. Vast hospitals and institutional networks, including those for mental health and corrections, are under state management. The administration of criminal justice depends primarily on state courts and in increasing measure on state police. About half the states manage public welfare programs directly, the other half through their local units. These and other functions illustrate the importance of competent, imaginative, and vigorous state administration.

A dramatic, nationwide instance of neglect in application of state powers is the modernization of local government. Under American constitutional law the 50 states have absolute and exclusive authority for the creation and dissolution of their local governments. While state constitutions often impose limitations, there is a wide area within which state legislatures can move—but have not—to correct deficiencies that plague the nation's 80,000 local units.

The cost of state operations, as such, is rising steeply. Total direct expenditures in current dollars nearly tripled, from $10.8 billion in 1952 to $31.3 billion in 1965, and per capita costs more than doubled in constant dollars. Expansion continues, at 7 to 10 percent annually. Excluding defense, the national government's purchases of goods and services as a share of the Gross National Product fell from 3.8 percent in 1940 to 2.3 percent in 1966,[1] while the corresponding state-local share of GNP rose from 8.0 percent to 10.3 percent. In 1966 the states and their local units employed 8.3 million persons, more than triple the 2.6 million civilians in federal service. Although local governments have three times as many employees as the states, state employment exceeds federal when defense and related functions are excluded.

State aids to local units of government rose at about the same rate as direct state expenditures, from $5.0 billion in 1952 to $14.2 billion in 1965. During that period, federal grants to the states more than quadrupled from $2.3 billion to $9.9 billion, while aids to local units almost quintupled from $237 million to $1.16 billion. Direct state expenditures were one-sixth of total governmental costs in 1965, the same as in 1932; but with defense-related items excluded the states' share of the total has risen sharply in recent years.

The conditional character of grants-in-aid has affected both policy-making and administrative processes. The idea of three levels or "layers" of government, each performing its own distinctive functions independently of the others, becomes obsolete. National, state, and local levels are all involved to some degree in education, health, welfare, transportation, hospitals, maintenance of law and order, sanitation, recreation, housing and slum clearance, and almost every other governmental function. State and local politics even impinge on locational and other aspects of defense, space, and postal services. As perceptive observers have noted, the three-level "layer cake" of former times has given way to the "marble cake" of a newer federalism.

The legal framework of federalism, as a system of "distributed self-government," and the fine distinctions drawn in interpretation of the United States Constitution are matters of profound concern to the American people. But pragmatic considerations often supersede legal and philosophical arguments. In the longer run the role of the states in the federal system will increasingly be determined by the capability with which they function and the vigor with which they meet their obligations.

REASONS FOR INACTION BY THE STATES

The frequent failure of the states in coming to grips with the fundamental economic and social issues within their province, and in coping with the chaotic fragmentation of local governments in most parts of the country, may be largely explained by four major kinds of handicaps.

1. Geographic Handicaps. Boundaries set long ago limit state size and jurisdiction, so that rational solutions for some major problems are beyond the reach of any one state.

2. Outmoded Structures. Innumerable deficiencies in the organization and management of state government serve as self-imposed handicaps against effective action.

3. Inadequate Use of Resources. Some states lack the resources, and many the determination, to raise sufficient revenues, leading to an increasing reliance on the national government for financial support of state and local services.

4. Political Weaknesses. Many states do not have the kind of political party organization necessary for building leadership on fundamental issues and for sponsoring highly qualified candidates for public office. In some states this extends to absence of any meaningful two-party system.

Geographic Handicaps

The boundaries of many states coincide reasonably well with the economic and social interests of the citizens, containing resources and population adequate for economies of scale in state services. Even where population is small, geographic isolation may justify separate statehood—as in Alaska and Hawaii. But some states are severely handicapped in solving their most pressing problems because of awkward boundary locations. Metropolitan areas containing parts of two or more states are illustrative, as are river basin problems wherever major rivers form state boundary lines.

Since no state, acting alone, can be expected to solve multi-state problems, there is an obvious need for active interstate cooperation. Occasional and slowly increasing use has been made of interstate compacts, which the United States Constitution has authorized since 1789. Still, the potential utility of this device is largely unrealized. Uniform state laws have been drafted on a number of important subjects, but comparatively few have been widely adopted.

A new form of interstate cooperation, exemplified by the Appalachian Regional Commission, is now emerging under federal auspices. It has federal and state co-chairmen, and is largely financed by federal funds. A similar pattern is being applied in New England, the Upper Great Lakes, the Ozarks, and elsewhere. This approach highlights the need for interstate cooperation, seeking to overcome past failures to take advantage of opportunities for joint action by the states on their own initiatives.

Outmoded Structures

Although there are partial exceptions, most state governments are burdened by obsolete structural organizations that are often fixed in their constitutions. This generalization extends to all three branches of state government.

Archaic Constitutions. In spite of the need for modern structural frameworks, only seven states have adopted new constitutions since 1945, including recently admitted Alaska and Hawaii. In some other states there are strong new indications of public concern, but most have shown little popular interest in the subject.

Unresponsive and Ineffective Legislatures. Past refusals by legislatures to reapportion themselves in conformance with clear state constitutional mandates have contributed to popular distrust of state government. There is also a widely held view that all governmental powers should be limited and restricted. Partly for these reasons, and partly through sheer inertia, most state legislatures are hemmed in by severe constitutional barriers. For example, 29 legislatures still meet in regular session only once in two years. Time limits of 40 to 195 days are imposed in 33 states. Many houses are unwieldy in size; only 19 lower chambers have less than 100 members. Few have committee systems designed for modern needs. Constitutional limitations in specific fields of legislative action are common, notably in taxation and appropriations.

Executive Weakness. Only half a dozen states give their governors the means for exercising administrative authority commensurate with their responsibility for faithful execution of the laws. Independent departments, agencies, boards, and commissions abound, inhibiting most governors. Eleven states deny their governors a second consecutive term and 13 others a third, reducing gubernatorial ability to provide political as well as administrative leadership. Such factors, together with low pay and inadequate staff assistance, discourage able persons from seeking the governorship.

Uncoordinated Court Systems. A few states have taken important steps to rationalize their court systems, but most have done little. Some or all state judges are elected in 41 states, most commonly by partisan ballot. Often tenure is too short and compensation inadequate.

Inadequate Use of Resources

Collectively, the states have been reluctant to use their broad powers of taxation. Local governments have gradually claimed the lion's share of property taxes, and federal taxation of personal incomes has circumscribed state levies in this field. The states have fallen back on federal or selective sales taxes for more than half their tax revenues. Negative attitudes toward taxation in any and every guise have been more strongly represented in state legislatures than in Congress or local legislative bodies, particularly where reapportionments were long delayed. In January 1967, there were 17 states without a broad-based personal income tax, 13 without such a levy on corporate incomes, and eight without a general sales tax.

Nevertheless, in recent years several states have added new taxes and raised rates on older levies, under pressures for better state services and increases in state aid. These changes, coupled with revenue by-products of the rapid rise in GNP, have left the majority of states in a strong financial position. However, those with small populations and large land areas are hard pressed despite heavy federal aids, and those containing large metropolitan concentrations are in above-average difficulty. Many others would have serious financial troubles if more of the urgent demands being made on them were met.

State long-term debt outstanding on June 30, 1965, totaled $26.2 billion, less than half of it on "full faith and credit." On that date, the 50 states had cash and security holdings of $20.0 billion, exclusive of trust accounts. Meanwhile, many of their local governments were in grave difficulty. The vacuum created by state inaction has drawn the national government into law enforcement, highway safety, antipollution measures, conservation of natural resources, and many other fields where state responsibility is supposed to be primary. It is possible for a state to be "financially sound" and policy bankrupt.[2]

Political Weaknesses

State politics are characterized by vigorous two-party competition in many instances, permitting a healthy exploration of public issues. Several states are under one-party domination, however. In 12 cases more than 80 percent of all members of the 1966 legislatures were members of the same political party. Since 1900 all or all but one of the governors from 13 states have been of the same political party.

Students of politics in one-party states point out that primary elections and runoffs give considerable opportunity for choices between candidates and their political positions. But is also clear that popular participation in primary and general elections is customarily far less than where strong two-party competition exists. Control of governmental affairs by repressive "machine politics"–like that in many rural and urban communities–is often found in states under one-party domination. We are, therefore, gratified to note a recent trend toward the development of two-party systems in New England, Southern, and border areas where one-party government has been deeply rooted.

State and national politics are intertwined, to the degree that national parties are described as "federations" of state parties. In 1966, 48 of the 100 members of the United States Senate were former governors or state legislators, or both. In the United States House of Representatives there were 160 former legislators and three ex-governors. Often the main objective in holding state office is advancement to a national position. This helps to explain why state election campaigns tend to focus on national issues, particularly when they are held with national elections.

There is some advantage in linking state and local elections with national contests. All levels of government are increasingly involved in the administration of the same functions. More voters customarily participate in state elections when they are held at the same time as national contests. Direct costs of elections and total campaign outlays are likely to be lower. Joint elections may also help to strengthen the two-party system, because weak state parties can gain more support for state and local candidates when tickets are headed by attractive persons running for national office.

Despite these apparent advantages, concentration on national campaigns distracts serious attention from issues and candidates at state and local levels.[3] The choice for governor, for example, is frequently affected by opinions concerning a potential for national leadership–in the Presidency, the Vice Presidency, or the Senate–rather than upon executive abilities for managing state affairs. Subordination of state problems, policies, and leadership to broad national trends may lead to defeat of outstanding state legislators, solely on the basis of identification with the party losing a national contest.

Such factors have led Kentucky, Mississippi, New Jersey, and Virginia to hold state elections in odd-numbered years, while Louisiana uses an earlier month in Presidential years. State affairs are thought to command more intelligent attention than would be possible with concurrent dates. Citizens of all states should seriously weigh the advantages and disadvantages of separate elections. There is an intermediate alternative already in use where state elections coincide with Congressional contests in non-presidential years.

If the states are to make independent policy decisions, their political institutions should have a degree of separability and a vitality of their own. The machinery of party organizations and nominating procedures ought, therefore, to receive careful attention. For example, consideration should be given to Connecticut's "challenge primary," which is intended to overcome the proven disadvantages of both the direct primary and the nominating convention. It permits primary contests, but only when convention losers have significant support. Every device designed to elicit greater popular interest and participation should be weighed. But vitality in state politics must depend most of all on fundamental substantive matters, on which governors and legislatures must provide leadership.

[1]Excluded from "goods and services" are transfer payments, as from insurance trust funds and interest on the public debt, estimated at $46.6 billion in fiscal 1968; this sum would equal more than 5 percent of GNP.

[2]For a more detailed discussion on the subject of federal-state-local finance see *A Fiscal Program for a Balanced Federalism*, a Statement on National Policy by the Research and Policy Committee of the Committee for Economic Development, June 1967.

[3]A classic local effort to make use of national issues was seen in a Chicago campaign billboard of the 1920's, "Elect George F. Harding County Treasurer–No League of Nations, No World Court."

9 State Legislatures in the Seventies

The Citizens Conference on State Legislatures

The states have often been described, in civics textbooks and political science quarterlies, as the "keystone of the governmental arch." In the real world, they have generally been regarded, at least in recent memory, as among the last bastions of political reaction and regression. State legislatures, in particular, have been thought of–to the extent that anybody has bothered to think about them at all–in essentially negative terms, as vehicles for preventing the passage of "progressive" legislation or for perpetuating archaic or unjust practices.

But attitudes are changing, and state legislatures themselves are changing. The inability of the federal government to deliver on many of its promises and programs, and the plight of local jurisdictions–smothered with problems that exceed their boundaries and their budgets –have forced growing numbers of Americans, as well as state officials themselves, to reconsider the role of states in dealing with our problems, in particular those of our urban areas and of our environment.

The states, we are beginning to discover, occupy a critical position within the federal system, and they have a wealth

The Citizens Conference on State Legislatures is the broad-based study group concerned with improving the performance of state legislative bodies.

of powers that have remained largely unused. If they begin to take advantage of that position, if they begin to use those powers creatively, they can do much to help cope with our major problems and to enable federal and local government to cope with them far more effectively.

We are rediscovering the states and their legislatures not out of filial respect for our forefathers, or a fine regard for our political heritage, but for the most pragmatic of reasons: our federal system simply will not work well without them, and it is the only system we have. . . .

In recent years, almost every important study of urban or environmental problems finds the states of critical importance. In 1967 the National Commission on Urban Problems (authorized by Congress and appointed by the President) issued an exhaustive and enlightening report on our "urban crisis": what it is, how it happened, what can be done about it. The Report found the states to be in an ideal position—"close enough to the people and yet enough removed from petty parochial interests—to become major constructive forces in dealing with urban problems." After a raft of recommendations for action that states are uniquely qualified to take on urban problems, the Report concluded:

> States have tended to become forgotten members of the governmental family. By using powers they already possess, by assuming new authority when necessary, and in providing funds, they occupy a unique position to help bring urban areas out of confusion. State governments are close to the people and the problems, but bring enough perspective to bear to help release urban areas from the excess of localism. State action of the kind we recommend, where the states are willing to help pay a significant amount of the costs as well as to exercise their authority, can help restore a genuine sense of community to our cities and their surrounding areas.

Another example: The 1969 report of the National Committee on Urban Growth Policy concluded that such a policy required a direct and active public involvement in land deployment, mainly on the part of the states under a scheme by which, with the help of federal loans or grants, they would buy up land, put in the necessary public facilities, develop a detailed plan for its use, and then sell it to private developers with the proviso that they adhere to the plan.

To undertake such an enterprise presumes a degree of sophistication which is characteristic of only the most advanced kind of an institution. The states, and especially their legislatures, have not been in a position to move into such complex areas. But more and more of the problems of the 1970s are in these complicated areas. By virtue of their unique powers and position, the states have an especially important and "relevant" role to play in our political life. The problem is that the powers and position of the states are not new. They have always been there, but states have been unwilling or unable to use them. There is good reason to believe that many of our urban and environmental ills would never have developed, at least in such acute form, had the states been willing to act creatively and constructively. Why, then, should we think that states will change? Why should we even care whether or not they do change? Why not leave things up to federal or local governments, and let them slowly squeeze the states out of the picture?

THE STATES AND THE FEDERAL SYSTEM

There are at least two reasons for not letting the states wither away. First, the federal and local governments are doing a poor job of dealing with our problems. Both are trying to do things they cannot do well: the federal government is trying to run local programs and local governments are trying to tackle problems they have not the money or the power to handle. Our federal system, we are learning, is designed so that federal and local governments cannot perform their own functions unless the states perform theirs. As political scientist Charles Merriam once remarked, if the states did not exist, we would have to invent them, or something like them. For our federal system to work, the states have to work. The only alternative is to install an entirely new system. And that is the second reason for not just letting the states go: short of revolution, we simply do not have the option of scrapping the system we have and starting it over again.

We do, however, need to do some serious restructuring and revitalizing at all levels of our political system, and especially at the level of the states. "In these times," one experienced political observer has remarked, "our kinship is not so much with the Year 2000 as with the Year 1776. We are back to the basics of organizing a new society and providing for its governance."[1] We are back to the same kinds of concerns that occupied the first framers of our governmental institutions. Those old questions of checks and balances, separation and sharing of powers, allocations of function among different levels and different branches of government, have once more become the most contemporary of questions. For those questions, as our forefathers well knew, go to the very heart of the democratic process—they determine how we make the decisions that shape the world we share with others—how we make public choices. . . .

In recent years, the federal government has increasingly stepped in where states have failed—either dealing directly with cities and localities, or employing the states as purveyors of federal programs. But even among the most enthusiastic proponents of these federal programs there is increasing disappointment and disenchantment with the results. Experts differ on why these programs have not lived up to expectations; indeed, different programs may well have faltered for very different reasons. But there is evidence, and a surprising amount of agreement, that whatever other reasons may be involved–poor design, low funding, unrealistic expectations–many of these programs have failed because they were essentially attempts to administer and operate from Washington hundreds and sometimes thousands of local endeavors. In the words of Charles Schultze, the Director of the Bureau of the Budget under President Johnson: "As a control center, the [federal] government can handle defense and space, hand out checks, and regulate industry. But when it comes to aid to programs in education, pollution, manpower, poverty, health, and urban renewal, it is no longer possible to sit in Washington and operate them effectively."[2]. . .

The federal government, therefore, is apparently overreaching and overextending itself; and localities are impotent. In the middle are the states. Under our federal system that is precisely where the states are supposed to be. They are, on the one hand, supposed to give us the advantages of local government (its closeness to the people and the problems) without its disadvantages (parochialism, shortsightedness). They are, on the other hand supposed to give us the advantages of a central government (broad perspective and powers, large human and financial resources, a single focus) without its disadvantages (remoteness, inflexibility, arbitrariness). They should, when they are doing their job, offset the centralizing tendencies of the federal government, which are useful for broad policy planning, revenue raising and redistribution, and similar functions, but which are terrible for dealing with down-to-earth and close-to-home needs and problems. And they should offset the atomizing tendencies of local government, which, theoretically at least, ought to be close to its constituency but is rarely organized or able to handle a whole problem of any size or seriousness.

The states, in short, ought to function under our system as middlemen and mediators, as means of avoiding both overcentralization and excessive localization. We seem to be suffering from both these afflictions at the same time, mainly because the middle ground has been, by and large, a vacuum. The states have not filled it, and they are the only institutions that can. . . .

What is required, therefore, is a genuine realignment of roles and responsibilities in which each level of government does what it does best, a genuine sharing of powers and problems among all levels of government. If that realignment is to occur, it will and must be achieved primarily through the resumption by the states of their role and their responsibilities, under the federal system, in meeting the needs of contemporary America.

The federal government may have to assist states in reassuming this role–perhaps through assuming a greater portion of the cost of welfare or sharing with the states some portion of federal revenues. But in the main it is the states themselves which are responsible for the atrophy that has occurred, and it is the states which must once more assert themselves. The federal government has not, for the most part, moved into areas where the states were functioning effectively. It has, instead, moved into areas where states were failing to function; and the result has been in fact, a rather large increase in the *operations* of state government. . . .

There seems to be no "ideological" opposition to enabling and encouraging states to do more. Rather, the opposition appears to be largely pragmatic; it stems from a deep-seated disbelief that the same states which, by refusing to employ their powers to deal with pressing public problems, let the problems mount and their powers grow musty with disuse, will suddenly put those powers to work where the problems are.

There is, however, reason to believe that there is underway a resurgence of responsibility in the states. *Business Week* recently surveyed the states and reported that they "are trying to lift themselves by their own bootstraps. Some are faltering, most are overdue, and the record is spotty. But a surprising number of governors and legislatures are starting to come to grips with the problems many have ducked up to now; planning, regional development, education, economic development."[3] Twenty-eight states, according to *Business Week*, now have offices of planning and community affairs–with significant powers, such as property-tax assessment. More than a dozen states have their own programs for housing and urban development, including mortgage assistance or loans for low- and middle-income housing. Up to now, education and building codes have been mainly local functions. But Michigan is thinking of taking over a portion of the revenues for education (from the local property tax) for redistribution from more to less affluent school districts. Some half-dozen states have mandatory statewide regulations for multifamily dwellings, and others are working on model building codes.

The states, in sum, are an old idea whose time has come around once more.

THE LEGISLATIVE LAG

Legislatures are the main, although not the only, "drag" upon the capacity of states to function as full partners in the federal system. They are hampered and hamstrung by a host of restrictions on their powers and operations. Some of these restrictions are internal, stemming from the legislature's own rules, traditions, and practices. Some of them are external, contained in the state constitution or resulting from the low popular esteem in which they are held. In their structure, size, procedures, salary level—all those aspects of organization and operation that determine how well they can or cannot work—they are all too often equally as outmoded, and not always as picturesque, as the antique chambers in which many of them assemble, or the bright brass spittoons with which those chambers are still sometimes adorned. It is not simply in their ornateness, or in the musty old odors they often exude, that many of our statehouses remind us of museums. . . .

THE ROLE OF STATE LEGISLATURES

Some argue that the cumbersome qualities of legislatures are a good thing—that they ought indeed to operate as obstacle courses. Thus, the argument goes, they prevent hasty and ill-considered decisions; they insure that any decision reached will be thoroughly and carefully considered. But too many legislatures seem designed to prevent their members from reaching any decisions at all, much less reach them democratically and intelligently. The problem primarily is one of balance, as are most important questions concerning state legislatures—balance between the need to make decisions and the need to make them democratically, between the need to decide and the need to deliberate, between the need to respond and the need to reflect. But simply preventing or postponing decisions does nothing to ensure that they will be made wisely; it ensures only that they will be prevented or postponed.

There are also those who, while they are aware of the need for effective action at the state level, regard the relative weakness of state legislatures as a good thing. What we need, they argue, is a strong executive and a legislature that lets him have his way. But there are a number of difficulties presented by this argument.

Assuming that a strong executive will do the "right" things, there is no guarantee that even a "weak" legislature will simply go along with a governor. The one great power that nearly every legislature has is the power to be negative and to do nothing. What most legislatures do not have are the resources they need to act positively, to react constructively and creatively to executive proposals as well as to initiate and develop proposals of their own. When the governor fails to exercise leadership every legislature should be in the position to take up the slack by proposing programs to deal with pressing needs and problems.

The concept of checks and balances, of the separation and the sharing of powers, requires that you have some powers to share and separate in the first place. It requires, in addition, that these be powers of relatively equal weight. Presently, there are very few legislatures that can compete on equal terms with the executive branch; they must, therefore, simply sit back and wait for executive initiatives, and once those initiatives are made, they must assess them often on the basis of information supplied by the executive. Problems in today's world are simply too complex to be dealt with from a single perspective. Nobody is the possessor of ultimate wisdom, however much we may disagree about who has the lion's share of it. "If we don't have an effective check on the Executive," a seeker after that office recently remarked, "through the power of the Legislature to consider, scrutinize, and reflect popular opinion, then we do not have a republican form of Government; we have instead an elected monarch."[4]

There is great need in this country for genuinely responsive, representative institutions that can help resolve social conflict and reach social settlements. We desperately need institutions which differing groups, interests, or factions can regard as offering them a full hearing and a fair shake. We need a place other than the streets where they can settle their differences. We need institutions that every group can accept as *authoritative*, that make decisions every group can accept as legitimate. We need institutions that reflect the various views and values of the citizenry and respond to them in informed and intelligent ways. And these are the chief functions that a legislature–rather than an executive–ought ideally to perform. They are, as John Wahlke has said, "the principal political functions of a legislature in a democratic system: to 'represent' both the individuals, groups and interests which make up the society and the communal interest of preserving and improving the aggregate society itself, and to 'legitimize' in the eyes of citizens the decisions made by government."[5]

More fully perhaps, as Yale political scientist James Barber explains, in its representative function, the legislature is the miniature of the larger society, a kind of necessary but less perfect substitute for "direct democracy of the town-meeting variety."[6] Its rational, decision-making function revolves around the idea that "the people are best served by a government that is better than they are. The complexity and volume of decisions that the legislature must make requires that it be better.". . .

A DEMOCRATIC DECISION-MAKING BODY

There is no single ideal legislative structure, no magic number of committees, no perfect number of members, no exact set or sequence of rules and procedures. With legislative as with architectural structures, form and function are inseparable. While the broad functions of every state legislature are the same, the forms that in one state will enable a legislature to fulfill its functions may not work equally well in another state. Every state differs from every other, groups of states differ from other groups, in terms of geography, climate, history, economy, population density and composition, and per capita income. The "ideal legislature" is simply the one that best meets the needs of its state–that is, a genuinely democratic decision-making body, reflecting the various views and values of its citizenry on the one hand and responding effectively and authoritatively to their needs and problems on the other.

In no state does such a legislature exist.

[1]Horace Busby, address before the International City Managers' Association (Detroit, Mich.), October 21, 1968.

[2]*Business Week*, October 17, 1970, p. 101.

[3]October 17, 1970, p. 102.

[4]Howard Samuels (candidate for the Democratic nomination for Governor of New York), "Legislative Reform: Up from Chaos," position paper issued in 1970.

[5]Heard, p. 151.

[6]James Barber, *The Lawmakers* (New Haven, Conn.: Yale University Press, 1965), p. 251.

10 Too Costly Politics

Herbert Alexander

From: *National Civic Review,* Vol. 58 (February 1969) pp. 50–55, 82. Reprinted by permission of the author and publisher.

Herbert Alexander is director of the Citizen's Research Foundation, a non-profit study organization based in Princeton, New Jersey.

Why has the federal corrupt practices act not been changed in 43 years, or the Hatch act provisions relating to political finance in 29 years? In the face of both continuing, widespread criticism of existing law and lip-service to reform, why is there a lack of remedial action? Both parties say they favor reform—only the incumbents fail to vote for it. Often they don't even have a chance to vote for it.

Few would deny the gravity of the problem. Political costs are high and escalating. Given our present system of financing politics, a succession of unhappy incidents relating to fund raising is practically guaranteed. The magnitude of the problem is bound to be great in a system where 500,000 public offices are filled by popular vote, not counting nomination campaigns. There is great diffusion and duplication of fund raising appeals. The high cost of politics could refer to the ill effects on the voter at one level, and on the decision-making process at another level, as well as to the dollar amounts.

The unexpected passage by the Congress in 1966 of a tax subsidy for *Presidential* elections has caused rethinking about the form further reform should take. But it should also cause rethinking about the means of achieving legislative change in the field of political finance at the federal and state levels.

The 1966 enactment–which provided for a combined tax check-off and subsidy only for general election campaigns for President–passed on the last day of the second session of the 89th Congress without any visible support of the public, press or opinion leaders. In a four-month period Senator Russell B. Long, chairman of the Senate Finance Committee, introduced, guided and managed passage of a major subsidy bill, without reference to an elections or appropriations committee in either house. No hearings had been held on the House side, and the measure got through as an amendment to another bill. On its own it no doubt would have faltered. As it was, it remained in force only seven months and was made inoperative pending congressional approval of a substitute –which has not yet come. But the important thing was that a subsidy bill could pass the Congress at all.

For more than a decade, public and congressional support had been mounting for tax incentives for political contributions, but their adoption at the federal level had always met resistance. Tax incentives were a familiar concept, not too much unlike deductions for church, charity and welfare. Four states–California, Hawaii, Minnesota and Missouri–had adopted tax deductions before 1966, and Arkansas has since done so. Yet there was considerable opposition. On the other hand, one could not demonstrate strong congressional or other support for subsidies for political activities. Apart from a few vocal advocates, dating back to President Theodore Roosevelt in 1907, they had not attracted substantial backing. Suddenly Senator Long's bill appeared, and passed. The support of a persuasive, skilled, determined and powerful advocate brought the issue to the fore.

Political finance is not a pocketbook issue, or one which clearly affects the lives of many constituents. The appearance of a concerned legislator in a position of power is a fortuitous circumstance. But, in a bicameral system, action in one house is not enough, and only press and public pressure may then force action in the other.

The Congress moves slowly, and it is easy to write off forward movement as futile. One disappointment may be noted in the failure of the Joint Committee on the Organization of the Congress to say anything meaningful on the subject of the administration of campaign fund reports, despite a surprising amount of testimony received on the topic. One can point to the action of the Senate Rules Committee in 1966, which reported out a stale and unimpressive disclosure bill. One can point to the problem in the House, where there was considerable bipartisan resolve and determination in the Committee on House Administration to report out a meaningful bill on disclosure, publicity and limitations. After many years of futile attempts, the subcommittee on elections reported out a strong bill with much bipartisan support. Yet opponents were able to delay the bill in full committee for more than a year and then get it killed in the House Rules Committee.

Surely legislatures can better organize to meet the challenges of political finance. When President John F. Kennedy made recommendations to the Congress in 1962, based on the report of the President's Commission on Campaign Costs, he proposed separate bills covering a broad range of legislation including public reporting, tax incentives, political broadcasting and transition costs. In the Senate the recommendations were referred as a package to the Committee on Rules and Administration. In the House, however, the package was not referred to the equivalent Committee on House Administration but to the Committee on Ways and Means. In each case the proposals were then separated and each bill re-referred to a committee of appropriate jurisdiction. In fact, each of the four bills went to four different committees in each house, and none of them dealt with the President's ideas on the package as a whole. Might it not be in order to establish special or joint committees on occasion to deal with the subject comprehensively?

The major political parties have not played a major role in trying to influence legislation. Each national party chairman has urged congressional action, but has not devoted enough time to lobbying for legislation, to seeking to get petitions of state chairmen or similar action that would attract congressional attention, and having party representatives testify when public forums are available, as in hearings before congressional committees. With notable exceptions, incumbents, whether Democrats or Republicans, are products of the present system. Whether liberal or conservative, they have arrived successfully under the present system, so they are reluctant to tamper with it.

From 1907, when President Theodore Roosevelt suggested subsidies in a State of the Union message, until President Kennedy appointed a bipartisan Commission on Campaign Costs in 1961, no President took any major initiative in this field. President Kennedy twice sent proposals to Congress based on the commission's report. The commission proposals were endorsed by all recent former Presidents and presidential candidates and the two national party chairmen, and they received a favorable press. Yet this support could not be translated into major legislative action. It was then two years until President Lyndon B. Johnson stated his intention in his 1966 State of the Union address to make his own proposals to Congress.

Reform of political finance can rarely if ever be an overriding issue because it is meaningful to relatively few—mainly to candidates, political activists and "do-gooders." The salience of the issue will be in proportion to the number who are concerned. Until recently there has not been much mileage in the issue of either excessive expenditures or questionable sources. Now, in varying degrees and circumstances, the financing of politics is slowly becoming an issue. But no great organized portions of the population are yet disturbed by it.

Apart from the broadcasting industry, which does lobby with respect to political uses of the airwaves, there are no powerful, concerned industries. Church groups generally abstain. Service groups are usually tax-exempt and unable to work for reform. Business groups have seemed more concerned about erosion of the tax base or budget balancing than about erosion of the electoral system.

The role of the press has been understressed, yet it was crucial in developing several cases. As inadequate as federal law has been, recent revelations have vindicated the publicizing of campaign fund data. Digging, even with inadequate tools like campaign fund reports, can prove productive. The combination of the unsavory disclosures before the Kefauver Crime Committee and a thorough newspaper investigation was crucial in the development of the Florida law of 1951. But the ingredients of a modern reform movement were missing in the 1950s, and the Florida enactment inaugurated a major improvement only in that state.

The states have often been berated for failure to meet their responsibilities in many fields. Where great amounts of money are needed, or federal-state powers divided, there are perhaps excuses for state inactivity. But in housekeeping functions, where states have basic jurisdiction under the federal constitution, they have not done well. In the field of elections states have shown little concern, imagination or resourcefulness. Reapportionment was forced on most states by the courts.

To improve corrupt practices legislation or public reporting statutes does not require great appropriations. Only Oregon and Washington provide voters' publicity pamphlets and only Oregon and Kentucky summarize campaign fund reports. The costs to Oregon for voters' pamphlets in 1966, including publication and distribution, were $85,770 for 1,000,600 copies in the primary, and $79,118 for 930,000 copies in the general election. A combined total of $33,853 was recovered from candidate fees paid for inclusion in the volumes, which are additional to their filing fees but minimal nevertheless. Costs in Presidential election years are somewhat higher.

Tax incentives at the state level are relatively inexpensive, yet only five states have adopted them. And in each case they have adopted the least costly and least effective form, tax deductions rather than credits. The only state for which data could be obtained is California. It is estimated by the state franchise tax board that for 1966 the tax deduction for political contributions was taken on 75,000 taxable returns, approximately 2 percent of the total number, and the revenue loss was $250,000.

During the 1967 legislative session the tax structure was changed and it is estimated that for 1968 about 100,000 returns will contain the deduction, at a revenue effect of about $500,000.

Few states can boast about their registration or election-day procedures. Most mature democracies consider these a proper function of the state. But not American states, which leave citizen participation to private or party initiative. Accordingly, parties and candidates are subject to added financial pressures to get these jobs done, and often are led to a condition of reliance on labor organizations and other special interests to help achieve fuller citizen participation. Expenses related to registration and getting out the vote are probably the largest single political cost at the local level. There are more than 175,000 election districts in this country. Volunteer labor suffices in some places, but in many areas the election district captain of each party may spend $100 or more just on election day for workers, watchers and drivers.

With reference to registration, Idaho pays deputy registrants, one in each precinct, to keep rolls up to date, and door-to-door canvassing is authorized. California authorizes the appointment of large numbers of deputy registrars and permits counties to pay them for each new registrant. Alaska and North Dakota do not require prior registration, and a few other states permit registration at the polls in rural areas. A few states now permit mobile registration units. But most states fall far short of these desirable procedures which may cost a few dollars but are important ways to relieve parties and candidates of some of the financial pressures on them.

Election costs in primaries have escalated in recent years. It is ironic that primaries are so expensive, for they are adopted to give the people a voice in the choice of candidates who were being chosen in "smoke-filled rooms" by small groups of large contributors and party bosses. Now it requires wealthy supporters to finance primary campaigns in which the voice of the people can be heard. A return to convention designation would surely result in lower political costs, but must be weighed against the advantages of popular voting to nominate candidates.

State consideration of nomination procedures is long overdue, as is reform of party election procedures. To give the states their due, they have assumed responsibility and costs for administering primary elections, which once were private affairs paid for by the parties, and still are in a few states. But in some states filing fees are too high and tend to exclude or screen out some potential candidates. Only North Dakota subsidizes limited travel expenses for national convention delegates, which is appropriate at a time when broader public participation in delegations is being advocated.

Another state concern should be the number of elected officials. The costs of putting so many of them into office are huge. Still another state concern should be political use of state-supported educational television stations. In 1967 the Florida legislature took unusual action permitting the state Department of Education to grant $25,000 to interconnect seven ETV stations to carry interview-panel type programs with 1968 U.S. senatorial candidates. The experimental project was designed to determine whether candidates could reduce campaign costs if they got meaningful ETV exposure.

Better enforcement of existing laws could provide a real impetus to improvement. But enforcement has been lax. The reasons are understandable–difficulty in finding evidence, lack of respect for present law, partisanship, reluctance to prosecute members of one's own party or even of the opposition party for fear of retribution when that party assumes control. Enforcement agents are appointed or nominated through party processes and are reluctant to prosecute. Lack of enforcement, combined with public indifference, results in few legal cases dealing with political finance. A real pressure for change could come from the courts, just as *Baker* v. *Carr* stimulated redistricting. Might not legal suits overturn certain current practices if grounds were related to the lack of enforcement; failure to comply; failure to administer properly; interpretations of law in obvious violation of legislative intent; the right of the voting public to know; and the public character of political parties, campaigns and operations?

The lack of comparability and uniformity in state laws is remarkable. Many of them have for many years conflicted with federal laws relating to candidates for federal office. Some recent bills in Congress would declare the inapplicability of a state law inconsistent with federal law, and would encourage state election officials to develop procedures to eliminate the necessity of multiple filings by using copies of federal reports to satisfy state requirements. To ensure uniformity and local availability, copies of federal filings would be deposited with the clerk of the federal district court in the state of origin of the candidate or political committee. At present the uneveness of information available is great, and in several Presidential primary states no public reports are required at all.

Apart from the National Municipal League and, recently, the Committee for Economic Development, few organizations have contributed much to this field. Whatever institutional and procedural reforms result from the work of such groups as the Council of State Governments; Citizens Conference on State Legislatures; uniform law groups; and national conferences of governors, secretaries of state or attorneys general will be inadequate unless qualified state officials are elected to office free of obligations to large contributors and special interests.

Despite the presence of numerous political scientists at recent state constitutional conventions, as delegates and advisors, the newly written documents have not significantly upgraded political parties or the electoral process (save for redistricting provisions). Thus, parties continue to compete ill-sanctioned in a restrictive universe, without full legal or constitutional status that might help secure sounder means of financing.

In some states legislative or gubernatorial commissions have been established to recommend changes, but the results have been disappointing. The terms of reference too often relate to limitations and publicity, neglecting a consideration of how laws can be designed to assist candidates and parties to raise necessary funds or reduce current expenses. In New Jersey the state legislature enacted a bill to set up a commission, which was appointed but made no progress and no report and went out of existence. In New York funds for a legislative study were available but no meaningful action was taken.

In Kentucky in 1966 the results were more promising and a registry of election finance was established, though it took substantial, concerted efforts on the parts of citizens' groups; a governor committed to improvement; a Governor's Committee on Campaign Expenditures; the state Legislative Research Council; an influential press and broadcast coverage. The spark plug was the Kentucky Government Council, an independent and nonpartisan group representing various elements of the population. But it could not have succeeded without stimulating the cooperation of other groups such as the Kentucky Farm Bureau Federation; the Kentucky, Louisville and Junior chambers of commerce; Kentucky AFL-CIO; League of Women Voters; Kentucky Bar Association; Associated Industries of Kentucky; County Attorneys Association; and the Democratic and Republican state central committees. Still the 1968 session of the legislature repealed the registry, which was saved only by the governor's veto.

In a state without such a pivotal organization, or the ability to enlist the cooperation of other groups, or a committed governor, the results are understandably desultory. In Massachusetts, Connecticut and Iowa initiatives have been taken by secretaries of state, who in most states have responsibilities in this field. In Hawaii the legislature requested the Legislative Reference Bureau to make a report and recommendations, which it did last year. In New Jersey in 1965 the Citizens' Research Foundation undertook a study of the financing of the gubernatorial election.

There is a structuring and maturing of issues, and most eventually have their day. But whether the day will be exploited to produce comprehensive and meaningful legislation is another matter. There is some danger in premature maturing of issues, and it is easy to do a little and claim reform is accomplished. The aborted federal subsidy proved, nevertheless, that subsidies as well as tax incentives can be enacted. But the need for comprehensive legislation remains, covering both reform and financial assistance to candidates and parties.

Despite all the obstacles and the lack of strong leadership to date, progress will surely be made at the federal level in the near future, perhaps as part of new evaluations of the nomination and election processes. Given the barrage of criticism of our political system, and charges about its lack of responsiveness, it will behoove the states to move ahead with courage and imagination. Else, once again, they may have missed an opportunity to lead, this time in a field in which their jurisdiction is clear and the need is great.

Federalism and the Urban Scene

INTRODUCTION TO CHAPTER FOUR With 73 percent of the U.S. population (149,300,000 people) living in urban areas, there is little doubt that the problems of the city represent one of the major domestic issues facing the nation during the decade of the 1970s.

Our cities are experiencing a crisis of such magnitude as to cause many government officials to wonder whether local government, in its present form, can continue to survive. This crisis has been manifested in several ways: by the physical decay of the urban core of the city, by the deterioration of municipal services, by the racial antagonism prevalent in many urban areas, and by the financial shortages threatening to push the cities into bankruptcy.

In this chapter, the major problems of urban America will be analyzed from the perspectives of governmental structure, finance, social relationships, and the provision of urban services. Each of these categories involves issues that are clearly intergovernmental in nature and will require solutions carried out by policy-makers at all levels of government.

THE NUMBER OF LOCAL GOVERNMENTS

As indicated by Table 1, there are over 81,000 units of local government, including, cities, towns, villages, and special districts. This number has been relatively stable over the past two decades. While there has been some decrease in school districts (because of consolidation or elimination of non-operating districts), the number of other special purpose districts has been rapidly increasing.

OVERLAPPING LAYERS OF GOVERNMENT

Because of state constitutional provisions, local customs, financial exigencies, and the desire of citizens to have local government that is "close to home" we often find several local governments having jurisdiction in the same area. For the homeowner, such duplication often means inefficiency in the provision of services and a higher tax bill. For the government involved, such a situation means that no one unit can effectively govern.

TABLE 1 Types of Government in the United States, 1957–1967

Type of Government	1967	1962	1957
Counties	3,049	3,043	3,050
Municipalities	18,048	18,000	17,215
Townships	17,105	17,142	17,198
School Districts	21,782	34,678	50,454
Special Districts	21,264	18,323	14,424
Total	81,248	91,237	102,392

Source: Bureau of the Census, *Census of Governments*

POLICY-MAKING AND ADMINISTRATION

Unlike the national government, local governments lack strong executive leadership and sufficient, professional staff assistance for administering many programs. One consequence of this situation has been near chaos on the local level. There has also been increased reliance upon the state and national government for assistance in formulating and administering programs.

LACK OF COOPERATION BETWEEN MUNICIPALITIES

One of the most serious governmental problems is that of coordination and cooperation between municipalities. In the past, local governments have been notorious for their disregard of neighbors when building new facilities or planning for urban growth. Each city tends to look inward towards its own problems, rather than seeing them as part of a common difficulty faced by all those dwelling in a particular area.

FINANCIAL PROBLEMS

Several financial problems face our cities. One is a lack of adequate taxable resources (or tax base). State constitutions often severely restrict the types and amount of taxes that can be used by local units of government. Income taxes are often prohibited, and sales taxes frequently are administered by the state. Consequently, the largest single revenue source for municipalities is the property tax. While this tax is a prolific source of funds, it has several disadvantages, such as inequities in administration and regressivity in impact upon different income groups.

A second difficulty results from the fact that some communities are wealthier than others, and often this wealth bears no relation to the physical needs of the community. Thus, a small suburb may be able to raise large amounts of money because of wealthy industries, or wealthy people residing within its borders, while a neighboring city burdened with ghettos and crime may lack a sizable tax base.

Finally, there is the question of distribution of funds within the federal system. Cities have often been on the short end of the stick when federal or state funds are disbursed. Rural domination of Congress and state legislatures, priorities in other areas such as defense, and unequal distribution of taxing powers are largely responsible for this situation.

SOCIAL RELATIONS

From the perspective of human needs, there are many challenges facing the city. One that has been the subject of considerable attention in the past decade involves race relations. A trend that has continued throughout the last ten years has been the pattern of migration to northern central cities by southern and rural blacks. Several cities now have a majority, or near majority, of non-white inhabitants. For example, the 1970 Census reports the following proportions of non-white residents in major cities: Washington, D.C. 71.1 percent, Newark 54.2 percent, Baltimore 46.4 percent, and Cleveland 38.9 percent. Concurrently, there has been an outward movement of white middle class residents to the suburbs. This tendency has led to increased racial polarization and to continuing tension between the "inner city" and its environs.

Nor are urban social problems confined to those relating to race. There is often conflict between different occupational and social classes inhabiting a common area. Similarly, achieving harmonious relations among various ethnic groups is also a goal that is not always satisfactorily achieved.

PROVISION OF SOCIAL SERVICES

Another crisis facing the cities has resulted from severe deterioration of municipal services. This can be seen in all fields: sanitation, health care, public safety, education, welfare, water supply, and recreation. Part of the problem can be attributed to money (or lack of it), part to the rapid urban growth in some areas and decay in others, and a large share to inefficiency and the inability of local governments to function adequately.

RESPONSIBILITY FOR ACTION

Even this brief listing of some of the problems faced by cities suggests that there is a great deal that must be done before solutions to urban ills can be effected. The selections in this chapter will further explore some of the points raised above and attempt to explain how policy with regard to urban America is formulated by each level of government.

READINGS IN THIS CHAPTER

Federalism and the City—The Present Response: Feld

Professor Feld's article, written for this volume, indicates the degree to which federal and state governments have been actively involved in the urban field. An introductory section briefly traces the present role of local government in the federal system, stressing points such as new implications of local home rule, the growth of suburbia, and trends in population growth. The main portion of the selection closely examines the responses of the states and federal government to the plight of the cities, and suggests ways in which the effectiveness of these responses can be assessed.

The conclusion focuses attention on prospects for future action by federal and state governments and on other factors—such as financial pressures, shifting racial balances, court decisions, and public sentiment—which are likely to encourage this action.

The Metropolitan Dimension: Zimmerman

Metropolitanism stresses another aspect of intergovernmental relations: the interaction of governmental units on the local level. For several decades, there has been considerable interest among scholars in the possibility of restructuring government in metroplitan areas, so as to provide a more "rational" framework for patterns of urban living and the provision of urban services.

This selection examines the question of governmental reform from a variety of perspectives and mentions the most common proposals: consolidation, federation, "metro," voluntary agreements, and councils of government.

In a concluding segment, the benefits and pitfalls of reform proposals are described, and an assessment of the feasibility of future change in government structure is provided. While Professor Zimmerman's article does not settle the dispute over the merits of the various proposals, it does provide one of the clearest explanations of what all the shouting is about.

Federalism and Community Control: Suzanne Farkas

The impact of federal and state programs on urban areas goes far beyond the financing of services or the restructuring of local governmental units. Involvement by the federal (and to a lesser extent state) government also results in changes in the nature of local politics, budget practices, and issues debated within the community.

One of the trends found in recent urban programs, particularly those conceived by the Nixon administration, has been a movement toward increased decentralization of decision-making to the local level. This is in line with President Nixon's concept of the New Federalism and is a step that has been advocated by many observers of the urban scene. Professor Farkas notes that there are several benefits that can be derived from such a plan: greater local control over resources, more responsible action on the part of local officials, increased citizen participation and a possible reduction in the size of the federal bureaucracy needed to administer the large number of urban-oriented programs. She warns, however, that there are also dangers inherent in this approach, such as the unequal distribution of resources and a realignment of the present balance of power in the federal system.

Alternative Approaches: Downs

The final selection presents a unique framework for analysis of urban governmental patterns. Professor Downs suggests that a number of factors not mentioned by the previous authors have a considerable impact upon the pattern of urban development, and the nature of the response to this pattern that has been shown by all levels of government. In what might seem to be heresy to some urban planners, Downs suggests, for example, that urban population may actually *decline* instead of expand during the next several decades. He also notes that the trend toward building new cities (rather than preserving old ones) may not be desirable from a social and financial perspective.

Downs argues forcibly that government must take steps to control urban growth through planning, government intervention, and economic limitations. He similarly proposes a series of policy alternatives in the fields of housing, the growth of suburbs, and the financing of local government. If all or most of these recommendations were adopted, there is little doubt that a major change in the entire range of government programs directed toward urban areas would result.

11 Federalism and the City: Where Do We Stand Today?

Richard D. Feld

Given the nature and severity of urban problems, there is little doubt that virtually all of the cities' ills will require assistance from higher levels of government to insure a lasting solution. Consequently, it seems appropriate to begin with an examination of the role played by the state and federal governments with regard to the cities, and then to assess how effective each level of government has been in carrying out its responsibility in this field.

Original article prepared for this volume.

Richard Feld is Assistant Professor of Political Science at the University of Houston. He is the co-author of a recent article dealing with political recruitment in Houston.

THE ROLE OF THE STATES

State involvement in local affairs can be traced back to the colonial period. As part of the heritage of common law, state constitutions, with few exceptions, have affirmed the idea that cities owe their existence to the states and can be created or destroyed at will. This so called "creature theory" of local government is expressed by "Dillon's Rule," which states that municipalities can exercise only those powers expressly granted to them in writing and that in the case of a dispute over interpretation of municipal power, courts will rule in favor of the state rather than the local entity.[1]

Toward the end of the nineteenth century, the principle of home rule, or local autonomy for the cities, was given more favorable attention and the emphasis of state control was made less restrictive. At this time there was also the beginning of a movement toward providing increased technical and financial assistance to the cities.

Accompanying the assertion that the states continue to have a major responsibility in the field of urban affairs, there have been numerous suggestions concerning how this responsibility could be exercised. One solution often presented is that the states should establish some form of an Office for Local Government which would advise communities of availability of state and national funds, undertake studies of the needs of local government, and provide a mechanism for coordination of local, state, and national policies. There is usually mention of steps which would strengthen the structure of local government, such as improved annexation laws, more stringent requirements for incorporation of new communities, and passage of legislation encouraging interlocal cooperation.[2]

Two groups that have been actively involved in the campaign for increased state involvement in and assistance to local government have been the Advisory Commission on Intergovernmental Relations (ACIR) and the Committee for Economic Development (CED). The ACIR has called for a "package" of powers to be given to localities in order to enable them to operate more effectively. This package includes increased planning powers, control over land use, state involvement in interlocal agreements, and authorization for the creation of functional single or multi-purpose authorities which would operate over a broad geographic area.[3] In a recent report, the CED also issued a call for state assistance in effecting a realignment of local government.[4] Noting that the nation's cities often lack the vision and dedication (as well as the financial resources) to solve many of their problems, the Committee suggested a program incorporating reforms such as: reduction in the number of local governments, elimination of many overlapping layers of government, modernization of the county, revision of state constitutions so that they more accurately reflect the needs of urban residents, and changes in grant programs to encourage increased local efficiency.[5]

STATE RESPONSE TO THE URBAN CRISIS

The states have responded in a variety of ways to these proposals. Several have adopted all or most of the recommendations discussed above, while others have chosen to institute different types of programs.

Technical Assistance to Municipalities

In line with recommendations made by several study groups, most states have established an Office for Local Government which provides technical advice, information about grants from the federal and state governments, and other advisory services. As of 1970, 42 of the states had established an agency of this type. A few states, notably California, New York, New Jersey, and Pennsylvania have given added powers to their urban agencies, allowing them to supervise annexation and incorporation procedures, land use controls, and the planning of "new towns" to alleviate overcrowding in the existing cities.[6]

Financial Assistance

Currently, the states provide over $6.5 billion to local governments to be used for a variety of purposes. Most frequently, states give grants to help defray the cost of education, highways, welfare, and health services. These are usually given as earmarked funds which must be spent for a particular purpose. One of the problems with the system of grants commonly in use is that it often discriminates against many of the larger cities. Because of previous rural domination of most state legislatures, aid formulas were written in a manner that favored rural areas and the more wealthy suburban communities at the expense of the cities. This pattern is changing as legislatures become more responsive to urban needs, but the process is a gradual one.

Elimination of Constitutional Restrictions

In the past decade, over half the states have taken steps to remove or soften many of the constitutional restrictions on the powers of local governments. Usually this means granting more home rule to municipalities, raising or eliminating tax and debt ceilings, and passing legislation that allows greater flexibility in the operation of local government.

Permission for Interlocal Cooperation

Over 75 percent of the states have now passed legislation authorizing local governments to enter into agreements between themselves for the joint provision of services, or contractual arrangements which facilitate providing services over an areawide basis. These provisions are important from several perspectives: they can effect monetary savings as a result of economies of scale, they discourage duplication of effort, and they help reduce the need for creation of special districts which can lead to unnecessary governmental proliferation.

Reapportionment of State Legislatures

As a result of the Supreme Court rulings in the cases of *Baker vs. Carr* (1962)[7] and *Reymolds vs. Sims* (1965)[8] state legislatures have been required to redistrict themselves to be in conformity with the dictum "One man, one vote." As of 1970, there has been almost total (although somewhat reluctant) compliance with these court orders. To many observers, this action has the potential for being one of the most significant ways of obtaining state aid for urban areas.[9]

The State Response: Has It Been Sufficient?

Without doubt, the role of the states in urban affairs has increased significantly over the past two decades. As we have seen, many states are beginning to take steps designed to aid their cities and a number of successful programs have been initiated. However, a great deal more could be done. In general, state programs have often been narrow in scope and have concentrated largely on planning or restructuring of local government rather than on the broad spectrum of urban needs. Financing for programs has also been quite limited, and considerable opposition to urban aid frequently exists among rural and suburban legislators.[10]

THE FEDERAL GOVERNMENT AND THE CITIES

Because of the inability or unwillingness of many states to fully assume the responsibility for providing urban programs, the federal government has become increasingly involved with the plight of urban America. Depending upon how narrowly one classifies the term "urban development," between 175 and 200 distinct federal urban development programs can be identified. They cover a wide variety of services such as highways, mass transit, education, housing, public health, welfare, employment, and construction of municipal facilities.[11]

Virtually all of the nation's programs directed toward the cities are administered directly on a federal-local basis, without using the states as an intermediary. Large-scale federal involvement in urban affairs began in the 1930s with the passage of the Housing Act of 1937; in 1949 it was re-enacted with major revisions that attempted to further encourage housing construction and the elimination of urban blight. The second part of this act contained provisions for one of the most controversial aspects of the housing program–urban renewal–which embodied the concept of destruction of dilapidated housing and its replacement with more suitable living units. Housing Acts passed in 1954 and 1962 re-enforced the earlier statutes and still sought to attain the ever-elusive goal of decent housing for all Americans.[12]

During the Kennedy and Johnson administrations, several new approaches to housing problems were explored. Three of the most controversial ones were low-cost private housing (the "235 program") and the rent-supplement and interest-subsidy apartment projects.[13] In each case, the goal was to allow low and moderate income families to purchase homes or rent apartments at rates they could afford. These programs have continued, with some modification, under the Nixon administration. The details are administered by the Department of Housing and Urban Development (HUD) or the FHA and stress the involvement of non-profit corporations and private developers in the housing process.

The federal government has also sponsored other programs in the field of low and moderate income housing such as Project Turnkey and Operation Breakthrough. These are experimental efforts designed to encourage mixed income residential developments and to discover low cost methods for the construction of housing units.[14]

In the 1960s there was also greater involvement by the federal government in many of the other problems facing the cities. Two of the most comprehensive programs adopted during this period were the "War on Poverty" administered through the Office of Economic Opportunity (OEO) and the Model Cities Program directed by HUD. These are particularly significant because they reflect a broadened approach to the solution of urban problems. Instead of dealing with individual aspects such as housing or transportation, the two programs seek to provide for a large variety of urban needs through a common administrative structure. For example, the OEO oversees the Head Start Program for preschool children, the Job Corps, and the Community Action Agencies, which design the bulk of projects for poverty area residents. The Model Cities Program also stresses the use of a single agency to coordinate many projects. Another common feature of both programs is the concept of local citizen involvement in the planning and implementation process. This is done in order to insure that those being helped have a voice in selecting the programs most relevant to their needs.[15]

Federal Assistance: How Effective Has It Been?

The programs mentioned above are only a few of the many ways in which the federal government has become involved in the urban crisis. While the amount of federal aid is growing and is impressive in terms of dollar amounts, there has been mounting criticism of the way in which this aid is being administered. Unlike the state assistance programs, which generally involve providing technical services or funds for capital construction, federal programs often deal directly with social issues and involve a restructuring of many practices that have existed for long periods of time. Consequently, there have been several drawbacks to the approaches adopted.

In the case of housing, there have often been undesirable consequences, such as the perpetuation of patterns of racial segregation, of the isolation of the poor in perpetual high-rise ghettos, and the producing of sterile architectural designs which detract from rather than enhance the physical surroundings of the city. Perhaps the most serious complaint, however, relates to financing. Several studies have indicated that considerably less than 10 percent of the total housing needs of the nation are met by the various federal programs, and that at present levels of expenditure little permanent improvement in the housing supply can be expected.[16]

Urban renewal presents another case in which good intentions have often failed to solve a particular problem. As several critics have noted, the "bulldozer approach," or total destruction of large segments of neighborhoods, has only resulted in overcrowding in adjacent neighborhoods, and in maintaining the patterns of race and social class that previously existed.[17] Because of the rededication of large portions of renewal areas for commercial use, it is often found that the actual amount of housing available for the poor is less than when the project was started.

Model Cities and the War on Poverty have also come in for severe criticism. It has been charged that the amount of funding is inadequate, that the projects do not help those who need it most, that political turmoil and distrust is caused by the sponsoring agencies, and that there is lack of imagination in the design and execution of the projects that are adopted.[18]

An overriding issue affecting virtually all federal activity is that of coordination. As a result of the haphazard way in which many programs have been developed, there has been little cooperation among the many agencies involved in administering financial assistance. Even within a single department, such as Housing and Urban Development, there is often little knowledge of the impact of one program upon others already existing. This situation causes many difficulties for the cities. They are often confused about application procedures, and they may be frustrated in their own attempts to achieve a unified planning process. The large number of agencies directing programs also means extra effort on the part of cities to keep themselves informed of the various types of assistance that are available.

Citizen Reaction to Federal Programs

In assessing the impact and effectiveness of government programs, the response of local residents in the cities should also be considered. In recent years, this response has been more vocal, and the number of protests against federal activity have steadily increased. Objections have been made by both supporters and opponents of many of the new programs.

Citizens favoring many of the federal programs, including those living in poverty areas, have alleged that they are not given the opportunity for meaningful consultation over expenditure of funds, selection of projects, and election of neighborhood councils. Many representatives of the poor have also charged that large amounts of federal funds are siphoned off through graft, political favoritism, racial prejudice, or ineptitude, so that the actual amounts reaching them are quite small.

Opponents of federal programs, particularly in the field of housing, have argued that the values of their homes and the esthetics of their neighborhoods are damaged by inadequate site selection and the overburdening of municipal facilities. There is also the claim that racial and social integration is being forced upon only one segment of the community–the less affluent whites–while other sections of the city are unaffected. Finally, local leaders have contended that the Model Cities and War on Poverty programs have encouraged radicalism and engendered, rather than extinguished, racial hostility.[19]

The protests in several large cities such as Philadelphia, Los Angeles, Chicago, and Houston have helped to re-emphasize the point that uniform regulations and a large (and often unwieldy) bureaucratic administrative procedure often tend to antagonize citizens and turn them against programs which they otherwise might support. It can also be viewed as an encouraging sign, however; sufficient local interest can insure that even "big government" is made responsive.

The Nixon Approach to Urban Affairs

The Nixon Administration is making a concerted effort to reverse the trend towards centralization of governmental power at the national level. While this effort is being directed mainly at the states initially, a similar logic applies to the local level as well. Thus, while there has been a continuation (and even expansion) of several of the urban-oriented programs initiated during the Kennedy-Johnson period, we can also expect to see more proposals for revenue sharing between federal and local governments and more suggestions for delegating increased authority for administration to the localities.[20]

GOVERNMENT POLICY AND URBAN AFFAIRS: IMPLICATIONS FOR THE FUTURE

In the previous pages we have focused on the impact of local, state, and federal government decision-making on urban development. We must now speculate about the nature of future activity in this area.

One feature that is readily apparent is the pervasive nature of the problems affecting municipalities. We have seen that these problems are multi-dimensional in scope and require broadly based solutions rather than a single narrow approach. Consequently, money alone is not the answer to the crisis facing the cities. Nor will new housing, increased employment opportunities, beautification of the physical environment or resolution of social conflict single-handedly solve all urban ills.

This complexity points to another conclusion: the degree of involvement by all levels of government will steadily increase. Examples of this intergovernmental concern have been previously mentioned–the programs initiated by state and federal governments, and the measures taken to promote interlocal cooperation within a metropolitan area. This trend will mean that a greater amount of financial and technical resources are available and that a more comprehensive approach to the total problem can be achieved. It will also further emphasize the degree of interdependence existing among units of government in the federal system.

A third aspect of governmental activity in urban affairs relates to the actual results achieved by the policies being pursued. As we have seen with Model Cities and the War on Poverty, there are often a variety of harmful unintended consequences that occur along with any benefits which may accrue. Examples could be cited from many projects: the new civic center that destroys a neighborhood that has just been rehabilitated; the urban renewal project that replaces less than half the number of residences torn down so that adjacent areas become overcrowded; the new expressway (financed largely with federal funds) that increases congestion in the downtown area; and the welfare system that penalizes people who seek employment to improve their economic situation. Another issue that compounds this problem relates to the lack of agreement over what policy alternatives should be followed. Federal and state governments have not spoken with a single voice on this issue, nor have the cities that have been recipients of financial aid. In fact, we can find many instances where two or more levels of government are pursuing totally different objectives within the same program. Academicians have also been unable to achieve a consensus. Indeed, given the division over goals that exists among social scientists, there is considerable doubt as to whether a unified policy can ever be realized.

Many questions concerning the fate of our cities remain unanswered. While there is general agreement that somehow the cities must survive and be transformed into viable political entities, the actual details of how this survival is to be insured have not been decided. This will be one of the major tasks facing policy-makers in the years ahead. If an effective approach to the solution of urban problems is to be found, there will have to be a coordinated effort made to reach agreement on many of the fundamental principles of this approach, and to make certain that the tools necessary for achieving the stated objectives are available.

[1]John Dillon, *Commentaries on the Law of Municipal Corporations*, 5th ed. (Boston: Little, Brown & Co., 1911), I, sec. 237, pp. 448–50. For a complete discussion of home rule legislation and its importance to metropolitan areas, see Neil Littlefield, *Metropolitan Problems and Municipal Home Rule* (Ann Arbor: University of Michigan Law School Press, 1962).

[2]These proposals have been strongly supported by the Council of State Governments, which is comprised of representatives from each state. See John Bollens, *The States and the Metropolitan Problem* (Chicago: Council of State Governments, 1956); and Council of State Governments, *State Responsibility in Urban Regional Development* (Chicago, 1962).

[3]Advisory Commission on Intergovernmental Relations, *Governmental Structure, Organization, and Planning in Metropolitan Areas*, (Washington, D.C.: Government Printing Office, 1961) pp. 18–25.

[4]Committee for Economic Development, *Modernizing Local Government* (New York, 1966). Similar recommendations were included in a later report by the same organization: *Reshaping Government in Metropolitan Areas* (New York, 1970).

[5]Committee for Economic Development, *Modernizing Local Government*, pp. 17–18.

[6]A listing of the states that have established Offices of Local Government and a summary of the powers of these agencies is provided by: House Report No. 1270, 90th Congress, 2nd Session, *Unshackling Local Government* (revised). Report by the Committee on Government Operations, Appendix 1 (Washington, D.C., 1968).

[7]369 U.S. 186 (1962).

[8]377 U.S. 533 (1964).

[9]Many cities have found to their surprise, however, that reapportionment has not been a panacea for curing all their problems. Frequently, it has been observed that suburban legislators (who also have gained strength as a result of reapportionment) align themselves with the rural interests in opposition to the wishes of the cities they surround. Also, since the cities now have several representatives instead of the one or two they formerly had, there may be disputes over who is the leader of the urban delegation, and over what programs are most beneficial. For further discussion of these points, see Robert Heath and Joseph Melrose, Jr., "New Lawmakers" *National Civic Review*, LVIII (October 1969) 410–14; and George C. Roberts, "A Districting Dilemma," *National Civic Review*, LIX (June 1970), pp. 303–7, 313.

[10]For a detailed discussion of the accomplishments and failures of state government in the urban field, see Alan K. Campbell, ed., *The States and the Urban Crisis* (Englewood Cliffs, N.J.: Prentice Hall, 1970.)

[11]A summary of the major federal programs directed toward urban areas is given in Executive Office of the President, Office of Economic Opportunity, *Catalog of Federal Assistance Programs* (Washington, D.C., 1967). A more recent listing of programs admini-

stered by HUD is also available: U.S. Department of Housing and Urban Development, *HUD Programs* (Washington, D.C., June 1970).

[12]As pointed out by several authors, the total amount of financing currently provided for public housing, and the number of new housing starts each year, are inadequate to meet the demand for sound living quarters. For a discussion of this problem, see Nathaniel S. Keith, "An Assessment of National Housing Needs," *Law and Contemporary Problems*, Vol. 32, No. 2 (Spring 1967), 209–19.

[13]Sec. 235, 236 of Housing and Urban Development Act of 1968 (PL90-448); also Sec. 221d (3) of National Housing Act of 1935 (P.L.73-479) as added by Housing Act of 1954 (PL83-560) and as amended.

[14]For a discussion of these new approaches and an evaluation of the entire public housing program, see Joseph Birstein, "New Techniques in Public Housing," *Law and Contemporary Problems*, Vol. 32, No. 3 (Summer 1967), 528–49.

[15]The War on Poverty was officially passed by Congress as part of the Economic Opportunity Act of 1964. The Model Cities Program grew out of the Demonstration Cities and Metropolitan Development Act of 1966. A full discussion of these programs, including an excellent analysis of problems of coordinating bureaucratic structures, can be found in James L. Sundquist and David W. Davis, *Making Federalism Work* (Washington, D.C.: The Brookings Institution, 1969).

[16]For further discussion of these issues, see Lawrence M. Friedman, *Government and Slum Housing: A Century of Frustration* (Chicago: Rand McNally, 1968); Nathan Glazer, "Housing Problems and Housing Policies," *The Public Interest*, VII (Spring 1967), pp. 21–25, and William H. Ledbetter, Jr., "Public Housing–A Social Experiment Seeks Acceptance," *Law and Contemporary Problems*, XXXII (Summer 1967), pp. 490–527.

[17]Several recent studies have been highly critical of various aspects of the urban renewal process. These include Martin Anderson, *The Federal Bulldozer: A Critical Analysis of Urban Renewal* (Cambridge, Mass.: MIT Press, 1964); Harold Kaplan, *Urban Renewal Politics* (New York: Columbia University Press, 1963); and Peter Rossi and Robert Dentler, *The Politics of Urban Renewal* (New York: The Free Press of Glencoe, 1961).

[18]Sundquist and Davis, *Making Federalism Work.* A report issued by a Presidential Study Commission (under the chairmanship of Edward Banfield) also contains criticism of the way in which the Model Cities Program is presently administered: Report of President's Task Force on Model Cities, *Model Cities: A Step Towards the New Federalism* (Washington, D.C., August 1970). Additional suggestions for changes in scope and direction of these programs are found in Kenneth B. Clark and Jeanette Hopkins, *A Relevant War Against Poverty* (New York: Harper & Row, 1969).

[19]Daniel Moynihan's *Maximum Feasible Misunderstanding* (New York: Free Press, 1969) describes some of the problems involved in managing programs directed toward the urban poor. One of the most comprehensive series of studies relating to citizen participation and the effects of the Model Cities and War on Poverty programs can be found in a symposium on planning social intervention in *Social Science Quarterly*, Vol. 50, No. 3 (December 1969).

[20]One approach of President Nixon has been to try to coordinate the activities of federal agencies involved in urban programs, while also allowing greater discretion at the local level. For a description of this policy, see John Fischer's article "Can the Nixon Administration be Doing Something Right," Harpers Magazine (November, 1970). Other indications of the directions being taken by the Nixon Administration can be seen in the President's recent messages.

12 Metropolitan Reform in the U.S.: An Overview

Joseph F. Zimmerman

The metropolitan problem, variously defined, has been accorded recognition since the early part of the 20th century, and numerous proposals have been advanced for a restructuring of the system of local government to solve the problem. With relatively few exceptions, reorganization proposals have been rejected by voters who apparently have been influenced more by arguments promising to keep the tax rate low and the government close to the people and free of corruption than by arguments stressing the correction of service inadequacies and the economical and efficient provision of services.

Interest in the structural reform of the local government system appeared to reach its peak in the 1950s. Frank C. Moore wrote in 1958 "that more surveys have been initiated in the last five years than in the previous thirty."[1] Seventy-nine of the 112 surveys initiated between 1923 and 1957 were launched between 1948 and 1957, compared to one or two per year from 1923 to 1948.[2]

The number and nature of surveys underwent a significant change in the 1960s, primarily as the result of require-

From: *Public Administration Review*, Vol. 30 (1970), pp. 531–43. Reprinted by permission of author and publisher.

Joseph Zimmerman is Professor of Political Science at the State University of New York at Albany. He has written several articles dealing with metropolitan cooperation and state-local relations.

ments in various federal grant-in-aid programs. A sharp rise in transportation and comprehensive land-use studies occurred. The number of transportation studies rose from 15 in 1960 to 118 in 1966, 154 in 1967, and 198 in 1968.[3] Comprehensive land-use studies increased from 15 in 1960 to 48 in 1966 and 73 in 1967, but decreased to 71 in 1968. Studies concerned with governmental organization declined from 40 in 1960 to 34 in 1966 and 29 in 1967. Thirty-six such studies were launched in 1968. Although the results of a comprehensive canvass of metropolitan studies are not currently available, it appears that there has been a vast upsurge since 1968 in the number of governmental organization studies, particularly in the South.

THE CONSOLIDATIONISTS

Nineteenth century metropolitan reorganization took the form of city-county consolidation without referenda in Boston, Philadelphia, New Orleans, and New York City. In addition, entire towns were consolidated by legislative edict with the central city; Charlestown, Dorchester, and Roxbury were consolidated with Boston. And annexation also commonly was used by the central city to keep pace with urbanization.[4]

The leading consolidation advocate in recent years has been the Committee for Economic Development (CED), composed of 200 prominent businessmen and educators, which maintains there is a great need for a revolutionary restructuring of what is labelled an anachronistic system of local government. In 1966 CED urged an 80 percent reduction in the number of units to no more than 16,000, with increased reliance being placed upon reconstituted county governments everywhere except in New England, where the proposal was advanced that towns should be consolidated or closely federated to form metropolitan governments.[5] Interestingly, CED in February 1970 recommended "as an ultimate solution a governmental system at two levels."[6]

When we speak of consolidation we may refer either to the consolidation of functions which occurs when a function is shifted to a higher level of government—this is labelled centralization by some—or to a consolidation of units of government. The creation of a metropolitan federation also may be referred to as a type of consolidation in view of the fact certain functions are taken away from municipalities and assigned to the newly created upper-tier unit.

City-county consolidation may be complete or partial. In a complete consolidation, a new government is formed by the amalgamation of the county and municipal governments. Partial consolidation may involve the merger of most county functions with the cities to form a new consolidated government, but the county continues to exist for the performance of a few functions required by the state constitution. A second from of partial consolidation involves the merger of several but not all municipalities with the county.

TWENTIETH-CENTURY CONSOLIDATIONS

Prior to 1947 there was relatively little 20th-century interest in city-county consolidation. The Hawaiian Territorial Legislature did merge the City and County of Honolulu in 1907 without a referendum, but only three proposals for consolidation in other areas reached the ballot and each of the proposals was defeated.

Louisiana voters in 1946 approved a constitutional amendment permitting a home rule charter to be drafted for the Baton Rouge area. Voters in 1947 approved a charter providing for the partial consolidation of the City of Baton Rouge and East Baton Rouge Parish effective in 1949. The city, parish, and two small municipal governments were continued and a city-parish council was created. It is composed of the seven-member city council and two members from the remainder of the parish.

After rejecting a consolidation charter in 1958, voters approved a similar charter in 1962 creating the Metropolitan Government of Nashville and Davidson County. The charter created an urban services district, and a general services district, and authorized a separate tax rate for each district based upon services provided. Six small cities were exempted from the consolidation, but may disincorporate and join the urban services district when it is expanded to their area.

The next major partial consolidation occurred in the Jacksonville area as the result of a 1967 referendum when a charter consolidating the City of Jacksonville and Duval County was approved. The voters of three small cities and a town voted to retain their separate corporate status. Patterned largely upon the Nashville model, the new city has a general and an urban services district.

A minor consolidation—Carson City and Ormsby County, Nevada—received voter approval in 1969. A more major consolidation occurred in the Indianapolis area on January 1, 1970, as the result of the passage of an act by the Indiana Legislature consolidating the city and Marion County.[7] This consolidation is particularly noteworthy in that it is the first one in the northern United States, as well as the first one implemented without a popular referendum since 1898 when New York City was formed by a five-county consolidation. . . .

CONSOLIDATION IN THE SOUTH

With the exception of the Indianapolis-Marion County merger, all 20th-century city-county consolidations and a major semiconsolidation, Dade County, have occurred in the South. Furthermore, a three-judge annexation court in Virginia in 1969 allowed Richmond to annex 23 square miles of territory and 44,000 residents; the largest annexation in terms of population and area in the state's history.[8] The city had sought to annex 51 square miles of territory and 72,000 residents. And indications, as reflected by the creation of charter commissions, are that most consolidations in the next few years will occur in the South.

What factors, other than general geographical location, are common to each area or to each reorganization plan where consolidation has occurred or current interest in consolidation is strong? Even a superficial analysis of the areas indicate that they possess a number of similarities with each other and dissimilarities with metropolitan areas in other sections of the United States.

Number of Units

There were relatively few units of local government in each metropolitan area prior to consolidation, and each unit had a small population with the exception of the central city.

The partial consolidation in the Baton Rouge area involved only four units, and the partial consolidation in the Nashville area involved only seven municipalities, six of which are small and were exempted from the consolidation. In Duval County there were only five municipalities and six special districts; only four of the special districts had property-taxing powers. Aside from Jacksonville, the largest municipality had a population of 16,000. And the four small municipalities were given the option of remaining out of the consolidation.

In the Charlotte area there are only six municipalities and one special district with property-taxing powers. Other than Charlotte, the largest municipality has a population under 5,000. We find a somewhat similar situation in the Savannah area where there are six small municipalities, four of which have a population under 5,000. In the Chattanooga area, three of the six municipalities have a population under 5,000, and in the Charleston area six of the eight municipalities have a population under 5,000.

Dade County with 27 municipalities is the exception, and the fact that there were such a large number of municipalities may account at least partially for the fact the two-tier approach was adopted. Proposals were made in 1945, 1947, and 1953 to consolidate the county and the City of Miami, but were defeated.

Partial Consolidations

The Nashville and Jacksonville reorganizations were partial consolidations in that the few existing small municipalities were given the option, by referendum, to remain out of the consolidation, and all chose to do so. The Baton Rouge consolidation retained the city, the parish, and two small municipalities. The Dade County reorganization provided only for functional consolidation and not for the merger of governments. And most of the proposed consolidations in the South offer the smaller municipalities the option of continuing their separate corporate existence.

Use of the County

An established government, the county, was utilized as the base to build the new metropolitan government. This strategy improves the prospects of creating an areawide government with sufficient powers since it usually is easier, under state enabling legislation, to restructure the county government than to create a new regional unit. In the South, the county traditionally has been a stronger unit of government than in the Northeast. In North Carolina, for example, the county can perform nearly all urban-type functions.

Irving G. McNayr, the second manager of Dade County, in a 1964 speech, stated: "Realizing that the county's inadequate tax structure and lack of long-range plans for operating special districts held little hope for expansion of urban services throughout the county, the citizens of the unincorporated area began supporting the new concept for an areawide government with broad powers."[9]

Incremental Consolidation

City-county consolidation is not entirely new in most southern areas, as partial consolidation has occurred incrementally over the years and citizens, consequently, were accustomed to look to the county for solutions to areawide problems.

In the 1940s the Dade County school system was created by the consolidation of 10 school districts, a county health department was created by the consolidation of all municipal health departments, and a county port authority was created to operate all airports and terminals. In 1948 Miami turned its hospital over to the county.

In the Jacksonville area health, tax assessing, tax collecting, voter registration, and planning and zoning had been consolidated prior to 1967.

Charlotte-Mecklenburg County currently have consolidated school, public health, and public welfare systems, and jointly finance a single agency responsible for elections, a second agency responsible for planning, and a third agency responsible for property tax administration. According to a recent report, "only thirty percent of combined city and county expenditures are in areas where further consolidation or joint financing arrangements would appear to deserve consideration."[10]

Special Service Zones

The consolidations, starting with the Baton Rouge one in 1947, rely upon special service and taxing zones. A separate tax rate is established for each zone based upon the number and level of services provided. The use of service zones has made consolidation more appealing to residents of unincorporated territory, and proposed southern consolidations provide for the use of service zones.

Dade County is not allowed by the Florida constitution to utilize tax and service zones. This means that residents of unincorporated territory receive urban services from the county and pay *ad valorem* property taxes to the county at the same rate as residents of the 27 municipalities who do not receive these services from the county.

Lack of a Competitive Political System

The political system in southern metropolitan areas is, in general, not highly competitive. In 1957 Edward C. Banfield wrote, "it will be difficult or impossible to integrate local governments where the two-party system operates. . . . In effect, advocates of consolidation schemes are asking the Democrats to give up their control of the central cities or, at least, to place it in jeopardy."[11]

The term "No-party system" has been used by Edward Sofen to describe the absence of powerful political parties in Dade County.[12] In Charlotte, elections are nonpartisan, but all councilmen are Democrats. Partisan elections are used in Mecklenburg County, and two of the five county board members currently are Republicans; the system, however, is not highly competitive.

Scandals

Scandals in Nashville and Jacksonville worked in favor of the consolidationists. In Nashville prior to the referendum there were charges of police scandals. Jacksonville was plagued by a high crime rate and insurance and police scandals. In November 1966 the grand jury indicted two city commissioners, four councilmen, the recreation director, and the city auditor. In addition, the tax assessor resigned and the city's 15 senior high schools were disaccredited shortly before the referendum.

Racial Overtones

There were racial overtones attached to the Nashville and Jacksonville referenda campaigns, as it was charged in each case that consolidation was designed to dilute the growing black voting strength in the central city. It has been suggested that Richmond's 1969 annexation of 44,000 persons, most of whom are white, would help to offset black political strength in the city. Prior to annexation, an estimated 55 percent of the population was black. It must be pointed out, however, that City Manager Alan F. Kiepper testified at the annexation trial the city's need was for land for new industry and housing. Only 6.4 percent of the city's land prior to annexation was vacant, whereas 27.7 percent is now vacant. The city maintains that the annexation will strengthen the economy of the metropolitan area by providing a more realistic economic base for the central city.

State Senator LeRoy Johnson of Atlanta has charged that the 1969 bill providing for the consolidation of Atlanta and Fulton County was designed not as "an effort of extending the tax base of the City but from an effort of curtailing and limiting the Negro voting strength."[13] Mr. Johnson pointed out that nearly 50 percent of Atlanta's population is black and that a black vice-mayor, five black aldermen, and two black school board members were elected in the fall of 1969. Nevertheless, a black has never been elected to a county office.

Motivations for consolidation are many and varied. Although the growing political power of blacks in central cities may predispose a number of whites to favor consolidation, it must not be overlooked that the deep and growing fiscal crisis of many central cities is a major reason why certain groups favor consolidation. If conditions in the central city, which increasingly is becoming black, are to be improved, new financial resources must be found. A metropolitan government would be in a position to mobilize considerably larger resources than a central city to solve the most pressing problems in the area.

The Nashville consolidation was endorsed by a number of prominent blacks, even though black voting strength would be decreased from approximately 40 percent in the city to 25 percent countywide. According to 1960 census data, 37.9 percent of Nashville's population was black and 19.2 percent of the county's population was black. Currently, approximately 19.3 percent of the population of the consolidated government is black.

Professor Brett W. Hawkins analyzed the 1962 Nashville referendum and pointed out that "both whites and nonwhites in the old city voted against Metro, and by very similar percentages."[14] He concluded that the racial factor was relatively unimportant and that blacks and whites may have voted in the same manner for different reasons.

Prior to consolidation there were two blacks serving on the 31-member Nashville City Council and none on the 55-member county court or in any other local office. Currently, five members of the metropolitan council are black; 35 of the 40 members are elected by districts. All other elective offices are held by whites. There is a black attorney in the Metropolitan Department of Law, a second black attorney in the Office of Public Defender, and one black has been appointed a judge of the Court of General Sessions.

Jacksonville had a population which was 42 percent black in 1967, yet black areas voted in favor of the consolidation which was endorsed by civil rights groups and resulted in black population dropping to approximately 23 percent of the total population. Fourteen members of the 19-member Jacksonville City Council are elected by districts, and blacks felt that this system would guarantee them increased representation. L. A. Hester, former executive director of the Local Government Study Commission of Duval County, has testified that the most popular aspect of the proposed consolidation was district elections.[15] The proposed electoral system was designed to guarantee blacks three seats immediately, with prospects of two or more additional seats in the future. Whites favored district elections because they felt that blacks had been exercising the balance of power in the at-large city elections. There is some evidence that suburban whites favored consolidation to prevent the blacks from capturing control of the core city.

Two blacks were elected to the nine-member city council shortly before the referendum creating the consolidated government was held; the first time a black had been elected to local office. Currently, there are four blacks on the 19-member council, three elected by districts and one at-large. Furthermore, a black has been elected to the school board and another black has been elected to the Civil Service Board. A black has been appointed head of the Motor Pool Division, a second black has been appointed a legislative aide to the mayor, and several blacks have been appointed to the Community Relations Commission and other advisory boards.

The black population in Dade County in 1957 was approximately 15 percent, but no black had ever been elected to the Board of County Commissioners or any other elective county office. The nine-member county board presently has one black member, and the black population has increased to 18 percent of the total population. Blacks have been appointed to a number of top offices, including the director and assistant director of the Housing and Urban Development Department, director and assistant director of the Welfare Department, director and assistant director of the Community Relations Board, executive director of the Fair Housing and Employment Commission, head of the Waste Division of the Public Works Department, and head of the Children's Home in the Youth Services Department.

Other Factors

The fact there is less industry in southern metropolitan areas compared to northern areas is of some significance, as it may indicate a lesser role played by manufacturing interest groups in the areas' politics. Table I clearly indicates that white-collar employment is of much greater importance than manufacturing. Although no hard evidence has been produced, it is possible that northern industrial firms which have found a haven in suburbia from central-city woes may be opposed to consolidation or the creation of a federation if it appears that their taxes will be increased substantially to help solve central-city problems. Conversely, central-city industry may favor creation of a metropolitan government because of the tax relief it would afford.

Finally, Nashville annexed 49.46 square miles of territory and 82,000 citizens subsequent to the defeat of the proposed consolidation charter in 1958, and the threat of further annexations helped to persuade outlying areas to vote in favor of consolidation. Voter rejection of two proposed Virginia mergers–Winchester and Frederick County in December

TABLE 1 Percent Employed in Manufacturing and White-Collar Occupations, Selected Metropolitan Areas, 1960

Area	*Mfg.*	*White Collar*	*Area*	*Mfg.*	*White Collar*
East Baton Rouge Parish, La.	24.4	41.0	Fulton County, Ga.	19.3	44.3
Davidson County, Tenn.	23.1	45.9	Cook County, Ill.	34.1	45.3
Dade County, Fla.	11.6	46.3	Erie County, N.Y.	36.9	43.3
Duval County, Fla.	13.2	45.4	Genesee County, Mich.	50.7	33.4
Mecklenburg County, N.C.	22.8	45.7	Lehigh County, Penn.	45.1	38.9
Hamilton County, Tenn.	31.1	40.0	Mahoning County, O.	41.9	37.4
Charleston County, S.C.	23.2	39.0	Monroe County, N.Y.	42.8	45.8
Charlottesville, Va.	15.1	49.1	Summit County, O.	44.7	42.1

Source: United States Bureau of the Census, *U.S. Census Population: 1960,* Vol. I, "Characteristics of the Population," Tables 33 and 36 (Washington, D.C.: U.S. Government Printing Office, 1963).

1969 and Charlottesville and Albemarle County in March 1970–have led to the initiation of annexation proceedings. The threat of continued annexation in time may make county voters more receptive to a merger.

THE SEMICONSOLIDATIONISTS

The semiconsolidationists advocate a two-tier system of local government in metropolitan areas, the upper tier to handle areawide functions and the lower tier of municipalities to handle local functions. The metropolitan county, federation, and metropolitan special district are the three varieties of two-tier systems which have been employed. Each may be viewed as a type of semiconsolidation in that certain functions are consolidated at the upper-tier level. A new unit of local government, the upper tier, is formed by a decision to create a federation or a special district, whereas an existing unit is utilized in the case of the metropolitan county. Under federation, of course, a number of lower-tier governments could be consolidated as they were in the Toronto area in 1966.

A metropolitan county may be developed either by the incremental approach or the revolutionary approach. Los Angeles County, which developed as a major provider of urban services since the turn of the century, represents the first, and Dade County, Florida, which adopted a home rule charter in 1957, represents the second. It must be pointed out that Metropolitan Dade County simultaneously is a two-tier and a single-tier system. There is a two-tier system in the 27 areas of the county where there are municipalities, but there is only one local government in unincorporated areas–the county.

Opponents of metropolitan Dade County challenged its constitutionality and entered a total of 155 suits affecting aspects of the new government during its first three years; the courts ruled in favor of the county. Attempts were made to emasculate the government by charter amendment in 1958 and 1961, but each was defeated. However, two amendments weakening the power of the county manager were approved in 1962; his administrative orders creating or combining departments and his appointments of department heads were made subject to the approval of the county commissioners.

In 1963 voters approved amendments providing for the at-large election of one commissioner from each of eight districts. More recently, voters in November 1968 defeated a proposed amendment consolidating all police and fire-fighting functions on the county level.

In spite of the fact the Dade County League of Municipalities has led a strong fight against metro, city-county cooperation has been common and the county provides services to a number of cities on a contract basis.

In addition, cities gradually have turned functions over to the county under the charter provision authorizing a city council, by a two-thirds vote, to turn over functions. To cite two recent examples, Florida City and North Miami turned their fire departments over to the county in 1968 and 1969 respectively.

Pressure for the creation of a regional government for the San Francisco area has been growing for a number of years. In March 1969 the legislature's Joint Committee on Bay Area Regional Organization (BARO) introduced a bill creating a 36-member board to be in charge of a nine-county regional government which, in terms of functions, would be limited to reviewing applications for state and federal grants, signing joint agreements with local governments, and preparing and adopting a regional general plan.

The Association of Bay Area Governments (ABAG) has recommended since 1966 that it be converted into a regional government, and a bill was introduced in the 1969 legislature creating a 14-member Bay Area Transportation Authority to prepare a plan for highways and mass transportation facilities. However, no action was taken by the legislature prior to its adjournment.

THE STATISTS

The creation of state authorities has been a third major organizational response to metropolitan exigencies. Massachusetts in the late 19th century created three state agencies, a metropolitan water district, a metropolitan sewer district, and metropolitan parks district in the Boston area; they later were merged to form the Metropolitan District Commission. In more recent years, other state authorities were created in eastern Massachusetts.

New York State, under Governor Nelson A. Rockefeller, decided in the 1960s to use its plenary authority to directly solve areawide problems and adopted the authority approach. Both statewide and regional authorities have been created for special purposes: Urban Development Corporation (UDC), Environmental Facilities Corporation, Job Development Authority, Metropolitan Transportation Authority, Niagara Frontier Transportation Authority, Capital District Transportation Authority, Central New York Regional Transportation Authority, and Rochester-Genesee Transportation Authority. UDC, for example, may override local codes and laws by a two-thirds vote of its nine-member board of directors.

The rationale for the creation of state authorities is a simple one: only the state has the authority and resources to solve critical metropolitan problems. Other reasons for the use of authorities in New York State include a desire to avoid the constitutional debt limit and civil service, and to remove items from the state budget and annual appropriation processes.

A different state approach has been adopted by Minnesota whose legislature created in 1967 a 15-member Metropolitan Council for the seven-county Twin Cities area. Fourteen members are selected from equal population districts by the governor who also appoints the chairman at-large.

The Council assumed the functions of the abolished Metropolitan Planning Commission, and was granted authority to review and suspend plans of special districts in conflict with the Council's development guidelines. The Council initially also was authorized to appoint a nonvoting member to the board of each special district, conduct research, operate a data center, and intervene before the Minnesota Municipal Commission in annexation and incorporation proceedings. Contracts subsequently signed with the Metropolitan Transit Commission and the Minnesota Highway Department provide that the Council is responsible for metropolitan transportation planning. And the Governor's Crime Commission designated the Council as the criminal justice planning agency.

THE ECUMENICISTS

Coming into prominence during the 1960s primarily as the result of conditional federal grants-in-aid, the ecumenicists hold that metropolitan exigencies can be solved by inter-local cooperation within the existing governmental framework. In particular, ecumenicists maintain that conjoint action will be stimulated by the development of areawide plans identifying problems and mechanisms for their solution.

Comprehensive metropolitan planning is a form of intergovernmental cooperation which may be traced in origin to the Regional Plan for New York and Its Environs completed in 1929 under the sponsorship of the Russell Sage Foundation. By 1961 it was generally concluded that areawide planning had been ineffective because of a schism between the planners and the decision makers. In that year, the Advisory Commission on Intergovernmental Relations suggested that planning should be the responsibility of an organization composed of local elected officials and private citizens, and indicated its opposition to the creation of commissions "comprised solely of part-time commissioners, and dominated by professional planning staff."[16]

The sharp increase in the number of metropolitan planning agencies since 1963 resulted from a conclusion reached by the federal government that areawide planning is the most feasible method of guaranteeing coordinated development of metropolitan areas. A decision was made by Congress in 1965 to involve local elected officials in the planning process, and was implemented by the Housing and Urban Development Act of 1965, which made organizations of local elected officials–councils of governments (COG's)–eligible for the receipt of grants for the preparation of comprehensive metropolitan plans.[17] The following year Congress provided an additional stimulus for the formation of commissions by enacting a requirement that all local government applications for federal grants and loans for 30 specified projects must be submitted for review to an organization responsible for areawide planning "which is, to the greatest practicable extent, composed of or responsible to the elected officials of a unit of areawide government or of the units of general local government."[18] This requirement promoted the formation of a COG or planning commission in each of the 233 standard metropolitan statistical areas.

Until 1965 most commissions were composed of nonelected officials and COG's generally were composed only of elected officials.[19] The 18 COG's active in the spring of 1966 were strictly voluntary associations of governments seeking to identify problems and develop a consensus for coordinated remedial action.[20] The 1966 act led a number of planning commissions to convert themselves into COG's while retaining their original names and others to change their membership and names. Furthermore, several COG's assumed responsibility for planning. As a consequence, it no longer is possible to make a clear distinction between the two types of organizations.

Several early appraisals of the COG movement were relatively optimistic regarding its future potential.[21]

During the past three years, however, there has been a growing consensus that the potential of COG's, a form of voluntarism, is limited in view of the increasing magnitude of metropolitan exigencies.[22] Any organization built upon cooperation between local governments with widely differing socioeconomic makeups and aspirations is predestined to experience serious difficulty in attempting to develop a program, based upon conjoint action, to solve major problems. The fact that a COG member from a given community ratifies a proposed plan of action does not necessarily mean that his community will take steps to initiate the plan. COG's have developed and helped to implement programs to solve minor problems, but no COG has successfully implemented a program to solve a highly controversial problem such as housing in the metropolis.

Furthermore, COG officials are beginning to question whether regional organizations are becoming "arms of the federal government."[23] Board Chairman Joseph L. Fisher of the Metropolitan Washington COG maintains that most federal grants-in-aid received by his COG are dedicated to specific purposes and "virtually all of the one-quarter of our total funds that come from the contributions of local jurisdictions is used in matching and otherwise accommodating the specific activities that federal and state agencies would like us to undertake."[24]

CONCLUSIONS

The continued existence of a fractionated local government system is attributable to political inertia, strong opposition to reorganization, and the failure of the federal and state governments to promote a rationalization of the government of metropolitan areas. The constitution and statutes in most states inhibit or prevent a reorganization of the local government system, and federal and state grants-in-aid have strengthened the ability of smaller units of government to survive. Should the ecumenical approach succeed in solving major areawide problems, the pressure for a major overhaul of the governmental system will be reduced.

Barring a dramatic reversal of federal policy, it is unlikely that the 1970s will be a decade of metropolitan reform. The current interest in consolidation in the South may prove to be transitory, and it is unlikely that interest in consolidation will become widespread elsewhere without federal or state encouragement.

If either the federal or state government decides to promote a rationalization of the local government system, it is probable that the prescription will call for the use of revenue sharing and grants-in-aid to encourage the creation of a two-tier system, as it is less disruptive to the existing system, allows for uniformity in certain functional areas and diversity in other areas, and would not be as susceptible as consolidation to promoting alienation between citizens and their governments. If a federation is not formed, a number of urban states probably will follow New York State's lead and create authorities to solve problems transcending local political boundaries.

The formation of a megalopolis as metropolitan areas grow and amalgamate with each other has effectively limited the use of the ecumenical, single- and two-tier approaches to smaller areas. The only governments able to cope with the major problems of an interstate megalopolis are the state and federal governments, and this means that greater reliance will be placed upon direct federal and state action, interstate compacts, and federal-state compacts.

[1]*Metropolitan Surveys: A Digest* (Chicago: Public Administration Service, 1958), p. vii.

[2]Daniel R. Grant, "General Metropolitan Surveys: A Summary," in *Metropolitan Surveys: A Digest, op. cit.,* p. 3.

[3]See *Metropolitan Surveys* (Albany: Graduate School of Public Affairs, State University of New York, published annually).

[4]John C. Bollens and Henry J. Schmandt, *The Metropolis* (New York: Harper and Row, Publishers, 1965), p. 438.

[5]*Modernizing Local Government* (New York: Committee for Economic Development, July 1966).

[6]*Reshaping Government in Metropolitan Areas* (New York: Committee for Economic Development, February 1970), p. 19.

[7]*Indiana Acts of 1969,* chapter 173.

[8]"Virginia Capital Wins Big Annexation," *National Civic Review* (October 1969), p. 436.

[9]Irving G. McNayr, "The Promise of Metropolitan Government," paper delivered at a Boston College Conference, May 26, 1964 (mimeographed), p. 2.

[10]*Single Government* (Charlotte, N.C.: Charlotte Chamber of Commerce, 1968), p. 12.

[11]Edward C. Banfield, "The Politics of Metropolitan Area Organization," *Midwest Journal of Political Science* (May 1957), p. 86.

[12]Edward Sofen, *The Miami Metropolitan Experiment* (Bloomington: Indiana University Press, 1963), pp. 74, 86, and 212.

[13]"Abolish Atlanta Gains in Georgia," *The New York Times,* November 9, 1969, p. 65.

[14]Brett W. Hawkins, *Nashville Metro* (Nashville: Vanderbilt University Press, 1966), p. 133.

[15]"Statement by L. A. Hester," *Hearings Before the National Commission on Urban Problems,* Vol. 3 (Washington, D.C.: U.S. Government Printing Office, February 1968), p. 272.

[16]*Governmental Structure, Organization, and Planning in Metropolitan Areas* (Washington, D.C.: Advisory Commission on Intergovernmental Relations, 1961), p. 34.

[17]Housing and Urban Development Act of 1965, 75 STAT. 502, 20 U.S.C. 461 (g) (1965).

[18]Demonstration Cities and Metropolitan Development Act of 1966, 80 STAT. 1255, 42 U.S.C. 3301-14 (1966).

[19]Royce Hanson, *Metropolitan Councils of Governments* (Washington, D.C.: Advisory Commission on Intergovernmental Relations, August 1966).

[20]Joseph F. Zimmerman, ed., *1966 Metropolitan Area Annual* (Albany: Graduate School of Public Affairs, State University of New York, 1966), pp. 5–6.

[21]*ABAG Appraised* (Berkeley, Calif.: Institute for Local Self Government, December 1965), p. 19; "The Association of Bay Area Government–A Gathering Force," *Bulletin* (San Francisco Bureau of Governmental Research, April 1, 1965), pp. 1–2; and Samuel Humes, "Organization for Metropolitan Cooperation," *Public Management* (May 1962), p. 107.

[22]Joseph F. Zimmerman, "Metropolitan Ecumenism: The Road to the Promised Land?" *Journal of Urban Law* (Spring 1967), pp. 433–57.

[23]"Chairman Urges Assessment of COG's Future Status," *National Civic Review* (March 1970), p. 158.

[24]*Ibid.*

13 The Federal Role in Urban Decentralization

Suzanne Farkas

From: "The Federal Role in Urban Decentralization" by Suzanne Farkas is reprinted from *American Behavioral Scientist,* Volume 15, Number 1 (September/October 1971) pp. 15–35, by permission of the publisher, Sage Publications, Inc.

Professor Suzanne Farkas formerly taught at New York University and Queens College of the City University of New York. The editors of this volume were saddened to learn of her untimely death last year at the age of 32.

The term urban decentralization has become a political symbol, connoting multiple meanings with vague rhetoric. It is an attractive ideal because it symbolizes attempts to find formulas for social justice, democratization, and liberal, redistributive politics, and because it exhibits a kind of sociointellectual empathy with the disadvantaged. As used here, urban decentralization refers to proposals for greater citizen participation in large urban governments by restructuring them into smaller, multipurpose units to which considerable "community control" or political authority over policy and administration would be devolved. Variations of this concept have been proposed by the Committee for Economic Development, the Association of the Bar of the City of New York, Americans for Democratic Action, Mayor John V. Lindsay, the President's Commission on Urban Problems, and many scholars, civic leaders, public interest organizations, and government officials.

The purpose of this article is to show that while most often urban decentralization has been approached as a matter of reforming or restructuring local government, it is a concept and an empirical possibility more appropriate for analysis as a complex issue in intergovernmental relations. In fact, the addition of community governmental subunits would probably considerably alter the existing intergovernmental system.

Federal urban policy, as it has operated in many large cities, has contributed either directly or indirectly to many of the problems which urban decentralization is intended to address. At the local level, therefore, the movement is largely aimed at compensating for the substantive and structural by-products of past federal urban programs. Moreover, the existing intergovernmental pattern of federal city-aid programs would probably restrict the range and nature of policy choices and program control by decentralized units, although a substantial and accommodating change in this pattern might be possible. In addition, it seems likely that political decentralization of urban government would result in further centralization of political control by the federal government. However, in the absence of this kind of strong policy control by a higher authority with a broad constituency, multipurpose urban decentralization is less likely to change the balance of political influence in cities. In fact, it might have a conservative effect on urban public policy by reinforcing the power biases of a federal structure of government. Some of the complexities underlying the concept of devolving political authority in the urban context can best be seen by analyzing the intricate relationships between urban decentralization and the theory and practice of federalism.

While, on one hand, a strong role for the federal government offers the greatest possibility for urban decentralization to be redistributive as to resources and political influence, on the other hand, even the New Frontier and Great Society programs have not been as redistributive as is generally believed. Nevertheless, it seems probable that if a strong relationship between the federal government and the large cities had not developed, the distribution of resources and nature of policies by local governments acting alone might have been even less attuned to the needs of the disadvantaged. Since this author is generally disposed to favor some form of urban decentralization for New York City, this article examines some of the constraints and possibilities for decentralization that attends the federal role with the hope that some liabilities might be avoided.

This discussion is limited specifically to the federal role in urban decentralization. It is therefore necessary to indicate at the outset that several important points have been deliberately omitted, and that in some cases the impact of federal programs has been overemphasized for clarity of argument. Only those aspects of federal programs which bear on urban decentralization will be discussed, although these programs have had many other dimensions. Also, most of the urban conditions cited as examples or as problems addressed by the decentralization movement had multiple causes and result from failures in city and state policies as well as from federal urban policy. The federal government's contribution to urban structural fragmentation or racial segregation, for example, was a reinforcing of existing local trends or community norms; movement to suburbia, in addition to being encouraged by Federal Housing Administration mortgages, was also stimulated by the "development of a transportation capacity and by an image of suburbia as a place preferable to the central city."[1] However, throughout the article, only the federal government variable will be mentioned.

SUBSTANTIVE BY-PRODUCTS OF EARLY FEDERAL URBAN PROGRAMS

Although the direct federal urban-aid programs which began in the 1930s have had many beneficial effects, they have also played a role in reinforcing several of the structural and substantive aspects of what is currently referred to as the "urban crisis." In fact, federal urban programs have generated enough unanticipated substantive consequences that their reverberations can be held to constitute a failure of federal urban policy. Perhaps nowhere are the ramifications of these policies more clearly seen than in the results of early federal housing and urban renewal programs, although these programs were the "backbone" of federal urban policy. To a large extent, they did not produce the promised advantages for their stated beneficiaries (including the large cities themselves) and worked against the interests of those without power.

Federal Housing Administration and Veterans Administration mortgages were used by middle-class whites to move to the suburbs, thereby depriving the central city of a major source of revenue-producing residents; rings of "beltways" and highways built under the federal highway program later facilitated the exodus from the central cities of many job-producing and revenue-generating businesses. Although federal programs may have been reciprocal with local tendencies, the probabilities are that no more than a fraction of this dispersal from the central city would have taken place without the combination of these three federal programs[2] (Sayre, 1971). More important, the FHA and V.A. mortgage programs and the earlier highway programs represented *choices* by the federal government. The result of these choices was to spend considerable resources outside the central cities for the benefits of the suburban, automobile-oriented middle class instead of spending those resources inside the central cities for the benefit of the urban poor and for those dependent on mass transit.

In requiring racial homogeneity of neighborhoods where mortgages were insured, the FHA program also reconfirmed patterns of a racial segregation. Early federal public housing and low-rent housing programs frequently complicated the urban housing problem still further. In some cases, eligibility requirements, racial equity formulas, and various other regulatory, discretionary, or statutory factors combined to exclude the blacks, the very poor, and large families.[3] Thus, in many cases, the programs benefited primarily tenants who were white, employed (therefore financially dependable), and those who could afford twenty percent of their income for rent.[4] "Some housing authorities limited the number of public assistance recipients they would accept, and others would not admit any."[5]

In other places, the same housing programs served to concentrate the very poor and the blacks into "public housing slums," creating pockets of discontent and disrupting middle-class black neighborhoods.[6] Moreover, although there is considerable debate on this point, many scholars have found that at least in their earlier stages, both the housing and the urban renewal programs indirectly accelerated a shortage of urban housing, especially through the requirement that the number of substandard dwellings demolished must be equal in number to those constructed. Also, there is some indication that those whose homes were bulldozed to make way for commercial establishments ended up in housing of even poorer quality.[7]

Finally, by defining "slums" mainly as physical conditions of aged housing, mixed land uses, and high densities, the urban renewal program destroyed many stable urban ethnic communities whose social structures had prevented several of the forms of social pathology that are increasing in large cities.[8] Once the housing and urban renewal programs became expediting vehicles for concentrating the powerless and the needy into central cities, and once the liberal mayors made these groups part of their electoral base, the mayors were no longer free to endorse programs which would disperse them, and "gilding the ghetto" became a "legitimized" political necessity.

Thus early federal urban programs had spillover effects of reinforcing racial discrimination, ghettoization, depletion of urban taxation resources, immuring the slums, and exclusion of those who most needed help. However, at the same time, they geographically concentrated those who suffered most, but who had the least access to the governmental process. In time, geographic concentration then provided a political base from which to demand power and participation. One might argue that the area of housing and urban renewal may not be typical, and that programs in education and health, for example, have had a somewhat different tradition. Nevertheless, the housing-related programs were the main thrust of federal urban programs for many years, and federal policy in this area can be criticized for accepting as appropriate those forces which might have been counteracted.[9] It is not surprising that within large cities, initial impetus for urban decentralization came in demands for community control from ghettos of the nonwhite poor, whose living conditions to some extent reflect past federal housing and urban renewal policy.

STRUCTURAL BY-PRODUCTS: INSTITUTIONAL INCAPACITIES

Many other problems to which the urban decentralization movement is addressed result either directly or indirectly from failures in federal policies toward the cities. The history of direct federal-city relations shows a consistent effort by the large cities to strengthen themselves as general-purpose units of urban government through a federal-urban alliance, a need which stemmed from their untenable financial situations, their underrepresentation in state legislatures, and from the inabilities of state governments to deal with large-scale urban problems. Instead, however, federal-city categoric grants built programs which enhanced the strength of vertical, functional bureaucracy at the *expense* of local government institution-building.

The same housing and urban renewal programs which had abetted the ghettoization of the poor were perhaps leading examples of the building of functional bureaucracies which were not accountable to public constituencies. Although these programs did have specific purposes, they were highly discretionary as to implementation. Broad decisions which determined what groups would benefit from public programs were delegated to interested parties, usually both the federal and local administering agencies and their clientele groups. This kind of federally legislated liberalism was found in most federal urban programs. It drained urban elective leadership of accountability because policy responsibility remained the province of organized support groups and administrators. An example may be seen in the relations between Local Housing Authorities, mandated by federal law to be "independent" of urban elected officials, and the National Association of Housing and Redevelopment officials, the professional interest group of those who administered these housing agencies.[10]

This type of closed circuit interaction excluded incoming groups that tried to make demands for services; they could not break into the established decision-making pattern. Thus the federally induced functional bureaucracies, essentially "given" to their first set of beneficiaries, diffused the public power of urban government and crippled it in responding to the needs of new constituencies. Against this background, urban decentralization can be analyzed as the answer given by a new black constituency that was not accommodated by the established federal urban pattern. In one sense, it can be seen as an attempt to consolidate political power at the local level to compensate for the fragmentary effect of federal programs which weakened the capacity of urban governments to respond to the needs of new clienteles.

The internal fragmentation and weakening of urban government by the creation of vertical access and alliance channels for line bureaucracies (some of which would have been otherwise subject to its control, and some of which might have otherwise not existed) was further exacerbated by the tendency of the federal government to give grants to special districts or independent commissions. One of the more significant consequences of this trend was that valuable sources of political currency for bargaining in city decision-making and for inducing policy trade-offs became less accessible to elected urban officials. Of course, there is little empirical evidence to suggest for what purposes and to whose benefit the mayors might have used their trade-off powers. Nor can it be assumed that strong general urban governments would have been somehow "better" without federal constraints, or that special districts and independent authorities might not have been just as common in response to local debt limits, and so on. The point is that the interbureaucratic "constant" undermined the role of elected legislatures and executives so that their responsiveness or lack of responsiveness to their constituencies made less difference.

The effects of federal programs on internal city sources of political currency has been especially apparent with federal funding for "hardware services" such as transportation, bridges, or airports, and for housing programs in the creation of L.H.A.'s and L.P.A.'s. First, jurisdiction over these typically becomes lodged in a commission which, although not completely autonomous, usually has considerable independence from control by individual local governments. This has lessened the authority of general local governments over the location and operation of facilities. Since decisions on subway stops, transit routes, and bridge connections have such great ramifications for land values and community development, they are sources of powerful political leverage which were made less available to urban chief executives. For example, an effect of refocusing transportation-related decisions for New York City in an independent commission was that the mayor is deprived of the capacity for inducing outer areas of the city to accommodate publicly assisted housing by promising a subway extension for that area in return. Second, some analysts believe that when the federal government went into the business of such high capitalization services as bridge-building or water and sewer facilities, it removed a strong incentive for contiguous small cities in metropolitan areas to consolidate in order to share the large cost burden.[11]

Fragmentation of urban government is not in itself an evil. In fact, the existence of plural power centers may under some conditions open a system to more alternatives and to more interests. But fragmentation can also mean such dispersal of political power that urban government cannot act (i.e., respond to demands and support), and citizens are less able to locate responsibility for services. In the case of large cities, the functionalism and internal fragmentation that were by-products of federal urban programs have interfered with "the ability to bring even a minimum level of coordination among . . . independent programs."[12] Finally, dispersal of urban public authority places limits on the ability of urban governments to decentralize, because power and authority that is not first centralized in city government cannot be devolved by it.

The need for national uniformity of administrative regulations and for local agency feedback under federal programs meant the introduction of much "rationalization" or "certainty" into the range of local bureaucratic reactions.[13] To the extent this was true, federal urban programs have indirectly discouraged flexibility and innovation in urban bureaucracies by promoting efficiency and similarity instead. In that the capacity of urban agencies for flexibility and innovation is crucial for responsiveness to differing local needs and for ability to accommodate citizen participation, this, too, has restrained the potential institutional outreach of general-purpose urban government. In fact, the federal government's attempt to solve urban problems directly has in itself not been conducive to building strong local decision-making machinery. The urban decentralization movement has reacted to this by stressing the idea that "activity should be to help community agencies, not by providing the traditional social services to them but by helping them in an educational way to develop the capacity to make decisions."[14]

Finally, in contributing to the weakening of urban parties, federal urban programs accelerated the disintegration of the base for organizing geographically concentrated political influence, and of the coordinating networks which had mitigated some aspects of urban fragmentation. The party machines had helped make a place for the newcomer and the disadvantaged in urban political life and to build a focus of loyalty toward local institutions by enhancing the neighborhood as a meaningful social, economic, and political base. In the past, the patronage system, the party's role in performing social welfare services, and party maintenance of close ties between national and local organizations were important elements in gaining access to bureaucracy, absorbing and integrating minority groups, and maintaining accountable elected leadership.

However, when these elements weakened, it was the federal bureaucracy as opposed to the local that absorbed more upward-bound minorities, and the federal government's grant programs which pushed aside the parties' "community welfare" services, while in the process creating "islands of functional bureaucratic power."[15] Parties and bureaucracies represent two different kinds of decision-making–geographically oriented and functionally oriented–and represent very different interests. Federal urban programs enhanced the latter type of representation, which does not afford the maximum advantage to newly concentrated urban minority groups.

The concept of urban decentralization is in many ways analogous to the concept of the old urban political machine, and the movement toward community control can be viewed, for analytic purposes, as an attempt to replace its latent functions while adjusting to the changed role of the federal government. Moreover, from the perspectives of urban whites as well as of urban blacks, advocacy of decentralization may be interpreted as a search for legitimate authority rather than as a rejection of governmental leadership. In organizing representation and political power geographically rather than functionally, it might increase the political influence of the concentrated black minority. It might also encourage visible political leadership with a community mandate for action, and by bringing service agencies into neighborhoods, strengthen government accountability and administrative control. Community control of jobs would replace the parties as sources of upward mobility. Viewed from this perspective, urban decentralization seeks to further legitimize public authority and represents a demand for consolidation rather than for diffusion of political power.

THE FEDERAL VARIABLE IN URBAN POLITICS

Despite the undesirable side effect that early federal urban-aid programs did not seem to build general urban political viability, they were advanced by urban lobby groups made up of the large cities themselves in order to maintain urban financial viability.

Although ideally cities would have preferred a financial subsidy, the federal government gives out only "programs"–"formula"-type programs where federal control over the actual beneficiaries is somewhat looser and the percentage of federal payments relatively larger, and a large number of "pilot"–type programs, where federal controls are more stringent, federal design more precise, and the percentage of federal payment smaller with respect to requirements for local matching funds.[16] In general, however, the funds for federal city-aid programs are earmarked, controlled, reinforcing of autonomous bureaucracies, contingent on yearly appropriations, and unstable. But the chosen strategy of the cities was to try to compensate for "money with strings" by lobbying to influence the *substance* of the federal programs.

The numbers of these programs proliferated rapidly. Between 1962 and 1966 alone, the number of categoric federal programs operating in urban areas increased from 160 to 349.[17] The impact and implications of these programs have made the influence of the federal government a significant variable in urban politics and power structures. Federal legislation, standards, and administrative guidelines constrain the free interplay of local political forces, and unstable levels of program funding introduce a permanent uncertainty of agenda.[18]

But most important, since "politics" may be defined as the competition over decisions affecting allocation and uses of social and financial resources, the input of earmarked federal funds has a particular implication: the amount of federal funds in a city's budget represents an "amount" of decisions made in the federal arena—outside that city and not subject to effective control by its own political processes.

Federal funds, for example, make up about one-fourth of the expense budget of New York City. Clearly, urban politics can no longer be understood without consideration of the federal role, and analysis should focus on the extent and nature of its impact rather than on whether it is a significant variable. In fact, urban government in many respects *is* intergovernmental relations (as is state and federal government as well). Responsiveness of urban government to its citizens is affected by priorities that are set elsewhere, and the attentiveness of urban leadership to its immediate constituency is distracted by the need to win over a federal audience.

Federal grant programs act as constraining factors on urban government in a variety of subtle ways, as, for example, by the very multiplicity of conditions attached, or by the availability of one kind of program over another that may not meet local needs. Perhaps more constraining, however, is the usual requirement that the local unit supply some percentage of the program costs. To the extent that this means that participation makes the city budget even less flexible because funds are less available for intracity use, and to the extent that decentralization would require a greater amount of flexible city revenue, one can readily see the implications of this for financing urban decentralization. However, "the evidence is not clear as to the impact that aid has on the local jurisdiction's employment of its own funds. In suburban jurisdictions, it is clear that aid is generally stimulative of the amount of local funds raised, and, therefore, may in fact increase the total amount of resources available for allocation by local governments' jurisdictions. In other words, aid is not replacive of local effort. To the degree it is not replacive, it becomes simply additive to what would otherwise be available."[19] Nevertheless, when federal eligibility standards require the establishment (or abolition) of a particular kind of unit or official, the effects of federal programs on urban government become even more apparent. In fact, they "frequently support inadequate . . . structures by providing financial assistance to . . . ineffective and uneconomic units."[20]

By the 1960s, the adverse effects of federal programs on the capacities of general-purpose local government units became apparent to officials and observers. Urban government was believed to be more fragmented, more difficult to administer, and less accountable since the growth of its involvement with federal urban programs. The deprivation and alienation of the masses of urban poor became necessary inputs to public policy at all levels of government. Partly in response to these problems, the federal role in urban politics took on a somewhat unexpected dimension. The concept of devolving authority to subunits within the cities and creating mechanisms for more citizen participation in program-planning gained favor among the federal agencies concerned with the cities.

There followed a surge of interest in decentralization and participation in federal programs. The Community Mental Health Act of 1963, Title II of the Elementary and Secondary Education Act, the Poverty Program, and Model Cities all gave an impetus to the decentralization movement, and "citizen participation" guidelines were added to some of the older programs such as urban renewal. Paradoxically, the professionals in the federal government encouraged lay involvement at the local level (it was primarily the newly recruited, sometimes temporary federal officials who served as catalysts for this encouragement). But the steps were taken without considering what degree of decentralization was really possible within the basic framework of federal-city relations, and without a clear awareness at the start of how far one was willing to go.

The new efforts were grafted onto the existing system, but without abandoning the old fiscal dependency, the practices of guidelines, controls, and audits, or the continuation of the regular categoric grant system. The curious result was a further centralization at the federal level carried out in the name of decentralization at the local level. A great deal of confusion has thus been created. What is the likelihood of any genuine means of political decentralization occurring within the present complex and tangled pattern of federal-city relations?

URBAN SUBUNITS AND FEDERAL CONSTRAINTS

Federal urban programs in their present forms seem to restrict the realistic possibilities for urban political decentralization. Given the power of federal money and inevitable federal controls, they could circumscribe the community control, or extent of self-government, within decentralized units. Any plan for urban decentralization or governmental restructuring would have to consider the effects of the proposed plan on eligibility for, optimum use of, and distribution of benefits from federal urban programs. In this sense, the federal role in urban decentralization is, at minimum, to create a checklist of requirements imposed by the federal government to be compared with intended local items. When a federal program on which a city depends requires specified administration (by a designated unit or official; over a certain area; for a given population; including or excluding citizen participation), the possible forms decentralization can take are thereby predetermined by the "federal role." In other words, proposals for internal restructuring of urban governments would have to be tailored so as to provide that either the "decentralized" unit or the city would retain eligibility for federal programs.

Possibilities and alternatives for urban decentralization are also affected by the fact that where federal programs have become entrenched, functional bureaucracies through their vertical, intergovernmental relations are as important a focus of resources and decision-making as general units. Therefore an urban decentralization plan must find some way of rearranging and controlling these functional coalitions, or the degree of community control might be restricted considerably.

The degree of independence of a decentralized unit to make its own decisions would most likely be limited by several types of conditions attached to federal programs. Some federal urban programs require comprehensive planning by a citywide agency, some require approval through a regional agency, some must be authorized by a city council, and still others must pass through the state.

Perhaps the best example of the possible difficulties for decentralized units is the Workable Program condition attached to Title I of the National Housing Act (mostly urban renewal). Eligibility to participate in this major source of grant funds requires a coherent, citywide, workable program, including a master plan for major land uses, thoroughfares, and community facilities; plans for improving building and housing codes and for meeting low- and moderate-income housing needs; and arrangements for housing the families displaced by all forms of government activity.

Although these requirements may be highly desirable, one can readily see how they might create difficulties for the idea of "community control of decisions" by a decentralized unit of urban government. Facilities for sewage treatment and narcotics rehabilitation, for example, are usually not wanted within anyone's immediate neighborhood, while schools and parks are desired by each. Who is to decide which goes where? Would a central city government retain authority to locate low- and moderate-income housing? If so, a "decentralized" unit would not have much say in the structure of its neighborhood. In short, the Workable Program requires some way of making distributive, redistributive and regulatory decisions.[21] Another good example of a type of federal program (aside from the necessarily regional ones of mass transit, airports, or planning grants) which would probably constrain the possibilities for policy control by a decentralized unit is the Vocational Rehabilitation Program.[22]

One might imagine an "ideal" arrangement whereby federal grants might go directly to subunits which could negotiate directly on program coordination. However, the federal government's supervision of federal urban programs is not organized in a manner which would make this feasible. Consequently, experiments in which a community group has handled the federal Neighborhood Development Program, for example, encountered difficulty because the *federal* agencies were not set up to deal with neighborhoods. This is not to say that current restrictions with the present intergovernmental aid system are evidence that a new system of urban decentralization could not work; it is meant only to point out that changes in the local arena would have to be accompanied by changes at the federal level.

But there might be other, more abstract, conditions which could pertain. First, the greater the number of subunits, the less potential access they would have to federal agencies, and the slower these agencies might be in processing applications, reviews, and requests.

Second, many subunits might have difficulties meeting the requirements for either cash or noncash matching contributions to the federal programs, or for relocation facilities. And if the enabling "cash" or "noncash" credits were provided for them, the subunits might in effect be controlled by their benefactor. On the other hand, federal aid formulas based on need might be able to compensate for both liabilities. Also, one can assume that decentralized units could be more effective in some functional areas than in others.[23]

Third, all decentralized units would be negotiating with a source of "higher" authority to get a share of federal largesse. Organization theory and coalition strategy suggest some behavioral probabilities and some possible consequences. It is not unlikely that the decentralized units might compete with each other to where the greater power resides (as current units–cities and states–already do). Under these conditions, urban decentralization might permit even greater control by a more centralized government that could effectively play the far larger number of subunits off against each other and enable itself to gain more political currency to use for policy trade-offs.

Some form of coalition strategy among decentralized urban units would seem likely in a system where the competition is for either the same resources or for mutually exlusive policy choices. Generally, this results in "lowest common denominator," or consensus politics among unit allies, and in strong tendencies toward group cohesion and oligarchy (rather than democratization) within units competing for better bargaining positions with other governmental counterparts. In short, if neighborhood politics were a zero-sum game, decentralization would not work; if it were not, decentralization probably could not be radical.

Finally, expectation that urban decentralization would necessarily result in reductions of "red tape," increased capacities for action, or in neighborhood control over public services implies some possible misperceptions about American federalism. The ongoing debate over which unit should control what government function suggests the inaccurate concept that different governmental functions are performed at separate "levels of government." Since in fact almost all functions or services are shared among all levels, a decentralized unit could be at most another "shareholder," but could not "control" a service. Thus it could not avoid intricate relationships with its copartners. It is possible that the more units exercising power over a function, the more potential checks there could be against action and the greater the possibilities of encountering "red tape." This is not to make an argument against decentralization, but it is to suggest that a very careful division of power over functions would be necessary.

In light of the above discussion, it seems likely that federal urban programs in their present form would operate at least as restrictively on any decentralized urban unit as they do on centralized city governments. There is no reason to expect decentralized units with direct federal ties to be any more free from federal guidelines and fiscal control than present centralized city bureaucracies. Some scholars view community control by black neighborhoods within large cities as comparable to "community control" in many white suburbs.[24] One might point out that this comparison loses some force of argument in light of the impact of federal grants. Because of their wealthier tax bases and lower-density populations, the suburbs cited would have more freedom *not* to participate in federal programs than would a decentralized urban subunit which would probably have a greater need to rely on outside funding.

CONFLICTS AND CONTRADICTIONS IN FEDERAL URBAN POLICIES

The net results of earlier trends of federal programs in the cities, coupled with federal efforts in the 1960s to involve target area populations in decentralized citizen planning and program implementation, is an enormously complex intergovernmental pattern beset by internal strains, although not necessarily with insurmountable contradictions. On one hand, the categorical grant formula has not been abandoned. On the other hand, there is an effort by many to either replace or to superimpose on this some form of "no strings attached" general revenue-sharing, or program consolidation in the form of "special revenue-sharing." And while the Nixon administration has begun to use federal programs in such a way as to strengthen general units of local government, it is simultaneously attempting to channel increasing numbers of federal grant programs through the states (seen by some as the traditional "enemies" of the cities). Perhaps most important, however, some federal officials believe federal stimulation of urban decentralization may run *counter* to the administration's efforts to strengthen general units of state and local governments, or that urban decentralization would substantially decrease the strength of the city governments which the federal government is attempting to bolster.[25]

Goals for comprehensive planning and maximum efficiency of service delivery coexist in the same federal programs with what appear as the mutually exclusive goals of maximum citizen participation and neighborhood policy control.[26] In fact, federal incentives and policy guidelines encourage opposite trends with great frequency. Decentralization of services to neighborhoods, metropolitan area consolidation, and regional councils of government, for example, were all recommended in a single Presidential Commission on Urban Problems in 1968, the Douglas Commission.[27] These directions are not mutually exclusive; however, the fact that they *could* be reconciled is adequately understood. For example, "it was this misunderstanding which caused the Berkeley people to lose their fight for decentralized police districts. Had they been willing to accept a combined centralized-decentralized system, it probably would have been accepted by the voters."[28] The point is that the federal government has made little attempt to clarify a very confusing picture.

Perhaps most important, however, the federal programs that encouraged decentralization have undergone several transformations. The Poverty Program is particularly noteworthy. At first it required "maximum feasible participation" by the poor to decrease their alienation and powerlessness. Private community groups constituted as Community Action Agencies (CAA's) were directly eligible to receive, administer and set policy for using federal funds, a departure from the usual requirement that only public bodies could be vehicles for the use of public funds. But perhaps most radical, the CAA's could use poverty funds to organize their communities politically to gain better access to bureaucracies. Some organized against their own mayors. In this case, the federal government had used its redistributive capacities to change the balance of political power in cities.

The Model Cities Program was similar. Department of Housing and Urban Development guidelines indicated that, since neighborhood life could be improved only by action of the people themselves, "HUD will . . . outline performance standards for citizen participation which must be achieved by each City Demonstration Agency. . . ." Here, too, the federal government had shown its capacity for legislating a form of political decentralization within urban governments and had provided incentives for new elites to compete with established structures.[29]

However, subsequent federal decisions responding to a variety of pressures changed both programs. Amendments and administrative adjustments carefully circumscribed citizen participation, prohibited political activities, and ensured local governments of de facto control.

It is ironic that the upsurge of interest in citizen participation and local control by both citizens and local government resulted from influence exerted by the federal government. Yet the whole sequence of events—federal initiation of the programs, their variable funding, control over operating guidelines, and even the reversal in direction towards more control by city hall—points out the extent to which political decentralization at the local level has meant political centralization by the federal government. Control by city government had in important respects been replaced by control by the federal government. In fact, among the explicit motives for creation of the original Poverty Program was that community action would be "a mechanism for enabling federal officials to exert leverage on city officials."[30]

Despite the reversal of several federal decentralizing guidelines, both programs have had long-lasting effects for urban decentralization. They gave more impetus to the idea and began a wave of advocacy for greater citizen participation in all federal programs and for a restructuring of decision-making within urban governments. This added to an awakening realization by citizen groups that they could organize and attract enough attention so that urban government would have to respond. And, where citizen participation was already well developed, the federal attempt at containing the trend had little effect, because it had become politically unwise to ignore community groups.

When the possibilities offered by citizen participation groups for forming political alliances were perceived, they were actively encouraged by those for whom coalition strategies could be useful. The federal government had shown the uses of community groups when, at first, it had put itself in place of the city in direct alliance with the groups it had funded locally. Well-organized citizen groups now provided potential allies for their city hall program units in efforts to gain cooperation from other city bureaucracies, for mayors versus administrative agencies, for federal officials in exerting influence in urban politics, and for various other combinations.

INTERGOVERNMENTAL IRONIES AND THE POWER BIAS OF FEDERALISM

Federal experiments in the Model Cities and Poverty Programs suggest that, if there were further decentralization efforts patterned along similar lines, the likely result would be more centralization of control by the federal government. But ironically, if the federal government did not impose controls, it seems possible that urban decentralization might have a conservative effect on urban public policy by reinforcing the power biases of federalism.

The most important question to be asked about a federal role in urban decentralization is "Who will benefit?" The answer may depend on whether the federal government could play a role in financing the poorer units and in enforcing uniform standards for social justice.

Many proposals for decentralization of urban governments conceive of multifunctional subunits which would have a "federal" relationship with the "centralized" city government similar to that between the states and the national government. But there is a relationship between political structure and power bias. Thus, to the extent these proposals are intended to be "liberalizing" and to redistribute political influence, they must find some way to compensate for the fact that federalism as a political system usually has a structural bias toward conservatism, minority rule, and veto politics.[31]

Intracity federalism might well magnify the power biases of the system still further. It would create another and lower multiunit layer of governments sharing power over functions, with each unit having the right to make or to prevent policy. Very small subunit groups might be able to engineer veto majorities within single subunits, although constituting only small numerical majorities with respect to citywide policy preferences. Policy-by-subunit minorities could be at the expense of the "freedom" and "democracy" of dispersed minorities, of citywide policy majorities, and of any dissenting minority within the decentralized unit.[32]

The extent to which any of these projected possibilities might pertain under urban decentralization would, of course, be a function of many variables, the most important being the structure, powers, and numbers of "levels"–or the design–of the decentralized system. The extent of minority representation within subunits, for example, might depend on whether the subunit-governing bodies were elected by districts or at large. Moreover, the premise that the power of veto might be used at lower levels to prevent change while at the higher levels, power would be more likely to be used to advance liberal and redistributive causes may be more soundly based in theory and history than might be true of future political behavior under urban decentralization; in other words, it might be possible that a veto at the local unit level would be used to prevent *reactionary* policies of the higher unit, or that it could be the higher unit that might use its power to "override efforts of social reform by such subunits."[33]

Nevertheless, both the theory and practice of federalism in the United States suggests that the greater the scope of the veto power held by these units, the more one might expect the power biases of federalism to be reflected. In other words, decentralization, albeit conceived as democratization in the form of more freedom for local neighborhoods, could result in reinforcing the power of increasingly smaller numerical minorities at increasingly lower levels of government. *In calculating a possible redistribution of influence, therefore, one must be aware that the size and shape of the subunits planned would automatically "gerrymander" the beneficiaries of decentralization.*

In short, what is described may be termed a *concentric* federalism that keeps reducing the size of the local tyrannies that could prevent increasingly larger-sized majorities from carrying out policy.

In this sense, federalism is veto politics. And since the right of veto acts to prevent change, the unstated bias of federalism is preservation, or conservation. Furthermore, multiplying points of governmental access widens the arena of political conflict. A system of multiple layers of decision-making is likely to give an advantage to those interests which could organize at several levels. It can also institutionalize stalemate by enabling the "undoing" at one level of that which was done at another. In that most proposals for urban decentralization (except the Committee for Economic Development Plan) contemplate adding at least one, and sometimes two, "layers" of government, great care would have to be taken to compensate for the risk of triggering these proclivities.

Intracity federalism with substantial power to neighborhoods may therefore have some liabilities for its own goals. It might diminish political resources for positive policy and reduce the capacities of units to produce change. Moreover, it could freeze the status quo that existed at the time of the initial federalizing bargain, permitting the groups and leaders already strongest in a subunit to entrench themselves. In the New York City Model Cities Program, for instance, it is largely the middle-class oriented, older leadership (rather than "new recruits") that has participated–to increase the power in the community they already had or to inhibit "a new program from threatening an extant program in which the participant has a vested stake." Moreover, the two-year agenda illuminated the triumph of the veto process over the capacity to produce positive change; "the community brought the city to a standstill . . . through the tedious process of exercising negative power sanctions."[34]

PROSPECTS FOR THE FUTURE

A possible caveat for urban decentralization may be its emphasis on structure of government as a source of social change. At most, political structure is only one of the myriad forces influencing urban policy outcomes and their beneficiaries. It can refract rather than reflect the prevailing ratios of influence, but if government structure discourages the convergence of strong existing interests, decision-making will shift to the interstices of institutions and procedures.

In fact, the structure of local governments may have less impact on their policies than do such factors as type and size of constituency, strength of interest articulation mechanisms, vertical bureaucratic relations, and political culture. Recognizing the input of these variables becomes especially important to those for whom the central purpose of urban decentralization is the redistribution of political power.

Changing the balance of power between those with access and resources and those without requires a regularized source for both reallocating financial resources and for social justice, or redistributive, policy outputs. Thus, most decentralization proposals call for varying types of automatic, intracity budget-sharing to redistribute urban finances (either directly or in the form of services) on the basis of need and population.[35] However, it does not seem highly likely that a substantially redistributive formula could be resolved within the internal arena of urban government. Political decentralization would make the extent of redistribution among units a matter of record. The more visible the fact of resource redistribution (especially when the process is accessible to interested groups), the greater the intensity of conflict, and the greater possibilities that the formula would merely ratify the existing configuration of political forces. Without redistribution of resources among units, those which could raise least would get least, and without a mechanism for redistributive policy, relative disadvantages could become even more cumulative. Thus, lacking compensatory politics and significant resources to allocate, the virtues claimed for citizen participation, community control, and decentralization might all lose operational meaning for most of their intended beneficiaries.

It has been historically true, however, with respect to central (national) government participation in shaping the urban environment, that the higher the level of government, the easier it has been to reallocate government expenditures and to produce redistributive social policy. In addition to their access to greater resources, officials at the higher level are further removed from the arena of conflict and have broader and more heterogeneous constituencies in which to balance demands and support.[36] Perhaps the most appropriate role for the federal government in urban decentralization might thus be to act as a countervailing force and as a redistributive agent. As such it could

1. provide incentives for positive change to counterbalance potential conservatism;

2. change the balance in access and political power between the advantaged and the disadvantaged by guidelines to direct the social impact of federal programs; and

3. equalize the financial capacities of the subunits to ensure equitable public services.

If the federal government were to move in these directions, one might be quite optimistic about the possibilities that federal policy could take constructive directions to help implement decentralization without at the same time overcentralizing federal controls. While this article has emphasized the negative aspects of past federal activity in urban areas, it has done so in order to point out that federal urban policy would have to change to accommodate a system of urban decentralization, and in order to stress the intergovernmental nature of the concept. Any system which would attempt to meet legitimate demands for efficiency, effectiveness, and a socially appropriate redistribution of resources, while at the same time try to maintain some kind of local, small-unit input, must combine both centralization and decentralization. Such a combination would not attempt to bring together inconsistent forces, but rather, would "attempt to structurally meet what are inevitable tendencies in any kind of organizational system."[37]

However, the problems of federalism preclude simple panaceas, and the debate over urban decentralization is ultimately one of the more refractory issues of American intergovernmental relations. It involves the roles of many actors–national, state, regional, urban, and neighborhood–all sharing powers and functions in a complex arena. It highlights the need for national priority-setting without crippling local institutions and initiatives, and for drawing on private energies without bringing confusion to the administration of public affairs. And in order to energize relations between citizens and government, it underscores the need for thought and ingenuity.

[1]Mathew Holden, Personal communication. June 3, 1971.

[2]Wallace Sayre, Personal communication. June 10, 1971.

[3]Suzanne Farkas, *Urban Lobbying: Mayors in the Federal Arena.* (New York: New York University Press, 1971.)

[4]Charles Abrams, *Forbidden Neighbors.* (New York: Harper & Row, 1963.)

[5]Alvin Schorr, "How the poor are housed," in W. Wheaton et. al. (eds.) *Urban Housing.* (New York: Free Press, 1966.)

[6]*Ibid.,* p. 234.

[7]Scott Greer, *Urban Renewal and American Cities.* (New York: Bobbs-Merrill, 1965.)

[8]R. Krikus, "White ethnic neighborhoods–ripe for the bulldozer?" (New York: American Jewish Committee, Middle America Pamphlet Series, 1970.)

[9]Alan Campbell, Personal communication. June 8, 1971.

[10]Theodore Lowi, *The End of Liberalism.* (New York: W. W. Norton, 1969.)

[11]James Q. Wilson, "The mayors vs. the cities." *Public Interest.* (Summer, 1969).

[12]John DeGrove, "Help or hindrance to state action? The national government," in A. K. Campbell (ed.) *The States and the Urban Crisis.* (Englewood Cliffs, New Jersey: Prentice-Hall, 1970.)

[13]Victor Thompson, "Bureaucracy and innovation." Presented at the American Political Science Association, New York, 1966.

[14]S. M. Miller, "The future of maximum feasible participation." May, 1968 (unpublished).

[15]Wallace Sayre and Herbert Kaufman, *Governing New York City.* (New York: Russell Sage, 1965.)

[16]W. G. Farr, Personal communciation. June, 1971.

[17]Edward Banfield, "Revenue sharing in theory and practice." *Public Interest* (Spring, 1971).

[18]Office of Economic Opportunity, *Catalog of Federal Domestic Assistance.* (Washington, D.C., 1967, 1970.)

[19]Alan Campbell, ed., *The States and the Urban Crisis.* (Englewood Cliffs, New Jersey: Prentice-Hall, 1970.)

[20]Daniel Grant, "Urban needs and state response: local government reorganization," in A. K. Campbell (ed.) *The States and the Urban Crisis.* (Englewood Cliffs, New Jersey: Prentice-Hall, 1970.)

[21]Theodore Lowi, "American business, public policy, and case studies." *World Politics.* (1964.)

[22]Farr, Personal communication. 1971.

[23]Marilyn Gittell, Personal communication. June, 1971.

[24]Alan Altshuler, *Community Control.* (New York: Pegasus, 1970.)

[25]W. Sorrentino, Personal communication. Department of Housing and Urban Development, May 20, 1971.

[26]Judson James, "Federalism and the Model Cities experiment." (unpublished), 1971.

[27]National Commission on Urban Problems (1968) *Building the American City: Report to the President of the United States.* (Washington, D.C., 1968.)

[28]Campbell, Personal Communication. 1971.

[29]U.S. Department of Housing and Urban Development "Citizen Participation." CDA Letter 3, MCGR 3100.3, November 30, 1967.

[30]Altshuler, *Community Control*, p. 185.

[31]William Riker, *Federalism: Origin, Operation, and Significance.* (Boston: Little, Brown, 1964.)

[32]*Ibid.*

[33]Campbell, Personal communication. 1971.

[34]S. Mann, "Participation of the poor and Model Cities in New York City." Prepared for discussion at the National Academy of Public Administration, (May, 1970.)

[35]Donna Shalala, *Neighborhood Governance: Proposals and Issues.* (New York: Institute of Human Relations, 1970.)

[36]Alan Walsh, *The Urban Challenge to Government.* (New York: Institute of Public Administration, 1969.)

[37]Campbell, Personal communication. 1971.

14 Alternative Forms of Future Urban Growth in the United States

Anthony Downs

The prospect of further large-scale urban growth in the United States has evoked cries of alarm from many observers. One such cry (the "Columbus Challenge") warns that we will have to build as many new homes, roads, schools, shopping centers, and the like from 1960 to 2000 as we did from the time of Columbus up to 1960. A second demands that we build a large number of completely new, free-standing cities to cope with population growth and avoid continuing the supposedly chaotic horrors of urban sprawl. Another commonly heard exhortation urges the U.S. to develop a "national urban policy" or a "national land policy" before we become submerged in "megalopolis."

In my opinion, these and other similar views lack an adequate framework for viewing future urban growth and development as a whole. Such a framework should allow us to explore alternative ways in which future growth might occur and to design one or more effective strategies for shaping it.

This article sets forth a classification of alternative future forms of urban growth, some factors relevant to deciding which

Reprinted by permission of the *Journal of the American Institute of Planners* Vol. 31, (January 1970), pp. 3–11.

Anthony Downs is currently Senior Vice-President of Real Estate Research Corporation, Chicago, Illinois. He is the author of numerous articles and books dealing with urban economics and fiscal problems of American federalism.

are most likely and which are most desirable, and some policy implications for influencing this growth. Limited space permits me to present only an overview and basic conclusions, rather than any detailed analysis justifying the many admittedly arbitrary judgments involved.

CLASSIFICATION OF GROWTH FORMS

Defining the most likely forms of future urban growth requires an inherently subjective and arbitrary selection of a few combinations of key factors out of thousands of possibilities. Urban development involves dozens of important variables, each of which could reasonably take on several different future values. Some of these variables are:

1. Location of new growth in relation to existing metropolitan areas.
2. Contiguity of new growth to smaller existing communities located beyond the continuously built-up portions of metropolitan areas (including outside such areas).
3. Type of planning control (such as unplanned and highly fragmented, planned-unit development, or citywide).
4. Level of quality standards required in new construction.
5. Degree of public control over new urban development.
6. Degree of public subsidy for new urban development.
7. Distribution of housing subsidies among various income groups.
8. Degree of social class integration.
9. Degree and nature of racial integration.
10. Mixture of transportation modes.

Just considering these ten variables, and several arbitrarily chosen values for each one, yields at least 93,312 logically possible combinations—each representing a potential form of future urban growth! Clearly, it is impossible to formulate practical policy analysis on the basis of so many alternatives; drastic narrowing down must occur.

I accomplished this by using only variables 1, 2, and 3 to form possible future growth alternatives, thereby shifting consideration of the remaining seven to other parts of the analysis. I further reduced the many possible combinations of values for these three variables by eliminating those which seemed either internally inconsistent, or unlikely to accommodate large-scale new growth. The remaining ten combinations form my candidates for a standard classification of alternative forms of future urban growth in the United States:

1. *Redevelopment* of older neighborhoods in central cities or older surburbs through clearance and rebuilding. It has two forms:

a. *Unplanned redevelopment* (by individual parcel-owners with resulting highly fragmented patterns).
b. *Planned redevelopment* (under planned-unit-development type of control).

2. *Peripheral sprawl* with unplanned development control, either on the edges of the continuously built-up portions of metropolitan areas, or beyond those edges but still within commuting range.[1]

3. *Planned peripheral growth* on the edges of the continuously built-up portions of existing metropolitan areas. It has two forms:
a. *Peripheral planned-unit-development* (under planned-unit-development type of control).
b. *Peripheral new cities* (under comprehensively planned, citywide type of control).

4. *Satellite growth* beyond the continuously built-up portions of existing metropolitan areas but within commuting range of them. It has three forms:
a. *Scattered satellites* (under planned-unit-development type of control).
b. *Satellite new cities* (under citywide type of control but not contiguous to existing smaller communities).
c. *Satellite expanded cities* (under citywide type of control but contiguous to existing smaller communities).

5. *Nonmetropolitan growth* beyond commuting range from any existing metropolitan areas. It has two forms:
a. *Nonmetropolitan new cities* (under citywide type of control and not contiguous to any existing communities).
b. *Expanded nonmetropolitan communities* (under citywide type of control but contiguous to existing communities).

Admittedly, it might be desirable to modify this scheme under some circumstances. For example, scattered development along interstate highways outside of metropolitan areas might be considered "nonmetropolitan sprawl." However, I believe the ten basic forms of urban growth set forth above will form an adequate framework for most analyses of future urban development.

Two important aspects of these alternatives should be emphasized. First, they are not mutually exclusive. All of them could occur simultaneously within a single state, and the first eight could even occur simultaneously within a single metropolitan area. Second, these alternatives are not equally probable. In fact, far more future urban growth is likely to be peripheral sprawl than all the others combined. Public policies can influence the relative likelihood of these alternatives, but they hardly start with even odds.

KEY FACTORS FOR URBAN GROWTH

Before any policy conclusions can be drawn concerning these alternative forms of future urban growth, it is necessary to understand certain key factors related to such growth. These factors form the basis for my later policy implications.

Size of the "Urban" Explosion

Among urban futurists, a prevalent cause of alarm is the "explosion" of urban population they foresee. Extreme estimates indicate that total U.S. population will *double* from 1960 to 2000, rising from 180.7 million to 361.4 million. This gain of 180.7 million in forty years is derived from the U.S. Census Bureau's highest-fertility projection (Series A), which assumes fertility rates typical of the peak postwar years.[2] But, since 1957, U.S. fertility rates have plummeted 30 percent. Hence, they are already down to the level assumed by the Census Bureau's lowest-fertility projection (Series D), which indicates a gain of 101.9 million from 1960 to 2000.[3] If fertility rates keep on falling (as I believe they will), then even this projection may be too high.

Another consideration centers on the definition of "urban." The Census Bureau officially considers any place containing 2,500 or more inhabitants as "urban." I believe the word "urban" as used in popular and expert parlance really should be defined as "pertaining to metropolitan areas." In 1960, about 63 percent of all Americans lived in metropolitan areas. However, those areas captured about 80 percent of total U.S. population growth from 1950 to 1960, 83 percent from 1960 to 1966, and somewhat less than that from 1966 to 1969. Assuming that such areas receive about 80 percent of future U.S. population growth, Table 1 indicates future "urban" growth defined in terms of these metropolitan areas. The table shows why believers in Census Series A are still reciting the "Columbus Challenge." According to their estimate, metropolitan areas will more than double in population from 1970 to 2000. However, I think they are wrong–and by a huge amount.

TABLE 1 "Urban" Growth, 1960 to 2000

U.S. population projection used	Millions	As percent gain over 1960
My estimate	55.0	49.2
Census Series D	80.5	71.7
HUD estimate	96.4	85.8
Census Series A	144.6	128.8

Linking the Two "Urban Frontiers"

It is useful to simplify the incredibly complex welter of urban problems by viewing them as clustered around what I call two "urban frontiers." One is the *Frontier of Deterioration* in older central cities and suburbs, especially in ghetto areas. The other is the *Frontier of Growth* on the periphery of built-up portions of our metropolitan areas.

At present, most public policies treat these frontiers as completely separate from and totally unrelated to each other. One set of policies focuses almost entirely on improving central cities and ghettos as though they were hermetically sealed off from the suburbs. This includes most public housing, most urban anti-poverty programs, most urban job training programs, most housing code enforcement programs, a great deal of the urban Aid-to-Families-with-Dependent-Children, and even many mass transit grants. The one apparent exception is the federal highway-aid program. Yet, even its effect has been mainly to link downtowns and suburbs more closely, thereby making it even easier to bypass deteriorating areas within central cities.

On the other hand, plans for further suburban development deliberately exclude ways to use such expansion to help solve inner-city problems. Low-income housing is systematically blocked out of growth areas, even though suburban industrial firms are desperately short of unskilled labor. Only token efforts are made to introduce minority group workers into suburban building trades, in spite of critical shortages of construction workers in many areas. Thus, "natural" ways to simultaneously alleviate inner-city unemployment and suburban labor shortages are ignored. Metropolitanwide plans drawn up by federally supported regional planning agencies almost never contain any explicit consideration of where minority group members–especially Negroes–will live in the future. Yet the expansion of such groups provides the single most important dynamic force in many big central city housing markets. But it is "too hot to handle" for politically powerless metropolitan planning agencies, who are often fearful of their segregationist suburban constituencies.

"Extra" Costs in New Cities

Accommodating future urban growth in new cities involves several real costs larger than the costs of alternative forms of development. These "extra" costs result from the following key characteristics which differentiate new cities from other forms of urban growth.

1. Comprehensive Planning at a Citywide Scale. This requires centralized control over land use and development in a very large area *before*

anything is created on that land, so it generates the following added costs (as compared to growth at lesser scales of planning control):

a. The added costs of assembling a large enough site to accommodate 100,000 people (or whatever number is considered to be "city-sized") and holding parts of that site vacant during the first stages of development–which may last years.

b. The cost of developing and operating new institutions for centralized planning and control of such a large-scale activity.

c. The cost of overcoming the obstacles to new city development created by existing fragmented landownership and government institutions. A great deal of extra lobbying skill, waiting time, and money is needed to wrest comprehensive planning opportunities from them.

2. Distance from Existing Metropolitan Facilities. In nonmetropolitan new cities or expanded cities, where residents are beyond range of existing facilities, the following extra costs arise:

a. The *initial* loss of return on, or initially inefficient operation of, facilities that must be built immediately with a capacity to handle a large population long before that population itself arrives. These facilities include public infrastructure (such as roads, sewer and water facilities, high schools, and public buildings) and private enterprises (such as shopping centers and industrial plants).

b. The *total* costs of duplicating elements of existing metropolitan areas that now have enough excess capacity to serve many more people. Examples are some museums, universities, libraries, concert halls, public buildings, theaters, and business firms. No new facilities like these would be required if growth occurred peripherally or in satellites not too far from existing central cities.

3. Housing Everyone and Everything in Brand-new Quarters. Not all households, business firms, or other institutions can afford brand-new quarters. But in a new city, everything is brand-new. Yet society cannot operate a large community without the services of many low-income households and many low cost business firms. To enable these entities to survive in a new city, some form of public subsidy must be extended to cover the higher cost of their occupying new structures. This subsidy would not be required by peripheral growth. Then, such households and firms could occupy older quarters in the existing inventory of structures in each metropolitan area. Some subsidy for such entities might be required by satellite growth, but some low-income workers could commute from lower cost housing existing elsewhere. Moreover, these are not trivial costs. Housing costs are now so high that over one-half the households in the U.S. cannot afford even to *rent* newly built, modestly designed, appropriately sized apartments without spending an inordinate fraction of their incomes on housing. So unless almost all residents of a

new city are relatively affluent–which is impossible if the city is to operate efficiently–a large fraction of its residents will need subsidies to live there. The same is true of many businesses.

Thus, to the extent that any future urban growth strategy emphasizes new cities, it compels society, early in the development process, to pay extra public expenditures as compared to peripheral or satellite growth. True, if those extra public expenditures are eventually offset by extra benefits and if public authorities own most of the land in new cities, then they may eventually recapture enough profits and land value appreciation to repay this large initial investment. This appears to be happening in Great Britain. Nevertheless, public authorities will still have to make some arrangements to pay the extra initial costs of new cities in order to bring them into being.

Lessons from European Experience with Growth Controls

For several decades, many European nations have been exerting significant controls of various types over their own urban growth. In my opinion, their experience indicates some significant conclusions relevant to future policies affecting U.S. urban growth.

Any attempt to exert significant public influence over the nature, location, magnitude or physical form of urban growth requires public ownership or other direct control of a significant part of the land in major metropolitan areas, especially on their growth peripheries. Leaving most of the control over land use in private hands, especially where private ownership is fragmented into thousands of small parcels, as in the U.S., makes it impossible to impose any real guided development policy on even one metropolitan area. This conclusion implies that creation of any overall "urban growth strategy" or "urban land policy" would involve radical *restructuring* of traditional land ownership and control arrangements in the U.S. Also, development of any significant number of nonmetropolitan new cities, or even peripheral or satellite new cities, will require *public* ownership of much of the land in those cities.

Creation of relatively independent nonmetropolitan new cities is an extraordinarily difficult achievement of dubious long-run value. In Great Britain, public agencies promoting new town development have for decades exercised financial and administrative powers vastly greater than any currently contemplated in the U.S. Yet after more than twenty years of effort, only about 2.5 percent of all new housing construction in Britain occurs in new towns. Moreover, British government planners have virtually abandoned formation of additional nonmetropolitan new cities. They now favor peripheral new cities adjoining middle sized metropolitan areas beyond commuting range from London or the big Midlands industrial centers. This policy shift is essentially an attempt to escape many of the extra costs of nonmetropolitan new city development described above. To the best of my knowledge, in Sweden and the biggest Soviet cities, all so-called new cities are either peripheral or satellite in nature.

A crucial determinant of the physical form which publicly controlled urban growth takes is the type of transportation serving new-growth areas. The decision to plan such areas around public mass transit (as in Sweden and the Soviet Union) influences the physical form, density, and structure of the communities concerned, as does the universal decision to build them around automobiles in the U.S.

Any decision to shift major emphasis to mass transit in U.S. urban growth areas would cause radical transformations in the patterns of development typical of such areas during the past twenty-five years.

Rapid construction of new urban facilities to accommodate large-scale growth cannot be achieved through clearance and redevelopment; it must be done on initially vacant land. Even in the Soviet Union, clearance and redevelopment of built-up areas takes much longer than construction on peripheral vacant land. In Paris, after ten years, the huge La Defense urban redevelopment project had finished only 600 net new housing units (in addition to those needed for relocation); while a single public housing project on suburban vacant land housed over 40,000 residents eight years after its inception. These facts simply reemphasize a conclusion long established by U.S. urban renewal experience: the average redevelopment project takes from six to nine years.

Deliberately slowing down the growth of major urban centers—especially the national capital—is extremely difficult. With all their powers, Soviet urban authorities have been unable to prevent the Moscow area from continuing to grow rapidly. Although British authorities have had some success in shifting growth out of the center of London, there is still pressure to locate more activities within the London metropolitan region. The economic, political, cultural, and psychological advantages of being "where the action is," or at least within easy range, strongly favor peripheral or satellite expansion, rather than nonmetropolitan growth.

SPECIFIC POLICY IMPLICATIONS FOR THE UNITED STATES

In our diffused political system, creating a rational urban development strategy is extraordinarily difficult, even within a single metropolitan area. My own experience on the National Commission on Urban Problems convinces me that certain specific policy objectives must be attained before we can create any such strategies. These objectives are aimed at expanding the possible forms of future urban development beyond peripheral sprawl, which now encompasses almost all urban growth. They do not form a single urban development strategy in themselves, rather they are the foundations on which several such strategies might be built. Each of these objectives can be achieved through one or more tactics.

Increasing the Quantity of New Housing Built

The first key objective is *building much more new housing each year than in the recent past, and subsidizing much of it to improve housing conditions among the poorest and most ill-housed citizens.* I do not believe the U.S. will come very close to the ten-year target of twenty-six million new units (including six million subsidized units) set forth in the Housing and Urban Development Act of 1968.[4] Nevertheless, it is clear that we must build more units than in the recent past if we are to prevent a worsening housing shortage. Also, since many of the households in the worst housing are very poor, they cannot possibly afford to rent or buy new units.

Opening Up the Suburbs

The second key objective needed to widen our choice among future forms of urban development is *opening up the suburbs and outlying portions of central cities to new low and moderate income housing.* This is desirable not only for all the reasons cited above, but also because we cannot build large numbers of housing units for such groups within central cities. There is not enough vacant land there, and that which exists is needed for nonresidential uses. Creating new housing through relocation and clearance is impractical. It is time-consuming, expensive, and simply defers the problem by compelling poor people to move somewhere else, and most new jobs are being created in the suburbs. So it makes sense to put housing for low and moderate income households there also.

Escalating the Level of Planning

A third key objective relevant to future urban development is *escalation of the level of planning so that "spillover effects," now ignored by most developers, will be effectively taken into account.* Most building is done by owners of relatively small parcels. They do not, and cannot, pay much attention to how their own behavior affects their neighbors. They have very little control over their neighbors' projects except for that provided by zoning ordinances, which are vulnerable to court overthrow. This fragmentalized approach to new growth leads to "hodgepodge" development that is aesthetically disastrous and often inefficient. In order to achieve more fully integrated planning of urban growth, it is necessary to escalate the level of planning control to larger areas.

Several tactics would accomplish this. The first has already been discussed: shifting zoning and other land use control powers away from smaller communities to larger ones.

A third tactic for escalating the scale of planning is bolstering state planning powers and creating new institutions to carry out urban development at a citywide scale. This would involve three different kinds of institutions. The first would be a *national framework organization* charged with creating and administering national policies toward urban development. It could be part of the Department of Housing and Urban Development or an offshoot of the new Council of Urban Affairs. Its functions might include (1) developing national migration and population-growth policies; (2) coordinating all federal programs relevant to new cities; (3) coordinating land acquisition and disposition policies of all federal and some state agencies; (4) administering direct financial assistance to both state enabling organizations and actual developers of new cities; and (5) forming other national policies toward urban growth.

The second type of new institution would be *state or regional enabling organizations.* They would make it easier for private or public developers to overcome existing institutional obstacles to large-scale urban development. Possible functions for them include: (1) creating statewide plans for shaping future urban growth (including selecting sites for new cities if any are built); (2) controlling the location of major public investments like universities and highways; (3) granting franchises to developers to build new cities on specific sites; (4) establishing multipurpose taxing districts to help finance public improvements needed in urban growth; (5) using powers of eminent domain to assemble large-scale sites or create "land banks" or "buffer zones"; (6) "writing down" the cost of assembled land with federal funds so some housing on it could be occupied by low-income households; and (7) suggesting needed changes in existing zoning, subdivision, building code, and other regulations to help improve urban growth patterns.

The third type of new institution would be *operating development organizations,* created to plan and build large-scale new developments. These could be fully public corporations (like New York's Urban Development Corporation), quasi-public organizations, or fully private organizations benefiting from special powers exercised by the state (as private developers benefit from the eminent domain powers of local urban renewal agencies). They would carry out most of the initial planning, land assembly, public infrastructure construction, and some residential and other construction required for large-scale new developments. Since it is impossible to select from the menu of different possible organizations for such development any one best way applicable everywhere, national legislation should be designed to encourage formation of many different kinds of enabling and operating development organizations.

Broader Financing of Local Governments

A fourth objective critical to expanding our choices among forms of future urban growth is *widening the financial base of most local governments.* We cannot expect narrowminded thinking to disappear from most small communities as long as existing local government financial structures provide strong incentives for parochialism. Suburban resistance to the entry of low-income residents is partly—perhaps even mainly—a matter of fiscal self-defense. When low-income residents move into a wealthier community, they generally bring many children. The added cost of educating them is larger than the added tax revenues produced by the housing in which the low-income families live. Thus, every new low-income family represents an instant deficit to the local government and instantly higher taxes on all existing residents. We can hardly expect rational citizens to disregard these conditions by welcoming more low-income neighbors at their own expense. Americans have also traditionally resisted mixing with "lower class elements" after having escaped from those same elements themselves, so not all suburban hostility to low-income residents is fiscally motivated. Yet, we will never reduce that hostility unless we first remove its economic causes. I believe we must shift a large part of the financial burden for key local government activities—particularly schools and welfare—away from local property tax bases to a much broader base. That base could either be much larger property taxing districts encompassing whole metropolitan areas, state funds, federal funds, or federal funds channeled through the states (as the President recently proposed).

Other Objectives

Other key objectives that would expand our future choices among forms of urban growth include *reducing the diversity of existing building codes, zoning rules, and other local regulations,* and *reducing the cost of producing housing.* These are the focal points of Operation Breakthrough now being carried out by the Department of Housing and Urban Development. The first is necessary so that builders can capture more of the economies of large-scale production and marketing than in the past. At present, more than 8,000 legal entities in the United States issue building and/or housing codes. Almost all these codes are significantly different from each other. It is nearly impossible for housing developers of truly nationwide scope to come into being, since they must tailor their products to these immense local variations in requirements.

Reducing housing costs significantly would surely be desirable, but I doubt if it will happen. Most of the cost of occupying housing pays for land and financing, rather than for building the unit. In fact, technical innovations in construction will have to be incredibly significant just to keep the cost of housing from continuing to rise, given the acute shortage of skilled construction labor, rising land costs, and zooming interest rates. In my opinion, unless we drastically reduce the size and quality we require in newly built units, we will never have truly *low-cost* new housing. Obviously, new units for low and moderate income households will still require major subsidies.

CONCLUSIONS

The following conclusions represent what I believe are the most important implications of the foregoing analysis:

1. Future urban growth in the United States through the year 2000 will be much smaller than most official projections indicate, though it will still represent significant expansion of existing metropolitan areas.

2. Peripheral sprawl will undoubtedly be the dominant form of future urban growth throughout the U.S. Whether it will be almost totally dominant or just largely dominant will depend upon the extent to which the key policy objectives set forth here are actually achieved.

3. Nonmetropolitan new cities or expanded communities are not likely to capture any significant fraction of the nation's future urban growth, in spite of their current vogue in planning literature. The extra costs of these forms of urban growth mean that peripheral or satellite alternatives to peripheral sprawl are far more likely to occur.

4. Formulation of any one "national urban strategy" or "national land policy" is neither likely nor desirable. It is not likely both because of our diffused decision-making structure and because the necessary preconditions for real alternatives to peripheral sprawl do not yet exist. It is not desirable because diversity both within and among metropolitan areas makes a multiplicity of "urban strategies" better than just one.

5. State governments are the best focal points for development of any overall strategies controlling future urban growth or even for increasing our choices among forms of future urban growth. They are the only institutions that combine metropolitanwide perspective, decisive powers to override local governments, and sufficient local knowledge and local political roots to make use of such powers acceptable.

6. The proper federal role in shaping future urban growth should probably be one of structuring effective financial incentives for state governments to assume major policy responsibilities, financing subsidies needed for socially and economically "balanced" new development, and continuing to sponsor innovative approaches to key urban problems.

7. Developing effective alternatives to peripheral sprawl, or even mitigating some of its socially segregating effects, will require major changes in deeply rooted existing political and other institutions. These include local control over land use and zoning, local financing for schools, fragmented planning of new development, and the ability of individual landowners to engage in real estate speculation. The traumatic nature of these changes to many citizens can hardly be overestimated. In fact, they are likely to occur only if the failings of existing arrangements become far more pressing and obvious than they are now in most areas.

8. The choices Americans make among alternative forms of future urban growth will ultimately depend on the way they resolve certain key ambiguities among their own desires. On the one hand is a widespread feeling that future urban growth could be improved through more comprehensive planning and less haphazard decision-making. On the other hand is the traditional desire of individual Americans to control their own small parcels of land and their own small local governments and to gain from speculating in land values. But more comprehensive planning and continued fragmented control over development are mutually exclusive; we cannot simultaneously enjoy the benefits of both. As Pogo said about racism, "We have met the enemy, and he is us."

[1]The second form of growth I have called *peripheral sprawl* includes another form that might be more logically called *satellite sprawl.* It is not on the edge of existing cities (hence peripheral) but away from that edge (hence satellite). Yet the term *satellite* implies a cluster of some type, rather than more scattered development. Moreover, *peripheral sprawl* is used by many observers to refer to *all* scattered development outside existing built-up areas, both on the edge and farther out but within commuting range. Thus, I have adopted this dual definition.

[2]All data on official population projections are derived from U.S., Bureau of the Census, *Statistical Abstract of the United States, 1968* (89th Edition, Washington D.C.: GPO, 1968), pp. 7–9.

[3]*Ibid.*

[4]A detailed explanation of this belief is presented in "Moving Toward Realistic Housing Goals," Kermit Gordon, ed., *An Agenda for the Nation* (Washington, D.C.: The Brookings Institution, 1968), pp. 141–78.

Chapter FIVE

The Welfare Debate

INTRODUCTION TO CHAPTER FIVE In discussing the politics and administration of welfare we are essentially dealing with the plight of the poor in our society: those who are unable, for a variety of reasons, to earn a sufficient income to support themselves or their families. One of the first problems encountered in an examination of this topic is how poverty is defined. Economists point out that at least two definitions can be employed: (a) the *absolute standard,* or subsistence level, and (b) the *relative standard,* or concept of deprivation. The use of each of these standards has distinct implications for the programs that have been developed.

The subsistence level, or bare minimum necessary to support human life, has been placed at different levels by a number of sources. Some suggest the figure of $3300 for a family of four as the poverty level; others suggest that a figure of $4000 would be more appropriate. It is also necessary to take into account the place of residence of an individual in making these calculations. A family living in an urban area needs a higher income than one in a rural area, and a family living in New York City would need more income than one living in Houston. Using a figure of $3700 for a family of four as the poverty line, we find that about 38 million people, or one-fifth of the U.S. population, lives in poverty.

Looked at from another perspective, the figures above grossly understate the actual situation. Accepting the concept that poverty is a *relative* as well as absolute measure, many more people are living in some form of economic hardship. For example, in 1970, the Bureau of Labor Statistics estimated that the cost of living in a "moderate" fashion had risen to $11,236 for a family in the New York-New Jersey area. For the nation as a whole, a moderate standard of living required a minimum income of $10,200 for this same family of four. Thus, it can be argued with considerable logic that any family earning below this minimum is being deprived of some of the economic necessities of life.

Government on all levels has taken various steps to try to alleviate the need of those living in poverty. This assistance has taken a variety of forms: programs of general relief sponsored by the states; a system of welfare jointly administered by the federal-state and local governments; the enactment of programs in specific areas such as public housing, education, health, and sanitation; and the creation of training programs and employment services to encourage recipients of public assistance to end their dependency on these funds.

The welfare program discussed in the present chapter grew out of a series of amendments to the original Social Security Act of 1935. This act provided for the first time a method for the federal government to give aid to the needy who fall into certain specified categories, such as Old Age Assistance, (OAA), Aid to the Blind (AB), and Aid to Dependent Children (ADC). In recent years, two additional categories of federally aided programs have been established: Aid to the Permanently and Totally Disabled (APTD) and Medical Assistance to the Aged (MAA). In 1965, Medicaid, a companion to Medicare, was also added. Under the Medicaid program, those who are classified "medically indigent" (regardless of age) are eligible to receive support for a number of medical services.

THE PRESENT PROGRAM—ADMINISTRATIVE PROBLEMS

In 1971, there were approximately 14 million persons receiving welfare benefits from all of the categorical programs. The annual cost of the welfare program has been approximately $15 billion dollars, shared among the Federal, state, and local governments.

The largest, and most controversial, of the welfare programs is the one providing aid to families, now renamed Aid to Families with Dependent Children, AFDC. This category includes families where the father has deserted, where the father is unemployed, or where (for other reasons) a woman is the head of the household. The AFDC program, as well as the other categorical programs, is administered under a complex procedure: the federal government provides a portion of the funds (depending upon the wealth of the individual states) and establishes the overall regulatory framework for distribution of funds and determination of eligibility. The states, however, have the main responsibility for actually disbursing funds to the recipients and maintaining the lists of those eligible. In some states the county or city also plays a role in this process. As a result of this procedure, several problems have arisen. There is often considerable discrepancy in the amount of payment received by recipients in different states. For example, a family of four in Mississippi may receive a payment of fifty dollars per month, while a family of the same size in New York may receive over three hundred dollars. Another problem involves interpretation of the various regulations concerning eligibility for assistance. Some states have in the past established lengthy residency requirements, have insisted upon adherence to certain codes of personal behavior, have refused to give assistance if the husband continues to live with the family, and have made work rules that are virtually impossible to follow. Consequently, many persons eligible for assistance have been denied aid, and others have been forced to live on an extremely low payment because of the particular rules existing in their states.

PROPOSALS FOR REFORM

Because of these and other difficulties, there have been numerous proposals for reform or overhaul of the welfare system. Most of these proposals involve a greater role for the federal government and a more uniform system of administration. The major proposals that call for changes in the present welfare system include:

1. The Negative Income Tax. This is a plan which would utilize the facilities of the Internal Revenue Service. Stated most simply, every person would file a tax return. Those with income under a poverty level set by Congress would, instead of paying a tax, receive a payment from the national government.

2. The Guaranteed Annual Income. Under this proposal, the federal government would establish a poverty level. Those with income below this level would receive payment from the national government of at least a specified amount.

3. The Nixon Family Assistance Program. This is essentially a form of guaranteed income coupled with work requirements. Under this plan, a minimum level of payment would be given to all recipients, and this amount could be supplemented by the states. The "working poor" would also be eligible for assistance and recipents would be required to register for job training or employment.

4. The McGovern Proposal. The plan outlined by Senator McGovern originally envisioned a system in which every person in the U.S. would receive a set amount of money (tentatively set at $1000). Those persons with incomes over the poverty level would have to return a portion of this money and when a cut-off point (such as $20,000) was reached those above this level would return substantially more in taxes. A recent modification suggested a system that would be similar to the negative income tax discussed above. Under this new proposal, a family of four would be guaranteed an income of $4,000 by the Federal government. As a work incentive, those with higher incomes would be eligible for some aid until the cut-off point of $8,000 was reached.

The exact form of the welfare system that will emerge from Congress still has not been determined. There is little doubt, however, that a new plan will be devised, and that a major overhaul of the existing programs will be accomplished.

READINGS IN THIS CHAPTER

American Values and the Poor: Dorothy James

This selection traces the background of the current welfare program and examines the attitudes of Americans toward the poor in our society. Professor James suggests that despite the wide variety of programs that have been established, and the large amounts of money spent on them, most of the efforts in this field have been hindered by our reluctance to make lasting efforts. This reluctance can be traced back to values long held sacred in our society: laissez faire, the concept of "survival of the fittest", the "Protestant ethic", and the "Horatio Alger myth" (all one has to do is work hard and he will be successful). It is also suggested that there is an underlying racism present in much of the administration of the welfare programs, and an unwillingness by government officials to provide enough assistance so that the cycle of welfare dependency could be ended. Many specific examples of this are shown: the failure of public housing and urban renewal, inadequate food stamp programs, lack of medical care for the poor, and halfhearted efforts to win the "War on Poverty."

The Nixon Plan: Elliot Richardson

Former Secretary of Health, Education, and Welfare Richardson outlines the essentials of President Nixon's proposed welfare reforms and suggests how the President's plan would overcome many of the shortcomings of the existing welfare system. In his testimony before Congress, Richardson discusses the ways in which the government's proposals will reduce costs, simplify administration, and provide an incentive for recipients to seek gainful employment. One of the major problems relating to the Nixon proposals centers over the question of incentives: how can a system be devised that will give enough money to a family for necessities, but at the same time not discourage other low income families from working. The Nixon plan tries to remedy this by two measures: (a) allowing the working poor to keep some welfare payment in addition to their income; and (b) to require all able-bodied recipients to work, so that the alternative of being unemployed is not open to them.

Government Policy Towards Employment: Gerald Rosenthal

From the depression era of the 1930's to the present, the national government has become increasingly concerned with the problem of unemployment in our society. Professor Rosenthal traces the background of several pieces of legislation designed to help the economy achieve "full employment." He notes that the decade of the 1960s was a period of many important innovations in the field of manpower training, such as the Manpower Development and Training Act, the Job Corps, and several other programs administered by the Office of Economic Opportunity and the Department of Labor. This period was also one of greater participation by state and local governments in the employment field. The author suggests that the innovative programs adopted in the 1960s can serve as support for a further expansion of governmental activities during the present decade. The main objective of virtually all of the programs involving manpower training and job placement is to develop the skills of an individdual, and to create jobs that will enable him to utilize these skills. If successful, these governmental programs can be an important feature of the nation's social welfare policy, since they encourage a pattern of self-sufficiency, rather than one of dependency and despair.

15 Reflection of American Values in National Policy Toward the Poor

Dorothy B. James

Public policy toward the poor has always borne the mark of America's adherence to the liberal tradition, with its emphasis on individualistic materialism and antagonism toward comprehensive social planning. As one study indicated, in comparison with other western democracies the United States "is more reluctant than any rich democratic country to make a welfare effort appropriate to its affluence. Our support of national welfare programs is halting; our administration of services for the less privileged is mean. We move toward the welfare state but we do it with ill grace, carping and complaining all the way."[1]

From: Dorothy B. James, POVERTY, POLITICS & CHANGE, 1972, pp. 49–71. Reprinted by permission of Prentice-Hall, Inc., Englewood Cliffs, New Jersey.

Dorothy James is Associate Professor of Political Science at Herbert Lehman College of the City University of New York. She has written extensively in the fields of American politics, public policy, and welfare administration.

PRIOR TO THE NEW DEAL

One consequence of adherence to natural law, then *laissez faire* liberalism during the eighteenth and nineteenth centuries, was a preference for *private* and *voluntary* rather than *public* assistance to the poor. Thus, institutional charities (churches, political ward bosses, ladies societies), individual beneficence (such as Carnegie libraries), and privately sponsored Settlement Houses were the primary sources of assistance to the poor until the twentieth century.[2] Even after the more active governmental role allowed by organic liberalism had gained widespread acceptance, a substantial minority of American "conservatives" adhered to this *laissez faire* philosophy. . . .

In dealing with the Depression President Herbert Hoover unwittingly assisted in making clear to a majority of Americans the necessity for a positive governmental role. Throughout his lifetime, President Hoover spoke glowingly in favor of *laissez faire.* Therefore, when faced with those difficult years he stressed *voluntary* cooperative efforts to cope with the multiple problems of finance, agriculture, business, and labor. Continuous failures slowly laid the groundwork for public acceptance of a more decisive role for the federal government.[3]

Nevertheless, the dominance of materialistic individualism in American values may still be seen in a wide variety of empirical measures of political attitudes.[4] Invariably, since the 1930s a majority of Americans have supported only those welfare policies which have approached poverty by attempting to enable *individuals* to cope more effectively with the *existing* American economic, social, and political system (old age pensions, social security, unemployment compensation, aid to education). Consistently, any attempts at a more fundamental redistribution of reources, which are based on less materialistic or individualistic philosophies, have been attacked by the majority of Americans as "radical" and "socialistic." Available data indicate that there is widespread antagonism to "sharp shifts toward general or abstract socialist principles."[5]

THE NEW DEAL AND THE DEVELOPMENT OF WELFARE

President Franklin Delano Roosevelt came not to bury Capitalism but to restore it. Sharing the dominant American belief in the value of private property and free enterprise, he aimed at a return to high production, high employment and balanced government budgets, but in dealing with widespread poverty President Roosevelt inaugurated the most far-reaching set of programs in the nation's history. For example, on August 14, 1935 an omnibus Social Security Bill was enacted that made provision for a federal/state system of unemployment insurance; a federal program of old age insurance; federal grants to states for old-age assistance; aid to the blind, dependent children, maternal and child health services, and public health programs.

Despite public rhetoric antagonistic to their alleged "socialist" or "collectivist" tendencies, these programs were fully in accord with the tenets of organic liberalism. The American social and economic systems were assumed to be basically sound, merely needing to open greater employment opportunities in order for the poor to enter the work force without further help.[6] Poverty was considered a temporary condition due to unemployment, agricultural depression or the dependence of youth, or it was considered a condition due to individual problems such as blindness, or old age. Welfare was assumed to be a temporary measure which would end with rising employment and national income. Consequently, little attempt was made to coordinate programs or to consider their broader social implications. (Creeping it may have been, socialism it definitely was not.)

Once the Depression had passed, it again became difficult to induce the American people to formulate public policy for the poor. . . .

The impact on the poor of the widespread adherence to materialistic individualism and racism is most clear in the administration of these welfare programs: There the basic American equation of material possession with moral worth has been made obvious. Russell Conwell, the post Civil War Gilded Age's major apologist of the clergy, would have approved of the spirit in which our welfare programs have been administered, as they have accorded with his precept that: "It is all wrong to be poor."[7] The consequence of such an attitude has been a welfare system that is *paternalistic, punitive, and inadequate.*

The system is paternalistic in that it treats recipients as children, destroying initiative by depriving them of the ability to control their expenditures. They are told how, where, when, and for what their money should be spent. Social workers have unlimited discretionary authority over recipients' fiscal, physical, and emotional affairs. They may make inquiries at any time of day or night, and are held completely responsible for either opening or closing a case, for budgeting, and for supervising any necessary procedures.

The system is punitive because it is based on the assumption that the poor are morally unworthy. Therefore, eligibility for public assistance depends *on how great* a sacrifice the recipient is willing to make–economic need alone is *not enough* to warrant asking for relief: "There is an implicit assumption in these requirements that a really needy person will not be a newcomer, will not sin, will have nothing to hide and therefore will submit to whatever searches of his physical premises are asked of him, and will accept intrusion into his emotional privacy by the welfare agency that dispenses services along with money."[8]

Provisions under Aid to Dependent Children not only penalized stable families but also discouraged economic initiative on the part of the poor. A family could receive no payments whatsoever if a male in the household worked, no matter how low his income. Thus, a father whose job provided minimal income could economically hinder his children by keeping a job and the family intact. For example, a dishwasher who earned $60 per week and had a wife and three children could receive welfare payments of $48 per family member per month. *If he left his family,* New York City payments for a family of four in 1969 averaged $249.75 per month, or $62 per person per month, plus medical aid and other services–*and the income was tax free.*[9] To put it bluntly, the welfare system practically encouraged him to leave his family. It also dampened any economic initiative on the part of dependent children or their mothers because any income they received was automatically deducted from welfare payments. The net result was a *smaller* total income, since a job brought added expenses of carfare, meals away from home, clothing, and Social Security deductions.

THE PUNITIVE ASPECTS OF PUBLIC HOUSING

Another of the self-serving mythologies concerning the poor and welfare, which also is widely held among the American electorate, concerns public housing.

In addition to concern for welfare payments to the destitute, organic liberals recognized that man needed basic shelter and food to be free for development. As it became increasingly clear that millions of individuals could not provide these for themselves, liberals began to formulate public policy to that end. It was the 1937 Federal Housing (Wagner) Act which made the first attempt to have the national government bear acquisition and development costs of public housing. Subsequent acts broadened the scope in this area, so that by 1970 public housing assisted nearly two and a half million poor people, whose median annual family income was $2,800.[10]

This, however, was grossly inadequate to meet the need. It reached less than 10 percent for a variety of reasons.[11] Among them might be inadequate funding; the ambivalence of Congress for over a decade to commit itself to a sustained program; and the unwillingness of localities to provide such housing. For example, communities such as San Diego, California, or Des Moines, Iowa, have provided no public housing at all. Even where it was provided, it has tended to provoke high levels of antagonism from middle class groups against any plans to build low income housing on vacant land in their areas (particularly housing for nonwhites). Consequently, public housing has generally been built in poverty areas, causing severe dislocation problems for previous residents. Furthermore, for years, public housing has refused to accept troubled families as tenants, thereby excluding a large portion of the poor.[12] Even when these restrictions were softened, the most destitute were denied shelter because they lacked the money necessary to pay the minimal rent. . . .

By the 1960s liberals recognized the fact that the program they had intended to assist individual development had failed. The Kennedy and Johnson Administrations attempted to encourage social improvement rather than the earlier brick and mortar approach by rehabilitating the poor in public housing through the provision of social services. Four "concerted service" projects were developed in St. Louis, New Haven, Miami, and Pittsburg, California, to enhance public housing tenants' ability to achieve self-help and self-support. However, they proved a failure. . . .

THE FAILURE OF URBAN RENEWAL

Nationally subsidized urban redevelopment began with Title I of the 1949 Housing Act that provided funds for bulldozing "blighted" areas (generally defined as areas where the poor or nonwhites lived) which would be sold at a low price to promoters who would redevelop the areas.[13]

The resulting clearing and construction benefited the rich and badly hurt the poor. It reduced the supply of low-income housing by displacing residents in order to clear and construct projects which benefited non-residents, such as the New York City Coliseum or other commercial and business establishments. Many critics attacked the program as illogical and impractical on the ground that it fostered the forcible displacement of citizens, destroyed a great number of low-rent homes, and cost an exorbitant amount of the taxpayer's money.[14]

The 1954 Housing Act provided funds for more than bulldozing. It emphasized overall planning. As with low-income public housing, it remained highly controversial in local communities. Local control fostered racial and income segregation. Thus, the net impact of the program was not directly beneficial to the urban poor.[15]

INADEQUATE NATIONAL FOOD PROGRAMS

The same paternalistic, punitive, and inadequate national policies which have developed in welfare, public housing and urban renewal programs have also characterized national food programs. Not even this most basic of needs has been met for millions of Americans.

The development of food assistance programs was an indirect admission of the inadequacy of public welfare payments,[16] but it came slowly. Until 1964 only one major national program existed–the Commodity Distribution Program, established by the Agricultural Adjustment Act of 1949. This one was more concerned with aiding farmers than the poor. It was intended as a means to distribute selected farm products such as lard, flour, dried beans, and peanut butter, for which government price supports had previously been provided. It was never intended to be a complete diet, merely a supplement. Consequently, no attempt was made at nutritional balance (it was predominantly a diet of starches and fats) nor for an adequate quantity of food for subsistence.

Many obstacles related to class and racial bias prevented even this inadequate food assistance from reaching a majority of those who needed it. Local communities were unwilling to accept the program for several reasons. They were expected to provide space, facilities, and administrative salaries, all of which would cost local tax dollars which they were unwilling to spend on the "unworthy." Moreover, many local merchants feared (based on materialistic individualism) that the program would reduce their local sales.[17] Similarly, many local farmers believed that hungry people would be more willing to work in the fields when needed.[18] As a result, many rural counties discontinued the program during the harvest season to coerce the poor into harvesting crops.[19]

The difficulty that poorly educated people encountered in establishing eligibility, completing and handling forms, and coping with the administrative red tape involved were among further obstacles. In addition, recipients were required to go to food distribution centers, which were open only once a month, and carry home their entire month's supply of food at one time. Often the centers were inconveniently located. The elderly, ill or handicapped, or those with no transportation encountered many problems in receiving their commodity surplus foods.

Consequently, as recently as 1968, more than 500 of the poorest counties in America had no food subsidies of any kind, and three quarters of their poor received no help at all from any federal assistance programs.[20] Since then, participation has rapidly increased but the program has remained so inadequate that administrators increasingly favor the food stamp program. . . .

The degree to which the paternalistic, punitive administration and cost of the food stamp program have adversely affected the poor may be judged by the sharp drop in recipients when counties shifted from direct distribution of surplus foods to the stamp plan (both could not be provided in a county). Among all counties that shifted from surplus food to food stamps by 1968 "there was an average decline of 40 percent in persons participating."[21] The food stamp program simply failed to reach those who could not afford it. Nor was this a temporary drop due to administrative changeover, despite Department of Agriculture assurances to that effect. As recently as September 1969 a Senate committee found that: "Nationally only 21.6 percent of the poor people living in counties with food stamp programs participate in the program. . . . Only 116, or 10 percent, of all counties with food stamp programs reached 40 percent or more of their poor."[22]

In addition to the food stamp program, two further federally funded food assistance programs were established in the 1960s. They were designed to meet the nutritional needs of school children. The National School Lunch Act of 1964 provided low cost hot lunches, but many poor families could not afford the cost of $1.25 per week per child, and schools in poor neighborhoods lacked the facilities for the program. The Child Nutrition Act of 1966, which provided a school milk program, had similar problems. Thus middle-class children have benefited more from the school lunch and milk programs than have poor children.

Eventually, the inadequacy of food assistance programs could no longer be ignored. Public awareness of the problems was aided by a series of reports in 1967 and 1968 which left no doubt that starvation and malnutrition afflicted *millions* of Americans, and that government programs were seriously inadequate to meet existing need. . . .

This crescendo of criticism resulted in some changes in the food stamp and commodity distribution programs. . . .

THE WAR ON POVERTY

The same inadequacies which prompted liberals to develop the housing and food programs also prompted them to consider the nation's welfare policies. Unfortunately, despite a promising start, the resulting War on Poverty foundered on the familiar rocks of widespread public hostility to the poor, especially the nonwhite poor.[23]. . .

. . . Prior to President Johnson's administration, the men who would eventually be his top advisers for a few years had been made aware of the poverty problem. Several groups and individuals had already begun formulating proposals to cope with it. For example, in September 1963 President Kennedy appointed a Cabinet level Task Force on Manpower and Conservation. Shortly after his assassination, the Task Force reported that on the basis of physical and psychological examinations one third of the nation's youth would be found unqualified for military service, primarily due to poverty.[24] Meanwhile, research and the growing civil rights movement had documented the degree to which racial discrimination was responsible for much poverty.

All of these factors provided the background for the "war" that President Lyndon Johnson called on poverty in January 1964. It was intended to be a "total war on poverty" to eliminate poverty and restructure society by giving the poor a chance to design and administer antipoverty programs. In both its avowed intent to involve the poor in the decisions which affected their lives and in its lack of racial bias, it marked a radical departure from previous public policy toward the poor.

This innovation was possible because the Economic Opportunity Act of 1964, which provided its basic legislative authorization, was developed very quickly (between January and March) by a comparatively small body of men within the Executive branch who shared the same concerns, and who were Kennedy advisers remaining in the Johnson Administration.[25] Congress was merely asked to ratify the bill, which it did quickly (Summer 1964) and with relatively little change in the Executive proposal.

The most radical innovation of the Economic Opportunity Act was the concept embodied in Section 202 (a) (3) of "maximum feasible participation of the poor"–the basis for the Community Action Program. Analysis of its legislative history indicates that the provision became part of the law because it remained unnoticed in the EOA until after passage. It was inserted in the Administration's draft of the bill by a small staff group in the Bureau of the Budget and the Justice Department, after very little discussion, and received little attention in the bill's passage on Capitol Hill.[26] In fact, the legislative history of the entire EOA clearly states that it was not the reflection of a major change in American values, but of those of a particular small group of Presidential advisers. Once its provisions were applied the EOA raised a storm of controversy.

The Office of Economic Opportunity was established as part of the Executive Office of the President with broad coordinating responsibilities for poverty programs, such as organizing community action, job training, educational programs, legal aid, medical programs, and aid for migrant laborers. In order to reach the "inner city" poor and other disadvantaged groups the OEO often attempted to bypass state and local governments. Its vague mandate also brought it into conflict with established bureaucratic centers in federal departments, such as Agriculture, Health, Education and Welfare, Labor or Interior. Thus, it initially antagonized many established holders of political power, especially mayors of large cities, who were most directly affected by community action programs. Moreover, the public came to perceive the programs as having been designed primarily for ghetto residents. Consequently, in addition to general public hostility to the poor, widespread racism provided further impetus for attack on the programs. . . .

In short, the War on Poverty upset such a large body of Americans that it provided the incentive needed for eventual destruction or dilution of most of the programs through outright termination, inadequate funding, or pressure to change some to the point that they no longer filled the purposes for which they had been established. In fact, the degree to which individual provisions of the War on Poverty were altered under public attack correlated directly with the degree to which these same provisions attacked American values.

Project Head Start was least threatening, therefore least threatened. Embattled from the start, however, were the Master Teacher Program, which provided incentives for more competent teachers to work with the poor, the Rent Subsidy Program, which assisted ghetto residents in obtaining housing outside slum areas, and the Community Action Program.

The idea of giving people a voice in the programs which would affect their lives was the basis for the Community Action Program. It became the most controversial aspect of the "War," because it undercut the paternalistic, punitive, and racist assumptions of previous welfare programs. Funding was never equal to the task and leadership of programs was undercoordinated and weak.[27] By 1965, the intention that the poor would *plan* community programs was lessened to their *carrying out* those programs planned by "experts."[28] Increasingly, in many communities the poor were not given that much authority although there were some marked successes.

As the costs of the Vietnamese War made budget cuts necessary in domestic programs, Congress increasingly opposed appropriations for the War on Poverty. Whenever budgets have had to be tightened, poverty programs have traditionally been cut first. As the economic recession of the late 1960s and early 1970s deepened, both the Johnson and Nixon administrations and state and local governments followed this pattern. . . .

The War on Poverty did receive a great deal of publicity during the Johnson Administration but by 1970 analysts agreed that: "Most poor people have had no contact with it, except perhaps to hear the promises of a better life to come."[29] It certainly did not wage a "total war on poverty," as originally intended, which would eliminate poverty entirely. Nor did it even approach the restructuring of society.

MODEL CITIES

The problems that these programs faced with inadequate funding and general pressures which led to program dilution were also inherent in the

Model Cities experiment. As liberals increasingly criticized the urban renewal program, the growing frustrations and anger of urban blacks erupted in ghetto riots throughout the nation. This provided the impetus for reevaluation of public policy which resulted in the Demonstration Cities and Metropolitan Development Act of 1966 and which initiated the Model Cities experiment. The program attempted to find the uneasy balance between community groups (primarily black), which demanded community participation, and existing bureaucracies and elected officials, who wanted no further experiments such as the Community Action Program.[30] This program was supposed to concentrate resources in a defined target neighborhood in a limited number of cities. A Community Development Agency, directly related to both the Mayor's office and the neighborhood community, was responsible for the planning.

The experiment aimed to avoid lack of coordinated planning, a major weakness of the War on Poverty. The national Model Cities Administration was to supply funds for the planning effort, and supplemental funds for the resulting five-year plan. It also was to coordinate planning for the bulk of financing which would come from previous programs and agencies that were still functioning. . . .

In administering the program, during the Johnson administration, the Model Cities staff was divided between those who wished to strengthen community participation and those who wanted to work through City Hall. The Nixon administration, however, firmly disapproved of community involvement, as the Secretary of Housing and Urban Development, George Romney, announced that the Model Cities program was intended to be and would remain a local governmental function centered around the Mayor's office: ". . . . local government officials must exercise final control and responsibility for the content and administration. . . ."[31] Although it was not politically feasible to ignore well organized citizen groups, the Romney directive discouraged any local Community Development Agency from new or further organization. These shifts of emphasis about citizen participation generated confusion and bitterness among many participants in the Model Cities process.[32]

The coordination that Model Cities could achieve was seriously limited by its modest financial resources. Most national agencies contributed, but grudgingly, and those supplemental funds which were available to the program had to be spread too thinly to effect substantial control.[33] It was undercut further by the Nixon administration which placed far less emphasis on cities than had its predecessor, and extensively limited funds.[34] Thus, even as imaginative a program as Model Cities has tended to be grossly inadequate in financing and in the opportunities it provided for participation by the poor.

THE NIXON APPROACH

These recurrent problems of American public policy toward the poor were not changed by the Nixon administration, whose most innovative proposal involved a new approach to welfare problems of families with children. On August 11, 1969, President Nixon proposed that a Family Assistance Plan be enacted with a national standard for minimum welfare payments to families and a definition of basic eligibility. It would enable the poor to have a guaranteed basic annual minimum income with a work incentive system which would allow those receiving relief to keep a portion of their earnings. Thus, the working poor could keep the first $60 of all monthly earnings plus half of all income beyond that amount.

While this appeared to be a major change, the plan was couched in language that embodied all the assumptions underlying previous welfare policies, and had provisions which reflected them more fully.[35] Significantly, it was one of the weakest of the many plans which were being proposed by groups in and out of the government to deal with the obvious failure of the welfare system. Numerous alternative plans with broader coverage had been suggested at the same time but President Nixon chose the one with the narrowest coverage (only families with children), weakest structure, and lowest support levels ($1,600 for a family of four).

The paternalistic and punitive phases of the new plan were based on the familiar assumption that poverty was the poor's responsibility and that by changing the poor themselves poverty would end. The plan was largely the responsibility of Daniel P. Moynihan, based on his concept of a "culture of poverty." Every physically able adult family member, except the mothers of pre-school children, or those needed to care for the ill or handicapped, would be required to enter a work training class or accept a "suitable" job to remain eligible for assistance. The widest discretion concerning the "suitability" of the job, or the appropriate subject matter for work training programs, would be allowed state and local administrators because there were no specific minimum standards for either the types of jobs or wages to be offered. From their previous experience, many spokesmen for these groups anticipated highly discriminating and punitive administration of the program.[36] Further, it was only a partial means of dealing with poverty, for, as the government estimated, out of the five million family heads who were covered, only one half would be affected,[37] and the program did not attempt to cope with the poor persons who were not attached to families with children. The program also ignored the economic realities of a job market in which three problems seemed particularly significant: 1) the lack of child-care centers would prevent mothers from taking jobs; 2) newly trained welfare recipients would not be able to find work because there was a scarcity of jobs for those already trained and/or experienced; 3) increasingly, the available jobs required extensive education, which exceeded the scope and intention of the Nixon proposal. When the program ran into legislative difficulty it was dropped by the President. . . .

CONCLUSION

Poverty became the subject of national public policy relatively late in America's history, but since the nineteen thirties a number of programs have been enacted to deal with aspects of the problem. Despite the varied aspects of poverty with which they have dealt, these programs have tended to be inadequate, paternalistic, and punitive. There also appears to have been a general bias in the way in which most of these programs have been designed, with the result that they have often tended to benefit the well-to-do more than the poor. Consequently, national policies have tended to maintain and perpetuate American poverty.

[1]Harold L. Wilensky and Charles N. Lebeaux, *Industrial Society and Social Welfare* (New York: Free Press, 1965), p. xvii.

[2]Clarke A. Chambers, *Seedtime of Reform* (Ann Arbor, Mich.: University of Michigan Press, 1967).

[3]Albert U. Romasco, *The Poverty of Abundance* (New York: Oxford University Press, 1965).

[4]For a compilation and evaluation of most available empirical research on American political attitudes, see John P. Robinson, Jerrold G. Rusk, and Kendra B. Mead, *Measures of Political Attitudes* (Ann Arbor, Mich.: Survey Research Center Institute for Social Research, 1968).

[5]*Ibid.,* p. 35.

[6]Thomas Gladwin, *Poverty U.S.A.* (Boston: Little Brown, 1967), p. 28.

[7]Russel H. Conwell, *Acres of Diamonds,* (New York: Harper & Bros., 1915) pp. 15–25, 49–59.

[8]Gilbert Steiner, *Social Insecurity, The Politics of Welfare* (Rand McNally, 1966) p. 108.

[9]Statistics from *The New York Times,* August 12, 1969, 18:4.

[10]Gilbert Y. Steiner, *The State of Welfare* (Washington, D.C.: Brookings Institution, 1971), p. 122.

[11]*Ibid.,* p. 127.

[12]*Ibid.,* p. 125.

[13]For a discussion of the urban renewal problem, see Martin Anderson, *The Federal Bulldozer* (New York: McGraw Hill, 1964); Jewel Bellush and Murray Hausknecht, eds., *Urban Renewal: People, Politics and Planning* (Garden City, N.Y.: Doubleday, 1967); James Q. Wilson, ed., *Urban Renewal: The Record and the Controversy* (Cambridge, Mass.: M.I.T. Press, 1967).

[14]For example, see Anderson, *The Federal Bulldozer,* p. xix.

[15]Lawrence M. Friedman, *Government and Slum Housing.* (Chicago: Rand McNally, 1968).

[16]G. Steiner, *The State of Welfare,* p. 191.

[17]Roger L. Hurley, *Poverty and Mental Retardation: A Causal Relationship* (New York: Random House, 1969).

[18]Truman E. Moore, *The Slaves We Rent.* (New York: Random House, 1965).

[19]Citizen's Board of Inquiry into Hunger and Malnutrition in the U.S., *Hunger, U.S.A.* (Boston: Beacon Press, 1968).

[20]Hurley, *Poverty and Mental Retardation: A Causal Relationship.*

[21]G. Steiner, *The State of Welfare* p. 213.

[22]Prepared by the Senate Select Committee on Nutrition and Human Needs, *Poverty, Malnutrition, and Federal Food Assistance Programs: A Statistical Summary*, 91st Congress, First session, 1969, p. 29.

[23]For several trenchant discussions of this process, see Saul D. Alinsky, "The War on Poverty–Political Pornography;" and James Ridgeway, "The More Glorious War," in Chiam Issac Waxman, ed., *Poverty: Power & Politics* (New York: Grosset & Dunlap, 1968), pp. 171-79, 202-16; Sar A. Levitan, *The Great Society's Poor Law* (Baltimore: Johns Hopkins Press, 1969).

[24]John C. Donovan, *The Politics of Poverty* (New York: Pegasus, 1967), p. 26.

[25]For fuller discussion of the process, see *ibid.,* chap. 2.

[26]*Ibid.*

[27]Arthur B. Shostak, "Old Problems and New Agencies: How Much Change?" in Warner Bloomberg and Henry Schmandt, eds., *Power, Poverty and Urban Policy* (Beverly Hills, Calif.: Sage Publications, 1968); Roger H. Davidson and Sar A. Levitan, *Antipoverty Housekeeping* (Institute of Labor and Industrial Relations, University of Michigan and Wayne State University, 1968).

[28]Donovan, *The Politics of Poverty,* and Ralph M. Kramer, *Participation of the Poor* (Englewood Cliffs, N.J.: Prentice-Hall, 1969).

[29]Joseph Kershaw, *Government Against Poverty,* (Wash. D.C.: Brookings Institution, 1970) p. 161; Levitan, *The Great Society's Poor Law.*

[30]Judson L. James, "Federalism and the Model Cities Experiment," paper delivered at the Annual Meeting of the American Political Science Association, Los Angeles, September 8–12, 1970, p. 2.

[31]George Romney, statement before the subcommittee on Housing of the House Committee on Banking and Currency, Washington, D.C. (May 12, 1969).

[32]J. James, "Federalism and the Model Cities Experiment," p. 23.

[33]*Ibid.,* p. 25.

[34]*Ibid.*

[35]Reported in *The New York Times,* August 12, 1969, 18:3.

[36]For example, see George A. Wiley, Executive Director of the National Welfare Rights Organization, "Why Welfare Won't Work," *The New Generation*, Vol. 52 (Winter 1970), pp. 22–25.

[37]Secretary of Labor George P. Shultz, "The Nixon Welfare Plan," *The New Generation,* Vol. 52 (Winter 1970), p. 5.

16 A New Approach to Welfare: The Family Assistance Plan

Elliot Richardson

From: Testimony before Senate Finance Committee, 91st Congress, 2nd Session, July-August 1970, pp. 404-14.

Elliot Richardson was formerly Secretary of the Department of Health, Education and Welfare in the Nixon Administration. He has been one of the chief architects of the President's welfare reform programs.

This administration's analysis of the current welfare system began without preconceived notions or predetermined remedies, beyond the conviction that the antipoverty and welfare programs already on the books were not working. Rather than helping the poor to move out of poverty, they had perpetuated poverty and encouraged dependency.

The sole directive given to the analysis charged with reexamining the welfare system was to focus on the problems inherent in the custodial approach to poverty. If the system was found to be badly in need of repair, or if it was to be completely replaced, then the President wanted particular attention paid to the possibility of constructing a more remedial approach to welfare. If it were at all feasible, he favored a system directed toward encouraging the natural instinct of people to help themselves to become contributing members of our economic and social system.

Guided by this general approach, the administration's analysis of the problem began a few weeks before the inauguration, with the appointment of the President's Transition Task Force on Welfare.

After the inauguration, a special subcommittee of the Urban Affairs Council, chaired by former Secretary Robert Finch, continued the principal analysis. That examination of this very complex field continued unabated through numerous meetings of the Urban Affairs Council and ultimately involved dozens of experts in and out of Government.

The process was inductive, not deductive. The reform principles around which the family assistance plan was originally designed were shaped to overcome the specific deficiencies revealed by careful study of the current system. These principles, in turn, have determined the operational features of the plan. The whole was refined and strengthened through the patient and painstaking reexamination and reinforcement which it received at the hands of the House Committee on Ways and Means. I look forward to working with you, Mr. Chairman, the committee, and the committee staff to strengthen and improve the plan still further.

To this end, Mr. Chairman, I would like to review quickly the process that has led us to this historic stage in the Nation's development of a fair and adequate program of family assistance.

THE FAILURE OF THE CURRENT WELFARE SYSTEM

The first conclusion compelled by the administration's analysis of the current system was that it is not a system at all, but a confused clutter of many systems. From this has flowed disparity, inequity, and inefficiency.

1. Geographic inequities: The Aid to Families with Dependent children program is in reality 54 different programs in 54 different jurisdictions. It provides no national standards for benefits or eligibility ceilings. AFDC payments vary from an average of $46 per month for a family of four in Mississippi to $265 for such a family in New Jersey. The disparity in payment levels is aggravated by complicated State-by-State variations in criteria for eligibility and methods of administration. Each State has its own prescription of need standards, assets tests, incapacity tests, and requirements for school attendance and the age of children who can receive benefits. Furthermore, the day-to-day administration of the program has varied widely from State to State and locality to locality in terms of equity and responsiveness to the needs of recipients. . . .

2. Complex and inefficient administration: The paperwork and redtape associated with welfare have become notorious. Elaborate budgets of need are constructed, entailing an item-by-item investigation of the family's situation. State standards of need often bear little relation to actual payments, and complicated formulas using rateable reductions and maximum payments are applied to calculate actual benefits. Minute adjustments are made to reflect changes in the composition of the family

and the ages of its members, or as special needs arise. The resulting paperwork inundates social workers. The baroque administrative organization is fraught with error, and is largely incomprehensible to recipients and the public alike.

3. Services: The complex, localistic, and punitive character of the present welfare system destroys, in large part, the ability of the social worker to provide badly needed services to the recipient family. Not only are social workers overburdened with paperwork, but they are also forced into the role of policemen and guardians of the public purse—a role which has often been felt to be antagonistic to the client. This prevents social workers from becoming recipients' counselors. Thus most recipients are deprived of opportunities to talk with social workers and benefit from their professional training and skills.

4. Inequitable treatment of the working poor: The most striking defect of AFDC, however, and the reason that it cannot be reformed simply by adding national standards or streamlining administration, is its artificial restriction of eligibility. Since 1935, AFDC eligibility has been confined by the uncritically accepted notion that families headed by a full-time male worker do not need assistance. AFDC was accordingly designed for families headed by women and shaped by the belief female heads of households could not and should not be required to work.

The unfortunate truth, of course, is that the assumption on which AFDC rests—that the income of full-time workers is by definition adequate—is simply not valid for large numbers of families. In 1968, 39 percent of the poor families with children in this country were headed by full-time workers. Their poverty is seldom the result of a defect of character or a failure to try. It is rather the result of the inescapable fact that large numbers of jobs, for a variety of economic reasons, just do not pay an adequate wage—especially for persons with large families. . . .

Under current law, it is easily possible for a man on welfare who does no work at all to be economically better off than a man who works full time. But I believe that every man who is physically able to work should be required to do so, and that it should be in his interest to do so. Under present law, as a result of the 1967 amendments, AFDC—UF contains a work requirement. If a man complies with this requirement, however, he very often will be economically worse off than if he manages to evade the law. Thus we are telling him to penalize himself financially by taking full-time work. This is a greater sacrifice than we require of even the taxpayer in the highest bracket.

This inequity inflicted on the working poor is not rare. In 1968, over one and one-half million families—consisting of about 7.8 million persons—were headed by full-time workers and were still in poverty. Many of these people lived next door to welfare recipients who were economically better off than they were.

This unwise and unjust public policy has had predictable results in terms of social tension. First, an understandable discontent has been generated among those who are excluded and who see others no worse off than they are being assisted. Second, ominous racial overtones have developed, since current AFDC recipients—those who are helped—are about 50 percent nonwhite, while the working poor—those who are excluded—are about 70 percent white. This country can no longer afford to have one of its most important and needed antipoverty efforts viewed, by many of its citizens, as a divisive, unfair, and arbitrary failure. Such a view does not help to bring us together, does not promote understanding among people, and does not help to restore public confidence in the wisdom of our social policies.

5. Work disincentives: A further consequence of the exclusion of families headed by working men from AFDC is that it produces wrong-way work incentives—incentives which encourage less work, not more. We have created a program which penalizes rather than rewards work, a result out of character with our cultural heritage. . . .

6. Family breakup incentives: The exclusion of the working poor from federally aided assistance has yet another perverse effect—encouragement for families to dissolve, or for couples never to marry. In situations in which a full-time workingman is not making as much as his wife or the mother of his illegitimate children could receive in welfare benefits, the couple is better off financially if the man leaves the home.

The family stability problem, to be sure, is very complicated. It has many causes rooted in the complex social problems of industrialization and urbanization. We do not understand all the intricacies of family dissolution, nor do we have data that show a definite cause-and-effect relationship between welfare and family instability. But we do know that over 70 percent of the fathers of families currently on AFDC are "absent from the home," and that the present welfare system provides a prima facie incentive for breakup. Our current welfare law clearly discriminates against those intact, poor families who are making substantial efforts to work themselves out of poverty. This seems vicious and irrational. Socially, it is a self-defeating policy—one which the poor themselves see as exacting the pound of flesh of family breakup as the price for income supplementation.

7. Adult categories: The present system also produces severe problems for the adult assistance categories, although the crisis here is more muted. The same geographical inequities and administrative complexities exist for these categories as exist for AFDC. The adult programs also contain other features which are of more serious import.

In many States, the program of Old Age Assistance, Aid to the Blind, and Aid to the Permanently and Totally Disabled are funded at truly pitiful levels. Most of the recipients in these categories cannot be expected to work or receive substantial assistance from relatives or friends, but the system nevertheless allots them only tiny sums.

Also, the States control eligibility rules and administrative procedures, resulting in anomalous variations in assets tests, rules on relatives' responsibility, and work incentives from State to State.

THE BASIC PRINCIPLES OF FAMILY ASSISTANCE

Confronted with the glaring deficiencies of the existing welfare system, the President concluded that nothing short of fundamental structural reform would do. He could not in good conscience propose new patches on a jerry-built system defective to its foundation.

I want to emphasize again that this administration did not enter office determined to put into effect the specific kinds of welfare reforms which we have proposed. Neither the philosophy of the President nor our currently-restricted budgetary situation would have permitted us to propose such revolutionary and expensive legislative initiatives unless we were convinced that they were inescapably necessary.

The reform principles underlying family assistance are thus in every instance traceable to the foregoing analysis of what is wrong with AFDC. I have elaborated those wrongs in the hope that the committee would see that the recommended solutions flow from the basic defects of current law. I can summarize our cornerstone principles as follows:

1. Uniform national standards through establishment of a floor under welfare benefits, requirement of a new financial division of labor between Federal and State levels of government, and national eligibility rules;

2. More efficient administration through simplified application and benefit calculation procedures, separation of services from cash benefits, consolidation with other related programs, and Federal administration;

3. Strengthened work incentives and requirements through the elimination of "income notches," expanded training and day care, and mandatory work registration;

4. Inclusion of the working poor to achieve basic equity and anti-poverty effectiveness; and

5. Reform of adult categories to achieve more equitable and efficient programs.

I would like to discuss each of these fundamental points briefly before taking up the central question of the working poor in greater detail.

1. Uniform national standards: Family assistance will replace the 54 different State and territorial AFDC programs with a single program for families. We would also substitute a single integrated adult category system for the more than 150 different programs of aid to the aged, the blind, and the disabled.

We must recognize that Americans are mobile people, and that problems in one State have effects elsewhere. Poverty and welfare are national problems requiring national solutions. Foremost in any such national solution must be an effort to assure that citizens who live in different States do not receive grossly different treatment at the hands of their governments. We must insure that a minimum level of welfare support exists nationwide, for the problems of low-paying States like New York—and indeed, of the whole country—tomorrow. Family assistance establishes such minimum support levels: $1,600 per year (plus about $860 in food stamps) for a family of four, and $110 per month for individuals in the adult categories. . . .

2. More efficient administration: National uniform eligibility rules make possible another vital reform: simplification and streamlining of the notorious welfare paperwork and administrative morass. Family assistance terminates the present practice of basing benefits on minute investigations and computations of family budgets. Eligibility for aid would be determined on a simplified basis, which would include cross-checks of earnings data and sampling of recipients reports as protection for the system. . . .

3. Social services: . . . Family assistance would provide a new system for clients to be referred to State and county social service agencies from which they could obtain needed work-enhancing social services and counseling. These amendments require a complete separation of welfare eligibility functions and social services delivery, and incorporate a major program expansion in the area of foster care and adoptions.

Particularly important, in my estimation, is the proposed part B of the new title XX. It provides that if a Governor submits a consolidated plan which incorporates his social service program and one or more other HEW service programs, he may transfer up to 20 percent of the total funds from any one included program to another. This permits the States, for the first time, to shift Federal service funds among program categories to better meet their own State and local needs and priorities.

We believe that these new programs will revolutionize the current social services situation. The social worker will no longer be the policeman or the paper-ridden clerk, but will, in many places for the first time, be able to spend most of his or her time and energy counseling, advising, and generally assisting clients.

4. Inclusion of the working poor: As the members of this committee know, important issues are the most difficult ones. We think the single most important issue which must be faced if we are to have meaningful welfare reform is whether an income supplement for the working poor is essential. This is a difficult question for some of you. Many arguments support a negative answer. I believe, however, that an affirmative answer to that question is inescapable. Four principal considerations seem compelling to me:

(a) The need to provide equity: First, very simply, coverage of the working poor eliminates the harshest inequities of the present system. If we require that men must work to be eligible for assistance, how can we in good conscience fail to ensure that full-time workers are better off financially than people who don't work? Failure to supplement the incomes of full-time workers can make it profitable for them not to work.

(b) Reinforcement of the free market system: Second, we believe that granting public income supplements to low-wage workers is the only effective way of dealing with the poverty and inequities to which this group is subject while at the same time preserving a free market system. Our economy creates unparalleled opportunities for workers, but simultaneously creates disadvantages for a minority of workers. A significant number of jobs at the low end of the wage scale is an unavoidable result of a free market economy in which wages are set primarily by worker productivity and competitive forces. . . .

(c) Work incentives: Third, quite aside from arguments based on equity, it is impossible to establish a proper system of work incentives and at the same time exclude the working poor. . . .

(d) Antipoverty effectiveness: Fourth, we should extend income supplements to the working poor to attack fundamental problems of poverty. As the committee knows, 39 percent of the poor live in families headed by a full-time worker. At the same time, AFDC reaches only 35 percent of the poor children in the country. Family Assistance, on the other hand, will reach 65 percent of all poor people and 100 percent of all poor families with children. FAP payments to working families with children will move almost 2 million persons across the poverty line, and an additional 500,000 persons across the low-income line. . . .

5. Strengthened work incentives and requirements: As the committee knows, no principle in the family assistance plan is more important to this administration than strengthening the work incentives of the current welfare system. . . .

. . . To make the work incentives and requirements effective, we have included a comprehensive program of manpower training and child care, with over $600 million in additional funding. We plan to train thousands of FAP recipients each year, teaching them new skills and upgrading old ones. We also plan to provide day care for every FAP family which needs it, both while its breadwinner is engaged in training and after he has taken a job.

Building on the initiatives which this committee undertook in 1967, the family assistance plan relies on both incentives and a strengthened work requirement. Recipients must register for and accept work or work training to receive FAP benefits. If they do not comply with this requirement, they will lose $500 per year in benefits. I want to reemphasize that each and every able-bodied adult recipient, with limited exceptions strictly defined in the bill, is required to enter training or employment.

6. Incentives for families to remain together: Because we have included the working poor in our income supplementation, improved work incentives, and established penalties and requirements which are consistent with the basic philosophy of income maintenance, we believe that we have substantially reduced—and in many cases eliminated—the incentives for families to break up if they wish to supplement their incomes with public assistance. . . .

7. Adult categories: We have improved the adult categories in two significant ways. First, we have provided a national set of eligibility standards and a national minimum level of income for all recipients of these categories of aid. This will mean a great deal in simplifying administration, increasing dignity of the recipients, and eliminating much of the poverty which now plagues these people. I might add here that under this bill, an aged couple's minimum income from all sources would be greater than a poverty level income, and that a single aged individual's minimum income would be more than 80 percent of the poverty level.

The second major improvement in the adult categories is establishment of nationwide eligibility rules, following the same principles as family assistance, to replace the present complex of State-by-State variations. . . .

CONCLUSION

I have tried to explain and re-create for you some of the reasons we have made the decisions on the welfare reform which is before you today. We have presented, for your consideration, a program designed by reasonable men to meet a critical series of problems. It is, to be sure, not perfect. But then, it has been designated by men, and we are not perfect.

The problems demand the best that is in us, and we have given this issue our best efforts. I am convinced of the need for an income maintenance system to replace the current nonsystem.

We must remember that this system cannot solve the problems of severe labor dislocation, inadequate coverage of other social insurance programs–such as unemployment insurance and social security–or inadequate education. This program can only be expected to give us a new perspective from which to examine current and future welfare problems, and a new foundation upon which to build.

The issue of income maintenance and family assistance is exceedingly vast and complex. Finding solutions within it is an exciting challenge with great implications for the future of this Nation's poor, and indeed, of us all. . . .

17 Manpower Policy: The Role of the Federal Government

Gerald Rosenthal

The decade of the 1960s was a period of significant social and economic experimentation. Each of the many threads of social policy embedded in the fabric of experimentation represented a progression from the past; but, in some cases, new formalizations of social policies became evident and provided new frameworks around which to structure programs. Such a formalization is manpower policy.

While each of the programs which make up the federal manpower policy reflects antecedents in previous decades, the idea of a specific manpower policy is a fairly new one. As first formally articulated in the president's message on manpower in 1964, the objectives of an "active manpower policy" were:

1. To develop the abilities of our people.

2. To create jobs to make the most of those abilities.

3. To link the first two, to match people and jobs.

Each of these objectives is also served by other areas of social policy. Educational policy is certainly designed "to develop the abilities of our people" while

From: "Manpower Policy: The Role of the Federal Government," by Gerald Rosenthal, is reprinted from *American Behavioral Scientist,* Volume 15, Number 5 (May-June 1972), pp. 697-711, by permission of the publisher, Sage Publications, Inc.

Gerald Rosenthal is Associate Professor of Economics at Brandeis University.

the commitments embodied in overall economic policy include maximizing employment and the availability of jobs.

Perhaps more important is the fact that each of these tasks in our society has been primarily dealt with in the context of the private labor market. The function of the labor market is to provide a basis for matching people and jobs and to do this in a way that maximizes the degree to which individuals will undertake employment in economic activities, where their skills will make the greatest contribution to output and, therefore, which will yield to them the greatest income. In such a private market, people will tend to acquire those skills which will maximize their incomes (which society most desires). Changes in desired skills will be effected through changes in wages. While the existing skills in the labor force might tend to be somewhat stable, new entrants to the labor force will tend to move toward those jobs which embody the new, more highly valued, skills.

If this constant evolution of the skill "capital" in the labor force keeps pace with the changes in technology which adapt industry's requirements for labor, it is possible to implement technical change while maintaining high levels of demand for the skills of the existing labor force. If technical change occurs more rapidly than the labor force can adapt, either the pace of technical change must be retarded or the pace of labor force adaptation must be accelerated. In most cases, the national manpower policies have developed in response to observed deficiencies in the ability of the labor market to meet the twin social objectives of economic growth (served by effective utilization of the labor supply) and income adequacy (served primarily by the effectiveness of employment as a source of income). The moves toward formal manpower policies through developments in other areas of social policy represent such responses.

If the objectives of manpower policy are also served by other areas of social policy, why is it appropriate to consider manpower policy as a distinct area of endeavor? To some extent, the answer can be found in an examination of the earlier streams of development of the federal role in occupations education and training, job creation, and employment.

PRE-1960 DEVELOPMENTS

The federal role in occupational education and training might be dated from the Morrill Act of 1862 which provided grants of land for agricultural colleges. While these colleges formed the base for many higher education facilities in the western states, the agricultural emphasis was consistent with a simultaneous policy of opening western lands to agriculture and can be viewed as upgrading abilities of labor for emerging areas of employment opportunity and economic development needs.

With the skilled worker shortages of World War I came the development of the current system of vocational education, a federal-state program with an emphasis on providing formal training for nonprofessional occupations. The passage of the Smith-Hughes Act of 1917 provided the basis for what is now the largest source of such formal training. The original act emphasized education in agriculture, trade and industrial education, and home economics and established a federal board for vocational education. (This Board was abolished in 1933 and its responsibility transferred to the Commissioner of Education.) The emphasis was on training people with specific skills for specific occupations. The vehicle was an injection of funds to subsidize the development of vocational training within the educational system through grants and program reimbursement. Its objective was, again, to meet the manpower needs of a growing industrial society.

With the ending of World War II, another significant piece of federal legislation supporting training and higher education was passed–the Serviceman's Readjustment Act of 1944, known as the G.I. Bill of Rights. This Act provided a major impetus to upgrading the skills of the labor force by paying tuition and living allowances for returning servicemen receiving education or occupational training. Unlike previous federal efforts to support these activities, the payments were targeted to the individuals receiving training and not to particular occupations or educational institutions. While the legislation developed as a vehicle for assisting returning servicemen in reentering the labor force, the emphasis on education and training rather than strict monetary compensation was a significant departure from previous policies, as was the emphasis on individual choice as opposed to specific categories of skill requirements.

The last major federal effort in support of occupational education and training prior to the 1960s occurred in response to the Soviet launching of the satellite Sputnik. This display of technological accomplishment was quickly followed by a strong sense of national urgency in the need for trained scientific personnel. Only months later, the National Defense Education Act of 1958 was passed by Congress. This Act provided a program of fellowships and other aid to scientific and technical education, again reverting to the national strategy of serving economic development needs through federal support of training and education.

While the above developments emphasized the federal role in formal training, other legislation prior to the 1960s was directed at different aspects of manpower policy. The period of the Great Depression resulted in a number of particularly significant developments. The existence of mass unemployment highlighted the need for deliberate public efforts to supplement the private workings of the labor market. During the 1930s, such efforts took the form of efforts both to improve the actual job acquisition process and the direct creation of employment opportunities.

The former effort was primarily embodied in the Wagner-Peyser Act of 1933 which established the Federal-State Employment Service system. This activity provided a vehicle both for registering vacancies and for obtaining information as to jobs available by seekers of employment. This mechanism, designed to improve the matching of workers and jobs, is central to implementing many of the programs which make up our current manpower policies.

The Social Security Act, passed in 1935, provided a basis for the establishment of a system (or systems) of unemployment insurance for workers who were temporarily out of a job. The vehicle for registering for benefits was the Public Employment Office where recipients of benefits were to register for employment. As unemployment benefits cover greater proportions of the labor force, who, in turn, over time have cause to claim these benefits, the legitimacy of the Public Employment Office as "matcher" of men and jobs tends to increase.

The job creation effort was structured around a number of programs, most significant of which were the Civilian Conservation Corps and the National Youth Administration. Each of these programs provided direct employment and some small component of training. Although temporary, the experience with such programs influenced the development of more recent programs such as the Job Corps and the neighborhood Youth Corps.

The other major pre-1960 legislative commitment to serve the goals of a national manpower policy was the Employment Act of 1946. This legislation formalized the federal obligation to use the tools of aggregate economic policy to maintain high levels of employment. The Act provided no guarantee of employment. It set up the Council of Economic Advisers to monitor the economic state of the nation with particular emphasis on employment and the employment implications of aggregate fiscal and monetary policy. Unlike other legislation noted, the Act was directed at no particular segment of the population nor particular industry or area of economic development. Rather, the overall commitment served to legitimize a federal role in economic behavior previously held to be primarily a private market activity.

While each of these developing streams of national policy consisted of ad hoc pieces of legislation which responded to perceived social needs, two major labor market policy foci are evidenced. Much of the legislation is directed at investing in those forms of skill acquisition which will contribute most to perceived areas of economic development needs. The Morrill Act, Vocational Education Act, and the National Defense Act were all targeted to providing the skilled manpower pool necessary to support desired areas of economic growth. Legislation such as the G.I. Bill emphasized opportunities for individual choice leaving to the labor market the influencing of the nature of those choices. This dichotomy between general investment in human capital and targeted investment in particular skills basically reflects different views as to the efficiency of the labor market as a device to maximize the value of labor in the productive process. Neither approach places major emphasis on directly maximizing the effectiveness of employment as a source of income. To some extent, the general investment strategies of the G.I. Bill were justified by the expectation of postwar recession; the basic strategy was still on the supply side of the labor market.

The other major strategy is reflected in job creation programs and the Employment Act of 1946. These programs are directed at the demand side of the labor market. Here, too, a distinction can be made between general and specific policies. The aggregate economic policies embodied in the Employment Act of 1946 are directed at maintaining an overall high level of demand for labor. Such high levels of demand should contribute to more effective market choices on the part of the labor force. The job creation activities were specifically targeted to those who were not able to obtain employment by adding to the demand side of the labor market specific employment opportunities for the short run while aggregate demand for labor was insufficient.

In all cases, however, prior to the 1960s, policies were directed at overall social ends, either increasing capacity of labor force to contribute to economic growth or increasing available employment for the labor force as a whole.

THE DECADE OF THE 1960s AND EMERGING NATIONAL MANPOWER POLICY

By the late 1950s, a number of developments became evident which set the stage for a more formal integration and expansion of federal efforts to deal with manpower problems. Of major importance were the continuing high levels of unemployment following the recession of 1958 with unemployment rates over five percent during the recovery periods after 1958 and 1961. This contrasted unfavorably with the recovery experience after 1954 where unemployment dipped below the four percent level. The high levels of unemployment were accompanied by increased awareness of the significance of long-term unemployment as reflected by using up of unemployment compensation benefits and other survey data.

The concern with unemployment was heightened by an awareness of the implications of the postwar "baby boom." Significant increases in numbers of youth, high dropout rates after age 16, particularly among children in areas with the highest unemployment, and significantly higher unemployment levels for the 16-24 age group would combine to make the problems of unemployment get worse rather than better without specific efforts to deal with them.

The increasing concern with problems of unemployment and its uneven distribution within the country gave support to a growing concern with problems of poverty. The developments of the 1960s began to make it clear that significant numbers of the population were confronting long and extended periods of economic deprivation, not only due to lowness of income but to lack of availability of employment opportunity generally. In some cases, these problems reflected changes in population patterns. The significant shrinkage in employment opportunities in rural areas led to the identification of a number of parts of the country which were chronically economically depressed. The problems of discrimination, not only within the employment sector, but within education generally, led to a large addition to the potential labor force, particularly among nonwhite youth between 16 and 24, who were devoid of any significant skills or training with promise of employability.

The problems began to focus on significant areas of the country, where the level of economic activity was inadequate to generate jobs without regard to the training of the individual and the identification of growing groups in our population for whom employment potential was very low because of the lack of adequate education and training. In this latter group, not only were unemployment rates high, but labor-force participation rates were considerably lower than that which might be expected under circumstances of normal employment opportunity. This indicated that the unemployment rate was actually understating the potential need for employment in that population. Because the focus of the problem was on poverty, part of the solutions were sought in terms of income maintenance programs and development of that area of social policy. However, in the long run, the major thrust was felt to be increased emphasis on training and skill acquisition and, in regard to the chronically depressed areas, an overall strategy of economic development which had within it the promise of increased employment opportunity.

Prior to 1961, most of the federal efforts in these areas were limited to job placements under federal-state employment services and the earlier-mentioned emphasis on vocational education and, to a smaller degree, apprenticeship training. However, in 1961, the chronically depressed area problem had achieved sufficient significance to result in the passage of the Area Redevelopment Act. Although the major focus of the Act was economic development (loans for capital construction and federal investment in other areas of public capital), it also set aside money for retraining of unemployed workers when economic employment opportunities became available or were in the process of being developed. Under this legislation, unemployed persons who were selected to train were eligible to receive subsistence payments at levels comparable to unemployment compensation benefits paid in those states where the workers would receive the training. Thus, income maintenance payments were incorporated in a program of providing training opportunities. While the funding of the Area Redevelopment Act was limited and its coverage relatively narrow, the experience of training in the Area Redevelopment Act provided a basis for the development of a more concentrated federal effort in the area of direct manpower training.

This effort was embodied primarily in the Manpower Development and Training Act passed in 1962. The Act represented a major formal federal commitment to support the training of unemployed and underemployed workers and established a national program to provide that training. The Act noted "that even in periods of high unemployment, many employment opportunities remained unfilled because of the shortages of qualified personnel; and that it is in the national interest that current and perspective manpower shortages be identified and that persons who can be qualified for these positions through education and training be sought out and trained as quickly as is reasonably possible."

The components of that legislation included not only the program of occupational training but an emphasis on expansion of manpower research and the requirement of annual reports by the Secretary of Labor on manpower requirements, resources, utilization, and training. This means that the program had within it not only the training components, but additional activities ostensibly devoted to identifying the directions for such training and the encouragement of experimentation and demonstration of new methods of making such training effective.

Although the original emphasis was the retraining of experienced adult family heads who had been displaced by economic and technological change, as the program developed its emphasis has shifted to increasing attention to the training needs of the disadvantaged. After the initial year, the program of youth training was considerably enlarged and because lack of education served to preclude the effectiveness of occupational training of the hard-core unemployed, additional provisions were made for including basic education of MDTA trainees within the context of occupational training. By 1966, specific commitment in this redirection came in the form of a decision that 65% of the total effort should be directed at training the disadvantaged, with the remainder being devoted to meeting identified requirements for trained personnel in those occupational categories with identified skill shortages.

A significant aspect of the development of training programs under the Area Redevelopment Act and the Manpower Development and

Training Act has been continued emphases of the interrelationships among what had been previously independent programs. The connection around the training programs of employment services, vocational education, and problems of manpower projection provides an integration of essential components of a national manpower policy. These two pieces of legislation represent the primary legislative articulation of the components of such policy and the forms which such policies are likely to take.

While the Manpower Development and Training Act was the prime vehicle for formulating a national manpower policy, the Economic Opportunity act of 1964 contained a number of components which represent additional elements. The Job Corps had as its primary goal the provision of education and training for youths from low-income households who had no skills and, in many cases, no preparation for work, in a residential setting. It emphasizes basic education and reading skills, as well as training and has a strong rehabilitation perspective as well as actual job training objectives. The disadvantage of such a residential system is that the costs are extremely high. For many reasons, both those relating to cost and those relating to the social implications of operating residental settings for large numbers of impoverished youth, the Job Corps program itself has been highly controversial.

The Neighborhood Youth Corps, however, has been well received. Its objectives are provision of part-time employment to in-school youths and to help school dropouts develop employment and occupational potential. Although the congressional intent was two-pronged, in actual fact the Neighborhood Youth Corps turns out to be most significantly an income-support program. Very few of the projects provide remedial education and vocational training in a systematic way. Although most of the participants in the out-of-school program are high school dropouts, there has been difficulty in developing jobs for Neighborhood Youth Corps "graduates," and in many cases the employment experience provided while enrolled has little applicability in the employment market. The role of the program–particularly the in-school program–in providing income support and offsetting, to some extent, high dropout rates is likely to be its major significant contribution.

Title V of the Economic Opportunity Act established the work experience and training program. Its objective was the establishment of projects providing work experience and training resulting in welfare recipients and other "needy adults" becoming self-supporting. This program *specifically directed to welfare recipients* highlighted some of the inconsistencies between manpower development and work training strategies and the structure of welfare system. In many cases, welfare recipients were taxed 100% (that is, had their payments reduced by an amount equal to the value of their earnings). This provided a significant disincentive to the acquisition of employment beyond that which is provided for in the work experience and training project. It has been argued that this program represents a major step toward establishing the government as "employer of last resort," and that the increased emphasis on work experience and training within public assistance programs depends on maintaining employment opportunities at high levels, both by general economic policy and by the actual creation of employment, in order for such programs to manifest themselves in any significant reduction in welfare expenditures.

CENTRAL ISSUES

The above discussion of the major components of national manpower policy point up a number of issues central to a discussion of future developments.

Institutional Versus On-the-Job Training

The MDTA initially provided for two major types of manpower training; institutional training where federally paid instructors provide specific skill training and counseling in a site devoted to training, and on-the-job training (OJT) where workers are hired and trained while employed by a company with a training contract from the government. Institutional training provides trainees with allowances somewhat in excess of unemployment benefit levels. In addition, the government must hire the instructors and incur all of the costs associated with operating a training facility. In OJT, the government subsidizes the employer for the costs of training beyond those which would be incurred appropriately within the production process.

Institutional training tends to emphasize more general skills and is more consistent with a manpower policy devoted to overall investment in human capital. OJT is more specifically tailored to training in specific jobs within specific companies. The experience with MDTA shows a consistent shift toward OJT although institutional programs still represent a major share of the budget. This shift reflects both the higher costs of institutional training and the relatively poor posttraining employment experiences of trainees in the current periods of fairly substantial unemployment.

The shift toward OJT as a vehicle for government's intervention in training activities is also reflected in a move to OJT programs outside of MDTA. The major vehicle is the JOBS (Job Opportunities in the Business Sector) program. This is a cooperative venture between the National

Alliance of Businessmen and the Labor Department, directed at encouraging businesses to hire disadvantaged workers. (See Table 1.) Although initially focused on voluntary cooperation by businesses, increasingly business efforts are being stimulated by government training grants which reimburse cooperating industries for the costs of training. The increasing expenditures in this program illustrate the growing emphasis on private business in the national manpower policy.

Skills of People

The increasing emphasis on private market behavior in national manpower policy raises a significant issue about the appropriate federal role.

TABLE 1 Expenditures: Manpower Policy—1963-69

	Fiscal year (thousands)		
	1963	*1966*	*1969*
MDTA–Institutional	$55,219	$281,710	$196,629
OJT	851	57,939	56,429
JOBS	–	–	160,821

Source: Manpower Report of the President, 1970.

The resolution of such an issue depends on the overall objectives of such policies. In particular, whether the objective is related to issues of individual unemployment and income maintenance or at overall investment in human capital and its implications for economic growth. Both the split between institutional training and OJT and the increasing emphasis on training the disadvantaged indicate a move toward using national manpower policy as a vehicle for reducing individual unemployment. The shifts in MDTA from retraining workers suffering from obsolescence of skills to training the disadvantaged have required numerous amendments to the original Act and additional programs. By the late 1960s, over 27 job training programs were operational. These programs were authorized by 11 statutes and operated by 17 different federal agencies. This proliferation reflects the adaptation of manpower policies to shifting objectives with growing emphasis on targeting training to specific groups and specific jobs.

Manpower Policy and Welfare Policy

The shift toward training the disadvantaged is associated with a trend toward integration of manpower programs with welfare programs–in particular, those within the AFDC category. The earlier work experience and training program and the later WIN (Work Incentive) program specifically direct training efforts to public assistance recipients. More recently, interest is growing for requiring public assistance recipients to register for work with the Federal Employment Office in order to remain eligible for benefits. Such requirements are already operational in New York. While the percentage of AFDC recipients who are employable is not likely to be large, in absolute numbers such policies create a large pool of low-skilled job seekers for whom the promise of employment is held out as a matter of public policy.

Such requirements are built into the proposed Nixon Administration Family Assistance Program (FAP), but experience indicates that the effectiveness of such a requirement in reducing the welfare load is highly dependent on overall economic policies to increase employment, manpower policies to provide training, educational policies to provide basic education, and other welfare policies such as child care and the like, which are tailored to maximize the employment potential of the welfare population. This developing national strategy points out not only the degree to which the objectives of manpower, welfare, education, and economic policies are shared, but that the effectiveness of specific strategies within each depend for their success on other strategies within other areas of social policy.

The Future of National Manpower Policy

The experience of the period of the 1960s reflects a growing synthesis of programs and strategies around the development of an "active manpower policy." Such strategies, alone, cannot deal with the basic societal issues of rapid technical change, changing skill requirements in society, persistent long-run unemployment, and the impact of social and economic discrimination on participation in the fruits of society. The basic cornerstone of national policy must be an effective economic policy designed to maintain adequate employment opportunity. Without such a setting, the contribution to social objectives of manpower policy is severely limited.

The emphasis over the 1970s is likely to be in an integration of training and employment services targeted to welfare population needs. The success of such policies in serving welfare policy objectives will depend on the overall effectiveness of employment-generating policies. The short-run prognosis suggests a growing pressure for expansion of job creation activities, particularly in public service employment and through expanded New Careers strategies as an element of national manpower policies. Such policies are beginning to be manifested in growing interest in capitalizing on the growth in employment in certain areas, particularly health care, by federal programs to support the participation of disadvantaged groups in sharing the growth in employment.

This emphasis, together with the growing role of the U.S. Employment Service as a national labor market mechanism will probably provide most of the focus for national manpower policy over the next decade. In the longer run, an effective role for national manpower policy will probably require a shift toward better projection of manpower needs and integration of those findings into educational policies rather than the shortrun strategy of having manpower policies tailored to welfare policy needs. The political pressures of the 1970s will probably make this latter focus the major influence on national manpower policy in the near term.

1. Daniel Hamermesh, *Manpower Policy and the Economy.* (Cambridge, Mass.: General Learning Corporation.) 1971.

2. Sar Levitan, and Irving Siegel, *Dimensions of Manpower Policy: Programs and Research.* (Baltimore: Johns Hopkins Press.) 1966.

3. Garth Mangum, *The Emergence of Manpower Policy.* (New York: Holt, Rinehart & Winston.) 1969.

4. U.S. Government, *Manpower Report of the President* (Washington, D.C.: Government Printing Office. 1964, 1969, 1972)

5. Gerald Rosenthal, "Social policy components of economic planning," *Encyclopedia of Social Work.* (New York: National Association of Social Workers, 1971.) pp. 1377–1385.

6. U.S. Congress, Joint Economic Committee *Federal Programs for the Development of Human Resources.* (Washington, D.C., 1968).

Higher Education and the Federal Government

INTRODUCTION TO CHAPTER SIX Most of the nation's 2,300 colleges and universities have little direct association with the federal government. Congress has passed few laws regulating them (such regulation flows from state legislatures), and they receive relatively little money from the federal government (most of their money comes from state appropriations, gifts, return on investments, and tuition). But some universities are heavily dependent on federal assistance.

THE SCOPE OF FEDERAL SUPPORT

Large-scale federal aid to higher education dates back to the Morrill Land Grant Act of 1862, in which public lands were provided as sites for state universities. The Second Morrill Act in 1890 provided federal money to support instruction in particular areas (especially engineering and agriculture). The Hatch Act of 1887 and the Smith-Lever Act of 1914 established the Agricultural Experiment Stations and Agricultural Extension Service, respectively. During the Depression universities were involved in the Work Projects Administration and National Youth Administration. During World War II faculty members carried on a wide variety of war-related research, development, and engineering projects. After the war federal support for university research programs increased rapidly.

In fiscal 1963 colleges and universities received about $0.93 billion for research and development (R & D), mostly in the form of support for specific research projects funded by a variety of federal agencies, and in fiscal 1970 about $1.67 billion was spent for the same purpose (see Table 1). In fiscal 1963 university-administered research centers received about $0.70 billion and in fiscal 1970 they received about $0.96 billion. In fiscal 1963 miscellaneous federal assistance (scholarships, student loans, dormitory construction loans, etc.) totaled about $0.48 billion, and in fiscal 1970 the figure was about $1.56 billion. The totals represent nearly a three hundredfold increase since 1940 and a near tripling in the last decade. However, a slowdown in federal assistance began in fiscal 1967. Fiscal 1968, 1969, and 1970 saw cuts in federal assistance, if inflation is taken into account.

CHARACTERISTICS OF FEDERAL SUPPORT

Prior to fiscal 1965 federal college and university support stressed research and development, with only 22.8 percent of total federal obligations devoted to general educational programs. Fiscal 1965 brought a marked shift in emphasis toward construction of new facilities and general improvement of educational and training programs. In fiscal 1969, 45.5 percent of federal obligations to colleges and universities were devoted to these programs. After fiscal 1967 the percentage began to drop; in fiscal 1970 it was 37.4 percent. Responsibility for administration of the new programs was assigned by Congress to the Department of Health, Education, and Welfare. Other agencies which contribute heavily to colleges and universities are the Department of Defense, the National Science Foundation, the Atomic Energy Commission, the Department of Agriculture, and the National Aeronautics and Space Administration. Most of the research money is devoted to the natural sciences, medicine, and engineering. The social sciences and humanities receive relatively little.

Money for such things as scholarships and dormitory construction loans is distributed among many institutions. For example, in fiscal 1968, some 2,174 colleges and universities received federal money.[1] But much of the money being spent on research is concentrated in a few states and a few institutions. For example, in fiscal 1968 universities in California, New York, Massachusetts, Pennsylvania, and Illinois received a total of about $0.99 billion for scientific activities (mainly research and development), which represented 42.3 percent of federal obligations for scientific activities.[2] And within each of these states only a few universities received significant amounts of money. For example, in Massachusetts two institu-

TABLE 1 Federal Obligations to Colleges, Universities, and University Administered Research Centers, Fiscal 1963–1970 (dollar amounts in billions)

	Total Federal Obligations		College and University R&D and R&D Plant		University Research Centers		Miscellaneous	
Year	Amount	% increase in one year	Amount	% of total	Amount	% of total	Amount	% of total
1963	2.11		0.93	44.0	0.70	33.2	0.48	22.8
1964	2.35	+10.9	1.08	46.0	0.72	30.6	0.55	23.4
1965	3.03	+30.0	1.22	40.3	0.73	24.1	1.08	35.6
1966	3.78	+24.3	1.37	36.2	0.77	20.4	1.64	43.4
1967	4.10	+ 8.5	1.44	35.2	0.79	19.3	1.87	45.5
1968	4.20	+ 2.4	1.52	36.2	0.83	19.8	1.85	44.0
1969	4.35	+ 3.6	1.61	37.0	0.84	19.3	1.90	43.7
1970	4.19	– 3.7	1.67	39.8	0.96	22.8	1.56	37.4

Sources: National Science Foundation, *Federal Funds for Research, Development, and Other Scientific Activities: Fiscal Years 1968, 1969, 1970,* pp. 120–21; National Science Foundation, *Federal Support to Universities and Colleges Fiscal Year 1968,* pp. 3, 38; National Science Foundation, *Federal Funds for Research and Development and Other Scientific Activities: Fiscal Years 1969, 1970, 1971.*

tions received 75 percent of the money—the Massachusetts Institute of Technology and Harvard University. In Illinois, a state which contains about 140 colleges and universities, the University of Illinois, the University of Chicago, and Northwestern University received 79 percent of the federal money for scientific activities.[3] In fiscal 1968 roughly 5 percent of the nation's colleges and universities received 85 percent of the federal support for scientific activities.[4]

READINGS IN THIS CHAPTER

Introduction: Grayson Kirk

The article by Grayson Kirk is an analysis of the effects of federal research support on universities. The reader should remember that this article is drawn from a presentation made by Kirk before the Select Committee on Government Research of the U.S. House of Representatives. At the time of the presentation Kirk was president of Columbia University, an institution heavily dependent on federal assistance. Indeed, in the article Kirk notes that half of Columbia's operating budget came from federal sources. Kirk covers the following topics:

1. The impact of federal R & D money on the quality of teaching. "It is sometimes said that the students are shortchanged because the best teachers become absorbed in research, and reduce their concern with teaching or even cease teaching entirely."

2. The impact on the social sciences and humanities of federal support of the natural sciences and engineering. "We must ask whether this flow of funds into scientific fields has created a distortion or imbalance within the universities because the social sciences and the humanities have become the poor relations in the academic community subsisting on mere crumbs from the budgetary table."

3. The impact of federal money on pure research in universities. "A third contention is that Federal funds divert the universities from their true function, which is pure or basic research, to an undue emphasis on applied research."

4. The possibility that federal money leads to federal control of universities. "It is sometimes said that the universities may lose their independence because they have accepted such large grants and contracts from the federal government."

The Kirk article also includes a description of some administrative problems related to federal programs.

Alternative Modes of Support: Fawcett

The article by Novice G. Fawcett is also taken from a presentation before the Select Committee on Government Research. Fawcett opens his statement with two closely related points. "It is basic research—university research, if you will—that has given this country its position of world leadership, and without university research, that position cannot be maintained." "There would be no substantial research effort in American universities today without federal support."

After noting that most federal support of university research has been given on an individual project basis, Fawcett severely criticizes the federal government's near total reliance on this approach and advocates the use of institutional grants as well as project support. An institutional grant would be distributed within the university by the university administration.

There is a sharp contradiction between Fawcett and Kirk; Kirk completely supports the project support system and Fawcett criticizes it. It is probably not an accident that Columbia has been extremely successful in obtaining funds under the project approach (in fiscal 1968 only six other universities received more federal money than Columbia), while the institutions which Fawcett represented as president of the Association of State Universities and Land Grant Colleges believed that they were being shortchanged. They have consistently pushed for changes in federal criteria for distributing money. Fawcett represented this position in his presentation.

Impact of Federal Money on State Systems of Higher Education: Paltridge

So far the readings have concentrated on the impact of federal support on individual universities. This is because well over 90 percent of federal money is given to individual universities (or researchers in individual institutions). However, a growing number of federal assistance programs award money to states. The money is then distributed among the universities by some central state agency. In California this state agency is a college and university coordinating board called the Coordinating Council for Higher Education. The effects of the federal money on the California system of higher education and the Coordinating Council are described by James G. Paltridge.

[1]National Science Foundation, Federal Support to Universities and Colleges: *Fiscal Year 1968* (National Science Foundation, 1969), p. 22.

[2]Ibid., pp. 23–24.

[3]Ibid., pp. 9–10.

[4]Ibid., p. 22.

18 Federal Research Grants: The View from the Private Universities

Grayson Kirk

Our university involvement with the Federal research support program has been continuous; it has been expanding; and in all modesty I must say that it has been enormously fruitful in its results. The benefit derived by our country from the expenditure of these funds at Columbia has been incalculable.

If I had the time to do so, I could talk at great length about these research programs which we have been enabled to conduct because of Federal aid. It would be an interesting demonstration of how one university undertakes to do its best to serve this Nation. But this is not the purpose of my appearance. I have been asked to talk with you about the utility of the program, the problems it creates, and possible means whereby we can use the taxpayers' money so as to obtain maximum results with the greatest efficiency and economy.

Let me turn first to the influence which this Federal research support has had upon the universities. Naturally, I will speak primarily about our experience at Columbia, but I believe our situation is typical of that to be found in other leading universities both public and private.

From: Testimony before the Select Committee on Government Research, U.S. House of Representatives, November 1963.

Grayson Kirk is a former president of Columbia University.

First, has this great expansion of research activity impaired the effectiveness of the university as a teaching institution?

Let me begin by reminding you that the obligation of the university, considered in terms of the national interest, is just as great in the field of research as in teaching. This is what distinguishes the university from the college. If our universities were to confine their activities exclusively either to teaching, or to research, our country would suffer. The goal of the university must be to encourage both kinds of activity in proportions that are properly balanced.

It is sometimes said that the students are shortchanged because the best teachers become absorbed in research, and reduce their concern with teaching or even cease teaching entirely. Such generalizations are dangerous. The most effective university scholar is a man who combines teaching and research. . . .

I do not believe there is any danger that our major universities will be transformed into research institutes. Their current research commitments are far more of a positive aid than a detriment to teaching. At Columbia, more than 400 students in the final phases of their postgraduate training are participating in our federally supported research programs. We all learn by doing. These young people are having a research apprenticeship of a kind which they could not otherwise have, and one which will greatly increase their effectiveness as teachers and research scientists in the future.

Next, we must ask whether this flow of funds into scientific fields has created a distortion or imbalance within the universities because the social sciences and the humanities have become the poor relations in the academic community subsisting on mere crumbs from the budgetary table.

This may appear to be true but we must temper our judgment with certain other facts which are pertinent in this connection. The first is that financial needs for research in science and the humanities are vastly different. Except in the field of pure theoretical speculation, no one can carry on effective scientific research without a great array of costly equipment. . . .

Conversely, in the humanities, what, for example, does a professor of literature need for his research? He must have some time free from teaching, an assistant, travel funds, and access to a first-rate research library. In financial terms, with full allowance for the expenditures that such a library requires, the cost is relatively slight.

Moreover, because of the availability of Federal funds for scientific research, provided its costs are met in full for each project deemed worthy of Government support, the university can concentrate its own limited free funds to a greater degree upon nonscientific research fields.

Also, the availability of Federal funds for science has enabled many of the great foundations to direct more support to other fields of scholarly interest. I do not say that the humanities have all the research money they need today; I do say that their relative financial need is small and that to meet it in full would require further expenditures on a scale quite modest compared with the costs of doing the same for science.

A third contention is that Federal funds divert the universities from their true function, which is pure or basic research, to an undue emphasis upon applied research.

David Lilienthal has recently written that:

"The scientific 'boom' under Government sponsorship that followed the splitting of the atom has resulted in a rapid and disturbing alteration in the nature and functioning of our colleges and universities. Some of our major universities are becoming scientific dukedoms rather than institutions of higher learning. The scientists may still bear the honored scholarly title of professor, but in actuality they are the devisers, promoters, and administrators of projects being carried out under contracts or grants–and have little or nothing to do with teaching or basic research."

Frankly, I think Mr. Lilienthal should have studied the record more carefully before making such a charge. At least 80 percent of the Federal funds expended in support of research at Columbia goes to basic research. The remaining 20 percent flows to projects that we have undertaken at the request of the Federal Government because they have convinced us of our special competence to carry on certain activities of the highest importance to the security of the United States. It is unnecessary to remark that many who are familiar with these latter projects would regard them as basic rather than applied. What is important is that only a handful of our regular professors are concerned directly in them whereas hundreds of members of our academic staff with regular teaching duties participate with hundreds of students in basic research projects of the first kind.

Once again, it is my judgment that if any institutions have unduly sacrificed their primary commitment to basic research, this is not the fault of the Federal program which has always recognized the value to the Nation of encouraging universities to concentrate their work in the basic research field.

This, of course, is as it should be. Basic research is the thing university people want to do, and the thing they can do best. And one never knows when or how this research will suddenly develop practical applications of great importance. For example, the laser was conceived as a piece of apparatus to test certain fundamental ideas believed to govern emission and absorption of radiation, without any expectation that the outcome of the experiments would suggest the laser which now promises to revolutionize the whole field of communications. The dissertation submitted to our faculties by the doctoral candidate who performed this research contains little if any pretension to practicality. The results, however, speak for themselves.

Finally, it is said at times that the universities may lose their independence because they have accepted such large grants and contracts from the Federal Government.

Mr. Lilienthal observes that "when a third or half or more of a great university's funds come from the Government sources, the muffled tones some university officials use in discussing the issue is understandable." Well, gentlemen, I have no desire to muffle my tones about the issue because in my experience it is largely a strawman. In the past 10 years I can recall no instance when Federal agencies have used this financial lever to try to influence educational policy at Columbia.

We must bear in mind the normal process by which funds are made available. In almost every instance, the initiative comes from a person within the institution. A scholar wants to investigate something that has aroused his intellectual curiosity and he secures the approval of the university to ask support from the appropriate Federal agency. The university administration first sanctions his request and then approves the final terms of the arrangement before it is concluded. If by chance any inappropriate pressure were applied as a condition of the grant, the university needs only to reject the terms and the grant.

It is well recognized–and as fully in Washington as in the academic community–that the independence of our universities is a precious national asset the value of which permeates our whole social structure. I see no evidence that this independence is being–or is likely to be–impaired, simply because our Government has recognized that it can enrich and secure the Nation's future if it helps the universities carry on work which they want to do, which Government agencies are not well staffed to do, and which the universities could not do if Government funds were unavailable. I do not lose any sleep at night because nearly half of my university's gross operating budget comes from Federal research support.

Now let me turn briefly to some of our administrative and procedural problems.

The university, in the interest of all concerned, must interpose its central administration between its academic officers and Federal agencies. This is not always easy, because of professional relationships between scholars and Government officials, but unless this is done, the university could not maintain effective control over the volume and the nature of the federally sponsored activities which it undertakes. At

Columbia we handle this function through a special office of projects and grants.

Next, the university must exercise the greatest care to insure that its Federal funds are expended solely for the intended purpose, that they are expended frugally and efficiently, and that no financial benefit—other than the customary privilege of earning additional salary for services during the summer period—be made available to the individual professor. All of this, of course, is merely a matter of proper and carefully devised policies and administrative procedures within the university.

We do have two troublesome administrative problems. First, while we could not derive any profit from research operations, we cannot undertake much research that represents an actual out-of-pocket loss. This is so because we cannot in good conscience cover the deficit on research by appropriations from the precious unrestricted income of the university which is derived in large part from tuition and fees paid by students for their instruction. I do not propose to discuss with you the various rates of indirect-cost allowance set by different granting agencies. May I observe merely that the principle of full cost reimbursement—no more and no less—is of the utmost importance to the financial health of the Nation's universities.

At times it is said that a partial reimbursement should be sufficient because the universities should be prepared, if they wish to undertake research programs, to meet at least a part of the cost from their own operating budgets. The crux of the matter is whether the sponsored research is to be regarded merely as part of a Federal aid-to-education program or whether it is an investment in our country's scientific and technological future. As I have said, the universities simply do not have at their disposal any considerable amount of free funds which they could use for matching purposes. Therefore, the principle of less than full reimbursement would bring about a substantial reduction in the amount of research performed. The amount of Federal funds to be saved thereby would be small, and the national cost in other ways would be uncomfortably high.

The second source of our concern is over the amount and diversity of bookkeeping and accounting required. No one would advocate that the Government should fail to maintain a proper supervision over the use of its funds. But it would be helpful if the wide variety of accounting and reporting principles and practices now in use by the different agencies somehow could be made more uniform. . . .

Now we may turn to the basic questions, from the standpoint of the Federal Government, concerning the whole program. I shall comment very briefly on five possible areas of interest to this committee.

1. Is the emphasis on basic, as distinct from applied, research appropriate as a use for Federal funds?

It is always easier for the taxpayer to understand applied research because it is directed toward a tangible and specific product. Nonetheless, as I have indicated earlier, the national interest demands that basic scientific research be carried on at the greatest possible volume and momentum. Basic, rather than applied, research is responsible for our great advances in scientific and technological fields. . . .

2. Should the Government undertake, for purposes of administrative control and convenience, to channel university research support through fewer agencies?

My own university deals with a wide variety of Federal agencies, including the Public Health Service, the Navy, the Atomic Energy Commission, the National Science Foundation, the Air Force, the Army, and the National Aeronautics and Space Administration. I would oppose any effort to centralize further the research support function because the problems to be studied are so diverse and so complex that the quality of support would be impaired, even if the quantity were not, if too many kinds of support were to be filtered through a single granting agency. The present situation may at times appear to be confusing, but it is a productive confusion which is to be preferred to a more ordered sterility. . . .

3. Is it desirable to have greater uniformity in accounting and reporting procedures, and in indirect cost allowance rates?

I have just endorsed the present decentralization of Government support for research, first by agencies and then by separate programs within them, because we believe that this practice leads to the wisest technical decisions. . . .

4. Should Federal research funds be distributed more widely among our universities?

Everyone understands the reasons for the widest possible distribution of Federal funds. Whether that principle should be applied to research support depends upon whether–as indicated earlier–the whole program is to be viewed merely as aid to education or whether it is a national investment in scientific progress that must be made to yield as soon as possible the greatest possible productivity.

Financially, it is not really aid to education. The numbers of our students or of our academic staff have not grown substantially because of it, nor have our instructional budgets been relieved significantly. On the contrary, many contracts and grants do provide for something less than full reimbursement to the receiving institution. Therefore, the program is not actually aid to education but an investment in our Nation's scientific future.

If this is the case, then there need be no apology for concentration of support for research in those institutions, public and private, where the quantity and quality of scholarly manpower is such as to give the greatest promise of productivity.

As I see it, we have been–and perhaps still are–in an initial phase of growth of Federal support for research, designed to draw to the fullest possible extent upon the capabilities of our existing centers of excellence. This growth has been rapid because the funds could be absorbed immediately to good purpose by established communities of outstanding scholars. When their capabilities have been sufficiently implemented, further growth will become more gradual and will be connected with the spreading of new centers of scientific excellence throughout the land, and the men to staff these centers will have been given the finest possible training for their work. In other words, such concentration of support has been and is very much in the national interest, and especially at a time when the urgency for progress is so great.

5. Finally, is this large and growing expenditure of Government funds an appropriate use of public money?

The answer–and it is unequivocal–is "Yes." We live in an age when the future of our country depends to no small extent upon its scientific and technical progress. The rate of scientific growth accelerates constantly. Whether we speak of the conquest of outer space, the exploration of the ocean's depths, or the conquest of disease, our progress is such as would have been considered impossible a few years ago. Since our problems seem to be multiplying equally fast, our research effort becomes a vital part of our struggle for our national future.

The great universities of this country constitute one of our most precious national resources. They have placed themselves at the disposal of our people in order to expedite a great national research effort. The Government deserves praise for its foresight in developing and supporting the program. The universities have undertaken to administer it wisely and responsibly. From this joint effort all our people will benefit.

19 Federal Research Grants: The View from the State Universities

Novice G. Fawcett

The Association of State Universities and Land-Grant Colleges wants, first of all, to express its appreciation for these hearings and this study. . . .

It seems to us that your study will disclose two basically important facts–facts that can be taken as foundational stones upon which everything else will come to rest:

1. That Federal investment in basic research and training has produced dividends so important to the preservation and advancement of our material, social, and political well-being that the need for continuing and expanding that investment is no longer in question.

2. And that the basic consideration, then, becomes that of studying the mechanisms through which this investment is made in order to make certain that those mechanisms provide an effective means for enlisting the unique and vital services of the universities in the national interest without, at the same time, weakening the ability of the universities to perform these services.

It must surely be clear to all that there would be no substantial research effort in American universities today without Fed-

From: Testimony before the Select Committee on Government Research, U.S. House of Representatives, November 1963.

Novice G. Fawcett is a former president of Ohio State University and the Association of State Universities and Land Grant Colleges.

eral support. This is true if for no other reason than the cost of research in many fields today. This applies with special force to basic research, the type for which the universities have unique competence but also the type for which there is seldom any immediate commercial application and, consequently, any commercial or industrial sponsors.

But there are other–and perhaps more basic–reasons for this Federal involvement. We are today living in a national culture, civilization, and economy. The most important economic units in our Nation are national, extending from coast to coast, border to border, with thousands and even millions of stockholders dispersed throughout the country. Our potential sources of talent, too, are dispersed throughout the country, and it is in the national interest that they be developed, wherever they are. The highly trained men and women upon which the preservation and advancement of our well-being depends, is mobile. These people tend to go where opportunity exists to do the kind of work for which they have prepared. The income of these people has become one of our most important sources of national wealth and revenue, with taxation of this wealth having been largely preempted by the Federal Government–in part at least because of its mobility. We must think in terms of national interest and national involvement when we consider the need for a substantial research program.

There is, further, no other source of funds that is adequate to the magnitude of research effort that is vital to the maintenance of a highly complex, highly industrialized democracy. All other sources of university income–State and local appropriations, student fees, voluntary gift funds–are, and must be, almost wholly committed to the basically necessary task of attempting to meet the instructional needs of a rapidly increasing population in a society that increasingly demands higher educational achievement on the part of an ever-increasing percentage of its population. Only Federal assistance has made university research on a significant scale possible; and if this assistance is reduced or withdrawn, the research activity will of necessity be materially reduced. There simply will be no other choice for the universities. . . .

It must be understood here that I am talking about basic research, or that type for which the universities have unique competence and for which they provide unique conditions. This type of research constitutes only about one-tenth of the Federal expenditures for research and development.

This distinction between basic and applied research is important to the central question I have raised, even though, in the gray area between the two, the line dividing them is not always easily made out. A large percentage of the Federal assistance for research today is based on a purchase-of-service philosophy and an agency-to-individual contract mechanism that served admirably the urgent applied-research needs of World War II.

But, even though the philosophy and the mechanism have not changed materially, both the magnitude of the effort and the type of research needed have changed. The growth of the magnitude of the effort is well known and advertised. The significance of the shift in the type of research required, however, has not received sufficient attention. During World War II, we harvested our stock of basic knowledge without reseeding the plots from which the stock was taken in order to meet the vital imperatives of a world conflict for survival.

Since the war, then, we have rightly redirected a portion of our research effort toward this reseeding. This is inherent in the establishment of the National Science Foundation with broad responsibilities for basic research in the physical sciences and engineering and of the National Institutes of Health in medical science and health-related areas. Even the more narrowly mission-oriented agencies have found it necessary to direct at least a small percentage of their efforts toward long-range investment in the expansion of basic knowledge and theory.

This is the type of research for which the universities have unique competence. It flourishes best where career opportunities are made available to competent, dedicated scientists in an atmosphere that provides both freedom of inquiry and association with other inquisitive, informed minds, including those of advanced students, in order that the formulation of theory might complement and reinforce the search for knowledge and fact.

The purchase-of-service, agency-to-individual mechanism does not always serve well this type of research. It is difficult–sometimes even impossible–to organize a long-range exploration of basic phenomena in a particular area within neatly packaged one-, two-, or three-year projects, each with its own unit justification. The mechanism tends to drive a wedge between the instructional and the research functions of the university, to the eventual detriment of both. It discriminates in favor of the established scientist and against the newcomer. It contributes to the concentration of research competence within a few institutions, making it difficult for others to maintain and develop the resources needed in order that their ability to serve the Nation might be strengthened. The submission of proposals, the review-board mechanism, and the institution-to-agency liaison activity that are integral parts of the system are expensive in terms of the large amounts of money and the great number of individual projects now involved. Most important of all, the mechanism largely bypasses the institution itself and, in doing so, tends to deny to the institution the fiscal and administrative authority it needs to discharge its responsibilities for the programs.

Even though the approval of the institution must be attached to each proposal and each contract or grant, this approval amounts to little more than veto power, which if exercised, may result in the research worker taking his project with him to another university. Because of this, the system erodes the ability of the institution to direct its own development in research, especially in the less-affluent, less-prestigious institutions. Further, it makes it more difficult for the university's financial officer to exercise careful fiscal supervision over the project. In this situation, the university itself tends to be forced into a middle-management liaison role, providing career stability for prospective grantees and lending the prestige of the institution to the proposal.

Because of these difficulties with the grant-contract-fellowship type of relationship between the Federal Establishment and the universities, the Association of State Universities and Land-Grant Colleges has applauded and supported the general grants and the cooperative fellowship programs of the National Science Foundation and National Institutes of Health, both of which grant a greater degree of authority to the institutions over the development and management of the programs. . . .

During the legislative process establishing the National Science Foundation, the association vigorously supported attempts to get a provision calling for a geographical distribution to the States of a portion–perhaps 25 percent–of the funds made available to the foundation. We based that attempt on the tremendous record made by agricultural research through just such a mechanism. That attempt failed, as you know. We strongly feel that experience with the grant-contract-fellowship system provides still another demonstration of the merit of this suggestion for partial geographical distribution of research funds and hope that this committee will give it serious consideration and study in its deliberations. . . .

We believe that the interests of the country require support of basic research through an institutional-grant system as well as through continuance of the limited-term project system: Excessive reliance on the project system involves the difficulties and expense of attempting to manage thousands of individual projects through central staffs, review panels, and the like. More importantly, it involves a centralization of the function of judgment of what is and what is not likely to constitute an important and fruitful line of research. The whole history of research shows that it is unsound to place in the hands of any group–however wise, well motivated, and carefully chosen–the all-important responsibility of deciding what individuals, what projects, what institutions, should be selected to carry on virtually all of our research effort. There is a place–a most important and even major place–for the exercise of this kind of judgment in determining our research effort. This system has produced excellent results in many areas and should be continued. But we should not continue to place all our eggs in this basket.

There is an urgent need for attention to the largely missing component of our research effort: A program designed to strengthen institutional competence in research in a wide variety of institutions. We believe that in the long run, basic research will flourish better, be conducted more fruitfully and efficiently, under a general grants arrangement than under continued reliance almost wholly on the individual project system. A substantial decentralization of management and decision functions would make it possible for universities to build strong research staffs, to develop research competence through the association of research with teaching, and to reverse the trend toward separation of these functions within our universities. It would enable universities better to serve the Nation by organizing their programs around carefully formulated long-range objectives. It would grant institutional authority while imposing institutional responsibility. It would reduce the dangers involved in central domination of our research effort and would largely eliminate the inequities which result in the rise of pressures of various kinds to influence the awarding of research grants and contracts. We believe that a provision for a program involving both broad institutional support combined with a continuance–for some time to come at least–of individual support would be in the best interests of the country. . . .

20 New Organizational Structures and Functions for Administration of Federal Programs

James G. Paltridge

From: *California's Coordinating Council for Higher Education* (Berkeley: Center for Research and Development in Higher Education, 1966), pp. 122-36. Reprinted by permission of the author and publisher.

James G. Paltridge has written several books and articles on state university coordination in California and Wisconsin.

The burgeoning populations of most states in the union and the even greater increase in the number of youths desiring higher education have brought strains on already overburdened state governments. As a result, provision of vastly expanded public higher education facilities is almost beyond the ability of the states if they are to provide them in quantity and still maintain a desirable and necessary quality of education product.

Federal funds to higher education have been made available since the first recognition of federal responsibility in this area which was enacted into the Land Grant College Act of 1862. The "post-sputnik era" produced the National Defense Education Act of 1958. But it remained for the President-elect, John F. Kennedy, to set the pattern for the decade of the 1960s by defining a more highly educated population as a national resource and therefore a concern of the federal government.

The White House message on education sent to the 88th Congress, in which a national education act was proposed, emphasized the principles that federal financial participation must assist education and appointed an ad hoc committee to prepare a resolution setting forth the Council's opinions on the matter. It was approved by the Council in its January, 1961, meeting.[1] This resolution called upon President-elect Kennedy and the 87th Congress to consider a six-point program outlining suggested forms for federal aid to higher education.

HIGHER EDUCATION FACILITIES ACT OF 1963

The Higher Education Facilities Act of 1963[2] was the first massive appropriation of federal funds in support of national educational goals. It provided help to local, state, and private authorities so that they might build the necessary roads to reach these goals.

In January, 1964, the director of the Council reported on a meeting he had attended at the U.S. Office of Education earlier in the month and also reported that he had requested emergency state funds (such funds to be reimbursed when federal administrative funds were made available) to begin development of a state plan. Under date of January 14, 1964, Governor Edmund G. Brown wrote to the Secretary of Health, Education, and Welfare, designating the Coordinating Council for Higher Education as the state commission called for in the Higher Education Facilities Act of 1963.

In the April meeting of 1964, the Council received a report regarding progress in implementing the Higher Education Facilities Act of 1963. This report noted that the act would change the nature of the Council's responsibilities to a large degree. It continued, however, to point out that the Council and its staff must be very careful not to allow this new administrative responsibility to divert attention from the Council's highly important responsibility of long-range educational planning.[3]

CALIFORNIA STATE PLAN

The California Legislature confirmed the Council as the state commission and spelled out its responsibilities in connection with the act.[4] In the summer of 1964 the Council appointed a technical advisory committee to develop the state plan which would coordinate new programs with the overall Master Plan of 1960. The committee consisted of four representatives of the Association of Independent California Colleges and Universities, two representatives of the private colleges not members of the association, two representatives each from the University of California and the California state colleges, one representative of the California Junior College Association, and one representative of the California State Department of Education. At the November, 1964, meeting of the Council, unanimous approval was given to the state plan as developed by the Council staff and committee.[5] By certification dated December 28, 1964, the U.S. Commissioner of Education approved the California state plan as transmitted to him by the Council. This plan, in accordance with specifications in the federal act, is essentially a system for awarding points to individual college construction projects in order to establish fair priorities and make the most effective use of federal funds. The priority point system takes into account enrollment and capacity for growth, space utilization standards, availability of matching funds, enrollment of foreign students, increases in faculty salaries, and library expenditures. It gives special emphasis to library projects.

In late 1966, Congress authorized a three-year renewal and extension of the Facilities Act of 1963, though this may not be funded until the next Congress. The 1966 enactment adds a provision, not in the original act, for funding the necessary research and other costs of developing a long-range capital outlay plan by each state. These funds will be administered by local agencies, such as coordinating councils, and the planning work is to be done by them or under their direction. If fully funded, this will provide $400,000 annually to the California Council for the next three years.

HIGHER EDUCATION ACT OF 1965

The 89th Congress passed the Higher Education Act of 1965 and nineteen other acts providing federal support to education, the greater part of it to higher education.[6] Many, but not all, of these acts provided for state administration of the programs under a state plan prepared by an agency representative of the public and of the institutions of higher education in the state.

Early in 1965, the staff of the Council estimated that with the newly enacted programs approximately $860,000,000 in federal funds could be made available to California's public and private colleges and universities during the 1965-66 fiscal year. This figure did not include any student or institutional loans. It is now estimated that in 1966 this amount may quite possibly go up to over one billion dollars a year.[7]

It became increasingly apparent that the new federal programs and the proposed new state programs might be overlapping and to some extent duplicatory of existing programs. It also became clear that the detailed and explanatory information about the federal programs in the possession of the Council and its member institutions as well as in the state agencies and legislative committees was inadequate. Assemblyman

Charles Garrigus, chairman of the assembly education committee, introduced a measure, which was unanimously adopted, directing the Council to study the whole subject of federal programs affecting higher education, to conduct a survey of these federal funds, and to make recommendations for changes, either legislative or procedural, which would bring about better state coordination of these programs.[8]

In September of 1965, the Council made a number of revisions in the state plan to incorporate provisions of newly enacted federal legislation.[9] In preparation for this report, the staff reviewed the first year of operations during which ninety-one applications were received and processed, and considered the organizational and administrative procedures followed in the past year in relation to the requirements of the new federal acts. New staff positions were created and changes made in the priority points system. A system of dissemination of information related to the program was devised.

Funds for administration of the various state plans necessary under the federal programs generally are provided for under the acts. The Council has assigned the full time of an associate director to coordinate administration of these programs and has engaged additional staff people to handle this single function.

COUNCIL WASHINGTON OFFICE

In December, 1965, the staff of the Council reported on its liaison with federal funding agencies and stressed the need for improved communications, but it recommended against establishing an office in Washington. However, in the January meeting of the Council the director was urged by Council resolution to consider establishing a Council office at the Capitol.[10] The University, it was pointed out, had for some time maintained a permanent Washington office for liaison with federal agencies and foundations from which it receives grants and research contracts. The state college system had requested a budget appropriation to establish a small Washington office for this same purpose.

A number of public members questioned the wisdom of three or more California public higher education groups maintaining separate offices in the Capitol. Following the January meeting, an arrangement was worked out whereby the three groups would be housed in a single office in Washington with the Coordinating Council acting in an office management and coordinating capacity, but with the University and college representatives free to pursue grants and research contracts of direct interest to their own institutions. The legislature approved this arrangement.

TECHNICAL FACILITIES ACT

One of the nineteen federal higher education programs passed during 1965 was the Technical Services Act,[11] which provided for a $60,000,000, three-year program to establish state and regional technical service centers supported by matching federal grants to universities, local governments, and private enterprise. These centers are to disseminate the findings of science and technology to business and industry. Two primary areas of concern in this program are engineering schools and schools of business administration, both of which work closely with the business and industrial communities of the state.

The program called for the development of a state plan for allocation and distribution of funds within the state as well as for the development of a five-year plan. Very shortly after passage of this act, the governor appointed the University of California to draw up the required preliminary five-year plan and to administer the act.

The designation of the University for this administrative task was termed by other institutions a "hasty decision" on the governor's part. They argued that whenever a federal program involved more than one institution, the Council's advice should be sought on matters of administration and allocations. Prompted by this criticism, the governor wrote to the Council requesting its assistance, preliminary to the governor's approval, in reviewing the long-range plans for this program prepared by the University.[12]

DIRECT INSTITUTIONAL GRANTS VERSUS LOCAL (STATE) ADMINISTRATION

An increasing number of federal aid to higher education programs is being enacted with a provision for local administration and allocations by some state agency "broadly representative of the institutions and the general public." In most cases, the existing state coordinating agency qualifies or has been changed so that it will qualify and has been named for this administrative function. This has caused concern among some university administrators and their national associations. The land-grant colleges and universities traditionally have dealt directly with the federal government, and this practice provided a great deal of independence from state legislative and executive control. The American Council on Education, which generally has been favorable to state coordination, now appears to be opposed to further strengthening of the state's role with federal funds. ACE President Logan Wilson has commented: "All of these measures diminish the possibility of federal interference, of course, but at the cost of imposing another layer of state agencies between academic institutions and their sources of support."[13]

In the same paper, Wilson quoted David D. Henry, president of the National Association of State Universities and Land-Grant Colleges: "It was not expected that university involvement would be subsumed to state commissions and state plans in which the universities have little voice or influence, or that the executive departments of the Federal government would greatly decrease their regulatory power."[14]

Lyman Glenny predicts that with continued and mounting pressures from virtually all major states for more federal funds and fewer federal restrictions on their expenditure, administration and allocation by state agencies, rather than direct grants to institutions, will gain increasing support.[15]

In California, the idea of coordination of federal programs by the Coordinating Council seems to be well established, even though one exception was made in the case of the Technical Facilities Act. The Council has asked state officials and the legislature that it be consulted on all future agreements with federal officials, and assurance has been given that this will be done.[16]

THE CONSEQUENCES OF FEDERAL PROGRAM ADMINISTRATION

The full impact which the federal funding programs will have on the basic concepts of coordination can be appraised more fully only after institutions and state governments have had a few more years of experience in this new era. There is little question that these programs already have forced states to plan, to organize their efforts more highly, and to look further into their own futures. They have encouraged greater examination of the states' educational goals and individual institutional goals. While a certain amount of long-term planning was necessary in order to develop the state plans required under the 1963 act, the new 1966 legislation providing direct funding support for the research and study necessary to long-term planning will allow planning on a more scientific basis.

In California, the federal programs have given new authority and new breadth of activity to the coordinating mechanism. Blunt though it may be, the remark of one interviewee, who insisted upon anonymity, summarizes the new position of the Council now that it directly influences much of the funding of higher educational programs within the state. He remarked, "We subject every proposed new program [seeking federal funds] to analysis on a mutually agreed upon set of criteria, which is in the form of a scale, or point system. But if it doesn't fit into the Master Plan, it simply doesn't get funded."

The criteria on which this point system is based are occasionally challenged, and the Council's advisory committee has refined the procedure from time to time. Under this system, individual decisions on priority of funding become more clearly "programmed decisions" –subject to approval on the floor of the Council, but hopefully beyond partisan pressures and political influence. Thus the Council has greater influence–free to a large extent from the authority of the state legislature–to secure institutional compliance in the areas placed under its surveillance by the Master Plan directives. This very considerable influence, which amounts to *informal authority,* marks an important change in the Council, its organization, its operation, and its position of power in relation to the higher education institutions of the state, both public and private, as well as the agencies of state govenment.

New Council Functions and Organizations

The advent of the flood of federal programs in higher education since 1963 has created a whole new major area of functions for the Council. The two major programs, the Higher Education Facilities Act of 1963 and the omnibus Higher Education Act of 1965, required the preparation of highly detailed and technical plans for the intrastate administration of these funds.

Preparation of the state plan, in turn, implied the necessity for more thorough long-term planning of higher educational facilities and programs within the state. Toward this end, the Council requested the state department of finance to extend its long-term projections of population, general revenue incomes, and higher educational enrollments to the year 2000 rather than to the year 1975. While preparation and coordination of long-term plans for the public higher education segments of the state always have been regarded as functions of the Council, the requirements of the federal programs have given, and will continue to give, added impetus to these planning functions.

The administration of federal programs has required both procedural and organizational changes in the Council itself. An associate director and a number of analysts were added to the Council staff to give attention to this new function, which is fast becoming a major area of activity. Council procedures related to a number of its functions, particularly its review of segmental plans for new facilities and the relationship of these new facilities to educational programs, require coordination of institutional plans with available and appropriate federal programs.

New Role for the Council

The administration of federal programs within the state by the Council has brought about a number of significant changes in the role of the Council from that originally envisioned in the Master Plan. These stem, of course, from its authority to administer large sums of money which to a large extent are independent from the permissive authority of the legislature and of the state fiscal agencies. In the case of the Higher Education Facilities Act of 1963, the Council now directly authorizes by its own requisition the disbursement of funds by the state treasurer from federal funds held in his custody. In other cases, its advice on disbursements by the U.S. Commissioner or other federal officials is tantamount to final disbursing authority.

With these funds under its control, the Council has new sources of influence in shaping institutional plans as well as new sources of influence in its dealings with state officials and the legislature, for it is now an arbiter of educational programs, a *source* as well as a *coordinator* of budgetary commitments. Furthermore, for the first time in its history, the Council now is involved directly in the physical plans and, to some extent, in the educational programs of the independent universities and colleges of the state.

This new power, of course, is not without restraints, for it was authorized by statute and if used unwisely can be withdrawn by statute. It is true, also, that any institution may appeal a decision of the Council to the federal agency under whose jurisdiction general administration of the program was placed by the federal act.

Master Plan Compliance

The Council is in a much stronger position of authority to exercise each of the three functions prescribed for it under the Donahoe Act. Its *budgetary review* now must take into consideration the federally aided programs of each institution, and, hence, its recommendations are likely to have more influence upon those to whom its advice is rendered—the institutions, the state officials, and the legislature. It holds the prospect of exerting greater influence on matters involving appropriate *differentiation of functions* among the institutional segments, because if plans proposed for federal aid do not fit into the Master Plan, they are less likely to receive Council approval and priority. The Council now perceptibly exerts a stronger influence on development of *plans for orderly growth* of higher education and makes recommendations on the *need for and location of new facilities and programs.* The federal programs are forcing a greater degree of planning activity upon the institutions. The Council, in administering its own state plan, can better encourage and direct these planning activities.

Standardized Fiscal Reporting and Procedures

Still another imprint of the federal programs on the Council may be seen in the impetus that administration of these programs has given to the long-standing efforts of the Council to standardize the fiscal procedures and forms for reporting data of fiscal matters, student enrollments, space utilization, and other matters which have been of prime concern to the Council. The University, with its more sophisticated program budgeting procedures and data analysis systems, has set the pace for some time in this area. Since the advent of federal programs, the state colleges have applied new efforts to their long struggle to gain control of their own budgeting and accounting affairs. The Council now has placed with the legislature a detailed report to the joint legislative budget committee, advocating granting to the trustees of the California state colleges a broader authority for budget administration, and also has given its backing to the request of the state colleges for data processing equipment which will allow them to compile necessary reports and statistical data more completely and in less time.[17] These policies need to be extended to the junior colleges who are still laboring under budgeting and accounting procedures developed for school districts.

Segmental Relations

The power relationships surrounding the Council segment representing the private universities and colleges have been changed more than those of any other group in the Council. Heretofore, the "institutional interests" of this segment have been centered largely around their interest in the location of new public institution campuses and, to some extent, the development of new educational programs paralleling their offerings in neighboring public institutions. These have been about the only areas of competitive relations. Now, the private institutions are directly competitive with the public institutions for priority positions for funding of their projects proposed for federal aid. With this new ax of their own to grind, this segment can be expected to become more competitively active in a wider sphere of Council affairs.

The participation of junior colleges in the Higher Education Facilities Act of 1963, as well as in a number of other federal programs, gives them a new concern for Council deliberations on federal program funding.

More than ever, the public of the state through its legislature will look to the public members of the Council for assurance that monies are spent wisely and allocated fairly.

Council Leadership

The opportunities for strengthening the leadership role of the Council are increased considerably by the assignment of administrative and long-term planning functions in connection with federal programs. The records of the Council show evidence of no major conflict over the Council's administration of these funds, and this was confirmed in the interviews where it was pointed out that the Council staff's use of a technical committee on which analysts from all institutions are members has taken most competition out of the point system of arriving at priority allocations. Thus, the smooth operation of this function has added appreciably to the Council's leadership role on the part of both the institutions and the officials of state and federal government. The Council now has more authority in connection with its leadership role, and so long as this authority is used wisely and fairly in administering the state plan, its leadership role will be enhanced.

[1]Coordinating Council for Higher Education, *Minutes of January 5, 1961,* Sacramento, p. 6.

[2]U.S. Statutes, Public Law 88-204, 1963.

[3]Coordinating Council for Higher Education, *Minutes of April 28, 1964,* p. 7.

[4]California Statutes of 1964, Chapter 94.

[5]Coordinating Council for Higher Education, *Minutes of November 24, 1964,* p. 6. See also "California State Plan for the Higher Education Facilities Act of 1963," Coordinating Council for Higher Education, Sacramento, November 1964.

[6]See U.S. Statutes, Public Law 89-329, 1965. Also see "A Guide to Federal Aid to Higher Education," *College Management,* December 1965.

[7]Coordinating Council for Higher Education, *Staff Report 65-12,* June, 1965.

[8]State of California, Assembly Resolution 646, 1965.

[9]Coordinating Council for Higher Education, *Staff Report 65-17,* September, 1965.

[10]*Ibid.*

[11]U.S. Statutes, Public Law 89-182, 1965.

[12]Correspondence, Governor Edmund G. Brown to Dr. Willard B. Spalding, November 19, 1965, made a part of Coordinating Council *Minutes of Meeting of November 23, 1965.* See also *Minutes of January 25, 1965.*

[13]Logan Wilson, "Diversity and Divisiveness in Higher Education," in American Association of Junior Colleges, *Selected Papers,* 46th Annual Convention, St. Louis, Mo., 1964. p. 6.

[14]*Ibid.*

[15]Glenny, "Current Patterns in Coordinating Higher Education," *op. cit.*

[16]Council *Minutes of January 25, 1966,* p. 5.

[17]See Coordinating Council for Higher Education, "Budget Review in Public Higher Education," *Report 1022,* December 1965. Also, "Recognition of Fiscal Authority and Responsibility for the Trustees of the California State Colleges," *Staff Report 66-8, March 1966.*

Chapter SEVEN

Technology and Federalism

INTRODUCTION TO CHAPTER SEVEN Before discussing technology and federalism, "technology" must be defined; there is no universal definition of this term. Some authors think of technology strictly in terms of physical tools and methods for developing physical tools. Others argue that this definition is too narrow—that it is arbitrary to distinguish between physical tools and abstract methods (such as public administration) by which men and tools are organized to achieve complex goals. Victor Ferkiss in his book *Technological Man* agrees with this position and presents a definition of technology as "a self-conscious organized means of affecting the physical or social environment, capable of being objectified and transmitted to others, and effective largely independently of the subjective dispositions or personal talents of those involved." French philosopher Jacques Ellul feels that even a definition as broad as Ferkiss' is not useful. Ellul argues that his term "technique" offers a more useful category of analysis. For Ellul, "technique" is any complex of standardized means for attaining a predetermined result. Ferkiss' "technology" is subsumed under Ellul's "technique." Ferkiss objects that Ellul's term is so broad that it includes almost all human activities. Because our space is limited, we shall discuss only devices and methodologies which fit the first definition.

The question which this chapter seeks to answer is: What are the relationships between technology and the federal system? Four technological fields are examined: air and water pollution, creation and distribution of energy, computer and information systems in law enforcement, and weather modification.

The following propositions may aid the reader in his analysis of the articles in this chapter.

1. Technology is enormously important in the United States; technology presents tremendous opportunities and serious problems.

2. The effects of technology cross over political boundaries, including state and local boundaries. These effects can be negative (such as pollution) or positive (such as weather modification).

3. The federal system can delay solution to technological problems and thus exacerbate them.

4. Technology tends to encourage government growth in a wide variety of ways. And, to quote from the Daniel Elazar article in Chapter VIII "as the role of government in our society grows greater, all governments will continue to grow—in size, expenditures, and scope of activities."

5. The preceding hypotheses lead to the conclusion that local, state, and federal sharing of responsibilities will increase. Nevertheless, the political boundary-crossing quality of technology contains a powerful potential for centralization.

These propositions will be discussed in detail at the end of this chapter.

READINGS IN THIS CHAPTER

Air Pollution in Texas: Nathans

Philip Nathans' article focuses on the politics of air pollution in Texas. He describes the relationships between the many agencies in Houston, in Texas, and in the federal government which have responsibilities in this area. The Nathans article provides a close view of a typical heavily industrialized metropolitan area (population about two million) in a state which is typical in terms of pollution politics. In the course of his analysis he sheds considerable light on our five propositions.

The Energy Crisis: Muskie and Lippitt

The reader may believe that the term "energy crisis" is melodramatic, but it is a fact that the United States has begun to experience shortages of electrical power, petroleum fuels, and low sulfur coal. These shortages are documented daily in newspapers. In the summer of 1970, New York City experienced more than a dozen voltage reductions. In 1969 an electrical system covering Pennsylvania, New Jersey, and Maryland had over a dozen voltage reductions. Furthermore, in the last two winters there has been serious worry concerning the possibilities of fuel oil and natural gas shortages. U.S. petroleum reserves are declining (despite the Alaska North Slope discovery) while demand increases. Soon the U.S. will be obliged to import 50 percent of its petroleum. Nuclear power will help to alleviate some of these shortages, but due to various technical and legal problems, nuclear power has developed rather slowly.

The energy crisis is a multi-faceted phenomenon with a wide range of causes. One cause is greatly increased energy use on a per capita basis. In the 1960s U.S. energy consumption increased by 50 percent. Demand will increase even more rapidly in the 1970s. Furthermore, public demands for pollution-free energy production (including radioactive pollution) has slowed construction of new electrical power plants and oil refineries. Another cause of the crisis is that there has been little coordination of the production and distribution of energy in the United States. Federal and state governments are heavily involved in regulation of all phases of energy production and distribution. But there is virtually no coordination between the many federal agencies involved, and, in turn, no coordination between the states or between the states and the federal government.

In 1970 and 1971 Senator Edmund Muskie attempted to deal with one phase of the energy crisis with Senate Bill 2752, which was designed to promote intergovernmental cooperation in the control of site selection and construction of electrical power facilities for purposes of efficient production of electricity and environmental protection. The specific objective of the bill was to create a new set of federal and state agencies which would create a rational plan for designing and locating new electrical power generating plants. The bill never went beyond the committee hearing stage, but Muskie's introduction to his bill raises some of the major issues of the energy crisis.

Henry Lippitt discusses the problem of coordination between federal and state regulatory commissions. He argues that cooperation is often absent, resulting in irrational policies concerning power production and distribution and harm to innocent parties. He begins his analysis with cases concerning federal and state regulation of rates charged by two West Virginia gas companies. (The reader should not be discouraged by the technical terminology used in the first few pages of this article.) Lippitt's first case concerns a disagreement between the Federal Power Commission and the West Virginia Public Service Commission. The responsibility of these agencies is to investigate the financial situation of gas companies and determine their rates. The FPC-West Virginia commission disagreement caused the Hope Natural Gas Company to absorb $60,000 per year in expenses that were not reflected in its rates. Lippitt argues that mistakes of this sort are common.

Lippitt's study focuses on two key questions: "First, how can federal-state regulatory commission cooperation be encouraged? Second, how can federal-state regulatory conflicts be resolved?" He provides constructive answers to both questions.

The National Crime Information Center: Robinson

The FBI's National Crime Information Center (NCIC) is a network of teletype machines in local police stations connected by phone lines to state police computer centers, which are in turn connected to a central computer in Washington, D.C., operated by the FBI. The objective of the system is to provide law enforcement officers with immediate information concerning such things as stolen property, wanted persons, and revoked drivers' licenses. Local officials are encouraged to participate in the system by means of federal subsidies. Stanley Robinson, a free-lance computer programmer, is opposed to this system. He feels that the system as it is presently operated represents a direct attack on civil liberties, and that it could serve as the basis for a federal police system which would be even more threatening.

Weather Modification: National Science Foundation

Men now possess the ability to do something about the weather they have always talked about. Traditionally, weather modification has been identified solely with rain-making; this is still an important aspect of weather modification, but it is not the only one. Others include dissipating fog and suppressing lightning, hail, hurricanes, and tornadoes. In addition, man is beginning to accidentally modify weather with thermal and chemical pollution, and thought is being given to counteracting this. The National Science Foundation article is an introduction to the major political, economic, and social questions concerning weather modification. One major problem is that a change in the weather may not be beneficial to everyone in a given area. For example, rain-making may be beneficial to farmers but not resort hotel owners. Who is to decide when or if rain should be encouraged? Another problem is that the effects of weather modification are difficult to confine. It is likely that modification efforts in one state will be felt in adjoining states. There is also the problem of conflicting weather modification efforts; one can imagine local, state, and federal agencies conducting weather experiments with different objectives at a particular place and time.

THE FIVE PROPOSITIONS

In this section we reconsider the propositions set forth earlier. These propositions are rather solidly supported by the articles in this chapter as described below:

1. Technology is important. We have discussed air and water pollution, the likely possibility of severe energy shortages in the United States, a law enforcement information system which includes the names of 10 percent of the U.S. population, and a new technology which can make rain and lessen the intensity of hurricanes. Every reader is affected by these events.

2. The effects of technology cross over political boundaries. These four technological fields all demonstrate this quality.

3. The federal system can delay solution to technological problems and thus exacerbate them. This hypothesis does not apply to weather modification or the National Crime Information Center because they are not technological problems in the sense the term is being used here, but it applies to pollution and the energy crisis, which have been intensified by lack of federal-state coordination. However, it should be emphasized that a solution to state-federal coordination difficulties would not solve either problem because they have many additional causes.

4. Technology tends to encourage growth of government at all levels. Weather modification has been performed almost entirely by federal and state agencies; few private organizations are involved. The National Crime Information Center clearly involves more government spending at all levels. Nearly all analyses of the energy crisis include proposals for additional government research and the creation of new government agencies. And pollution has resulted in creation of many new city, county, state, and federal agencies.

5. Technology tends to encourage increased local, state, and federal sharing of responsibilities, but the overall tendency is toward greater centralization. Sharing is the basic philosophy of the National Crime Information Center, but, despite Stanley Robinson's projections, it is unclear whether it will result in greater centralization. Sharing has often been absent in pollution, weather modification, and energy production, but there are intense needs to improve sharing with the promise of great benefits if sharing is improved and severe losses if it is not. Rational planning in these three areas will require an increase in federal power; the problems they present are critical and they cannot be contained easily within a single state.

21 Air Pollution Control: A Case Study of Intergovernmental Relations

Philip Nathans, III

THE FEDERAL AIR POLLUTION CONTROL PROGRAM

For the past one hundred years, air pollution has been looked upon as a nuisance in the United States, but only recently has pollution been looked upon as a definite threat to the health and well-being of Americans. Prior to World War II, contaminated air was considered to be a purely local problem, and only small-scale local solutions were sought. With the increased scientific and technological advances of the postwar period, there resulted a considerable increase in the threats to environmental health.

Polluted air knows no municipal, state, or national boundary, nor can it be effectively controlled when its source lies outside the municipal or state jurisdiction of the affected area. In many regions of the country, the apathetic attitudes of local governments concerning air pollution control and the feelings of animosity which often pervade the relations between governmental units have greatly complicated control efforts. The scope of the problem is such that it requires both assistance and active participation on the part of the federal government.

Original article prepared for this volume.

Philip Nathans III is a graduate student in political science at the University of Houston.

Early Federal Control Efforts

Although many of the states reacted swiftly to the postwar surge of air pollution by enacting pollution control legislation, the federal government did not assume an active role in pollution control until 1955. The initial activities of the federal government under the 1955 legislation consisted of attempts to stimulate local control efforts, conduct research programs, and disseminate information; however, the grant-in-aid program provided by the act gave the federal government limited control over the state agencies. Up to five million dollars each year between 1955 and 1960 were authorized for appropriation to the Department of Health, Education, and Welfare for the purpose of making grants-in-aid to state and local agencies and entering into contracts for research and development on pollution with private agencies and institutions.

While the first national pollution control program resulted in the creation of a national air sampling network and the development of a series of valuable reports on community pollution problems, it failed to stimulate much growth in state and local programs. Six years after the initial grant-in-aid program was begun, only seventeen states operated control programs with annual budgets exceeding five thousand dollars.[1]

Control Under the Clean Air Act of 1963

The national air pollution control program became much more comprehensive with the enactment of the Clean Air Act of 1963. Congress established a committee on automotive air pollution and created federal criteria for clean air.[2] Under the 1963 act, the federal government could award grants directly to state and local agencies to assist them in developing, establishing, or improving control programs. This assistance program made awards in excess of nine million dollars possible for state and local agencies during the first two years of operation. These federal funds, coupled with increased spending by the state and local governments, created a 65 percent increase in total government funds available for pollution control.[3]

Further provisions of the act allowed federal action to abate interstate air pollution problems; however, careful scrutiny of the procedure for prosecution of interstate air pollution cases indicates that, with the proper hearings and notifications, a minimum of one year would be required for the Attorney General to bring suit against a violator. Federal prosecution of pollutors, thus far, has proven to be neither practical nor effective.

In addition, federal activity was authorized in the development of a comprehensive research program in motor vehicle pollution and sulfur oxide pollution. Congress encouraged a liaison between the Secretary of

Health, Education, and Welfare and the automobile and fuel industries. Only through a cooperative effort between government and industry could the program's aim of determining the effects of air pollution on health and property be accomplished.

To carry out the updated federal air pollution control program, Congress appropriated 12.9 million dollars for the 1964 fiscal year. Two years later, the annual appropriation had risen to 26 million dollars. With the financial assistance of the federal government, the number of states with air pollution control programs increased from seventeen states in 1963 to forty states in 1966. While the increased activity at the state level indicated a growing concern throughout the nation over air pollution control, it must be pointed out that a large majority of the states having pollution control programs limited those programs to research, development, and technical advice for local agencies. In 1966, only nine of the forty state control agencies included regulatory activities in their programs.[4]

Although the Clean Air Act of 1963 provided the basic framework for a comprehensive national control program, it was deficient in several areas. The act did not provide for the establishment of national emission standards for industry. Such standards are vital in the apprehension and prosecution of pollutors. In addition, the act lacked guidelines for establishing cooperative control regions, even though federal funds were provided for the creation of such regions.

Control Under the Air Quality Act of 1967

The federal approach to air pollution control and research was altered considerably by Congress in the Air Quality Act of 1967. The new program included a three-pronged attack on pollution: the adoption and implementation of air quality standards on a regional basis, national regulation of motor vehicle pollution, and updated research and development activities. The program to implement air quality standards on a regional basis was designed to stimulate cooperative activities where two or more communities share a common pollution problem. (Regulation of motor vehicle pollution included a fuels research program and the application of pollution standards to vehicles beginning with the 1968 model year.) The updated research and development activities included the construction of more sophisticated surveillance systems and the establishment of a cooperative regional, state, and local data gathering system.

To carry out the attack on air pollution, the federal government adopted two basic operating premises. The first premise was that the control of air pollution at its source is primarily the responsibility of state and local governments. The second premise was that the role of the federal government should be to provide leadership and assistance to the state and local governments.[5]

Under federal guidance, state and local governments were encouraged to create control agencies or to assign the task of air pollution control to an existing agency such as the state or county health department. The state agency was then expected to set air quality standards for pollutants for which air quality criteria and reports on control techniques had been issued by the federal government. When the standards were set, the state was required to adopt plans for implementation of the standards. With the approval of the standards and the plan of implementation by the federal government, the state was eligible for financial support from the funds authorized by the Air Quality Act and annually appropriated by Congress.

It should be pointed out that "the availability of grant funds has been an important factor in stimulating needed expansion and strengthening of state, local, and regional air pollution control efforts." In 1961, prior to the establishment of the federal grant program, there were 85 state, local, and regional air pollution control agencies with total budgets of 9.3 million dollars. At the end of 1969, there were 191 agencies with total annual budgets of 51.2 million dollars. Federal support accounted for 42 percent of the total.[6]

While the granting of federal funds is an important aspect of the national control endeavor, an equally important aspect is the manner in which the funds are granted. The federal government has attempted to make intergovernmental cooperation in the control of air pollution both desirable and profitable for those states and municipalities willing to work together. An agency serving a single state or local governmental unit is eligible for two dollars of federal aid for every dollar increase in its annual expenditure. However, an agency serving more than one municipality is eligible for three dollars of federal aid for each dollar increase.

Although the federal activities under the 1967 legislation provided considerable stimulation for expanded air pollution control efforts at all levels of government, there remained the problem of coordinating the air control program with other activities concerned with environmental maintenance. The interrelatedness of air, water, and noise pollution problems dictates that comprehensive solutions be sought on a grand scale.

The Environmental Protection Agency

In early 1970, President Nixon ordered a reorganization of the entire federal environmental maintenance program and placed all control activities under the authority of the newly created Environmental Protection Agency. To carry out its duties of total environmental maintenance, the agency was allocated substantial resources: an initial staff of over 6500 and a budget exceeding one and a quarter billion dollars.

Within the comprehensive agency program there remain activities which lie predominately in the area of air pollution control. The current air pollution control program includes the establishment of air quality standards, the regulation of motor vehicle pollution, research in low-polluting propulsion systems, making financial grants to state and local agencies, and conducting training programs at many colleges and universities for air pollution control personnel.

The success or failure of the Environmental Protection Agency to maintain a healthy environment may ultimately depend upon the attitudes and efforts of the public. To stimulate public involvement in control efforts the Agency has expended considerable energy in providing information to the public and encouraging public awareness of control endeavors. The public support ideology was aptly expressed by Dr. John Middleton: "The major ingredient in the effectiveness of state and local action will be the attitudes of public officials and citizens. If the citizenry truly wants clean air—and if control officials and the political decision-makers recognize this—we will be on our way to winning the fight against polluted air.[7]

As pointed out above, the federal air pollution control program of financial, technical, and research assistance to state and local governmental units has served to encourage state and local control programs. Such progress can continue only through a growing federal assistance program and a growing willingness on the part of state and local governments to cooperate with federal administrators.

The next section will reveal the efforts taken by the state of Texas to control air pollution. Special attention will be given Texas' role within the federal-state-local, or vertical, dimension of intergovernmental cooperative activities.

THE TEXAS AIR POLLUTION CONTROL PROGRAM

Texas has been chosen for this study of air pollution control because its reaction to the availability of federal funds and technical assistance is typical of several other states, and this study should help to explain the problems of air pollution control not only in Texas but also in a number of other states. Second, unlike such states as California and New York, where some scientists contend that the ecological balance may never return to a satisfactory position, Texas, with its vast expanses of land and its comparatively young urban areas, has an opportunity to develop a comprehensive control program before pollution of the state's resources reaches a disastrous and irreparable condition.

To illustrate the need for a comprehensive air pollution control program in Texas, certain facts concerning the demographic and economic make-up of the state will prove beneficial. The public services, such as refuse disposal and power generation, which must be provided for the state's eleven million inhabitants, greatly contribute to atmospheric pollution. The more than six million motor vehicles which are registered in the state are another major source of pollution. In addition, Texas leads the nation in oil and gas production and petroleum refining, industries which rank with iron and steel mills as major pollutors. Other Texas industries, such as chemical production, the cattle industry, and agriculture, are not without fault as air pollutors.

Early Control Efforts

In Texas, the pollution created by individual citizens coupled with the pollution created by the state's leading industries has necessitated control endeavors at the state level. Since 1967, air pollution control and research efforts in Texas have been the responsibility of the Texas Air Control Board; however, some earlier control activities were conducted by the State Health Department under its power to deal with public nuisances. In the absence of strict pollution standards, the Health Department was forced to seek prosecution of pollutors under the existing nuisance laws. It should be noted that the resulting set of court cases provided the Health Department with some general control guidelines if not a comprehensive body of pollution standards.

In addition to prosecutions under common law nuisance, initial activities of the Health Department included active campaigns against street dust and programs to stimulate more efficient incineration of refuse.

The Texas Air Control Board

In 1967, the Texas air pollution control program was reorganized in an effort to follow more closely the policies set out by the federal government in the national Air Quality Act. The state legislature, in passing the Clean Air Act of 1967, established the Texas Air Control Board. A revision of the act in 1969 specifically designated the board as: "the principal authority in the state on matters relating to the quality of the air resources in the state and for setting standards, criteria, levels, and emission limits for air content and pollution control."[8]

The Texas Air Control Board is composed of nine members who are chosen by the governor with Senate approval for six-year terms. Although four members of the board may be chosen from the general public, five of the members must meet certain professional requirements. The board must include a professional engineer, a licensed physician, an agricultural engineer, a specialist in industrial management, and a municipal administrator.

The board's duties are to develop a comprehensive control plan, gather information, conduct research, establish rules, and to instigate legal proceedings to compel compliance under the law. In addition, the board is charged to encourage actively a cooperative atmosphere among the other control agencies acting within the state. To accomplish this task, the board offers advice and consultation to local governments and industry and encourages cooperative agreements among the various political subdivisions of the state.

Clearly, a nine-member board, which meets as a physical entity only one day per month, could not possibly perform all of the duties mentioned above without assistance. The Clean Air Act authorizes the board to secure the personnel and laboratory services needed to carry out its duties from the State Health Department. There are currently 170 State Health Department employees assisting the board in its research and investigatory efforts.

Total federal and state expenditures for the control program amounted to only $823,975 for the 1970 fiscal year. Expenditures increased to over 2 million dollars in fiscal 1971 and over 2.5 million dollars in the 1972 fiscal year.

Control Activities in Texas

Although a lack of personnel and funds has not allowed the Texas Air Control Board to reach its full potential as a control agency, the board has made considerable progress in certain areas. In compliance with the rules of the federal government, the Texas Air Control Board has established both maximum standards for pollutants for which national standards are available and a comprehensive plan for implementing these standards. In addition, the board has instituted a research program, begun an active program of prosecuting pollutors, and provided technical assistance to local control agencies.

The emission standards established by the board are generally consistent with those recommended by the national control agency; however, certain deviations do occur. The Board has set a state-wide emission standard for each pollutant, but it has the authority to set higher standards in areas where air pollution problems are more acute. For example, the maximum allowable emission of sulfur dioxide in Galveston and Harris Counties is thirty percent less than that of the rest of the state.[9]

In some instances, the power to fluctuate emission standards by areas has led to strained relations between the board and municipal government officials. While control experts can see the need for higher emission standards in certain areas, many city councilmen and county commissioners view higher standards in their jurisdictions as a direct deterrent to the establishment of new industries.

Although the establishment of higher emission standards in certain areas of the state has been the subject of controversy, the presence of such standards has greatly facilitated the apprehension and prosecution of pollutors. Instead of relying on the general nuisance laws as grounds for prosecution, control experts can now measure the ambient air near escape stacks and easily detect the presence of unallowable amounts of pollutants. The result is a specific and scientifically proven charge against the offender instead of a vague nuisance charge.

Prosecution under such charges may be instigated by a local governmental unit in a civil suit for injunctive action or for the recovery of civil penalties; however, *the Air Control Board is always a party in the suit.* When a local government does so, the civil penalties recovered are divided equally between the state of Texas and the local government. Civil penalties recovered in a suit instituted by the Air Control Board without the aid of a local government are paid to the general revenue fund of the state.

Even though the establishment of emission standards has facilitated the prosecution of air pollution cases, the statute approach to controlling air pollution is not free from problems. The serious weakness of the statute approach lies in the fact that the emissions of each of the several escape stacks within a small area may be well under the emission maximums, but the sum total of their emissions may reach disastrous proportions.

In addition to the problem of setting fair and reasonable standards for emissions, the plans for implementing the standards have caused serious problems, especially at the local level. The Clean Air Act of Texas created a program by which the Texas Air Control Board may grant a variance to allow industries additional time to comply with emission standards and to install abatement equipment. A person, company, or governmental unit seeking additional time in which to eliminate offensive emissions must submit a petition for a variance to the board. Copies of the variance request are then sent to the mayor and health officials of the municipality and the county judge and health authorities of the county in which the source is located. If the local officials recommend the granting of a variance, the board will usually grant one without a hearing; however, if the local officials recommend the denial of a petition, the board will ordinarily hold a public hearing before acting on the petition.

Until recently, the Control Board decided variance petitions in accordance with the wishes of the local governments. Now, private citizens in many of the urban areas of Texas have begun to urge local officials to recommend the denial of variance petitions, and, in many cases, the local officials have complied with the wishes of some of their constituents even though the variances are necessary for the industries to continue their operations. The members of the Air Control Board, being removed from many of the local political pressures, realize that a variance is not a "license to pollute" for most industries, but it is a legitimate and necessary grant of time without which many companies would suffer tremendous financial losses. Moreover, the board retains the power to regulate pollution by specifying a maximum limit, somewhat higher than the state-wide limit, which even a company with a pollution variance may not violate. Therefore, the board has disregarded the wishes of local government officials in some variance grants, a practice which has caused ill feelings between the state board and local governments.

Powers Allocated to Local Governments

Although the state board is the principal authority in the state for air pollution control, it tries to follow a policy of non-interference with local governments which have an active control program, except when such a policy becomes impractical. No ruling, regulation, or order by the Texas Air Control Board can be enforced without assistance from local officials. In fact, most board regulations are the result of research and investigatory efforts by local control agencies. To gain the vitally necessary support of local control agencies, the Control Board practices a policy of close cooperation with local agencies whenever possible.

Close scrutiny of the 1969 revisions to the Clean Air Act reveals an awareness by the state legislature that an effective air pollution control program is ultimately dependent upon the activities of local governments. The Clean Air Act has reserved certain powers for the local governments, provided that the exercise of those powers does not conflict with the rules, regulations, or orders of the Control Board. Local governments may make inspections, file suits, enter into cooperative agreements, and pass ordinances and rules.

It should be pointed out that the grant of the aforementioned powers to local governmental units provides the foundation for an active air pollution control program at the local level, but the decision to employ any or all of these powers rests solely with the local government. In the absence of an active local control program, the state board must conduct investigations and file legal actions within the territorial jurisdiction of the local government. Although the state Control Board cannot coerce a local government to establish an active control agency, past experience indicates that most local governmental units prefer to begin a control program rather than experience overt state intervention within their jurisdictions.

If the local governments are to have major responsibility for the implementation of air control programs, there are a great many problems which must be overcome. The proliferation of local governmental units, coupled with increasing efforts by federal and state officials to introduce regional control programs, makes intergovernmental cooperation at the local level more necessary than ever before. The strained relations which often occur between local political officials are major obstacles to effective local control efforts and must be reduced. Local citizens must be informed of the acute hazards of air pollution and demand local activities to abate the problem.

The following section provides a case study of the air pollution control efforts by the federal, state, and local governments within the Houston Standard Metropolitan Statistical Area. The major purpose of the case study is to examine the federal, state, and local agency interactions in control efforts and the interactions of the various local governmental units within the Houston area.

THE HOUSTON AIR POLLUTION CONTROL PROGRAM

Several considerations have prompted the selection of the Houston SMSA for this case study of the intergovernmental relations involved in air pollution control. Houston's air pollution crisis, largely a result of the climate and industry of the area, was no small consideration in the selection process. In addition, the control efforts in the Houston area are similar to the control efforts in many other urban areas, and the problems of intergovernmental relations which are treated in this study are often found throughout the nation.

For analytical purposes, the intergovernmental relations involved in air pollution control have been divided into two dimensions: vertical and horizontal. In this study, the vertical dimension refers to the interactions between the federal, state, and local governmental units, while the horizontal dimension refers to the interactions between various local governments. Recent federal and state control efforts in Houston provide excellent examples of the vertical dimension of intergovernmental relations. Moreover, the proliferation of local governmental units in the Houston area indicates that examples of horizontal relationships are readily available for analysis.

The Houston SMSA includes Harris, Liberty, Brazoria, Fort Bend, and Montgomery counties. The 1970 census indicated 1,958,491 inhabitants in the area, a figure which indicates a 38.1 per cent increase over the 1960 census figure. The citizens are employed by high pollution industries such as oil refining and paper milling. The people and the industries within the SMSA are served by 214 local governmental units, a fact which has made intergovernmental cooperation vitally necessary not only in pollution control, but also in attacking many other metropolitan-wide problems.

The air pollution crisis in Houston is largely a result of the climate and topography of the Gulf Coast region. The fog which is quite prevelant in the marshy areas around Houston has the effect of holding pollutants from industry and individual automobiles in the air for long periods of time.

Control Agencies in Houston

With the acute pollution problem caused by the climate, industry, and local citizens, local control efforts are of the utmost importance. The first local control agency was established in 1953; however, prior to this date, a small amount of control work, primarily in the field of industrial hygiene, was done by the Texas State Health Department. In late 1952, the citizens of Green's Bayou, a community in east Harris County which has since been annexed by the city of Houston, requested the State Health Department to conduct an investigation of sulfur oxide mists which were forming along Green's Bayou. It was the opinion of the Harris County Commissioners Court that any air pollution control work should be done on the local level and under the auspices of the local heads of government; therefore, the Control Section of the County Health Department was created. This action clearly indicated a fear which is often found among local officials of the control which inevitably accompanies state or federal aid programs.

Financing the control program has been a particular problem from the beginning. The original intention of the commissioners court was for the various municipalities in the county to support the program on the basis of the 1950 census, at a per capita rate of six cents. In 1956, all of the municipalities in the county decided that air pollution control was a county function and the costs of the control program should be born by county taxes. The burden of support for the County Control Section has rested solely with Harris County since 1956.

Although funding has posed a difficult problem in Harris County, recent increases in the Control Section's budget have been significant. It increased from $101,108 in 1968 to $135,962 in 1969. Further increases led to a 1970 allotment of $260,045, which almost doubled the 1969 figure. By 1972 the figure had reached almost $480,000.

At present, the Harris County Control Section is staffed by forty employees. These forty people are responsible for the control of a 1732 square mile area, which in itself is sufficient evidence of a grossly inadequate program.

Since its creation, the Harris County Control Section has consistently been the most active pollution control agency within the Houston SMSA; however, two other control agencies have recently assumed an active role in the area's control efforts. The City of Houston Air Pollution Control Section and the City of Pasadena Control Section were created in the mid-1960s, largely as a result of the availability of federal assistance.

The City of Houston Control Section, which operates within the City Health Department, is staffed by approximately fifty employees. The budget for the Houston Control Section has been stable for the past three years at $481,000. Close to one-half of this total is federally funded. The City of Pasadena Control Section operates with a staff and funds well below that of its Houston counterpart.

The three local control agencies operating in the Houston SMSA have been assigned similar control responsibilities within their respective jurisdictions. Each of the agencies investigates complaints and makes routine inspections of public and private property within their boundaries of activity. In addition, each agency continually conducts laboratory analyses of air samples collected by their investigation teams. Finally, the agencies are available for consultation with private individuals and industrial officials concerning air quality regulations and control practices.

A major problem encountered in conducting the aforementioned activities is that each of the control agencies is restricted to operating within its own municipal or county jurisdiction. The nature of the air pollution crisis dictates that control activities be conducted across these jurisdictional boundaries. Far too often, one local agency is keenly aware of dangerous pollutants within its sphere of activity but is powerless to act because the source of the emission lies within another agency's jurisdiction.

The problem of effective control in a large urban area where many local control units are active can be solved only through cooperation among governmental units. Such cooperation is often stimulated by higher levels of government.

The Vertical Dimension of Relations

A basic outline of the legally permitted control activities with the vertical dimension of intergovernmental relations has been presented in the sections concerning the federal and state control programs. It is interesting to note that some of the recent practices of federal and state officials within the local jurisdictions are not clearly outlined in either the national Air Quality Act of 1967 or the Texas Clean Air Act of 1969. Such actions are justified by expediency rather than by a statutory requirement. This section will analyze the legal and extra-legal aspects of the vertical relationships present in the control of air pollution in the Houston area.

Attempts by the federal control agency to stimulate cooperative control efforts among the local governments in the Houston area include financial and technical assistance to them, research and investigations to determine air quality standards for the region, and the establishment of an air quality control region. Such actions are legal in that they are specifically allowed by the Air Quality Act of 1967.

Federal financial assistance to local control agencies in the Houston area has been available since 1963, and the City of Houston and the City of Pasadena Control Sections have been willing to accept federal funds. The Harris County Control Section, however, has not been willing to do so. The failure of Harris County to seek federal funds reflects a fear, real or imaginary, of the federal control which oftentimes accompanies federal funds, and it is not often conducive to vertical cooperation among governmental units.

Another of the legal activities performed by the federal officials in the Houston area, that of providing research and investigations to determine air quality standards, was seen recently in the preparation of the data necessary to establish an air quality control region. The federal agency cooperated with the Texas Air Control Board and the local governments in researching the air pollution problem and conducting an air quality analysis, which is necessary before an air quality control region can be established.

The most comprehensive action yet undertaken by the federal control agency to encourage cooperative control activities among the local governments in the Houston area is the establishment of the Metropolitan Houston-Galveston Intrastate Air Quality Control Region. The Texas Air Control Board, within the legal power granted to it by the Texas Clean Air Act, recommended the establishment of the air quality control region to federal officials. With the concurrence of the national agency, work was begun on the establishment of the region.

In the creation of the Houston-Galveston Region, the federal control officials had to consider such factors as the jurisdictional boundaries in the area, the urban-industrial concentrations, the cooperative regional arrangements, the pattern and rate of growth in the area, and the existing state and local air pollution control legislation and programs. In accordance with these considerations, the Houston-Galveston Region includes Brazoria, Fort Bend, Galveston, Chambers, Harris, Liberty, Montgomery, and Waller counties.

After the boundaries of the region had been determined, the Texas Air Control Board had responsibility for setting air quality standards in the area for all pollutants for which criteria and control techniques were available. It should be noted that these standards set by the State Board were required to be as strict or stricter than the previously determined federal standards.

Although the major purpose of the Air Quality Control Region is to stimulate intergovernmental cooperation, few cooperative programs have begun and the region remains little more than an administrative district of the Environmental Protection Agency. A major reason for the failure of the region to live up to initial expectations has been the fear on the part of officials in smaller municipalities and in county governments that the larger municipalities will dominate policy-making within the region.

In addition to the legally permitted or required activities mentioned above, there are numerous extra-legal actions being carried on by federal officials in the Houston area. The primary extra-legal activities in Houston have been endeavors of officials of the higher levels of government to stimulate local citizens to take a more active role in applying political pressure to local government officials for effective control. While the actual effects of addresses by elected officials of the higher levels of government cannot be measured, some of the local citizens may be stimulated to become active supporters of pollution control efforts through such addresses. In Houston, high schools, professional organizations, and private citizens are beginning letter-writing campaigns and establishing citizen's anti-pollution committees.

In addition to the extra-legal activities by politicians, federal control officials carry out important extra-legal functions. Every statement that a control official makes to the local news media has the potential to stimulate action at the local level.

The citizens of Houston have begun to take such an active interest in control work that the Chairman of the Texas Air Control Board was led to chastise another area for its inaction by stating, "If Houston city officials took the attitude that Amarillo did on air pollution, they would not simply be impeached, they would be lynched."[10]

While federal officials have been performing the legal and extra-legal actions mentioned above, state officials have not been idle in the

Houston area. Legal activities being performed in Houston by the Texas Air Control Board to stimulate local efforts include assisting the local control agencies in active prosecution of violators, and establishing air quality standards and an implementation plan in the area. Generally, the state investigations in the area entail a six-man state squad of investigators periodically checking on companies with variances which have expired. During the investigations the state officials are careful to stress that "inspections by state investigators are not attempts to supplant or discredit the city and county pollution control offices."

According to one newspaper, a problem which state investigators have encountered in the Houston area is that many industries seem to know when the state investigators are going to be making inspections and either shut down or curtail operations. Even if the state officials do not apprehend violators because of the curtailed operations, for the few days that the officials are in town Houstonians enjoy purer air than at any other time.[11]

Another legally authorized activity being carried out by state officials in the Houston area is the prosecution of pollutors. State activities in the prosecution of emission standard violators have included both direct instigation by state officials and participation by state officials in proceedings begun by local officials; however, most of the state participation in legal proceedings occurs in the latter manner. Action in these legal proceedings has ranged from a temporary injunction to a permanent injunction and a $17,500 fine.

The legally authorized state activity which has caused the most acute problem in the Houston area is the establishment and implementation of air quality standards. The Texas Air Control Board has set some standards higher in the Houston area than in the remainder of the state. While one might expect local officials to oppose such standards as deterrents to industrial development, Houston officials, realizing that nothing short of a natural holocaust could halt Houston's industrial development, have actually welcomed the strict standards in the area.

The implementation plan, however, has not been well received by local political officials. The granting of variances to industry is the major point of conflict in the state's implementation plan. Local officials have reacted to the demands of some of their constituents, notably private citizens, and have greatly curtailed recommendations to the Texas Air Control Board for the granting of pollution variances. For example, in March of 1970 city and county officials in the Houston area recommended that only one of eleven variance petitions be granted, but the Control Board granted a variance for six of the petitioners. Instead of cooperating with the state after such rulings have been made, local officials will often use the state board as a political scapegoat.

Other efforts by federal and state officials to stimulate cooperative control efforts in Houston do occur; however, this portrayal of the vertical relations involved in air pollution control points out the major problems occurring in such efforts. First, the local governmental units fear losing their identity in cooperative control efforts. Second, while the higher levels of government are endeavoring to stimulate cooperative activities among the local units, they oftentimes neglect the cooperation which is necessary between the various levels of local government. Third, pressures by citizens can cause political and control officials to make decisions which are politically expedient rather than helpful to the overall control program. Finally, even the cooperative activities which are being encouraged do not cope with the entire pollution crisis. This is only one dimension of the control activity. The horizontal dimension of cooperative control efforts is plagued with yet more problems.

The Horizontal Dimension of Relations

Like the vertical dimension, the horizontal dimension of intergovernmental cooperation in control efforts is characterized by legal and extra-legal approaches. Although such legal powers as prosecuting pollutors, entering cooperative agreements, making recommendations to the state board, and passing pollution ordinances are granted to the local governmental units in the Houston area, the local governments have had considerable difficulty in exercising these powers cooperatively.

Only recently have the Houston City Council, the Pasadena City Council, and the Harris County Commissioners Court begun to discuss cooperative control agreements. The discussions have centered around the consolidation of the three political subdivisions' control offices. A variety of merger plans have been proposed but tax support for a merged agency has posed a particular problem since consolidation was first discussed. City officials express the concern that city dwellers will be forced to pay twice for the same service if the city and county control sections are merged. This point has proved detrimental to other cooperative programs as well.

There are many extra-legal relationships present in the Houston area which act as direct threats to the consolidation of control programs in the area. The county has been very active in the prosecution of pollutors, while the cities of Houston and Pasadena have rarely prosecuted anyone. In addition, the approach to the granting of variances and other relations with the state board varies greatly between political and control officials, a fact which leads the political officials to keep a tight rein on the relationships of the local control officials and the state board. Finally, political officials fear losing their power to determine which industries will be prosecuted and which will escape prosecution.

The horizontal relations between local governmental units in the Houston area are hampered by other jealousies and concerns; however, the above problems are clear indications of those which arise in local control efforts. Reviewing the inherent difficulties of horizontal intergovernmental cooperation in Houston, they are: first, local officials are reluctant to consolidate control efforts for fear they will lose political influence; second, the execution of control efforts such as prosecution often differs vastly among governmental agencies; lastly, cooperation between local control experts and state officials is often undermined by the local political officials.

CONCLUSIONS AND RECOMMENDATIONS

The nature of the air pollution crisis justifies the use of all available means for active abatement programs. While considerable deficiencies are evident in the efforts of federal officials to encourage cooperation and active control at the state and local level, the fact remains that such efforts are vitally necessary if air pollution is to be controlled effectively. As the nation's large urban areas continue to grow, the federal government will possibly be called upon for increased financial and technical assistance in state and local control programs.

The current program of creating regional control offices has certain merits which cannot be overlooked as greatly simplifying control work at the state and local levels. The ability to cross jurisdictional boundaries, the establishment and implementation of regional emission standards, the consolidation of equipment and personnel, and the availability of increased federal funds under a program of regional cooperation can go a long way in cleaning the air around the sorely polluted metropolitan areas.

Assuming that the present approach is the most feasible and desirable, the air quality control regions established by the federal government, to reach their full potential as control agencies, must solve many problems. The federal government must allay the fears of local officials that their power will be usurped by the higher levels of government. Additional research must be conducted so that accurate emission levels may be established in the control regions. The help of industries must be enlisted in the pollution battle. Finally, Congress must continue to provide the federal agency with the funds necessary to carry out the national air pollution control program.

The federal government will continue to be dependent upon the state governments for assistance in stimulating control activities. The state of Texas assisted the federal government by promoting and actively researching the creation of air quality control regions. In addition, the state of Texas assumed major responsibility for the condition of the air throughout its boundaries instead of waiting for the federal government to do the job. Finally, state legislators have created the framework for an excellent control program in the passage of the Clean Air Act.

Texas can continue to promote active control of air pollution and can eventually eliminate a major portion of the problem if certain difficulties are overcome. The state agency must attempt to gain the trust of local officials without losing any of its power as the chief agency acting in the state to abate pollution. Like the federal government, the state must continually research the pollution problems in the state and endeavor to find more effective means of coping with them. More than anything else, the state must encourage enforcement of its rules and regulations at the local level if any success is to be made in pollution control.

Lately, local governments in the Houston area have made considerable progress in their control endeavors. Local control sections investigated the air quality in the area and have begun to prosecute actively industries which violate air quality standards. Moreover, local governments have begun to discuss consolidating their control offices to provide more effective means of abating the serious pollution problem in the Houston area.

The local governments in the Houston area are a long way from eliminating air pollution. To do so, they must approach cooperative activities with understanding rather than fear. Political and control officials must learn to cooperate in control efforts. More than anything else, local officials must endeavor to make their decisions in the light of those actions which will help to eliminate the problem, so far as politically feasible.

Unexplored Approaches to Pollution Control

In addition to the activities already being conducted by control agencies, there are several other avenues of approach to controlling air pollution which are yet unexplored. Industry in America is apparently the ever-present but often forgotten element in cooperative control activities. Control officials have been so concerned with the direct regulation of emissions by industries that cooperative activities between governments and industries have been neglected as a part of the overall pollution control program. With so many problems occurring in the cooperative government control programs, perhaps industrial officials could take a larger role in abating air pollution. Governments at all levels could establish tax programs whereby those industries which contribute huge amounts of pollution to the atmosphere would pay larger taxes than those industries which have installed abatement equipment. It would then be up to the industrial officials to balance the costs of taxation and the costs of installing various amounts of abatement equipment. Additionally, governments could offer inducements to industries to control their pollution in the form of large tax deductions on the depreciation of control equipment or direct government support for the installation and maintenance of control equipment.

Whether new methods of control are soon introduced or the direct regulation of pollution by government is continued for some time, the activities within the horizontal and vertical dimensions of intergovernmental cooperation which have been analyzed in this study will remain as significant attempts to deal with air pollution. Additional research is needed in air pollution control and should include topics such as informal decision-making and industrial participation in air pollution control which were not treated in this study.

The problems of intergovernmental relations discussed in this study occur not only in air pollution control but also in cooperative endeavors to cope with a score of other metropolitan crises. Whether the problem is urban housing, law and order, welfare, transportation, education, or health care, similar difficulties may occur in the cooperative efforts to deal the problem. At present, regional cooperation is being encouraged by the federal government not only in air pollution control, but also in such areas as urban planning, transportation, and comprehensive health care. This study of the problems of intergovernmental relations in air pollution control could be useful to the administrators of other cooperative programs in identifying and dealing with the problems they may encounter.

[1]U.S. Department of Health, Education, and Welfare, *The Cost of Clean Air: First Report of the Secretary of Health, Education, and Welfare to the Congress of the United States in compliance with Public Law 90-148* (Washington, D.C.: Government Printing Office, 1969), p. 11.

[2]U.S. Congress, House, *The Clean Air Act of 1963,* Pub. L. 88-206, 88th Cong., 1st sess., H.R. 6518.

[3]U.S. Department of Health, Education, and Welfare. *The Federal Air Pollution Program,* Public Health Service Publication No. 1560 (Washington, D.C.: Government Printing Office, 1967), p. 28.

[4]U.S. Department of Health, Education, and Welfare, *Today and Tomorrow in Air Pollution,* Public Health Service Publication No. 1555 (Washington, D.C.: Government Printing Office, 1967), p. 23.

[5]U.S. Department of Health, Education, and Welfare, *Progress Toward Cleaner Air,* Consumer protection and Environmental Health Service (Washington, D.C.: Government Printing Office, 1969), p. 2.

[6]U.S. Department of Health, Education, and Welfare, *Progress in State and Local Air Pollution Control Under the Clean Air Act,* Consumer Protection and Environmental Health Service (Washington, D.C.: Government Printing Office, 1969), p. 1.

[7]*Progress Toward Cleaner Air,* p. 6.

[8]*Clean Air Act of Texas, 1969, Vernon's Tex. Civ. Stat.*, art. 4477-5; (Supp. 1969).

[9]*Texas Air Control Board Regulations for the Control of Air Pollution,* p. 111-14.

[10]"Amarillo Lashed on Air Pollution," *Lubbock Avalanche-Journal,* Aug. 18, 1970, sec. B, p. 8.

[11]"Pollution Excuses Annoy Citizens," *Houston Post,* Feb. 15, 1970, sec. 1, p. 4.

22 The Energy Crisis

Edmund S. Muskie

Today we begin hearings on S. 2752, the Intergovernmental Coordination of Power Development and Environmental Protection Act of 1969. . . .

The purpose of this legislation is to provide a regional, intergovernmental mechanism in order to promote sound planning in electric power development; and, at the same time, protect the public interest with respect to the environmental impact of such development. The bill provides establishment of criteria to be administered by regional agencies in order to coordinate Federal, State and local efforts with respect to the planning and construction of electric power generation and transmission facilities. Such criteria would be subject to the approval of a Federal agency.

There is little argument over the fact that this nation will depend more and more on reliable and adequate electricity. We are told that within the next 20 years we must triple our power capacity if we are to meet population and corporate demands.

This will require the development of over 1 million megawatts of new generating capacity, and will involve the loca-

From: "Intergovernmental Coordination of Power Development and Environmental Protection Act" Hearings before the Subcommittee on Intergovernmental Relations, Committee on Government Operations, United States Senate, 1970

Edmund S. Muskie is a United States Senator from Maine. He was an early advocate of strict anti-pollution legislation.

tion and construction of over 250 new plants at an estimated cost of between $80 and $100 billion.

It will require the location and construction of over one-half million miles of high-voltage transmission lines requiring approximately 8 million acres of land.

This degree of effort to build up the Nation's power potential can have serious side effects on our environment, unless we act quickly and decisively to avoid them. The problems and their potential effects are self-evident.

By 1990, it is estimated that over 80 percent of the Nation's power generation plants whose daily use of water for cooling purposes will amount to from one-third to one-half of the total daily fresh water runoff of the United States. The thermal and other pollutant effects accompanying the return of this water to its original source are already a matter of national concern. Most important the unknown effects far exceed those that are known in this area—even to the experts.

In addition to the problem of thermal pollution, fossil-fueled power plants may pollute the air with sulfur oxide and oxides of nitrogens, beyond levels of environmental tolerance, unless new and costly technology is used. Atomic-fueled plants could add additional risks from plant accidents, transportation of fuel, dumping of radioactive wastes, the reprocessing of nuclear fuel elements, and the normal release of krypton-85 and tritium. The siting of large atomic power reactors in heavily populated areas may increase the risk potential.

Transmission lines present yet another set of environmental problems. There is increasing public concern over their appearance, and their deteriorating impact on scenic, recreational, and historic areas. Pressures to locate these lines underground will increase as the Nation's urban areas expand. Some progress has been made in developing the technology for placing transmission lines underground, but a great deal more needs to be done to bring the costs involved into line with those that are reasonable.

In initiating these hearings on this legislation, we recognize that there is an equation to be established between the need for additional power development on the one hand, and the protection of people and their environment on the other.

The electric power industry has consistently approached this problem in a haphazard manner. There has been no meaningful regional or national planning involved. Construction of generating plants and transmission lines has gone forward on a crisis basis to meet immediate demands consistent with cost savings rather than on the basis of long-range planned development. There has been no meaningful participation by government at Federal, State, or local levels in the process.

A major element that is lacking is responsibility with respect to our environment.

The Federal Power Commission has no jurisdiction over the siting and construction of steam electric plants and transmission lines. The Atomic Energy Commission is concerned only with the immediate health, safety, and defense aspects of atomic plants. State regulation is almost nonexistent. With the exception of two States, Maryland and California, there is no effective State jurisdiction over plant or transmission location, pollution standards, or aesthetic deterioration. On the local level, the only limitation is zoning.

In sum, we face two conflicting requirements—the sound development of electrical energy on a regional basis, on the one hand, and a maximum degree of protection to our citizens and their environment in the building of that energy potential on the other. . . .

23 State and Federal Regulatory Agencies —Conflict or Cooperation?

Henry F. Lippitt, II

The first case in which I ever participated before a federal regulatory agency was the Hope Natural Gas Company rate increase proceeding. In this case, Hope (its incorporators in the 1890's "hoped" that the company would eventually make a profit) was faced with a double-barreled increase in overall costs and a sharp reduction in liquid butane and propane prices–which had provided a substantial revenue credit to Hope's operations. After the sharp reduction ordered by the Federal Power Commission in Hope's annual revenues, based on Hope's 1940 operations, a reduction sustained by the Supreme Court, Hope finally found it necessary to file for one of the first rate increases to be brought before the Federal Power Commission, which was then rounding out its first ten years under the Natural Gas Act.

The Hope rate increase case was notable in several ways. Beside the fact that the FPC staff's chief depreciation witness wanted to recalculate all of Hope's depreciation accruals since the beginning of Hope's operations and the FPC staffs chief cost-of-service witness still showed "excess" revenues over cost of service

From: *Public Utilities Fortnightly* (March 26, 1970), pp. 33-38. Reprinted by permission of the author and publisher.

Henry F. Lippitt, II, is a Los Angeles attorney.

(even though a rate increase rather than a rate reduction was called for), the Hope rate increase proceeding was notable in the extent of the cooperation which the Federal Power Commission provided to the state regulatory commission which was the most concerned. First, the hearings in January and February, 1950, were held in Charleston, West Virginia, the headquarters of the West Virginia Public Service Commission (not too far away from Hope's Clarksburg, West Virginia, headquarters). Second, the regulatory "bench" consisted not only of FPC Presiding Examiner Farrington, but also Chairman Nethken of the West Virginia Public Service Commission. From time to time the other two West Virginia commissioners also shared the bench. The staffs of both the FPC and the West Virginia commission were active in presenting material for consideration by both commissions.

Eventually two decisions were issued. Both were based on the same record. Based on FPC Presiding Examiner Farrington's initial decision, the Federal Power Commission approved an interstate rate increase for Hope applicable to Hope's interstate deliveries out of West Virginia into Ohio, Pennsylvania, and New York. The West Virginia commission, using the same record, then authorized a rate increase applicable to Hope's intrastate deliveries to its thousands of retail customers within West Virginia. Certainly, the outer indication of "cooperation" between the Federal Power Commission and the West Virginia commission was an impressive one—to open the era of inflation which characterized most of the rest of the 1950s.

Unfortunately, however, the substantive results were less impressive. After making a cost allocation, even before the now well-known Atlantic seaboard allocation standards were determined, the Federal Power Commission separated Hope's overall cost of operations into jurisdictional costs subject to FPC jurisdiction, and remaining nonjurisdictional costs, including $168,336 annually of underground gas storage cost, subject to West Virginia commission jurisdiction. Based on this separation the Federal Power Commission then allowed Hope, using a 6 percent rate of return, a total rate increase of $1,703,937.

The West Virginia commission, however, took a different tack. Rather than allocating Hope's overall cost of service between jurisdictional and nonjurisdictional activities, the West Virginia commission took the position that West Virginia's low-cost supplies of natural gas, which were fully adequate to meet Hope's West Virginia peak-day and annual gas needs, should first be devoted to supplying—at low cost—the needs of West Virginia natural gas consumers.

As a result of this conflicting basis for decision, Hope found itself with $168,336 in annual storage costs which each commission refused to recognize for rate-making purposes. On exceptions before the FPC and after vigorous oral argument, the FPC grudgingly increased Hope's rates by an additional $97,226 but still assigned 5 percent of Hope's underground gas storage costs, rounded to $60,000 a year, to Hope's intrastate West Virginia sales. The West Virginia commission, however, refused to budge, and when the smoke cleared Hope had received approval for two rate increases, but "somehow" $60,000 a year of actually incurred costs, recognized by both commissions as part of Hope's overall cost of service, were left to be "swallowed" by Hope's parent–Consolidated Natural Gas Company. The situation is the same today. Hope's allocated cost of service, excluding some underground gas storage costs, provides the basis for FPC-approved jurisdictional interstate rate increases–but these same allocated underground gas storage costs are excluded as a basis for any remaining indicated increase in Hope's West Virginia intrastate retail sales rates.

FEDERAL-STATE CONFLICT CONTINUES

In the Columbia Gas System Amere case, the West Virginia commission again set low West Virginia retail consumer rates based on low-cost supplies of West Virginia-produced gas–even though the FPC used an allocated overall cost of service for the Columbia system's interstate rates subject to FPC jurisdiction. Amere's appeals to the West Virginia supreme court and to the United States Supreme Court proved unavailing, the appeals being denied without opinion. Since then, for the last several years, the Columbia system has been slowly trying to "realign" its system by separating its operating properties into companies subject "in full" either to the FPC's jurisdiction or the West Virginia or other state regulatory commission jurisdiction. Someday, when that alignment is complete, the Columbia system may escape the "unaccounted for" loss which even today faces Consolidated Natural Gas Company.

These cases suggest two questions: First, how can federal-state regulatory commission cooperation be encouraged? Second, how can federal-state regulatory conflicts be resolved?

In his recent presentation before the Senate Commerce Committee, FPC Chairman Nassikas discussed the necessity of "coordinated planning" through the mechanism of state and regional councils as a basis for meeting timely construction of new electric transmission facilities under the new "environmental standards" being imposed. Chairman Nassikas referred to the joint federal-state procedural mechanism under the Federal Power Act which authorizes the FPC to employ joint state-federal conferences to dovetail and implement all existing federal-state regulatory authority. In support of his suggestions, Chairman Nassikas referred to a number of Supreme Court decisions separating the FPC's interstate jurisdiction from the intrastate jurisdiction of the state regulatory commissions. Similar procedures are established under the Natural Gas Act. The FPC's Rules of Practice and Procedure have several pages outlining methods of "cooperative procedure" with state commissions. The difficulty is that, for all practical purposes, these sections of the Federal Power Act, the Natural Gas Act, and the FPC's Rules of Practice and Procedure are virtually "dead letters" at least when the FPC has to make a decision which will directly affect the work of one or more of the state regulatory commissions which must bear the brunt of the impact of the FPC's decision.

This is not to say that the cooperative procedure which Chairman Nassikas seeks with state regulatory commissions should not be continued. It should. The problem, however, is not merely to have cooperative state-federal conferences to "dovetail and implement" general planning concepts. The problem is to make certain that the point of view of the state regulatory commissions becomes a part of the FPC's decisional procedure. To be effective, this must not only be done on a "general planning" level, but it must also be done in specific cases where the FPC and state regulatory commissions are concerned.

HOW MUCH COOPERATION?

At present, under FPC procedure, a state commission gives notice of its intervention, or indication of interest, in a rate or certificate proceeding under the FPC's jurisdiction. Pursuant to that "notice of intervention" the interested state regulatory commission can present evidence by its own staff to participate in cross-examination and oral argument by its state commission counsel, presenting briefs, briefs on exceptions, and other statements to the FPC for FPC decision. Thus, under the FPC's present procedure, a state regulatory commission is treated in just the same manner as other participants to the FPC proceeding. This, of course, is not a "cooperative" method of arriving at a solution to the problem posed before the FPC—and which the state regulatory commission may be called on to absorb. It is a procedure under which the FPC's jurisdiction is considered "paramount" and the state regulatory commission is a petitioner like the other private parties whose interests are concerned, seeking to present argument to the FPC itself, and the FPC's presiding examiner, in order to arrive at a solution which may be in the state regulatory commission's best interest.

Certainly, this is not the way the framers of either the Federal Power Act or the Natural Gas Act expected the FPC to operate. The hearings in the early legislative history of both the Federal Power Act in 1933 and 1934, and the Natural Gas Act in 1937, indicated that the FPC, as a regulatory commission, was to be "first among equals"–rather than a "paramount" federal commission dispensing its idea of justice to applicants for its mercy, letting "chips" affecting the state regulatory commission's activities fall where they may.

Two simple facts are indicative of the present situation. Except for the initial two-day hearing in the Permian Basin Area Rate case (at Midland, Texas) and initial public hearings for hydroelectric project licenses under the Federal Power Act, neither the FPC as a commission, nor any of its presiding examiners, ever leaves Washington to hold hearings, or conferences, or issue decisions in an official capacity. Second, in the twenty years of FPC decisions following the Hope Natural Gas Company rate increase case in January-February, 1950, no FPC presiding examiner has ever shared the bench with an interested state commissioner. No interested state commissioner has ever been invited to participate, as a commissioner, in an oral argument before the FPC in any rate or certificate proceeding intimately involving the regulatory problems which may be thrust upon that state commission. No state commissioner has been invited to participate in an FPC conference in which the FPC itself is searching to arrive at a decision regarding a rate increase or certificate application affecting the state involved. Until some steps are taken along these lines, the concept of having the FPC "first among equals," acting cooperatively with other sovereign state regulatory commissions, will surely fail.

What can be done? Here are a couple of specific examples. In October, 1969, Colorado Interstate filed an $8.2 million annual rate increase with the FPC. About two-thirds of this rate increase, or $5.5 million a year, is applicable to Colorado Interstate's rates for gas consumed in the Rocky Mountain area, most of it in Colorado. Obviously, the Colorado Public Utilities Commission is keenly concerned with the outcome of these proceedings. At present, hearings on cross-examination of Colorado Interstate's case are scheduled to start before an FPC presiding examiner in Washington in July. Certainly, with the Colorado commission's keen interest and concern over the outcome of the proceedings, it would not be asking too much of the FPC to have at least the first day of public hearings held cooperatively by the FPC's designated presiding examiner with the Colorado Public Utilities Commission at the Colorado commission's headquarters in Denver. The same record taken in Denver might, thus, not only be a basis for hearing statements on behalf of Colorado interests most directly concerned but might also provide the Colorado commission with a basis for taking remedial action of its own, in its own jurisdictional sphere–considering such things as possible establishment of purchase gas adjustment clauses, and other rate-making problems concerning the

Colorado gas utilities which would be affected by the FPC's decision. If necessary, the remaining FPC hearings could be held by the FPC presiding examiner in Washington–so that the FPC staff might testify and present its testimony. Once, however, the records were made and the presiding examiner's initial decision issued, certainly an invitation to the chairman of the Colorado Public Utilities Commission to spend a day in Washington and participate, as a commissioner, in any oral argument which Colorado Interstate and the other interested parties might present would be a "minimum courtesy."

Taking Colorado Interstate, again, as an example. Colorado Interstate has recently announced the execution of a major gas purchase contract for the purchase of large quantities of oil well gas from two newly developed oil-producing areas in Wyoming. All of the construction by Colorado Interstate, by the producers in the fields, and the connecting pipeline involved, is to be carried out in Wyoming. Clearly, here is a situation in which the Wyoming Public Service Commission would be most keenly interested and concerned. Again, an opportunity would be presented here for the FPC presiding examiner to hold the initial hearings with the Wyoming Public Service Commission in Cheyenne, Wyoming. Later, the chairman of the Wyoming commission could be invited to Washington to participate, as a commissioner, in any oral argument or conference which the FPC might schedule to arrive at a decision to certificate the newly required gas supplies.

ELECTRIC VERSUS GAS COOPERATION

Under the Federal Power Act, even today, the FPC does conduct such initial one-day "public statement" hearings when a new hydroelectric project is to be licensed under the Federal Power Act. Certainly, there is no less a "public interest" in approving the certificate application or the rate increase of a natural gas company under the Natural Gas Act. Clearly, additional action is required by the FPC to discharge its responsibilities under the Natural Gas Act so that the "cooperative" procedure envisioned by the framers of the Natural Gas Act, and outlined by the FPC's Rules of Practice, does not continue to be a "dead letter"–implemented only in the "ivory tower" planning state but not applied to the hard "nitty-gritty" certificate and rate increase application cases where the bulk of the FPC's policy decisions are made, particularly the policy decisions which affect the work of the individual state regulatory commissions.

Perhaps, the objections to any such procedure are legion. Where is the money coming from? Which state commissions should be invited? When should the state commissions become involved? The answers to these questions will come with some thinking. Today, the FPC regulates over 3,600 independent producers of natural gas in the field selling gas subject to the FPC's jurisdiction. Yet, less than 10 percent of these, or only 275 produce nearly 95 percent of all of the gas moving in interstate commerce. Certainly, if every filing by every independent natural gas producer producing less than 2 million Mcf per year, or about $300,000 per year, were eliminated completely from regulatory control, there would hardly be a perceptible impact on the effectiveness of the FPC's producer regulation. Yet this would cut the numbers of "pieces of paper" filed in FPC producer rate cases by nearly 95 percent. Perhaps here would be an area in which FPC staff savings might be made–to provide a basis for additional FPC "cooperative" proceedings with the affected state regulatory commissions–and such a plan might even produce a surplus out of the FPC's present $18.5 million annual budget to cover some if not all of the $340,000 which the FPC asks to be earmarked for initiation of a National Gas Survey.

What about the second problem of the "poor" natural gas company with $60,000 a year of "unaccounted for" costs falling between the FPC and the West Virginia commission? Here, certainly, something of a more concrete nature is called for. While cooperation between the FPC and the various state regulatory commissions may go a long way toward solving the goal, it is by no means certain that this "cooperation" will achieve the desired ends. To date, it has not done so in any number of related fields in which the same federal-state regulatory commission conflicts have arisen. The fact of the matter is that every federal regulatory agency is acutely embroiled in questions which might better have been solved at the state regulatory level. Let me take another example in the natural gas field.

COOPERATION ON SAFETY STANDARDS

Some years ago, in the aftermath of the now famous Natchitoches natural gas explosion and fire, and Ralph Nader's concept of "unsafe at any speed," a public demand arose for additional supervision of pipeline safety in the natural gas transportation field. By then additional action by the affected state regulatory commissions (such as the California Public Utilities Commission) had adopted the American Standards Association B31.8 pipeline code, specifying the standards of wall thickness, elasticity, trenching and grading, and other requirements for the installation and operation of large diameter natural gas transmission pipelines. In California, not only was the ASA B31.8 pipeline code enacted but in a number of instances the permissive statements in the ASA B31.8 code (specifying "may") were enacted as "shall," imposing fixed standards on the natural gas transmission lines operating within the state.

Unfortunately, few other regulatory commissions followed this standard early in the game before the public demand for federal action came. When industry testimony was presented to the interested House and Senate Commerce committees, it was clear that a large "gap" existed in any regulatory commission supervision over pipeline safety. Then Congress determined to enact the Natural Gas Pipeline Safety Act and to appropriate up to $2 million (this year) to carry out enforcement under the act. Today the Director of the Office of Pipeline Safety is promulgating the same ASA B31.8 pipeline code standards which had already been widely adopted by the industry but which had not been made in the subject of either federal or state regulatory scrutiny and study.

This is not the only area in which the federal-state regulatory conflicts have occurred. The Federal Communications Commission and the state regulatory commissions have serious joint problems in regulating the newly emerging CATV systems and in determining the appropriate level for interstate long-distance toll calls and local telephone service. The Civil Aeronautics Board and the state regulatory commissions are increasingly enmeshed in the problem of regulating "third tier" air lines bringing traffic from outlying airports to central metropolitan area regional airports. The Interstate Commerce Commission and the state regulatory commissions are having difficult problems in railroad safety and railroad passenger train abandonments. In fact, the Federal Communications Commission decisions have gone so far in overriding the point of view of the interested state regulatory commissions in allocating costs to long-distance interstate telephone *versus* local intrastate service that the Senate Commerce Committee has proposed legislative creation of a Federal-state Communications Joint Board to regulate these relationships.

The effective answer to these questions lies in making a succession of decisions at the earliest stage. Where fire or other damage erupts from a ruptured pipeline—even by an independent contractor's bulldozer blade—the utility concerned should be quick not only to repair the damage, but to render assistance—financial, if necessary—to the people in the area who may be affected even though the ultimate liability may be on someone else. If so, no complaints to the state regulatory commission are likely to result. Today, however, the Office of Pipeline Safety is keenly interested and requires filing an accident report. Tomorrow, the question raised by the natural gas pipeline compressor station putting noise pollution into the atmosphere, or an old unsightly undeveloped gas field providing an "eyesore" to the community, must be answered. If the industry can take care of its own problems, this will end the matter. If it cannot, state regulatory commission jurisdiction is almost certain to be imposed. If state regulatory jurisdiction is absent or ineffective, then federal regulatory commission control will surely be imposed.

NEW LEGISLATION NEEDED?

But, what of the conflict between the federal and state regulatory agencies, when one of these events does occur? Cooperation, of course, should be the watchword. But if cooperation is not possible, what other possible resort does a utility have? Along these lines, I commend to your attention the recent proposal of the American Bar Association's Section of Public Utility Law for a bill granting federal district courts power to resolve the jurisdictional controversies arising between state and federal regulatory commissions. As Senator Tydings (Democrat, Maryland) said last October in introducing the bill: "The bill is in the public interest and eliminates needless litigation. Accordingly, it eliminates the costs of this litigation which will ultimately be borne by the utility consumer and taxpayer." The former chairman of the Maryland Public Service Commission supported the bill, saying it would provide an "impartial" forum for the settlement of such disputes without long delays. While the Federal Power Commission officially opposes the bill on the basis that it would "seldom be applicable" and that an enactment of the bill would "only result in unnecessary delay and duplication of the judicial level," it may nevertheless be expected that if there are additional controversies between federal and state regulatory commissions this may be the "way out." Certainly, it is difficult to argue with the concept of the bill. Merely having the legislation available "in the locker" might easily lead to the settlement of federal-state regulatory commission conflicts which at present go unresolved.

In 1954, after the FPC took jurisdiction over East Ohio Natural Gas Company's stub line from the Ohio border to Cleveland, and the FPC staff started to investigate the price applicable to Pacific Lighting's gas sales to San Diego Gas & Electric Company within California, the resulting furor (with firm support of the National Association of Railroad and Utilities Commissioners) led to the enactment by Congress of the Hinshaw amendment to the Natural Gas Act. This amendment provides specifically that the provisions of the Natural Gas Act do not apply to the transportation or sale of natural gas in interstate commerce if the natural gas is ultimately consumed within the state in which the gas is received. Similar legislation may be needed to preclude the FPC from requiring detailed sales and revenue information on intrastate gas sales.

In sum, in the past twenty years there has been little or no implementation of the FPC's authority instituting and carrying on any "cooperative" procedures with the individual state regulatory commissions—particularly with respect to the questions raised by specific rate increase or certificate applications filed with the FPC. The effect of this lack of "cooperative" procedure has, in a number of instances, brought about "conflicts" at the federal-state regulatory level. Either the problems giving rise to these conflicts must be solved at the outset by the industry itself, or by state regulatory commissions involved, in the exercise of their jurisdiction, or the questions will be ultimately decided by some federal agency, such as the FPC, in Washington. The alternative is to enact additional legislation defining federal and state jurisdictional boundaries and concepts, or providing a forum, perhaps in the federal district courts, where these conflicts can be resolved before they become major issues in the federal-state regulatory arena.

24 The National Crime Information Center (NCIC) of the FBI: Do We Want It?

Stanley Robinson

From: *Computers and Automation,* XX (June 1971), pp. 16-19. Reprinted by permission of the author and publisher.

Stanley Robinson is a free-lance computer programmer.

The FBI's computerized National Crime Information Center (NCIC) should be a growing source of alarm for all of us who are concerned with human rights–especially the rights of those who are black, poor, or politically unpopular. This article gives some of the reasons for alarm, and describes my challenge of local police hookup to NCIC. The challenge occurred in a New England Town Meeting in Wayland, Massachusetts.

NCIC is an automated nationwide police information network. Teletypes are installed at local police stations, connected by phone lines to state police computer centers, which in turn are connected to a central computer operated by the FBI in Washington, D.C. Records are stored and searched on-line with both state and federal computers. At present, the Massachusetts section, for example, provides "immediate information on stolen cars, missing and wanted persons, lost and stolen property, lost and stolen securities, stolen guns, outstanding warrants, narcotic drug intelligence, and suspended and revoked drivers' licenses and automobile registrations."[1]

These services, especially the narcotic drug intelligence, seem to have a potential for current misuse. Policemen are instructed, for example, to arrest "suspicious" persons for disorderly conduct to facilitate an NCIC check.[2]

However, I am far more afraid of the future of the system. I cannot give an authoritative future description of NCIC for these reasons:

1. Future plans are in a state of flux;
2. Officials responsible for those plans insist the planning is confidential, and the public will be notified only after decisions are made;
3. There is some variation in conception among the different sources I consulted; and
4. Part of the sales talk for NCIC is that it is infinitely flexible and expandable.

WHY THE ALARM?

NCIC plans to give its users electronic access to 19,000,000 individual citizens' arrest records–nearly 10 percent of the country's population–beginning this fall.[3] Euphemistically termed "criminal histories" (making it sound as if any person who was ever arrested has a history of criminality), these records will help police make decisions about arresting, searching, detaining, questioning, and investigating suspects and "offenders."

The shabbiness of using arrest records as a guide to police action cannot be overemphasized. At present, many forms of arrest records do not note dropped charges or results of trials and appeals. Even when complete records are kept, arrests that did not stick are listed, creating a suspicion–indeed a presumption–of guilt which can lead to further arrest and harrassment. As a local policeman told me, "a person doesn't get arrested unless he was asking for it." They believe that, judges believe it, employers believe it, and society believes it.[4]

PLEA BARGAINING

Moreover, convictions are frequently entered on arrest records as a result of the courtroom practice of plea bargaining. An attorney might get an arrested person acquitted of unjust charges, but an attorney costs money, and there is still a chance of losing, even on appeal, which costs more. Therefore many innocent defendants agree to plead guilty in exchange for a reduced fine, reduced or suspended sentence, or probation. The same idea extends to appeals of unfair trials; making an issue of anything is expensive and risky. (Several personal friends of mine have found themselves in this trap as a result of nonviolent political actions.)

Nowadays citizens can be arrested unfairly, searched illegally, charged with violating dubious laws (disorderly conduct, trespassing, blocking, loitering, or conspiracy), and railroaded into prison by ignorant or vindictive police, prosecutors, and judges.[5] The poor, the black, and the political radicals ("troublemakers") receive the highest incidence of this kind of treatment.[6] Yet, in the name of modern law enforcement, all these arrests and the convictions that go with them will go into the NCIC system.

THE INGREDIENTS OF A POLICE STATE

Computerizing and nationalizing records of arrests—complete or incomplete—and inviting local police departments to use them routinely—these are the ingredients of a police state. At the very best, discriminatory law enforcement and harassment practices will be cascaded, because an arrest becomes a justification for another arrest, and so on. I have never seen any evidence that this kind of law enforcement helps prevent crime. There seems to be growing evidence, however, of the day-to-day effect of such a system on citizens' lives. This is the chilling of free speech, free association, free petition for redress of grievances, etc. A telephone company manager recently explained this to me in this way: "It behooves a person to avoid arrest."

PROPONENTS OF NCIC SAY . . .

Proponents of NCIC argue that police already have five-minute telephone access to statewide and 24-hour access to nationwide arrest records of any person. They say NCIC will provide fairer, more detailed and accurate arrest records, distinguishing convictions from acquittals, for example. They say NCIC's fast response will allow cleared suspects to be released sooner, and arrested persons with clean records to be released on recognizance, thereby enhancing civil liberties. My response is that arrest records do not constitute probable cause for arrest, regardless of their accuracy; that detention without bona fide arrest is illegal in any case; that selective release on recognizance is really preventive detention in disguise; and that police access to records will be stepped up tremendously by NCIC, thereby damaging civil liberties irretrievably.

NCIC CONCERN ABOUT PRIVACY AND ETHICS

The Project SEARCH Staff (System for Electronic Analysis and Retrieval of Criminal Histories) has published a booklet[7] purporting to show that privacy and individual rights are being taken into account in their system planning. (Project SEARCH is now computerizing arrest records for a ten-state federally-funded demonstration.) The booklet is instructive. On page 1 it states: "criminal justice agencies require, in making decisions regarding a suspect or offender, knowledge of his prior involvement with the criminal justice system." And on page 19: "there is every reason to believe that (FBI) rap sheets . . . faithfully record the criminal histories of their subjects."

I found it difficult to read this booklet with any degree of objectivity, because of its countless euphemisms about "offenders" and "criminal justice"; it's a good illustration of the medium being the message.

POLICIES SUGGESTED BY SEARCH

In no way is the concept of discriminatory or politically-inspired arrest and harassment even touched upon as an area of concern, any more than the self-fulfilling properties of "criminal histories." The booklet presents many policy suggestions which are meaningful in the context of current law enforcement structures, such as improved accuracy and completeness, the exclusion of "information concerning juvenile offenders," and "further studies . . . to specify inclusion or exclusion of specific misdemeanors." However, let us examine four major areas:

1. The SEARCH prototype "does not include subjective evaluations . . . by police, judges, or detention authorities," just "hard data" on arrest, trial, and punishment. (If arrest, judgment, and parole decisions were made objectively, this world would be a different place today. I believe "hard data" is an utterly false description of arrest records, and one of the reasons why they are unsuitable for police access.)

2. Social security number, FBI number, operators license number, and "any miscellaneous identifying number" are part of each person's file. These are "not (to be used) as a device to permit linkages or data sharing with other information systems." (Who's going to believe that? It simply can't be enforced.)

3. Although highway patrols, registry authorities, prosecutors, judges, probation officers, and parole boards are to be given direct

access to all records, access is denied to the general public, defense attorneys and legal aid societies, and to the "offender" himself unless he submits to fingerprinting and his state submits itself to a law change.

4. A "code of ethics" pledges all participants in the system to limit their use to "criminal justice as a matter of government function," and other generally commendable pledges. (When the pledges do mean something, they do not seem to be enforceable or even checkable.)

The principal author of the booklet, Robert R. J. Gallati, also directs the New York State Identification and Intelligence System (NYSIIS)–the New York section of NCIC and a SEARCH participant. NYSIIS has been pointed out to me as a "model" for the national system in terms of human rights. Some rather bizarre misuse[8] and data theft[9] has occurred, but "civil liberties" and "due process" are supposedly enhanced by reducing illegal detention of suspects from 24 to 3 hours.[10] In order to check his record, however, an "offender" has to travel to Albany and pay a fee to NYSIIS.

A recent position paper[11] outlines at least four major concerns about data banks in relation to human rights:

1. loss of privacy through security loopholes;
2. transactions about individuals without their being notified;
3. merging and correlating dangerous information from diverse sources; and
4. operation without principled supervision.

NCIC has no features that satisfy a single one of these concerns.

OTHER REASONS FOR ALARM

Thus I regard NCIC to be dangerous because of its basic premise that police need arrest records of citizens, and can use them safely. However, there are yet more reasons for alarm as follows:

1. NCIC forms the basis for a total *gestapo* (literally "secret federal police") system, since the public has no access to its data, nor is any person notified of inquiries and transactions affecting himself. It could take the last vestiges of the "criminal justice system" entirely out of public hands.

2. The addition of surveillance data to NCIC is but a small step, technologically. The modern, aggressive style of surveillance and infiltration needs computer resources just like this, and there is reason to believe the NCIC system would be used for surveillance data.

3. NCIC could easily be used in the administration's preventive detention program and in gathering data for future "conspiracy" indictments.

4. The FBI runs NCIC. Its large scale undercover surveillance activities force one to view the FBI's ethics with suspicion, to say the least.

5. Computers are notorious for making mistakes themselves as well as transmitting unevaluated data, while policemen may well believe "anything a computer tells them."

WHO PAYS FOR NCIC? WHO SELLS IT?

The cost of NCIC equipment and operations, along with its substantial dangers to human rights, could hardly be ignored by responsible town officials in deciding whether to hook their police up to this system. The financing structure seems to be designed to circumvent this foible of democracy.

Towns in Massachusetts pay only their individual Teletype rental, about $2000 annually, to join NCIC. To ease towns in painlessly, a 40 percent federal subsidy is provided to reduce this rental cost. (Now that 131 towns are connected to NCIC, the subsidy is ending.) Expenses borne by the state, including phone lines and computer center operation, are also subsidized federally. The rest of NCIC, including development of SEARCH, is 100 percent federally funded, primarily by the so-called Safe Streets Act of 1968. We all pay for NCIC, of course. But the fragmentation of payments fosters a carefree feeling among budget-minded local and state officials that "somebody else" is paying.

Perhaps officials might be attracted to NCIC by its apparent bargain price, but still question its merits. To minimize this problem in our state, the sales staff of New England Telephone Company (supplier of lines and Teletypes) visited 117 towns in Massachusetts last year to educate local boards and committees on the need for NCIC in modern police operations. Quite by accident, I heard one of those sales talks. It was very smooth and professional indeed. Human rights were not mentioned. The officials present agreed "the advantages outweigh the disadvantages," and incorporated NCIC in their town's budget.

Because of indirect financing and professional selling, NCIC has begun operating almost entirely without the knowledge or approval of the public it fundamentally affects.

A CHALLENGE TO NCIC IN A TOWN MEETING

After I was defeated in an attempt to delete the NCIC budget line pending further investigation and a full explanation, I introduced the following motion on the floor of the Wayland, Mass., Town Meeting on March 8, 1971:

MOVED: That the Police Department be directed to include in next year's Annual Report a statistical tabulation of its usage of the NCIC computer system, including the following information if at all possible:

1) number of inquiries by type of inquiry and reason for inquiry;
2) results of inquiries, including arrests and known convictions;
3) a similar summary of information *entered* by Wayland police; and
4) troubles encountered (down-time, false arrest, invasion of rights, etc).

Despite angry opposition, the motion was carried by a majority vote of those present.

The reporting should accomplish one or more of the following objectives in addition to generating a list of features and how and why they are used:

1) stimulate discussion and questioning of NCIC by exposure to the public of its existence;
2) abate the chilling effect on free speech, association, etc., by removing the veil of mystery from NCIC operations;
3) deter questionable operations by the police by requiring an accounting of such operations (thereby opening them to criticism and veto);
4) convey the doubts of concerned citizens about NCIC to town fathers, police, state officials, legislators, and Congressmen;
5) stimulate public realization of the sham of the entire so-called "criminal justice system" in which NCIC is grounded; and
6) give people courage to demand public accountability of all governmental functions, computerized or not.

These objectives could be served even if the police misconstrue or falsify the required report! Actually, the report will be difficult to falsify because all NCIC transactions are logged verbatim at the state level, thus facilitating crosschecking.

Finally, if town officials actually fail to report as directed, perhaps because of secrecy statutes, then outraged citizens can demand removal of NCIC from the police department. (Wayland officials have indicated they intend to cooperate at the present time.)

Among the voters with whom I spoke, a tremendous number of factors affected their thinking on the issue of NCIC. Some of these factors include:

1) teenage offspring suffering police harassment;
2) Senator Ervin's hearings on data banks;
3) Arthur Miller's book and TV appearances;[12]

4) unemployment and blackballing;
5) runaway military actions, the war in Vietnam;
6) suspicious assassinations;
7) conspiracy indictments;
8) corrupt, vindictive auto registry practices;
9) police brutality and dishonesty;
10) computerized credit rating and billing;
11) the 1970 census;
12) Nazi Germany;
13) Distrust of Nixon-Agnew-Hoover-Mitchell-Burger-Blackmun;
14) preventive detention and no-knock;
15) official lies; and
16) general principles of public disclosure.

In fact, all repression and manipulation of the public trust could be related in one way or another to this alleged anticrime computer system.[13]

Personally, I think our souls felt a sense of renewal when we debated NCIC in our Town Meeting and we saw some hope of controlling or at least influencing the widespread implementation of this system.[14]

[1]*The 1970 Comprehensive Criminal Justice Plan for Crime Prevention and Control,* pp. 166-67. Commonwealth of Massachusetts, Committee on Law Enforcement and Administration of Criminal Justice, 80 Boylston Street, Boston.

[2]*Communication Breakthrough in the Fight Against Crime: National Crime Information Center.* Federal Bureau of Investigation, Washington, D.C. (1970). This 20-page booklet, prefaced by a letter signed by J. Edgar Hoover, is directed at policemen, encouraging them to use NCIC.

[3]FBI to Computerize Rap Files; No New Safeguards Planned," in *Computerworld,* September 30, 1970.

[4]"Misuse of Data in File by Honest Police Cited," letter in *Computerworld,* January 13, 1971. The letter describes discrimination against tenants based on arrest files.

[5]*What You're Up Against: A People's Legal Defense Manual,* Massachusetts Lawyers Guild, 70 Charles Street, Boston (1970).

[6]See *The Quality of Justice in the Lower Criminal Courts of Metropolitan Boston,* Lawyers Committee for Civil Rights Under Law, 15 Broad Street, Boston (1970). This booklet describes a rigorous statistical analysis of police and court discrimination against poor and black people. Readers should also examine "conspiracy" cases all over the country, now in progress.

[7]*Security and Privacy Considerations in Criminal History Information Systems, Project SEARCH Technical Report No. 2,* Project SEARCH Committee on Security and Privacy, 1108 14th Street, Sacramento, California. (July 1970).

[8]"Lawyer Seeks to Nullify Wall Street Fingerprinting Law," *Computerworld,* April 22, 1970. This article tells how 29 workers were fired because of NYSIIS arrest files, half of which showed no convictions.

[9]"Security Breach Leads to Police Data Theft," in *Computerworld,* February 10, 1971. This article tells of NYSIIS data reaching airlines, credit agencies, and private detective organizations by illicit means.

[10]"New York State Identification and Intelligence System," in *Computers and Automation,* March, 1971.

[11]"Data Banks-A Position Paper" by C. Foster in *Computers and Automation,* March 1971.

[12]*The Assault on Privacy: Computers, Data Banks, and Dossiers,* by Arthur R. Miller. University of Michigan Press, Ann Arbor, Michigan (1971).

[13]"The Theory and Practice of American Political Intelligence," by Frank Donner, in *The New York Review of Books,* April 22, 1971, gives an excellent detailed accounting of the assumptions and activities of the "intelligence mind" in this country.

[14]Shortly after this article was written, Massachusetts officials reportedly decided to "hold off" joining FBI arrest record system, building instead a far more modest, "limited" statewide arrest record network. (Although reported April 13, 1971, in *The Cambridge Phoenix,* state officials have refused to confirm these facts for me–while accusing me of not knowing what I'm talking about! Finally I obtained confirmation from a highly placed clandestine source.) Their reasons were "92 percent financial and 8 percent moral," according to my unquotable secret reporting to *conviction* of *"serious"* offenses only, and establishing formal control by *state* law enforcement groups instead of the FBI. I regard these changes as half-baked reforms; they ignore the basic political discrimination and repression fostered by arrest and "correction" reporting. For example, demonstrators who are beaten by police are often *convicted* of "assault on a police officer"; antiwar organizers are *convicted* of "conspiracy to incite riot"; and on and on. These are "serious" crimes. Moreover, the door seems open for 92 percent reconciliation with the FBI through negotiation of a subsidy. In short, NCIC is still dangerous.

25 Social, Economic, Legal and Ecological Aspects of Weather Modification

The National Science Foundation

Economic and social activities of communities, regions, or nations are influenced by the patterns of climate and weather. The changing seasons bring with them changes in the nature of individual and social behavior as people respond to these cyclical modifications of the environment. Even short-term weather incidents, such as a sudden snowstorm or a summer heat wave, may have effects on human behavior which can endure long after the weather incident has passed.

Relatively little is known about the processes of decision-making by which people respond to the normal variability of weather. The techniques for investigation are available, but the surface has scarcely been scratched with respect to what needs to be done. As the practicality of meaningful weather modification grows every day more promising, the social, economic, legal, and ecological implications involved demand an increasing share of attention. The human consequences of deliberate or inadvertent modification of natural processes must be understood and evaluated in advance. The extent and complexity of potential effects on human life and the ecology

From: *Weather Modification* (Washington: Superintendent of Documents, 1968), pp. 102-5.

The National Science Foundation is the federal agency with the major responsibility for funding scientific research projects and studying the characteristics of science and scientific personnel in the United States.

are only beginning to receive serious study by investigators in the many disciplines involved.

In fiscal year 1967, the NSF requested the National Center for Atmospheric Research at Boulder, Colo., to organize a task group on the human dimensions of the atmosphere with the objective of focusing attention on the social, economic, legal, and ecological aspects of weather and the possible impact of weather modification. The task group was chaired by Dr. W. R. Derrick Sewell of the University of Victoria, British Columbia, and included 12 other prominent social, economic, legal, and ecological experts from universities throughout the United States. After a year of study and discussion, the report has been published by the NSF in 1968 under the title "Human Dimensions of the Atmosphere" NSF 68-18. While this report tends to focus most of its attention upon weather modification, it nevertheless maintains a broad perspective throughout, with consideration being given to other alternative adjustments to variations in the atmosphere, and to problems relating to the increasing use of the atmosphere. Based upon estimates of probable technological success in the reasonably near future, the following questions were among those posed by the task group.

It is apparent from the rapid growth of weather modification activity during the past 20 years that those involved in this effort perceive important benefits from it. Several advantages are claimed for weather modification. It is generally fairly cheap, and the equipment involved can be moved from one location to another without great difficulty. Many farmers, for example, regard cloud seeding as an inexpensive gamble. If it succeeds in increasing precipitation (or reducing hail), it may make the difference between having a crop or no crop at all. If the effort fails, the investment will not have been large, and more often than not it can be shared among several farmers. Electric power companies that have undertaken programs to increase precipitation believe that the effort is an economical way of improving their operating efficiency. The gains from lightning suppression and from cold fog dispersal are also believed to be substantial.

Identifying the benefits and costs of the use or modification of atmospheric resources is not a simple matter. The dynamic nature and common property characteristics of the atmosphere lead inevitably to external effects. For example, no means have yet been found to confine the effects of using the atmosphere for waste disposal only to the users. Nor have means been found to confine the effects of modifying the weather to those who desire the modification. One farmer may need additional moisture, but his neighbor may suffer considerable losses if such moisture falls on his land too. Similarly, the precipitation which enables the hydroelectric power company to increase its profits may also ruin the vacation of the tourist. But these external effects are not always harmful.

In some cases, those who do not contract for weather modification may benefit from its results and may therefore experience windfall gains.

A complete evaluation of weather modification requires the identification of activities directly or indirectly affected by weather changes, and an analysis of the manner in which given changes result in gains or losses to such activities. A similar approach is required to determine gains and losses for different areas. In certain weather modification cases, for example, gains in local areas may be offset by losses in other areas.

Any evaluation of weather modification must also take into account that the effort is only one means of attaining specified objectives. Increases in food production, for example, may be obtained in many ways other than by augmenting precipitation in the arid West. Increases in electric energy production can be obtained not only by cloud seeding, but also by thermal power or nuclear power. The merits of weather modification, therefore, must be compared with those of alternatives to determine the most efficient means of achieving the desired objective.

WHAT IS THE POTENTIAL IMPACT ON BIOLOGICAL SYSTEMS?

Another important question raised by the expansion of weather modification activity relates to the potential impact on biological systems. Lack of moisture is the principal factor limiting the biological productivity of much of the earth. Added precipitation in water-short regions can doubtless increase yields of food and fiber from rangelands, forests, and cultivated croplands. However, such major weather modifications may also alter the balance among species of plants and animals, with sharp declines in the numbers of some, and inordinate growth in the abundance of others. In particular, major weather changes may result in the rapid spread of certain weeds, pests, and vector-borne diseases.

Plans for expanding weather modification must therefore take into account the possibility that the benefits of increased range, forest, and crop production will be counterbalanced in whole or in part by undesirable long-term effects on man's sources of food supply, his health, and his general environment. It is particularly important to identify those aspects of weather modification that are likely to have irreversible long-term consequences not foreseen by those whose primary objective is immediate increase in agricultural production or water supply.

ARE PRESENT LEGAL THEORIES ADEQUATE?

Are the principles underlying present legal theories of liability appropriate to cases of weather modification? This basic question has been the subject of academic discussion, but no definite conclusions have yet emerged. The general view seems to be that no urgency for answers exists so long as it remains impossible in specific cases to prove that the weather has in fact been modified in ways to cause particular results. However, the ability to modify the weather on a more consistent basis is rapidly developing. As this capability grows, the problem of proving occurrence and cause diminishes. Therefore, principles for compensating losses in weather modification cases will have to be determined. Principles need to be developed not only for settling claims of individuals against other individuals, but also for cases of individuals against governments, governments against governments, and perhaps nations against other nations.

WHAT TYPES OF CONTROL ARE REQUIRED, AND WHAT ROLE SHOULD GOVERNMENT PLAY?

The fact that weather modification efforts are increasing and that these activities have important external effects makes it inevitable that some form of governmental control will be required. What types of control are needed? Is it sufficient to require licensing of operations, or is it also necessary to require that information on results be furnished? At what level of government should control be vested? Should regulation be in the hands of local, State, or Federal authorities? Should the Federal Government control only those weather modification attempts that might affect more than one State or other countries, and leave control of other modification activities to State and/or local authorities?

Another set of problems is related to the proper role of the Federal Government in the management of atmospheric resources. Should this role be confined to regulation of the use of these resources, or should it extend to direct participation in development, as in modification of the weather? Are there particular characteristics of atmospheric resources and their management that call for government participation in development in the same way that certain characteristics of water resources call for such participation? In the case of water resources, the existence of indivisibilities, externalities, and the demand for certain public benefits (such as flood control and municipal water supplies) leads to public intervention and participation in development. Some of these features are also present in the case of atmospheric resources. The question arises as to which aspects of the management of these resources can best be performed by the public sector and which by the private sector. . . .

Chapter EIGHT

The Future of Federalism

INTRODUCTION TO CHAPTER EIGHT The articles in this volume have clearly demonstrated that American federalism is an "uneasy partnership" as our title suggests. It is full of tensions and conflict involving such problems as the energy crisis, pollution, and urban blight. Despite this, it remains a *partnership.* Many of its qualities are changing (in response to social and economic problems), but the partnership continues.

We have discussed the future of federalism in several of our chapter introductions, and there is no need to repeat our observations here. In this chapter we present the thoughts of two leading scholars in this field concerning the shape of the federal system in the years ahead.

READINGS IN THIS CHAPTER

Richard Leach and Daniel Elazar list the major forces which they believe will affect the future of federalism in the United States. Many of them tend to encourage increasing centralization:

1. *State and local governmental personnel who are unable or unwilling to cooperate with federal officials or unable to solve their own problems.* Many examples of this can be found throughout this volume. Sundquist and the Advisory Committee on Intergovernmental Relations emphasized the lack of coordination among governmental officials at all levels. The

Committee for Economic Development cited the failure of state governments to act in a responsible manner toward many serious problems of public policy. The Nathans article revealed that state and local officials are often unable to deal with pollution problems because of their lack of technical expertise. Furthermore, state and local officials may be unwilling to deal adequately with pollution because they are indebted to polluting industries or labor unions (perhaps because of generous campaign contributions or conflict of interest). Of course, this can also occur on the federal level, but it is somewhat more difficult for pollutors to gain a foothold in the large arena of federal policy-making. The Nathans article also revealed that officials of cities and counties in a particular locality are frequently unwilling to cooperate with each other because of various political jealousies; this leads to a paralysis of anti-pollution activities and an atmosphere of irresponsibility with these officials blaming each other for delays in the alleviation of pollution. There is also a common lack of cooperation between state and local officials on one hand and federal officials on the other. Often state and federal pollution regulations are inconsistent, and innocent businesses are whipsawed between them not knowing which regulations apply. The Lippit and National Science Foundation articles demonstrated that this can also occur in the fields of energy production and weather modification.

2. *The weak financial condition of many states and cities.* Our chapters on fiscal federalism, state government, and urban affairs all demonstrate that many state and local governments are in such dire financial condition that essential services including police and fire protection must be trimmed. Even rapidly increasing tax rates and deficit spending are sometimes insufficient to cover expenses especially in urban areas where the central city tax base deteriorates as people and businesses move to the suburbs. One solution to these problems is increased federal aid to states and cities which often brings federal control.

3. *Fragmentation of power among many government entities leading to a lack of coordination.* The urban, fiscal federalism, and technology chapters all support this point. A given locality may be governed by dozens of governments including towns, cities, school districts, water districts, counties, the state (and near borders sometimes two states), and the federal government. Furthermore, each of these entities is often divided into agencies which spend more time fighting than cooperating. The reader should note this point is closely related to the first two in this listing. Fragmentation is partially responsible for the financial condition of state and local governments and it also discourages cooperation among government personnel.

4. *The failure of many cities to provide safe, clean, and dependable environments.* To a large extent, this point is a result of the first three

points in this listing. In Detroit they say: "If the muggers don't get you the pollution will." And pollution and crime are not the only problems; many cities are noisy, dirty, and depressingly crowded. They are miserable places in which to live and work.

But Elazar and Leach also cite factors which tend to encourage decentralization within the federal system:

1. *The basic conservatism of the American people and their strong attachment to their cities and states.* There is little direct support for this point in this volume, but there is considerable circumstantial evidence. When policy problems arise which would seem to benefit from centralized direction, most policy-makers at all levels seek to utilize the federal system to solve the problems. For example, pollution, energy production, and weather modification would seem to be prime candidates for central policy-making, but every attempt has been made by Congress and the executive branch to encourage state and local initiative in these areas.

2. *The flexibility of the federal system, which has successfully withstood many drastic social and economic changes.* The selections in this volume do not bear on this point because our objective was to describe the current dynamics of American federalism and not its historical development.

3. *The considerable effort being invested to make federalism work.* The problems in the federal system described in this volume are widely recognized, and many imaginative solutions (such as revenue sharing) are being proposed; these are described in every chapter of this volume, and need not be listed here.

After balancing the forces for and against change, Leach concludes that if our major political problems are not at least partially solved, "the possibility of a major restructuring of federalism will rapidly increase." He hints that America may discard federalism in favor of an essentially unitary system. Elazar is much more optimistic about the possibility that the federal system as presently constituted will be able to deal with our problems.

26 The Resurgence of Federalism

Daniel J. Elazar

From: *State Government*, (Summer 1970), pp. 166–73. Reprinted by permission of the author and publisher.

Daniel Elazar is Professor of Political Science and Director of the Center for Study of American Federalism at Temple University. He is regarded as one of the foremost experts in the field of American federalism.

The great concern with problems of intergovernmental relations visible all around us today is accompanied by an apparent absence of sufficient understanding of the first principles of federalism, even among those who espouse the practices of intergovernmental partnership in the United States. When we speak of federal democracy and particularly of American federalism, we are not simply talking about convenient political arrangements that should be maintained because we are accustomed to them or about administrative decentralization that is valuable because it gets things done. We are talking about a comprehensive pattern of political organization that permeates every aspect of American political life from party politics to administrative law, a pattern based on three great political principles: *contractual noncentralization, territorial democracy,* and *multifaceted partnership.* Only when we understand those principles and the deeper meaning of federalism does the import of today's discussions take on its real significance.

Contractual noncentralization—the structured dispersion of power among many centers whose legitimate authority is constitutionally guaranteed–is the key to the widespread and entrenched diffusion of power that remains the principle argument on behalf of federal democracy.

Noncentralization is not the same as decentralization, though the latter term is frequently, and erroneously, used in its place to describe the American system. Decentralization implies the existence of a central authority, a central government. The government that can decentralize can recentralize if it so desires. Hence in decentralized systems, the diffusion of power is actually a matter of grace not right.

Noncentralization is used to describe a political system in which power is so diffused that it cannot be legitimately centralized or concentrated without breaking the structure and spirit of the constitution. The United States has a noncentralized system. We have a national–or general–government which functions in many areas for many purposes, but not a central government controlling all the lines of political communication and decision-making. Our States are not creatures of the federal government but, like the latter, derive their authority directly from the people. Structurally, they are substantially immune from federal interference. Functionally, they share many activities with the federal government but without forfeiting their policy-making roles and decision-making powers.

In contemporary social science language, centralization and decentralization are extremes of the same continuum while noncentralization represents another continuum altogether. In systems located on the former, it is rather simple to measure the flow of power one way or another. In noncentralized systems, however, it is a considerably more difficult matter. Simple evidence of national government involvement tells us nothing about the relative strength of the various power centers in policy-making administration. The primary diffusion of power makes "involvement" take on many different meanings. Or, to use another imagery, decentralization implies a hierarchy–a pyramid of governments with gradations of power. Noncentralization describes a matrix of governments with powers so distributed that the rank order of the several governments is not fixed; e.g., if the national government is primary in the field of foreign affairs, the States are primary in the field of education.

THE SPIRIT OF NONCENTRALIZATION

These theoretical principles have important and immediate practical consequences which lead to the primary operational fact of the American system–the necessity to involve all planes of government in virtually every activity of government in such a way as to give them an irrevocable share of the decision-making and executing processes.

The basic noncentralized relationship between the federal government and the States has been extended, de facto, to the localities as well. Even though the localities remain theoretically the creatures of their States, in fact they have gained a measure of entrenched political power because they have been able to capitalize on the spirit of noncentralization–the spirit of federalism, if you will.

Noncentralization makes it possible for local governments to develop policies and programs of their own within a system that is too complex to allow them the luxury of isolation; to acquire outside aids for carrying out those policies and programs; and to adapt those aids to their own needs.

The same principles of noncentralization have been extended into the private sphere, by permeation, in two ways. On one hand, it gives private interests a fixed place in the system that assures them of a political "say" that cannot be ignored. A good example of this is the evolving relationship between Washington and the scientific community. On the other, private organizations are also stimulated to organize along federal lines, diffusing power within their own structures to limit or prevent hierarchical decision-making. This is true whether we are speaking of the Chamber of Commerce or the AFL-CIO. State and local chambers are free to ignore the U.S. Chamber as they wish, and state federations of labor can choose their responses in like manner to their national body.

Noncentralization in the United States is based on territorial divisions, from States to precincts. The permanent boundaries of the former and the well-nigh permanent boundaries of their major subdivisions serve as strong bulwarks of noncentralization. As permanent boundaries, they offer continued opportunities for diverse interests to exercise power without fear or favor while, possessing the neutrality of so-called "artificial boundaries," they prevent the confinement of power to a few select interests. Since every interest, new or old, is located willy-nilly, in some formally defined political territory, every interest can gain some measure of expression more or less proportional to its strength, simply by making use of the country's political mechanisms.

Wayne County, Michigan, for example, was a locus of power for Yankee commercial and craft interests in the nineteenth century. With its economic transformation into an automobile center, it was politically transformed into a stronghold for "ethnic" and Negro autoworkers without having to significantly alter its basic political structure or institutions. The State of Florida, once a typical representative of traditional southern interests, now speaks for the pioneers of the space frontier and the new world of leisure. These changes have taken place without serious dislocations in the Nation's political system because of the existence of territorial democracy.

Noncentralization and territorial democracy are made operationally effective by the intergovernmental and public-private partnership that has grown up within the framework of the Constitution. This partnership is based on the almost universal sharing of functions previously described. Sharing involves a whole complex of deep-seated arrangements designed to recognize and accomodate national and local interests and preserve the basic integrities of the several governments that participate in the system, while mobilizing sufficient energy to maintain and develop positive public programs.

These principles permeate every aspect of the American political system. They are not simple features of grant-in-aid programs or intergovernmental consultations. Their influence is felt in the party system, the administration of so-called direct federal functions, the organization of our national defense and even in the realm of foreign affairs. Through them, the full implications of the federal bargain that unites peoples and polities is made meaningful in the arena where political ideas are ultimately put to the test.

THE REVIVAL OF CONCERN

These days we are indeed witnessing a revival of concern with federalism as a fundamental aspect of the American political system. Presidents Johnson and Nixon have repeatedly called for better federal-state-local relations. President Johnson and his cabinet met with the Governors of the States in Washington and in the field, to a degree unknown since the days of Teddy Roosevelt. Through Vice President Humphrey, direct lines of communication were opened with the mayors of our larger cities. Even more to the point, President Johnson issued executive orders and the Congress passed legislation strengthening the hands of the States and localities in cooperative programs. President Nixon is committed to continuing in the same direction. He has appointed Vice President Agnew as his liaison with the States and has located the newly created Office of Intergovernmental Relations within the Office of the Vice President. While Mr. Nixon's term of office has yet been too brief for a performance pattern to be established, his "New Federalism" has emphasized such concrete proposals as revenue sharing and the transfer of primary responsibility for manpower programs to the States. While the effects on the federalism of his proposed welfare reform, environmental pollution control and law enforcement programs are less clear-cut, his concern for federalism and the enhancement of state and local roles is apparent in all of them.

Beyond Washington, the new concern with the federal system is at least equally widespread. In the past three years, the country's leading periodicals–*Time, Life, Fortune, Newsweek* and *Saturday Review*, to name only a few–have featured articles, essays and editorial statements on the need for and virtues of a federalism that will strengthen all levels of government in the United States. Even *Commentary*, in its May 1967 issue, had an article on the virtues of utilizing federal principles to promote effective government, written by a member of the Eastern Establishment which has not been known to be particularly friendly to the traditional institutions of American government. Federalism is indeed "in" these days.

It is significant that this revived concern is not a renewal of the old cry of "states rights" by people who object to the new role of government in American life. Nor is it confined to state and local officials who feel burdened by pressures from Washington. The ordinary citizen, the intellectual, the conservative, the liberal–all seem to be sensing the basic strength of federalism.

Today's concern with federalism is based on the recognition of two fundamental facts: *that governmental activities must be shared by all levels of government to be effective and responsive to public needs*, and that *it is possible for all governments to grow in power simultaneously*. The first, in effect, holds that the various governments in the United States are more likely to share common interests that encourage or demand intergovernmental cooperation for their satisfaction or achievement than they are to be in conflict. The second recognizes that governmental power is not a limited quantity, a pie that must be redivided with every new program giving one government a greater share at the expense of the others, but rather that governmental power itself expands so that all governments may gain power simultaneously.

Careful students of American federalism know that both these facts have been true since the founding of the Republic. Despite a theory which held that the federal system functioned best when each plane was functionally as well as structurally separate, the necessity of shared interests and publics led to substantial intergovernmental cooperation in those fields where governments were active throughout the nineteenth century. The federal government, the states, and the localities cooperated in developing educational systems; in constructing roads, canals and railroads; in creating rudimentary public welfare institutions; in providing for the common defense; in maintaining a national financial system; and in numerous other ways after 1790. To do so they developed joint stock companies, exchanged personnel and technical assistance, and cooperated in inspections. These cooperative programs were financed primarily through federal and state land grants, permanent funds created by investing the proceeds, and even some cash grants-in-aid. As the role of government expanded, all governments grew in responsibilities, adding functions as their publics demanded them. By 1913, when the twentieth century brand of cooperative federalism emerged, a whole history of shared activities testified to the validity of both premises. In the area of program development and implementation at least, the changes in the velocity of government (the amount of government activity in relation to the total activity of society) have been reflected on all planes of government (federal, state, and local) without significantly changing the balance of power among governments.

PREDICTIONS OF FEDERALISM'S DOOM

The renewed concern with federalism in the most significant political circles would hardly have been forecast by most people even a few years ago. Three decades ago, leading political scientists were predicting the imminent demise of the federal system (a favorite pastime of Americans in every generation). Charles E. Merriam was calling for the creation of separate city-states to embrace the Nation's leading metropolitan areas and serve, in effect, as supposedly "more rational" federal administrative regions. Harold Laski, that brilliantly inaccurate British observer of the American scene, argued persuasively that federalism was obsolete and was rightly being replaced by a new quasi-collectivist pluralism. Franz Neumann was busy arguing that federalism had nothing to do with freedom but was an expedient device for unifying initially self-contained localities that could be dispensed with once unity was achieved.

Merriam, Laski, Neumann and their compatriots, it turns out, all missed the boat. Metropolitanization of the population has made Merriam's city-state idea progressively more obsolete. What if our great cities had been turned into city-states with their 1935 boundaries? Today they would be surrounded by people and communities still tributary to them but all located across state lines, further complicating interlocal relations. Even New York–the metropolis most afflicted by interstate suburbanization–has most of its suburbanities in Westchester County and Long Island.

Laski's vaunted pluralism has shown itself to provide no supportive structure of the kind necessary to maintain a sufficient diffusion of power to make diversity possible. Where it has been able to develop unfettered by federal structures and institutions, as in Great Britain and Western Europe, pluralist democracy has turned into a well-nigh crushing oligopoly coalescing big business, big labor and big government so that every interest seeking the ear of the latter must either appease the former two or become big and unresponsive to individual desires in its own right, often to the detriment of individual communities. If the influence of depersonalized oligopoly is less pervasive within our boundaries–and it is–I would argue that it is at least partly because our federal system has limited the power of the "bigs" to control access to or destroy communities and has kept all of them more permeable.

Finally, with the emergence of the new nations and the continued expansion of totalitarian and authoritarian systems in our century, we have learned that federalism is a system that functions meaningfully only in a democratic climate. Federalism is never simply a matter of merging disparate localities to form a larger polity–a way station to true national unity as Neumann and others have claimed, to be dropped when its expediential purposes have been accomplished. It is not a gimmick, but a legitimate approach to the problem of popular government in its own right. In fact, federalism is a major species of democracy, perhaps the most successful of all species of democracy. Federal democracy, the contractual linkage of polities and people in such a way as to preserve their diverse integrities while ensuring their unity, has turned out to be the most stable form of popular government even though it often gives the impression of great flux. Perhaps, indeed, its ability to handle flux is the key to its stability in a world of change.

If Harold Laski missed this point, another British student of the American political scene, M. J. C. Vile, whose work is more recent, has observed, "The United States is a federal country, in spirit, in its way of life, and in its constitution." Americans are beginning to consciously appreciate this fact once again. In a sense, it is being forced upon them.

The new concern with federalism is strongly influenced by the increasing awareness on the part of the people in Washington and elsewhere that nationally established programs do not become meaningful until they are translated into functioning ones at the local level. In a democratic society based on the idea of local control of public actions, this means that local cooperation is of first importance. And in a democratic society, local cooperation is not gained through coercive measures but through recognition of local prerogatives as well as local needs.

Moreover, certain policy makers are beginning to recognize some other elementary facts. I shall mention only two. It is becoming apparent that the reduction of the States' role in decision-making creates unmanageable log jams in Washington as every local government and interest assaults the federal bureaus in an effort to secure benefits from federal programs. It is becoming even more apparent that the only way to achieve coordination of the myriad of federal programs now available (estimates range from 160 to over 1,000 depending on how they are counted) is at the state and local level where they are translated to reality. For years, wise state and local officials have known that Washington's bureaus, with all the good will in the world, are too big and too diffuse to really work out interagency coordinating procedures at that level and that it is, de facto, a local responsibility to do so.

It is in the recognition of these basic truths and the right action they should call forth, that the future of federalism will be worked out. What of that future?

A FORECAST OF THE FEDERALISM OF THE FUTURE

Insofar as it is possible to forecast trends, we can see the following ones, always bearing in mind that the forecasting itself has an impact on the future it seeks to delineate.

1. *As the role of government in our society grows greater, all governments will continue to grow—in size, expenditures, and scope of activities.* American governments have grown consistently in all three since the establishment of the Republic. There is nothing on the horizon to indicate that this trend will be reversed.

Moreover, as long as the press of world affairs requires the federal government to devote something like 50 percent of its budget to paying for current military expenditures and another 15 percent to paying interest and costs from past wars, the growth of federal activities in the domestic field will continue to take second place to that of the States and their localities. This has been the case since the end of World War II. At the present time, the States and localities account for two-thirds of the total governmental expenditures for domestic purposes. This is a fair indicator of their political role as well.

At the same time, increased expertise at the state and local levels will not only improve the quality of their governmental services but will put the States and localities in a better position to negotiate with their federal counterparts. Not only will these professionals share the same professional values and long-range aspirations, with a consequent easing of communications, but they will also enable their governments to negotiate from positions of greater strength. This has been true of established programs in the past; the States and localities have gained greater control over cooperative expenditures whenever they have developed greater expertise to handle them.

2. *Sharing will be equally important in the future.* There will no doubt be changes in the respective roles of different governments and government agencies in specific cases. It is possible that functions now extensively shared will become more or less unilateral ones and vice versa.

While the argument for "turning functions back to the States" has continually run afoul of hard political realities (noncentralization in this respect prevents decentralization since Washington cannot give orders to decentralize so long as local interests use Congress to gain national assistance), this does not mean that specific shifts cannot occur. Moreover, new forms of sharing are likely to develop. Regional arrangements are beginning to loom large on the governmental scene, ranging from such long-term organizations as the Appalachian Regional Commission and its sister regional bodies in other depressed areas to special purpose conferences convened in a wide variety of situations. This new regionalism is promoting new kinds of cooperation in at least two ways: an increase in subnational planning of programs to deal with problems involving more than one State and the involvement of both the federal government and the States in joint policy-making, including decisions on the expenditure of federal funds, at the very beginning of new programs. Various approaches to regional cooperation are likely to be tried with increasing frequency over the next half generation, with varying degrees of success. The introduction of block grants and revenue sharing could open up new avenues for providing federal aid to States and their subdivisions without centralizing power in Washington. So, too, the establishment of minimum federal regulatory standards while encouraging the States to set higher ones and giving them the power to enforce both sets may open up new dimensions of federal-state cooperation.

The character of sharing over the next half generation is more difficult to forecast. One could simply conclude that old patterns will continue with minor adjustments. There are, however, some problems, almost perennial ones, which make the issue somewhat more problematical. It is entirely possible that the widespread recognition of sharing will lead to the use of sharing devices as a means to achieve de facto centralization. If the smaller governments are forced into a position where they must cooperate without really participating in decision-making, simply on the grounds that cooperation is expected of them, sharing will be formally preserved without achieving the goals for which it is intended.

In addition, there is the question of direct federal-local relations and the even more vital question of federal-private relations. One of the characteristics of the new programs of the 1960s has been the increased emphasis on federal aid to anybody. Thus, the federal government is not only developing more programs in which localities can deal directly with Washington to gain assistance, but is revising older programs to allow selective direct federal-local relations where none existed before. Though there are some tendencies to the contrary, it is likely that such relations will continue to grow in the immediate future. Since they involve project grants, they will tend to add to the complexity of the sharing process and may cause further distortions of the system.

In a more radical vein, traditional concepts of federalism are still being challenged by notions of pluralism. One consequence of this is that great national associations or corporations with powerful means to influence Congress are given responsibilities that might otherwise have been allocated to state or local governments. In some cases, there is every justification for this. In others, the issue is unclear. For example, the use of private industries to run Job Corps centers under federal contracts may or may not be the best way for the federal government to provide assistance to impoverished youth who need additional training. But the creation of local development corporations under federal aegis to combine federal and private powers for assistance to the ghettos would be fraught with dangers unless they were organized as elements of the state and local systems in which they were to function.

Federal-private relations are also a form of sharing and unquestionably help to perpetuate noncentralized government. At the same time, they may alter the shape of the system if they proliferate over the next half generation. There will be, almost certainly, pressures for their proliferation, particularly since the large corporations that have grown great as a result of federal defense spending are beginning to seek alternative ways to continue to draw upon the federal treasury for their profits in an effort to lessen their dependence on defense contracts. In one sense, this is all to the good since it will make future disarmament efforts easier on the economy. However, if these efforts are not fitted into the federal system, the States and localities may suffer from them while the oligarchic concentration of power at the national level, already evident in the "military-industrial complex," will sap the foundations of the American system of broad-based decision-making in the name of public-private partnership.

3. *The States will have to act constantly and with great vigor to maintain their traditional position as the keystone in the American governmental arch.* The continued central role of the States is no longer a foregone conclusion within the framework of American federalism. While it is not seriously possible to conceive of the States not playing a major role, the significance of their role will depend to a very great extent upon their responses over the next half generation to the challenges which confront them. Now that the federal government is meeting little public objection to its involvement in the range of domestic activities and direct federal relations with the localities are becoming equally accepted, it is possible that the role of the localities will be emphasized at the expense of the States. However, the very thrust towards regionalism indicates that sheer federal-local relations will not be sufficient to handle the dispersal of power and operational activity which is considered desirable in this country. The localities cannot confront the powerful federal government alone, nor can overall policy be made in Washington for the country as

a whole. Moreover, the States, by their sheer existence, have developed concrete patterns of politics and culture which infuse their localities with unique ways of doing things. Hence, they do not stand at a particular disadvantage in defining a positive place for themselves in the new federalism. But in order to do so, they will have to function like general governments and indeed like central governments. It will no longer be possible for them to rely simply upon their role as conduits funneling federal aid to their localities or local requests to Washington; nor will they profit by acting as simply another set of local governments. Rather, their strength lies in the fact that they are general governments with central government responsibilities toward their local subdivisions.

The Governors of the States show every indication of recognizing this and of seeking to capitalize on it. Such recent actions as the Interstate Compact on Education, which is a clear attempt on the part of the Governors to gain some measure of general control over educational programs within their States that have previously been highly fragmented, is one good example. The Appalachian program, which channels decision-making through the general organs of state government rather than through the specialized agencies, is another. The political situation of the next several years, which will encourage Republican Governors to make records in their States in order to gain support for their party from Democratic and independent voters at the polls, is likely to stimulate this kind of response. Democratic Governors will be forced to respond in kind, if only in self-defense.

The States will have additional advantages in defining their position because of the Nation's population growth. The sheer population size of the country is making the dispersion of political and administrative decisions necessary and desirable now, in the way that the problem of territorial size made such a dispersion necessary and desirable in the past. At the same time, the constant growth of population in the fixed number of States offers each State greater opportunity for internal viability. One need only look at the States of California and New York to see how this is so. States of some 18 million people, they are more populous than all but a few of the sovereign nations of the world and have larger budgets than all but five of them. California maintains an educational plant larger than that of any country with the exception of the Soviet Union. Four other States now have 10 million people or more and another five have in excess of 5 million. Such States are able to draw upon many kinds of skills from within their borders simply because they have enough people to produce a variety of talents. While they may never become as large as their giant sisters, sheer passage of time will enable most States to reach a stage in population growth that will give them greater flexibility as well as more money with which to function, thus adding to their potential for self-directed action.

4. *Localities will have to struggle for policy–as distinct from administrative–control of the new programs.* Despite the fact that federal-local relations are increasing and are likely to increase, the localities are not assured that these relations will continue to emphasize local decision-making with outside financial and technical assistance as in the past. The evidence is that the present pattern will be continued. Nevertheless, the localities will have to compete against the pressures for excessive equalitarian leveling and collectivist action that could make local control a relatively hollow achievement. These pressures will continue to be directed toward eliminating the policy-making powers of local government, particularly in the realms of housing, zoning, and urban development. The growth of expertise at the local level could help offset these pressures unless the new urban professionals themselves identify with these centralizing goals.

In their efforts, the localities would be wise to place increased reliance upon their States. The major pressures for direct federal-local relations that bypass the States come from the Nation's largest cities, whose populations equal or exceed the populations of many States and who consequently have adequate self-sufficiency and expertise to work directly with Washington without being at a great disadvantage. As the Nation's population decentralizes within the metropolitan areas and within the belts of urban settlement that are forming in various parts of the country, more people will be living in smaller units of local government. Since the chances for local consolidation have diminished and indeed the value of such consolidation has become increasingly suspect, there will be relatively few local units capable of dealing directly with Washington, simply by virtue of their lack of appropriate personnel. The States will provide assistance in most cases for a certain price, namely, a "say" in local decisions. While this price is not likely to be great–the States are also committed to the principle of local control–it will give the localities additional need to define their positions as well.

Only a full understanding of the implications of those principles and institutions will make the present concern with federalism a meaningful one and not just another rhetorical response to a period of intensive innovation at the national level.

Federal democracy has served America well for nearly two centuries as a primary means of preserving freedom while also allowing us to have energetic government able to respond to greater changes than government ever had to face before. Moreover, it has great promise for continuing to serve us equally well in the future if we understand its principles and use them properly.

27 The Future of American Federalism

Richard H. Leach

From: Tinsley E. Yarborough *et al.*, eds., *Politics 1972: Trends in Federalism* (East Carolina University Publications, March 1972), pp. 73–84. Reprinted by permission of the author and publisher.

Richard Leach is Professor of Political Science at Duke University. He is one of the leading scholars in the field of American federalism.

It is always folly to write about the future. But one sure thing with regard to the future of federalism is that it will continue to be with us, and indeed, that it will win new adherents, even as it did in early December, 1971, when six Arab Emirates came together in a single federation. Federalism, in short, is an idea whose day is far from waning. The American example has been followed in every part of the world, and it promises to continue to be utilized both by states presently federal in form and by those still in developing stages. The second sure thing is that federalism will continue to be debated on the one hand and to be developed on the other. Probably no governmental issue has evoked as much discussion over the years as the distribution of power in the federal system, and certainly no governmental institution has undergone as many changes as federalism. Both of these processes can be expected to continue in the future. Indeed, a structured reevaluation of federalism, designed to produce blueprints for necessary modifications, has just been launched as a part of the American Revolution bicentennial celebration. Under the name "Federalism

'76," the project proposes to undertake activity "to describe and interpret what our Federal system is, how it operates, and the role of the individual citizen in its functioning."

Through scholarly research and analysis, the preparation and dissemination of educational materials based on such analyses and other information, and a series of public discussions and dialogues across the nation, it is hoped that "a meaningful evaluation of our system of government" will emerge by the bi-centennial year, "thereby contributing to a renewal of faith in the nation's heritage and laying a solid base for moving forward."[1]

Both the process of Federalism '76 and its final products are much to be anticipated. Hopefully, its major impact will be on the extension among both public and private policymakers and the American public at large of a better understanding of the nature of American federalism and of its utility as an instrument of social change. For by and large the American public perceives of federalism–if it perceives of it at all–in an anachronistic frame, as a simple matter of division of power between national and state governments, rather than as a very complex matter, involving many governments and levels of government in the exercise of power. The public schools do not give a sophisticated understanding of federalism anywhere in the standard curriculum, and the nation's colleges and universities do not do much better for the relatively few students they reach. Given the basic importance of the federal system to American government, a remedy for this virtual ignorance of federalism on the part of the American people is badly needed. Federalism '76 may well be the spur to the development of such a remedy. It deserves both support and attention.

In the meantime, however, the future of federalism will continue to be molded by a number of forces, some known, some unknown, each subtly or directly inducing change.

First of all, and obviously, the future of American federalism will be intimately related to the future of the nation generally–to population growth and shifts, to economic development, to changing social conditions, and particularly to the maturation of the race question. No one can fail to perceive the centrality of the racial crisis to every aspect of American life. Two aspects of that crisis are particularly significant as they affect federalism: black Americans have increasingly shown their disdain for state and local government in particular, at least as presently constituted, and have begun to exert pressure to establish black communities as autonomous units of government. As W. H. Ferry recently described it, their vision "is not that of a New Jerusalem, nor is it that of (an integrated) national community. . . . It is a vision of a new federalism that will give 10 percent of our citizens the chance they are seeking to make whatever they want to make of themselves, their culture, and their community."[2]

At the same time, black Americans are conscious now as never before of their power *nationally* and have begun to exert that power at as many points in the national governmental process as possible. A national government of their making would be concerned with the achievement of full equality and would be harsh on those elements in our system which seem to retard that achievement. Since there is no doubt that federal division of power has aided and abetted segregation in the past, the implications of the black drive for equality on federal institutions are obvious. It is too early yet to predict safely what the outcome of black organization and pressure on those institutions will be. The failures of the federal form in Nigeria and Malaysia, however, point to the long-term incompatibility between racial conflict and traditional federalism.

Secondly, the future of federalism in America will be molded by the power points in the American governmental process. No exhaustive historical study has been made of the impact of presidents on the course of federalism, but given the fact that we have developed what amounts to a presidential system in twentieth century America, it would seem to follow that the future of federalism will be determined to some extent at least by the attention and perception present and future presidents bring to bear on it. Both President Johnson with his still-born "creative federalism" and President Nixon with his still adolescent "new federalism"—the first modern American presidents to be specifically identified with developments in federalism—would seem to serve as proof of the point. Indeed, President Nixon seemed well on his way late in 1971 to making an issue in federalism—growing public unhappiness over rising local taxes, especially property taxes—central in the 1972 campaign,[3] even as he had already sought in his administration to make the adoption of his revenue-sharing scheme central to the solution of major national problems. Whoever is elected president in 1972 and after will undoubtedly be forced to continue the precedent so set. But nothing in the American governmental system responds to one pressure alone; federalism in the future will thus also reflect the actions and beliefs of Congress (which is traditionally and locally minded and sensitive to the need to maintain division of powers), of the Supreme Court (which has moved contradictorily in recent years in both national and state power directions and probably will continue to do so), and of pressure groups and political parties (which for the most part have not identified themselves very closely with federalism, very likely because, as suggested earlier, in their misunderstanding of it, the American people do not take positions which force them to).

The pressures of state governors, other state officials and units of government, and mayors will be felt also. Present-day program administration in the United States is so much a joint enterprise of national, state, and local governments that the needs and demands of the "junior partners" in the federal system, increasingly well formulated and expressed as they are, can hardly be ignored. It is not without importance that most large cities now have their own lobbyists in Washington and that the National League of Cities and the United States Conference of Mayors form a solid phalanx of urban pressure on the national government on many issues.

In the third place, the future of federalism will be hinged to the improvement of public administration, to solution of the governmental manpower problem, to how well the crisis in metropolitan area government is solved, and to the resolution of the fiscal mismatch between the national government as major revenue receiver and state and local governments as major purveyors of services. Much of the operation of government at all levels is bureaucratic, and it is essential for successful operation that the various bureaucracies work well together. Yet the past has been marked by "conflict between professional administrators at the Federal level and . . . administrators at State and local levels, between line agency officials and elected policy-makers at all levels, between administrators of one aid progıam and those of another, between specialized middle-management officials and generalists in the top management category, and between standpat bureau heads and innovators seeking to strengthen the decision-making process at all levels."[4]

If federalism is to serve the people well, the future must see these conflicts resolved. Perhaps they would be resolved more easily if the quality particularly of state and local governmental personnel were improved. Too many state and local personnel systems are antiquated and patronage-oriented and so prevent the hiring and retention of professional people. As a result, state and local bureaucrats too often are "lacking in quality and experience, unimaginative, and too subject to negative political . . . pressures" to provide the kind of administrative cooperation that is required in the future.[5] The national government has recently begun to help the states and local governments overcome this problem, so that it may be less acute in the future. If the personnel problem may be diminishing, the problem of governing metropolitan areas remains largely untouched. Extreme fragmentation and division of power are still characteristic of the metropolitan areas where almost three-fourths of the American people live; indeed, between the 1962 and 1967 Census of Governments, 2,261 additional fragments of government were established in the nation's then 227 Standard Metropolitan Statistical Areas, the number of unifunctional, independent, special districts increasing most rapidly. The 1972 Census (Censuses of Government are taken only every five years) will show a further increase. As the Advisory Commission on Intergovernmental Relations concluded, such fragmentation divides "political responsibility for government performance . . . to the point of obscurity. Public control of government policies tends to break down when citizens have to deal with a net-work of independent governments, each responsible for highly specialized activities. . . . Each government is so circumscribed in its powers and in the area of its jurisdiction that important metropolitan action is virtually impossible for local governments to undertake."[6] Until this condition is alleviated, solution of the problems of urban America–the most critical substantive problem federalism must attack–will be retarded. It is not as if a wide variety of ways to alleviate the problem have not already been developed–interlocal agreements, merger, consolidation, councils of governments, etc.; the problem is securing agreement on which ones to utilize in individual metropolitan areas and in altering state constitutions and laws to make utilization possible.

That solution–and the solution of other problems as well–will be retarded in any case by the chronic poverty of state and local governments. The greatest tax potential lies with the national government, yet the greatest burden for services to be paid for by taxes is borne by state and local governments. Some sort of relief–whether it falls under the rubric of revenue-sharing or not–will have to be provided before too long, or an increasing number of American citizens in all walks of life will face a major deterioration of service, and federalism itself will be endangered. For a division of governmental power cannot be sustained for long if only one level of government has the resources necessary to undertake the tasks the people place upon governments. As the Advisory Commission on Intergovernmental Relations put it in its 1970 report, "No governmental theory or system . . . can be sacrosanct at the expense of serving the needs of the citizenry."[7]

The future of American federalism will also be affected by the increasing urbanization of the United States on the one hand and the quality of urban life on the other. The American farmer is disappearing; small towns and cities are struggling for survival against the onslaught of megalopolitanism; the center of American life is now the alabaster cities that were not mentioned until the fourth stanza of Katherine Lee Bates' poem and hymn, "America, the Beautiful." How to reverse the movement to megalopolis–if indeed it should be reversed–has yet to be found. What relation will a system of distributed governments designed for a dispersed agrarian population bear to a nation of people clustered in a few giant urban agglomerations? Are not they already, and will not they increasingly be, quite a different people from their farmer forebears? Once in megalopolis, what do people find? Not what many expected: "far too many of our great urban centers have become . . . obsolete, unmanageable . . . polarized . . . garbage-strewn, polluted, and great cesspools of crime, drug addiction, corruption, and despair."[8] People caught in such an environment are strangers to the American experience and may well demand changes in the traditional structure of American government to get at reform.

There is also considerable evidence that the country has already become so nationalized that continuation of a localistic system of government is already an anachronism. So mobile are the American people—one-fifth of them move every year—, so nation-wide is the job market and the market for goods, so uniform are the television and radio programs, newspaper contents, and other media presentations, so ubiquitous are the same powerful interest groups, that one could easily conclude that the local and regional differences classical federalism was designed to protect no longer exist in sufficient degree to warrant protection at all. In this view, state and local governments are superfluities, largely irrelevant to an attack on America's pressing problems; the national government alone can launch a successful attack. Not that some sort of local or regional agents of the national government would not be necessary to carry out many facets of that attack. They would be necessary. The point is, however, that they would be agents, even as counties have always been of state governments. Local units would then become very like Hamilton visualized them in the plan he presented to the Constitutional Convention in Philadelphia in 1787, "corporations for local purposes." Hamilton's perspicacity concerning so many other matters has been borne out by events; perhaps he was right all along in thinking that, in so large a country as the United States, the states and their local subdivisions were altogether inadequate "for any of the great purposes of commerce, revenue, or agriculture." One option open to America in the future, then, is a return to Hamilton's concept of sovereignty lying solely in the national government. Whether it is yet a viable option is doubtful; at present, Americans seem to have too much emotional attachment to existing states and cities to be attracted to the idea. Prolonged failure of those units of government to perform, however, could rapidly sour the traditional affection Americans feel for them and thus open the door at last to the Hamiltonian model.

It can also be demonstrated economically that the present federal arrangement is outmoded Economists argue that government serves three major economic roles: it constitutes a vehicle for necessary redistribution of income; it serves to stabilize the economy; and it allocates the nation's public resources to meet public needs. The national government alone, they argue, can fill those roles satisfactorily. The present division of power between units of government weakens government's ability to perform and so is an inefficient use of resources. A single government would be able to bring to bear on the public's problem a "scientific" approach, and through the use of planning and reliance on systems analysis be able to inaugurate policies which are impossible to get under way now. The economic argument does not imply that lesser administrative units would not be employed. It only declares that the nature and functions of those units would be determined on the basis of demonstrated needs and facts, not on the basis of constitutional or theoretical states' rights. Thus, where a certain service was found to be best performed locally, arrangements would be made to have it done so. Similarly, if others were determined to require a regional or national administration, appropriate units to provide that kind of administration would be established. The test of a governmental arrangement would then be how efficiently it delivered its service; the marketplace would provide the test. Of course, this line of reasoning can be hooted out of court, too. Americans are generally skeptical of economic criteria and economists are far from agreed on the analysis. On the other hand, they are used to seeing decisions in business and industry being made on economic grounds, and again, prolonged demonstration of the inefficiency of federalism may persuade them to accept those grounds in the governmental arena.

Finally, the future of federalism will depend on the nature of the ideas advanced for its alteration. Some of the proposals now circulating call for the creation of national cities, independent of the states in which they are located, as the way out for the most problem-plagued cities; for devolution of much power of local governments to neighborhood councils or community groups, as a way to bring government closer to local residents; for the development of regional units of government, as ways to fit structure to changing circumstances; for the adoption of a National Growth Policy and a National Land Use policy, as ways to guide future population growth and shift so as to prevent further environmental deterioration; and for the creation of new towns, as a way to side-step the issues in the old ones.

An even further departure from traditional federalism is the suggestion for a governmental ombudsman. An ombudsman is an intervenor on behalf of the people with government. Up to now, where one has been employed, he has represented individual citizens in claims against governmental agencies within a single unit of government. The suggestion has recently been advanced that the same idea be adopted to claims of local governments for services of the national government. The Joint

Economic Committee, in a report to the two houses of Congress early in December, 1971, recommended providing local units of government (and the same logic would apply to state governments as well) with a federally supported "modern professional equivalent of the old-time local political leader in the form of a paid intervenor elected by the popular vote in a general election every two years."[9] It would be the intervenor's responsibility to stand between local communities (and possibly states as well) and units of the national government, to help them solve their problems. It would be the intervenor's duty to cut through administrative red tape, through the "morass of bureaus and agencies . . . [the] endless series of paper-shuffling processes"[10] that now prevent local communities from taking advantage of existing federal programs, and find the answers to the questions the local communities were asking. The adoption of such a scheme would revolutionize the relationship between the national (or state) government and local governments, with obvious effects on the structure and processes of federalism. It is admittedly a radical suggestion (nearly half the members of the subcommittee which wrote the report disagreed or dissociated themselves from the findings), and unlikely to win many adherents, at least quickly. But the very fact that it was seriously proposed shows that something is seriously wrong with federalism as it presently functions.

Basically, the trouble is that federalism today is not satisfying the service demands of the American people, for to provide adequate services requires a positive assertion of governmental power. Federalism as conceived and long practiced in the United States is more concerned with limiting and restricting power. It has a negative thrust. It is based on the theory of limited government; it reflects the Founders' fear of aggregated power and their acceptance of small constituencies as the proper base of democratic government. Yet today it appears that the services industrialized and megalopolitanized man needs—clean water, clean air, satisfactory transportation, educational and recreational facilities, housing, to name a few—require the very centralization federalism was designed to prevent. In the face of service demand, small constituencies have been found wanting. In Senator Hubert Humphrey's words, "In activity after activity—from street cleaning to public safety—communities are barely able to meet even the most basic minimum levels of service. As a result, in all too many instances, the spirit has gone out of our cities."[11] In a contest between theory and tradition on the one hand, and modern man increasingly irritated by service inadequacies or deprivations (the number of virtually bankrupt school districts is growing rapidly) on the other, theory and tradition are likely to be set aside—unless the quality of services can be improved. Senator Humphrey is not alone in declaring that the American people "should have certain basic standards of service–standards of education, of health, of social services, of public services. This is their basic right."[12] The problem in a mobile society such as ours is how to maintain a basic standard evenly across the nation–and essentially that is a problem in federalism.

It is not easy to say how the problem will eventually be solved. Fortunately, the distinguishing characteristic of American federalism has been its capacity for adaptation and change. Indeed, federalism in the United States has been in flux since its adoption and nothing has happened to suggest it has lost that ability. Already we have begun to recognize the need for further adaptation and have even devised an institution for developing it. Acting on a specific recommendation of the Kestnbaum Commission, Congress in 1959 established the Advisory Commission on Intergovernmental Relations as a continuing body for study, information, and guidance on issues of federalism. The Commission is a bipartisan body of twenty-six members, who represent governors, mayors, county officials, state legislatures, Congress, the executive branch of the national government, and the public at large–most of the bodies involved in modern functional federalism. If its membership does not include group representatives, its procedures have been designed to insure that group points of view are heard. The Commission derives almost all its financial support from the national government, but it responds "to the needs of all three major levels of government." It "encourage(s) discussion and study at an early date of emerging public problems that are likely to require intergovernmental cooperation" for their solution.[13] It thus provides a regular forum to study and discuss trouble spots on the federal scene which might interfere with the effective exercise of power at any level of government–i.e., with the *rendering of adequate services*–and to make recommendations for their alteration or removal. Once recommendations are made, the commission works to implement them by stimulating and encouraging their adoption by national, state, and local governments. In the years since its creation, the commission has tackled some thorny problems,[14] and a large number of its recommendations have been adopted every year.[15]

Not only is the Advisory Commission on Intergovernmental Relations at work, but there are many other indications that the re-adaptation of federalism to the exigencies of the late twentieth century is of increasing national concern. Both Congress and the national administration are giving a large amount of attention to intergovernmental problems, as are state legislatures, governors, and city officials. Important political leaders now regularly address themselves to problems in federalism, and both major political parties included planks on federalism in their 1968 party platforms. The issues they were addressed to then are still with us, and the 1972 platforms will undoubtedly recommit the two parties to the effort to solve them. Federal, state, and local officials are alert to the problem, thanks in part to the Advisory Commission's prodding, but due also to a heightened sense of urgency in the wake of the urban disorders of the '60s and a resulting strengthening of their own structures. Universities have turned to problems of federalism and intergovernmental relations in increasing numbers, as have such groups as the National Association of Counties, the National League of Cities, and the U.S. Conference of Mayors. And even the business community is becoming aware there is a problem. As Federalism '76 goes into action, it can be expected to develop a greater awareness in the people as a whole of the need to reexamine and improve federalism in operation, which will react to force all the foregoing to step up their pace.

It is doubtful whether the final product of the current interest in federalism will be support for any of the drastic changes summarized earlier–complete nationalization; pragmatic marketplace federalism; the intervenor concept (can 20,000 to 40,000 new style "ward bosses" be imagined, someone asked); a rash of national cities, neighborhood councils, regional arrangements, etc. The American people are too conservative in their politics, still too localistic in their attachments, still convinced of the need for decentralization in their theorizing, still too personally oriented in their economic and social relations, to move very far away from the traditional basis of government in this country. What will happen if crisis follows crisis for another generation may alter that reluctance. But the immediate prospect seems to be for a continuation of the mild changes in federalism that are already taking place, namely, at the local level, of rationalization and consolidation of units of government; at the state level, of constitutional revision, legislative and executive reorganization, and the increasing assumption of responsibility for rendering urban services; and at the national level, of continuing simplification of the complex grant-in-aid program and the assumption of greater responsibility for financing essential services. The Advisory Commission on Intergovernmental Relations mounted the following as the "Agenda for the Seventies," and it would seem that if those can be accomplished in the decade, little more can be expected: restoring fiscal balance; adopting national and state urbanization policies; civilizing the jungle of local government; and massive state financial and administrative commitment to urban problems.[16]

If the business on that agenda can indeed be accomplished in the seventies, the American federal system will very likely remain undisturbed for several more decades to come. If it is not accomplished, however, the possibility of a major restructuring of federalism will rapidly increase. It is worth noting that two classes of mine, one an undergraduate class and the other a graduate class, have recently been analyzing the state of American federalism today and, almost unanimously, the students are pessimistic about the success of mild change and are bracing themselves for something more radical. The Advisory Commission itself, concluding a section in the *Twelfth Annual Report,* concluded that no attachment to a traditional way of doing things could be allowed to stand in the way of meeting legitimate service needs.[17] The seventies may thus well be the critical decade for the concept and practice of federalism in the United States.

Thus this will not be the last essay written on the future of American federalism. The debate about governmental power and the quality of life will continue for a long time to come, as will changes in the American condition. The result inevitably will be further alterations in the institutions of American government to accommodate new demands and new circumstances. American federalism has met the test in the past, despite sometimes a slight time lag. The seventies will prove whether it can continue to do so.

[1]*Federalism Seventy-Six.* Re-draft. October 16, 1971. Mimeo., pp. 2-3. The headquarters of Federalism '76 is in Washington, D.C., at Suite 400, 1700 Pennsylvania Avenue, N.W., 20006; Wendell Hulcher, former Mayor of Ann Arbor, Michigan, is its president.

[2]W. H. Ferry, "The Case for a New Federalism," *Saturday Review*, June 15, 1968, p. 17.

[3]See the Associated Press dispatch by Gaylord Shaw from Key Biscayne, Florida, December 3, 1971, as reported in *The Durham* (N.C.) *Sun,* December 3, 1971, p. 6-A.

[4]*The Federal System as Seen by Federal Aid Officials.* Committee Print. December 15, 1965. 89th Congress, 1st. session, pp. 95-99.

[5]*Ibid.*

[6]*Metropolitan America: Challenge to Federalism.* A report of the Advisory Commission on Intergovernmental Relations. Committee Print. 89th Cong., 2nd session (1966), p. 7.

[7]Advisory Commission on Intergovernmental Relations. *Twelfth Annual Report* (1970), p. 16.

[8]Senator Thomas J. McIntyre (D., N.H.), "To Make the Morning Last," an article in *Yankee,* December, 1971, reprinted in *Congresstional Record,* 117:S19078-9 (November 19, 1971).

[9]Quoted in the *Durham* (N.C.) *Morning Herald,* December 6, 1971, p. 7b.

[10]*Ibid.*

[11]Senator Hubert H. Humphrey, Speech to the National Municipal League's Conference on Government, Atlanta, Georgia, November 15, 1971, reprinted in *Congressional Record.* 117:S19088-89 (November 19, 1971).

[12]*Ibid.*

[13]Advisory Commission on Intergovernmental Relations, *Third Annual Report* (1961), p. 2.

[14]See Advisory Commission on Intergovernmental Relations, *Eleventh Annual Report* (1970), Appendix B, "Summary of Actions Taken by the Advisory Commission on Intergovernmental Relations," pp. 60-65.

[15]See Advisory Commission on Intergovernmental Relations, *Federalism in 1970.* Twelfth Annual Report (1971), Ch. 2, "Action on Commission Recommendations."

[16]*Ibid..* pp. 13-16.

[17]*Ibid.,* p. 16.